Ravel the Decadent

Ravel the Decadent

Memory, Sublimation, and Desire

BY MICHAEL J. PURI

OXFORD
UNIVERSITY PRESS

OXFORD
UNIVERSITY PRESS

Oxford University Press, Inc., publishes works that further
Oxford University's objective of excellence
in research, scholarship, and education.

Oxford New York
Auckland Cape Town Dar es Salaam Hong Kong Karachi
Kuala Lumpur Madrid Melbourne Mexico City Nairobi
New Delhi Shanghai Taipei Toronto

With offices in
Argentina Austria Brazil Chile Czech Republic France Greece
Guatemala Hungary Italy Japan Poland Portugal Singapore
South Korea Switzerland Thailand Turkey Ukraine Vietnam

Published by Oxford University Press, Inc.
198 Madison Avenue, New York, New York 10016

www.oup.com

Library of Congress Cataloging-in-Publication Data
Puri, Michael J.
Ravel the decadent : memory, sublimation, and desire / by Michael J. Puri.
p. cm.
Includes bibliographical references and index.
ISBN 978-0-19-973537-2 (hardcover : alk. paper) 1. Ravel, Maurice, 1875–1937—Criticism and
interpretation. I. Title.
ML410.R23P87 2011
780.92—dc22 2011012644

Publication of this book was supported by the AMS 75 PAYS Publication Endowment
Fund of the American Musicological Society

1 3 5 7 9 8 6 4 2

Printed in the United States of America
on acid-free paper

TABLE OF CONTENTS

ACKNOWLEDGMENTS

For their research assistance on behalf of this volume, I am grateful to the following people: Catherine Massip, director of the Department of Music at the Bibliothèque nationale de France (BnF) in Paris; the relevant staff at three branches of the BnF: Louvois, l'Opéra, and François-Mitterrand; Dell Hollingsworth and Richard Workman, music librarians at the Harry Ransom Center of the University of Texas at Austin; Fran Barulich, the Mary Flagler Cary curator of music manuscripts and printed music at the Pierpont Morgan Library and Museum in New York City; and Madame Claude Moreau of the Maison-musée de Maurice Ravel in Montfort-l'Amaury.

The following sources of support enabled me to visit these sites and complete my research: a Franklin Travel Grant from the American Philosophical Society, a Mellon Travel Grant from the Harry Ransom Center, and several grants from my home institution, the University of Virginia (UVa), including a Vice President for Research Grant, a Sesquicentennial Research Fellowship, and four Faculty Summer Research Stipends in the Humanities and Social Sciences. Costs for the production of this book were offset by generous subventions from the American Musicological Society 75 PAYS Fund and the Society for Music Theory.

This book has also benefited from the friendly, supportive, and intellectual environment that characterizes UVa's McIntire Department of Music, as well as the many fruitful interactions I have enjoyed when presenting my work not only at national meetings of the American Musicological Society and the Society for Music Theory but also in colloquia at the following institutions: the University of Wisconsin at Madison, the University of Texas at Austin, the University of North Carolina at Chapel Hill, the University of Pennsylvania, and Cornell University.

Above all, I cherish the input of specific individuals: Arbie Orenstein, whose incomparable knowledge of Ravel and enthusiasm for all related scholarship were indispensable to me, especially at the beginning and end of this project; Steven Huebner and Brian Hyer, both of whom read the full manuscript carefully and offered excellent, detailed feedback; Suzanne Aspden, Bruce Alan Brown, Eric

Drott, Walter Frisch, Dan Harrison, Denis Herlin, Peter Kaminsky, Lawrence Kramer, Deborah Mawer, Susan McClary, Robert Morgan, Jann Pasler, Alexander Rehding, Steven Rings, Marianne Wheeldon, and Richard Will, all of whom provided invaluable advice and guidance at various stages. This help notwithstanding, I take full responsibility for any remaining problems or errors in this text.

My deepest thanks are reserved for my family, former advisors, editor, and partner. My appreciation of knowledge, education, and the arts is a direct consequence of the values instilled in me by my late mother, Duane, and my father, Yogishwar; my relationships with my great friend of several decades, David R. Elliott, and the Baumanns—an artistic and erudite family who adopted me during my years of pianistic pilgrimage in Switzerland—have only heightened and deepened this appreciation. Every sentence of this book is an homage to the influence that my undergraduate and graduate thesis advisors, David Lewin and James Hepokoski, have had on me as researchers, teachers, musicians, and passionate, ambitious thinkers. For more than five years Suzanne Ryan has been not only a brilliant and visionary editor but also a patient and encouraging one, and I am proud to call her a dear friend. Sylvia Chong, my wife and fellow professor, has given me during the composition of this book more love, support, and intellectual companionship than I could ever have hoped for.

***

Earlier versions of chapters 3 and 5 appeared respectively as "Dandy, Interrupted: Sublimation, Repression, and Self-Portraiture in Maurice Ravel's *Daphnis et Chloé*," *Journal of the American Musicological Society* 60.2 (Summer 2007): 317–372, and "Memory and Melancholy in the 'Epilogue' of Ravel's *Valses nobles et sentimentales*," *Music Analysis* 29/ii–iii(2011): 1–37.

Ravel the Decadent

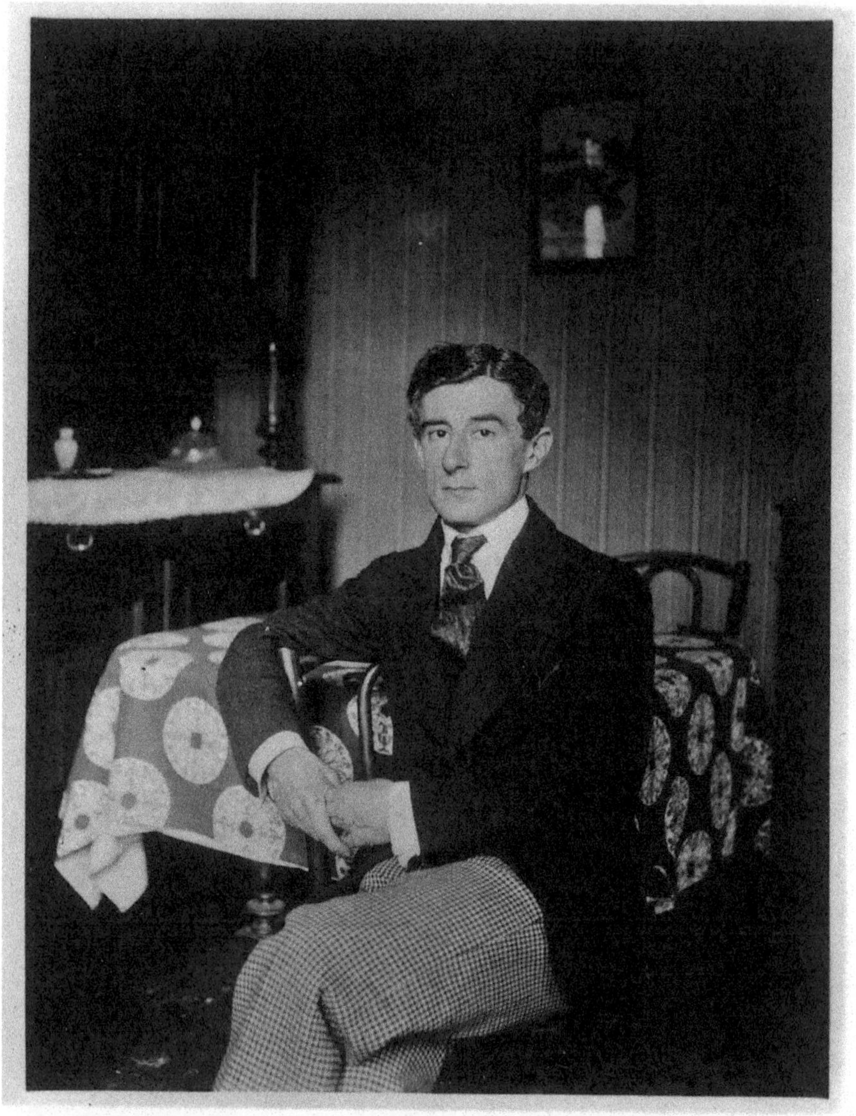

Frontispiece: Ravel, c. 1910. Used by permission of the Bibliothèque nationale de France.

Introduction: Memory, Decadence, and Music

The music of the French composer Maurice Ravel (1875–1937) is one of the great artistic successes of the twentieth century, as beloved for its beauty as it is esteemed for its craft. Nevertheless, serious attempts to get to the heart of this music—how it works and what it means—have appeared all too seldom. *Ravel the Decadent* seeks to break this cycle by providing a broad account of Ravel's music and relating it to contemporary trends in early European modernism.

When dealing with a specific repertoire, such as the output of a single composer, we often rely on preexisting critical terms to capture its particular style. In the case of Ravel, familiar and enduring terms include *imposture, artifice,* and *irony,* among others. In this book I propose my own set, which features the four mentioned in the title and subtitle: *decadence, memory, sublimation,* and *desire.* I do not necessarily intend my terms to negate their precedents and the interpretations they inform; the two sets mentioned here are actually quite compatible since imposture, artifice, and irony were all marked as typically "decadent" behaviors at the end of the nineteenth century in France.[1] Nonetheless, by highlighting the dynamism of Ravel's music—its vacillation between lust and lassitude, rawness and refinement, sentimental reminiscence and unsentimental oblivion—and associating this dynamism with both the mind and the body, I maintain that these terms open up novel and productive perspectives on Ravel. In this introduction I begin by surveying these phenomena during the period in question before delving more deeply into the complex topics of memory and decadence. I conclude by briefly summarizing subsequent chapters and indicating their relation to the key concepts.

Offering refuge from a hectic world and entry into the limitless and mysterious depths of the mind, memory fascinated French artists and audiences at the *fin de siècle,* appearing prominently in varied venues such as the *fêtes galantes* of Verlaine, the philosophy of Bergson, and the nostalgic effusions of Proust. Sublimation—conceived here as the transformation of some entity into a more elevated form of itself—counterbalanced memory by shifting emphasis away from the invisible interior and toward the visible exterior, as exemplified in the exquisitely stylized art and architecture of *Art Nouveau*, the *poésie pure* of Mallarmé, and the artifice-ridden scenarios in the prose fiction of J.-K. Huysmans. The increasingly rigorous formulation and legislation of behavioral norms, fueled by and fueling widespread anxiety about cultural degeneracy, only enhanced the allure of desire.[2] All three topics gained further ground through their close interrelation: Memory and sublimation converge in the idealization of the past, sublimation transforms expressions of desire from crude to seemly, and nostalgic desire engages memory to relive the glory days. Growing up during the height of the Decadence, an era in French literature and culture (1880–1900) that was preoccupied with these ideas, Ravel could hardly do otherwise than to incorporate them into his music.

Decadence in Majuscule and Minuscule

A thesis underpinning this book is that Ravel's music is indebted to the Decadence, a late nineteenth-century artistic and cultural phenomenon centered in France but influential throughout Europe. Ravel grew up when it was flourishing, was described in his youth by his best friend, Ricardo Viñes, as a "super-eccentric decadent,"[3] maintained a dandy persona throughout his life, was a devoted reader of writings by members and precursors of the Decadence (Verlaine, Mallarmé, Huysmans, Baudelaire, Bertrand, Poe, Barbey d'Aurevilly, Villiers de l'Isle-Adam, Klingsor, Lombard), set their poetry to music, and even reiterated his aestheticist position after World War One by declaring art to be "the supreme imposture" and confessing that Huysmans's novel *À rebours* (*Against Nature*, 1884), regarded then and now as the centerpiece of Decadent literature, "still rings true for me."[4] Despite this wealth of biographical evidence, very few scholars have attempted to draw out its consequences.[5] Instead, his music has most often been linked to impressionism, symbolism, and (neo)classicism, with only partial success: Impressionism captures the occasional luxuriance of its sound but does not jibe with its more mordant and dynamic qualities; symbolism highlights its esotericism and preciosity—an important overlap with decadent aesthetics, as we will see later—but ascribes to it a general orientation toward vague suggestion and metaphysics that it lacks; classicism and neoclassicism correctly register its preference for traditional forms and genres, diatonicism, and clear phrase divisions but displace it from its proper Decadent context in a gesture that would either cleanse it of any untoward associations or put it in its place as quiescent or even regressive art.[6] However, even if Decadence does seem to suit Ravel better than alternative aesthetic labels, it still has its own stumbling blocks, including a complicated relation with "decadence."

In comparison to "Decadence" its lowercase sibling enjoys a broader relation to history and culture. Some have argued that we should avoid using it—along with "degeneration" and "decline"—and treat it with extreme skepticism wherever we may encounter it. For one reason, it draws a false analogy between individuals and collective entities (a nation, a society, an institution), incorrectly attributing to the latter the life cycle of the former;[7] Gibbon's *The History of the Decline and Fall of the Roman Empire* (1776–1788), Nordau's *Entartung* (*Degeneration*, 1892), and Spengler's *Der Untergang des Abendlandes* (*The Decline of the West*, 1918) are only the more prominent examples of these misplaced metaphors. For another, it is often merely a term of empty invective used, in a spasm of fear and paranoia, to disavow anxiety over change and alterity.[8] Further, in the context of the early Third Republic in France it has been critiqued as an idle, ahistorical fantasy of the "literate few" that had little to do with wide-ranging, bona fide improvements in the standard of living for the urban masses.[9]

Even if we were to reduce the notion of cultural decadence to faulty reasoning, unjustified opprobrium, and indulgent self-delusion, it nevertheless remains an inescapable aspect of discourse and sentiment at the *fin de siècle* in France. The sense of decadence largely stemmed from the national trauma suffered during the Franco-Prussian War and its aftermath, including the occupation of Paris and the annihilation of the Paris Commune during the *semaine sanglante* of May 1871, and was subsequently fostered by a decline in the nation's prestige and power on the international stage, an economic depression lasting almost until the end of the century despite the expansion of capitalism on a global scale, a disorienting increase in democracy and colonialization, a decrease in birth rate, a loss of religious faith, and the erosion of the authority of the Catholic Church. At the beginning of the Third Republic, political and cultural leaders were apt to condemn and proscribe anything that might threaten the health of the nation, in particular viewing the Second Empire and its institutions as frivolous, profligate, and deleterious. However, as Jann Pasler has shown, the dissipation of Mac-Mahon's Moral Order policy in the 1880s made way for the gradual incorporation into national discourse of notions such as "grace," "pleasure," and the "decorative."[10] Moreover, despite the increasing prominence of what Robert A. Nye has called the "medical model of cultural crisis" in France,[11] its face had been made over by the 1900 World Exposition, shifting from the monumental exteriority of the Eiffel Tower to the organic interiority of *Art Nouveau*.[12] Standing firm against the increasing pressure to adopt conformist, bourgeois, materialist values for the sake of social progress, the Decadents—whether or not they accepted this label as an emblem of their countercultural stance—found themselves in a somewhat more hospitable environment at the end of the century, notwithstanding conservative retrenchments in the wake of the Dreyfus affair.[13]

To say this, however, is to assume that the Decadence extended at least until the end of the nineteenth century—an assumption that literary historians did not begin to make until recently. Previously, the Decadence was thought to occupy only a brief period of transition (c. 1880–1886) that led from Naturalism and Parnassianism to Symbolism and was punctuated by the September 18, 1886, Symbolist manifesto of Jean Moréas in *Le Figaro littéraire,* which overrode Anatole Baju's prior attempts at a Decadent manifesto in *Le Décadent littéraire et artistique*; though the Symbolist manifesto, according to Michèle Hannoosh, may not have amounted to much more than an "effort at public relations," Pamela Genova has affirmed that the term *Decadence* gradually fell into disuse after this moment while the less pejorative term *Symbolism* continued to gain ground.[14] Nevertheless, flying in the face of this narrative and its proponents, Jean Pierrot argued persuasively in his 1977 monograph, *L'imaginaire décadent,* 1880–1900, that the Decadence was no mere passing phenomenon of trifling significance but an important and durable one that stretched at least to the beginning of the twentieth century.[15] Moreover, the breadth of its concerns qualified it to be "the common denominator of all the literary trends that emerged during the last two decades of the nineteenth century" in France—a claim that recalls contemporary strategies by both Baju and Arthur Symons to use decadence as an umbrella term for avant-garde experimentalism.[16] Since this breakthrough, critics have underscored the importance of the Decadence by claiming it to have laid the groundwork for many cultural-intellectual phenomena, stretching from surrealism, futurism, and *Art Nouveau* to cubism, critical theory, and poststructuralism.

The issue of influence raises the question of content: What, if anything, gave the Decadence coherence as an artistic movement? First and foremost, it is a set of topics and stances, including antirealism, antinaturalism, antimoralism, antiprogressivism, *épater le bourgeoisie, fumisme,* individualism, aestheticism, refinement, dandyism, *fête galante,* perfectionism, machines, automata, *femme fatale, ange-femme,* esotericism, pessimism, alienation, isolation, escapism, ennui, spleen, *tristesse,* melancholy, unconscious, introspection, retrospection, futurism, exoticism, fantasy, dreams, medievalism, mysticism, idealism, metamorphosis, ornament, sensuality, music, synesthesia, hyperesthesia, androgyny, sexuality and sexual deviance, neurosis, morbidity, sadomasochism, and satanism.[17] The Decadence is also a motley group of artists whose work draws heavily on the preceding themes: Huysmans, Verlaine, Mallarmé, Barbey d'Aurevilly, Villiers de l'Isle-Adam, the brothers Goncourt, Rachilde, Laforgue, Moreau, Redon, Lorrain, Samain, Rod, Rodenbach, Maeterlinck, Péladan, Puvis de Chavannes, Klingsor, Mauclair, Maupassant, de Gourmont, Lautréamont, Rops, Mendès, Valéry, Schwob, Rollinat, Barrès, Lombard, Louÿs, and Mirbeau, among others; critics typically expand this list back in time to Romantics such as Poe, Baudelaire, Gautier, Chateaubriand, Bertrand, Rossetti, de Quincey, and Flaubert and laterally to foreign contemporaries such as Wilde, Swinburne, Beardsley, Moore, Klimt, D'Annunzio, and Richard Wagner, whose *Tristan und Isolde, Götterdämmerung,* and *Parsifal* all shone brightly in the constellation of Decadence.[18]

In addition to a thematic catalogue and artistic roster, the Decadence has also been identified—through the more general notion of decadence—as a style that emphasizes the detail at the expense of the whole, thereby reflecting in art the increasing isolation of the individual within modern society. Originating with Désiré Nisard's 1834 *Études de mœurs et de critique sur les poètes latins de la décadence*, this formulation of decadence-as-style was appropriated fifty years later by Paul Bourget for his *Essais sur la psychologie contemporaine* (1883), which correlates and explicates the writings of some early Decadents, including Baudelaire, Flaubert, and Renan. Despite the broad success during their time of both the *Essais* and their sequel, the *Nouveaux essais* (1885), this notion of decadent style would probably not have enjoyed such a rich posterity had Nietzsche not used it in *Der Fall Wagner* (*The Case of Wagner*, 1888), where it plays a central role in his critique of the composer as a decadent artist. Although this treatise has been prized mainly for its insights into Wagnerian aesthetics, poetics, and ideology, it is also an invaluable document for its account of European decadence. In this regard one of its signal contributions is its association of decadence with the legacy of Romanticism, set into relief by Nietzsche's description of Wagner as "the Victor Hugo of music" due to the grand rhetorical gestures that compose his operas.[19] Indeed, the French literary Decadence has come to be understood as a continuation, intensification, and critique of Romanticism—the "agony of Romanticism," as the title to Mario Praz's famous book put it so fittingly more than a half century ago.[20]

This sense of internal conflict—closely related to what David Weir has identified at the heart of Decadence as "the interference of mimesis and poesis," the simultaneous impulse toward the real and the artificial—is also found in Nietzsche as a central "symptom" of decadence: its dialectical nature.[21] This profound ambivalence, which is essentially a symptom of the nonidentity of the self to itself, is already evident in the poetry of Baudelaire: When the poet juxtaposes glorious antiquity with corrupt modernity in the poem "J'aime le souvenir des époques nues" or when he expatiates on the glories of the sunset in his critical writings on Poe and Gautier, he does not simply remind us of the depravity of decadence but also sings of the new "beautés de langueur" arising from it. Thus, we are merely confirming and elaborating what contemporary artists already understood about the dialectics of decadence, whether we describe it as " irritating irresolution"[22] or "perennial decay." Identified as an "insistence on *at once* mobilizing and undermining boundaries and differences," perennial decay surfaces in every instance of memory, sublimation, and desire in Ravel.[23] One example is the dandy, who simultaneously unsettles and reinstates the distinction between art and life—or, to put it more sardonically, one who is "both symptom and solution . . . a product of his time even as he railed against it."[24] A more musical example is cyclic form, whose thematic recollection both strengthens and weakens the traditional notion of form as articulation by overriding boundaries between movements while also establishing divisions within them.[25]

Decadent Affinities and Vignettes

Identifying Ravel as a Decadent composer opens up many new possibilities for historians and analysts. For one, it allows us to compare his music to Wagner's both directly and indirectly, as mediated through the many French Wagnerians at the *fin de siècle*—especially Ernest Chausson, who expressed the unremitting decadence of Maeterlinck's "Serres chaudes" in a set of *mélodies*. In addition, we gain a new purchase on the relation between Ravel and Debussy, whose decadence stretches from his settings of Verlaine's "C'est l'extase langoureuse" to Louÿs's *Chansons de Bilitis* and, further, to D'Annunzio's *Le martyre de Saint Sébastien*.[26] This approach also brings out affinities between Ravel and Satie, whose Rose+Croix period took place under the influence of one of the most important (and maligned) Decadents, Joséphin Péladan. Finally, due to the international reach of Decadence and its resonance with other strains of *fin-de-siècle* aestheticism and mysticism, we are able to forge connections between French music and a variety of other repertoires: Russian (Skryabin), Polish (Szymanowski), American (Griffes), Hungarian (the Bartók of *Bluebeard's Castle*), Austro-German (the Zemlinsky of *Der Zwerg*, Strauss of *Salome*, Korngold of *Die tote Stadt*, Pfitzner of *Die Rose vom Liebesgarten*, Schoenberg of *Pierrot lunaire*), and, even more recently, Decadence-indebted works in Britain (Britten's *Death in Venice*) and Italy (Dallapiccola's *Il Prigioniero*, based on a short story by Villiers de l'Isle-Adam, and Sciarrino's two Laforgue operas, *Lohengrin* and *Perseo ed Andromeda*).[27]

Decadent tendencies in all these repertoires can often be conceived in terms of memory, sublimation, and desire. However, the reader will probably have noticed that the earlier list of Decadent topics, despite being drawn from representative scholarship, does not include our privileged trio. Although critics may not have consistently identified them as such, they have been hiding in plain sight all along: memory in "retrospectivism," "introspection," and "the unconscious"; sublimation in "aestheticism," "refinement," and "dandyism"; and desire in "fantasy," "sensuality," and "sexuality," among other kindred terms. To learn more about their particular incarnation in Decadent writing, let us briefly survey the work of Verlaine, Mallarmé, Huysmans, and Baudelaire, all of whom were crucial for Ravel's artistic identity and development.

In Verlaine, memory is sentimental, nostalgic, melancholic, hedonistic, and intoxicating. It may cause a heady delirium ("Crépuscule du soir mystique") and even joy ("Colloque sentimental"), but it is so sensitive to the threat of oblivion that every paean to the past is simultaneously a lament over its loss. All three of our topics intertwine in his renowned collection, *Fêtes galantes* (1869): delicate scenarios involving the *commedia dell'arte* that sublimate desire into serenade and dance, leaving it deliciously unrequited.[28] Verlaine, now as then, represents Decadence in its purest sublimate. Even when he distanced himself from these works in "La dernière fête galante" (1889), proposing that desire be expressed in bacchanals rather than sentimental idylls, he increases his decadence. Not only does it encompass the dialectic of the idyll/bacchanal and their associated modes of sublimated/unsublimated desire, but it also manifests itself in playful ironies, exemplified here by a subtle intertexuality: The authorial persona that disavows the decadent Verlaine was actually participating in this decadence all along, as intimated in the earlier *fête galante* "La Faune," whose terra cotta satyr smiles as if mocking the melancholy lovers and their effete erotics.

The most famous faun of the Decadence, the narrator of Mallarmé's "L'après-midi d'un faune" (1876), is no mere statue, however, but rather a decadent subject caught up in the dialectics of memory, sublimation, and desire. A hybrid of man and beast, he wishes to slake his sexual desire by ravishing some nymphs but, impotent in his solitude, is constrained to sublimate his desire into music and play a "long solo" on his panpipes. Moreover, since he is unsure whether he ever actually encountered the nymphs, his mental processes become as mixed up as his physiology, blending memory and fantasy in uncertain proportions. For its volatile juxtaposition of the "subtleties of sensual pleasure" with the "bestial, frenzied cry of the faun," Mallarmé's poem earns special praise from the Duke Jean Floressas des Esseintes, the protagonist of Huysmans's *À rebours*.[29] If this novel is indeed the "breviary of Decadence," as Symons famously asserted less than a decade after its 1884 debut, des Esseintes is its greatest adept. Disgusted by his dissolute life in Paris, he flees the city for an eremitic existence in the countryside, where, in outright defiance of nature and reality, he attempts a total sublimation of self and environment, surrounding himself with decadent artifacts and striving for a "sexual insensibility of brain and body."[30] At first, his experiment succeeds: By restricting himself to a carefully designed universe of art, books, food, lighting, smells, and décor, he gains absolute control over his mind and senses and thus manages to keep at bay any unpleasant memories of his past. But the past eventually catches up with him:

> The confused mass of reading and meditation on artistic themes that he had accumulated since he had been on his own like a barrage to hold back the current of old memories, had suddenly been carried away, and the flood was let loose, sweeping away the present and the future, submerging everything under the waters of the past, covering his mind with a great expanse of melancholy, on the surface of which there drifted, like ridiculous bits of flotsam, trivial episodes of his existence, absurdly insignificant incidents.[31]

With this breakdown he loses control over both memory and desire. Bonbons that used to trigger pleasurable memories of "distant, half-forgotten dissipations" now "thrust before his eyes the bodily reality in all its crudity and urgency," reminding him of failed sexual relationships and burning his nostrils with the stink of nature.[32] Undone by his own, ultimately irrepressible "primal fervor," he becomes similar to Mallarmé's faun, his sublime composure shattered by the return of the repressed.

Among the real-life dandies that served as models for des Esseintes, Baudelaire looms large, even receiving an homage within the novel for having laid bare the decadent subject in its "irritable sensitivity of soul" and its "hybrid passions, exacerbated by the impossibility of obtaining complete satisfaction."[33] In the epoch-making *Fleurs du mal* (1857) Baudelaire defined the modern subject in its rivenness, a being torn between the extremes of *spleen* and *l'idéal*. This dichotomy is part of a broad psychological economy in Baudelaire that includes sublimation ("La beauté"), desublimation ("L'albatros"), myriad forms of desire—lust ("Le crépuscule du soir"), ennui ("Au lecteur"), aspiration ("Élévation")—and, last but not least, memory. As Walter Benjamin has suggested, "the *idéal* supplies the power of remembrance," whereas the *spleen*, an accomplice of oblivion, "musters the multitude of the seconds against it," as in "L'horloge."[34] In its literal invocation, memory is a pervasive and multivalent theme in Baudelaire: Witness its intoxications in "La chevelure," regrets in "L'irréparable," retributions in "Remords posthume," reminiscence in "Le balcon," redemption in "La cloche fêlée," devotion in "Harmonie du soir," and so on. When linked to *l'idéal*, however, memory extends beyond its literal invocations and flows into mystical concepts such as Baudelaire's *correspondances*. Benjamin rejects the common interpretation of *correspondances* as synesthetics and describes them instead as "data of remembrance" that result from an encounter with the vestiges of a former life; here, remembrance is the anamnesis of a prelapsarian existence in which humanity enjoyed a familial interaction with both nature and itself.[35] Benjamin continues by noting that, in Baudelaire's "La vie antérieure," which is an implicit ode to the *correspondances*, "the images of caves and vegetation, of clouds and waves . . . rise from the warm vapor of tears, tears of homesickness" that bespeak the unbridgeable distance between this prehistorical utopia and the decadent subject.[36]

Decadence in Ravel's Music

These literary influences left abundant traces in Ravel's music. In addition to the settings of Verlaine's poetry, which include both the *fête galante* "Sur l'herbe" and the rendering of oblivion in "Un grand sommeil noir," we find melancholic, quasi-moonlit serenades with a lutelike accompaniment in the middle movement of the *Sonatine* and the development section of the *Introduction et allegro*. For Ravel, sublimation, desire, and the sublimation of desire are elements of Mallarmé's legacy: Note his early setting of the poet's "Sainte," whose cyclical chordal patterns—to be played "piano sans aucune nuance"—capture the mesmerizing, inviolate sublimity of the poetic image, as well as the *Trois poèmes de Stéphane Mallarmé,* whose "Soupir" limns the quintessentially decadent gesture of rising toward the Ideal before falling back melancholically upon the Real.

Huysmans's *À rebours* does not receive a direct setting in Ravel's music, but it does garner an homage in an article the composer wrote in 1931. In addition to emphasizing its "major importance," Ravel claims—despite the untimeliness of such a confession—that his entire generation came of age through this novel, as previously mentioned.[37] None more so than Ravel himself, who, like des Esseintes, retreated to the suburban countryside, where he furnished and meticulously decorated a home after his own tastes;[38] upon completing his purchase of a home in Montfort-l'Amaury after the war, Ravel must have felt something like des Esseintes's "glow of pleasure at the idea that here he would be too far out for the tidal wave of Parisian life to reach him, and yet near enough for the proximity of the capital to strengthen him in his solitude."[39] Ravel's lifelong dandyism is further evidence of his strong identification with des Esseintes, whose mental breakdown in the novel—the shattering or "interruption" of the dandy's sublime exterior—arguably becomes part of the representation of the dandy in his music.

Baudelaire's influence on Ravel is also more a matter of general proclivities than direct citation, whose sole example is the epigraph for the "Habanera." Nevertheless, a few moments in Ravel are hard to conceive without the poet's precedent: Serenely retrospective codas in the first and third movements of the String Quartet exemplify Baudelaire's "l'art d'évoquer les minutes heureuses," and the wavelike reanimation of festive scenarios in the "Feria" of the *Rapsodie espagnole, Daphnis et Chloé,* and *La valse,* preceded as they are by processes of recollection and coalescence, bespeaks the operation of *correspondances* in conjuring up the past. In addition, two instants in Ravel stand out for sharing a phenomenology with Baudelaire's "A une passante," a classic account of glimpsing a beautiful woman within a quickly moving crowd that Benjamin wittily summed up as "love at last sight."[40] One is the final, tender embrace between Daphnis and Chloe (example I.1), which Ravel sets to a love theme whose premature truncation reflects the disruption of this idyllic vision by the bacchanalian revelers in the finale. The other is the breathtaking hiatus in the midst of the climactic end to *La valse,* reproduced in the middle of example I.2 as the piece's "backward glance."

These are only a few of the myriad instances in Ravel that respond well to a hermeneutics of decadence. While I discuss many of these in the book proper, I would like to consider here one of the composer's personal favorites, "Oiseaux tristes" from *Miroirs,* which juxtaposes two contrasting principles throughout: the sprightly innocence of birdsong and the brooding melancholy of its human auditor, as laid out in the schema of its opening measures (example I.3).[41]

Example I.1 Love at Last Sight 1: The Final Embrace of Daphnis and Chloe.

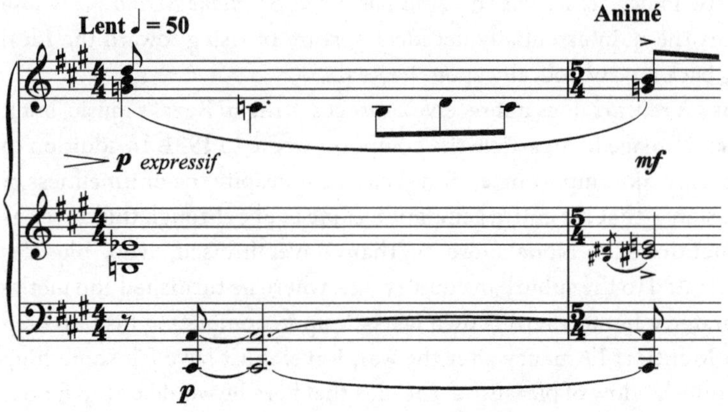

Example I.2 Love at Last Sight 2: The Backward Glance in the Coda of *La valse*.

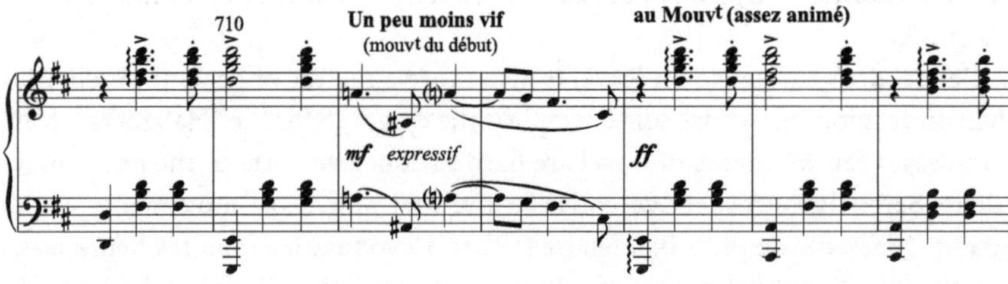

Example I.3 The Plunge into Melancholy during the Opening Measures of "Oiseaux tristes."

The next example reproduces the similar, albeit reversed, decadent configuration at the beginning of *L'heure espagnole,* whose initial melancholy (example I.4a) erupts into a chromatic wail (example I.4b) before various automata begin to dance and play their music (example I.4c).

However, as in "Oiseaux tristes," these sounds of innocence and provocations to childlike wonder ultimately do little to lighten the mood of the brooder, whose cycle of brooding and wailing continues unabated. Indeed, the sense of melancholy is so forceful here—especially because it is seemingly unmotivated—that it threatens to make the portrayal of the ennui-racked decadent appear more parodic than sympathetic. Rather than undermining the decadence of the frame, however, this double perspective augments it since the hypertrophied conscious-

Example I.4 The Decadent Frame of *L'heure espagnole*: Brooding (a), Wailing (b), and Wondrous Distraction (c).

ness and self-consciousness of decadence have always smoothed the path to caricature: In addition to the more general embrace of internal contradiction in the concept of perennial decay, witness the hyperbole of Huysmans's *À rebours*, the parodies of Laforgue's *Moralités légendaires*, the early self-parody of the decadent poets in *Deliquescences*, and the pastiche-cum-parody of Verlaine's "À la manière" series in *Parallèlement*, which paved the way for Proust's famous series of pastiches. Highlighting the decadent frame of *L'heure espagnole*—whose brooding motifs return periodically in the opera to reassert its initial premises—is a particularly rewarding application of our interpretive approach because it helps to answer a question that has troubled audiences since the work's premiere: Why did Ravel write such sad music for Franc-Nohain's lively sex farce?[42] From our perspective, it is because the opera is founded in a decadent experience of time as an existential prison; the prisoner here happens to be Concepcion, shut up in a clock shop filled with an audible "multitude of seconds" that would suffocate her if the "Spanish hour" did not offer momentary release by enabling her sexcapades.[43]

And so forth since every piece by Ravel is arguably inflected by decadent aesthetics. Nonetheless, if the Decadence ended just as his career was taking off, is it not anachronistic to describe Ravel as a Decadent composer? Before we formulate a response, we should first examine the two main justifications for terminating the Decadence around 1900. One is generational, based on the fact that several founding figures of the Decadence died around this time, including Verlaine (d. 1896) and Mallarmé (d. 1898). Despite the time-honored impulse to proclaim that an "era has passed" with the death of one or more cultural figureheads, this obviously does not preclude the possibility that a later generation will continue its concerns. Indeed, what would European modernism look like if the paradigmatic contributions of James Joyce, T. S. Eliot, and Thomas Mann, not to mention Ravel, had been leached of their decadent preoccupations? The other main justification is that the worldview of the Decadence was supplanted by a Nietzschean vitalism antithetical to it, but this model of opposition and succession is weakened by the dialectic between life and death that can already be found at the heart of decadence—just as Charles Bernheimer refuted the mutual exclusion of a supposedly organic naturalism and an inorganic decadence, revealing instead their dialectical interaction.[44] Thus, it need be neither anachronistic nor nonsensical to describe Ravel as a Decadent artist even if he were a bit belated. But what company he had, alongside his equally epigonal compatriots Valéry and Proust! Though composed during the second and third decades of the twentieth century, Proust's novel *À la recherche du temps perdu* (*Remembrance of Things Past*, 1913–1927) has been described by one of the most highly regarded historians of this period as "the supreme artistic expression of the *fin-de-siècle* mentality."[45] Fittingly, it also provides the basis for our exploration of memory from a decadent perspective.

A Conspectus of Memory, by Way of Proust

Memory is as fundamental to human life as it is vast as a field of study and thus continually inspires attempts at a survey while also threatening to defeat them. One strategy I have chosen to limit memory's conceptual sprawl is to adduce only those aspects that seem most helpful in understanding Ravel's music. Another is to choose a single text from this period as a central reference point for memory. For this role I have selected *À la recherche*, a three-thousand-page novel that not only features a deep and sustained meditation on memory but, as a landmark of decadent literature, also emphasizes those qualities that helped to make memory such a compelling topic for the decadents.[46] Stemming from a close reading of Proust and supplemented by insights from other relevant texts, the following conspectus of memory has a threefold purpose: to offer a general introduction to the study of memory, to provide a specific introduction to the discussion of memory in Ravel, and to ground the more occasional references to Proust in subsequent chapters of the book.

While the turn to Proust may be hardly surprising, it is rather unusual to compare his work to Ravel's—and understandably so. If Proust was the proverbial hedgehog, focusing his attention on the production of a single work as it gradually evolved over many years from *Jean Santeuil* into *Contre Sainte-Beuve* and finally into *À la recherche*, Ravel was a fox, producing numerous smaller-scale works in a variety of genres. Nonetheless, their lives resembled each other in several respects: They were born four years apart, were Parisian dandies, and ran in similar social circles. Although Ravel receives only an incidental mention in *À la recherche*, they clearly respected each other's work, as indicated by Proust's asking for the *Pavane pour une infante défunte* to be played at his funeral and Ravel's collecting all the volumes of Proust's novel for his personal library at Montfort-l'Amaury. A common orientation toward aestheticism, pastiche, and memory—all part of the decadent legacy—further unites them, as I have discussed elsewhere.[47] While my efforts to compare the two may seem unusual, they have precedent in many observations by other scholars, including some relatively recent remarks by Frederick Goldbeck and Marcel Marnat about the retrospectivism and perfectionism of these two artists, as well as an early essay (c. 1928) by Adorno, who noted that both treated the object of desire in an aristocratic manner by setting it at a distance and idealizing it—in other words, sublimating it.[48]

When I invoke "memory," I usually mean either the past become present or the ability to make the past present. Within the flow of time, the past becomes present either by continuing smoothly into it or breaking into it at a particular moment. How the past does so depends on what it is. Classic examples of memory-as-continuous-past include tradition, landscape, and race, all of which have been supposed to possess a "long memory."[49] Indeed, one of the most influential concepts in memory studies—Pierre Nora's *lieu de mémoire* [site of memory], which is ostensibly indebted to the *locus memoriae* of Western classical and premodern rhetoric—poses precisely this question of the continuity between present and past.[50] Ranging from monuments and festivals to anthems and literary texts, the *lieux* are vestiges of the past in the present—"no longer quite life, not yet death, like shells on the shore when the sea of living memory has receded."[51] In the course of defining the *lieu* Nora critiques modernity for its loss of collective memory, as well as its concomitant focus on individual psychology; in both respects he is echoing, wittingly or no, the arguments of Maurice Halbwachs's *Les cadres sociaux de la mémoire* (1925), in which the author excoriates Bergson for his conflation of memories with dreams and calls instead for the recognition of *la mémoire collective* in every aspect of life, including private, individual memory.[52] However, from a decadent perspective the obsolescence of tradition and a surging concern over the individual psyche do not simply give cause for lament but rather impel the creation of new and special relationships between past and present, lending each a valence of its own.[53] The degree of discontinuity between the two—the fundamental source for *la poésie de la mémoire* in Proust, according to Hans-Robert Jauss—depends on their temporal distance and qualitative difference from each other;[54] in general, the more distant the past is from the present and the more sharply its memory is distinguished against the backdrop of the present, the greater its potential to affect the present.

A well-known example of this value system is the dichotomy of "voluntary" and "involuntary" memory outlined by Proust in *À la recherche*, whereby an involuntary memory contrasts with a voluntary memory insofar as the former is unbidden by the conscious will and conjured up by sensation rather than the intellect.[55] Discontinuous with the present, involuntary memories are like electric shocks, entering through the body and startling the rememberer out of the oblivion brought on by the dulling effect of the mundane and the quotidian. (My comparison of memories to shocks alludes, of course, to the theorization of modern urban life by Baudelaire, who was also a major influence on Proust.)[56] Fusing notions of experience from Baudelaire and Proust, involuntary memory enacts the decadent scenario par excellence: Not only is the subject's gaze turned inward and backward on the past, but memory—especially in its involuntary mode—is also loaded with so much charge, derived from the original shock power of its object, that it acts as a powerful stimulant, jolting the jaded subject into heightened states of consciousness ranging from the ecstatic to the traumatic.

Three examples from Proust's novel, presented in the order of their appearance, help to demonstrate the difference between voluntary and involuntary memory, as well as the range of shock effects produced by the latter; citations from the three-volume English translation by Moncrieff, Kilmartin, and Mayor henceforth appear directly in the text.[57] The novel begins with the narrator's voluntary memory of his youth in the country town of Combray, centered around a bedtime scene that shows his childhood anxiety over being separated from his mother. Insofar as the narrator,

Marcel, has become accustomed to the memory of this scene, it has lost its appeal and has become drab, unrevealing, and lifeless. In the "felicitous moment" (*moment bienheureux*) that follows, he is suffering from ennui on a dreary day in the midst of his mature life in Paris, when suddenly, upon biting into a madeleine dipped in tea, he recalls the joyous part of his childhood in Combray—a memory to which he previously had no direct access. The exhilarating sense of transport and redemption he feels at this moment contrasts with the traumatic loss he feels at what we might call an "infelicitous" moment later on in the novel, when the gesture of bending down to take off his boots suddenly brings to mind a hitherto repressed memory of his dead, beloved grandmother. This particular involuntary memory shocks the false and oblivious present with its true and sudden "revelation of death," which strikes the narrator like a "thunderbolt," carving "a double and mysterious furrow" into his psyche (II, 787).

For Marcel, these moments of involuntary memory, intermittent and unexpected, are "foundation stones for the construction of a true life" (III, 262). For readers of the novel, they call attention to an important paradox of memory: how the return of past experience can be felt as something shockingly new. No one was more sensitive to this paradox than Proust himself, who has the narrator remark toward the conclusion of the novel how the felicitous moment of involuntary memory "causes us suddenly to breathe a new air, an air which is new precisely because we have breathed it in the past" (III, 903). This leads us to a second paradox, one that emphasizes a dialectical aspect of memory: Memory is indebted to oblivion for its shock effect, for it is oblivion that preserves the immediacy of the past by holding it in prolonged abeyance. Symbolized by the "vase clos" (sealed vessel), the preservation of memory in oblivion is so central to Proust that Shattuck identifies it as his "general law of memory."[58]

Recording experience and producing memories, memory does not float freely but belongs to a remembering subject, whether individual or collective. As an aspect of subjectivity, memory is included among the cognitive faculties that enable reflection and self-reflection. When memories are shared, memory turns out from the self-reflective subject and toward society; by making private experience public, memory builds communities by fostering communication, interaction, and self-knowledge among individuals and groups.

Memory also refers the self back to itself by serving the rememberer. While memory might have the simple goal of retrieving facts about the past, it can also fulfill less practical and rational aims, including the production of pleasure (as well as the exquisitely painful pleasure of the unrequitable) in and through the act of reminiscence.[59] Reminiscence can be pleasurable, regardless of content, for the intoxicating and autoerotic state of reverie it produces. However, this pleasure often depends on the specific content of a memory; enfolded within Proust's famous apothegm that "the true paradises are the paradises that we have lost" is the notion that certain moments in the past (rather than in the future or in some impossible, purely imaginary realm) are the ultimate objects of desire and therefore also the ultimate sources of pleasure (III, 903). The pleasure outlined by this apothegm is born of nostalgia, a particular mode of memory that can be thought to enhance the pleasure of reminiscence by mixing it with the pain of loss—an enticing prospect for the decadents, who were connoisseurs of pleasure in its more rarified forms. In the case of Ravel, one thinks immediately of the epigraph by Henri de Régnier that he chose for the *Valses nobles et sentimentales*: "the delicious and always novel pleasure of a useless activity," where the valorization of a "useless activity" resembles that of "wasted time" in Proust (another meaning of *temps perdu*).[60]

Beset simultaneously by the presence of the past in memory and the knowledge of its absence in the here and now, nostalgic subjects are, as Proust says, "amphibious," living in two temporalities at once (III, 544).[61] The pleasure afforded by reminiscence will continue as long as memory and interest can sustain it—which is to say, indefinitely, since memories often induce memory to produce further memories in a feedback loop or chain reaction. In the autobiographical "Berlin Chronicle," which forms part of his broad and deep reception of Proust, Walter Benjamin calls attention to this aspect of memory, declaring at one point that "he who has once begun to open the fan of memory never comes to the end of its segments; no image satisfies him, for he has seen that it can be unfolded, and only in its folds does the truth reside."[62] In this scenario memory maintains a perfect economy by meeting an infinite demand with an infinite supply. Moreover, the motivating role Benjamin assigns to truth echoes sentiments by Proust, who proclaimed that "the march of thought in the solitary work of artistic creation proceeds in depth, in the only direction that is not closed to us . . . toward a goal of truth" (I, 968). However, the justification for memory work need not be so simple or noble as this. As Proust shows in the characters of both Swann and Marcel, memory is just as easily motivated by jealousy and obsession—and thereby flirts with disaster since, as Proust warns us, "attachment to an object always brings death to its possessor" (III, 834).

Memory serves the rememberer by also being of the rememberer. At first thought, memory might seem to diminish the presence of the rememberer by casting its spotlight entirely on the remembered past. However, as Proust notes, this is a chronic misunderstanding of perception, whereby "one's egoism sees before it all the time the objects that are of concern to the self, but never takes in that 'I' itself which is incessantly observing them" (III, 474).[63] Consequently, perception is never objective but rather inescapably perspectivist—life in "perpetual error," as he puts it (III, 585). One trace of memory's error may be its mannerist emphasis on "some distinctive feature that had struck us," thereby "making a woman who has appeared to us tall a sketch in which her figure is elongated out of all proportion" (I, 978). Another is the omission of some elements, the effect of memory's dialectic of remembering and forgetting. Upon noting that people do not remain as immutable in memory as they do in a painting, Marcel declares that "oblivion is at work within us, and according to its arbitrary operation they evolve" (III, 1022).[64] To put it even more dramatically, memory does not merely transform the remembered past but recreates it with every act regardless of whether we have noticeably altered the image of the past from one recollection to the next. Proust mentions this aspect early on in the novel, having the narrator spontaneously correct his understanding of memory's relation to the past: "Seek? More than that: create" (I, 49). The underlying, potentially unsettling realization here is that the mind does not hold memory apart from fantasy but rather allows one freely to penetrate the other; Freud came to similar conclusions around the same time, as his earlier notion of the falsified "screen memory" gradually gave way to the stronger claim that remembering shares with dreamwork the latter's array of transformations upon mental content (condensation, displacement, symbolism, etc.).[65] By remodeling memory on creation rather than reproduction, Proust's modest substitution of *créer* for *chercher* has momentous implications—and not only for the title of the novel (*À la* ré-création *du temps perdu*?). For one, the creativity of memory keeps alive the dialogue between present and past, simultaneously satisfying and frustrating our desire to comprehend the past since all of our interpretations of the past are as provisional as the shape of any particular recollection. For another, Proust also proposes that creativity can feel mnemonic, as if entities newly created in the present were merely returning from the past in an instance of Platonic anamnesis (III, 912).[66] Once we pay heed to this complex interference between present and past in memory, we may sense the dissolution of other hoary, memory-related dichotomies, including remembering/forgetting and truth/fiction.[67]

Broadcasting the perspective of its creator, memories become a mirror of the self, reflecting modes of understanding and perception available to and characteristic of the self at different points in time, especially at the bounding points of the original experience and its present recollection. When Marcel recalls his dead grandmother, he realizes how memories, especially involuntary ones, have the "power . . . of installing alone in us the self that originally lived them" (I, 784). For a dandy like Proust, memory could even be thought to sublimate life into a form of art, refashioning the past in such a way as to lend it a coherent style. For instance, when Marcel recalls a heterogeneously decorated dining room, he notes that his memory has retroactively imposed upon it "a cohesion, a unity, an individual charm that are not to be found even in the most complete, the least spoiled of the collections that the past has bequeathed to us" (I, 581). For Marcel, this homogeneity is a sign of mature artistry, as exemplified in the work of various fictional characters: the actor Berma, the composer Vinteuil, and the painter Elstir.[68] On the one hand, when the past becomes homogeneous, its details lose their revolutionary potential to break off from the whole and puncture the present as involuntary memories. On the other, the homogeneous past can also be an idealized past insofar as the creative and sublimating aspects of memory shape it to fit preconceptions of beauty. For Marcel, memory most often behaves this way when memorializing desirable women in his life, whether it be Albertine, silhouetted against the sea at Balbec, or Gilberte, "embowered always in a hedge of pink hawthorn" (I, 578), or the Princesse of Guermantes, whose noble profile is forever impressed into his memory as upon the gold of a glorious medal (II, 659).

A fragile thing, susceptible to the vicissitudes of the body to which it belongs, memory simultaneously preserves the self and exposes it to mortal danger; it is no coincidence that one of the most widely read treatises on memory during this period, Théodule-Armand Ribot's *Les maladies de la mémoire* (1881), attempts to explicate memory from the standpoint of its pathologies—having too little (amnesia) and too much memory (hypermnesia) are equally symptoms of ill health, whether caused by falls, decrepitude, fevers, manias, hysteria, or the like.[69] Memory's inherent orientation toward the self can also be thought to foster narcissism and solipsism, two behaviors that threaten to isolate and deactivate the individual, thereby decomposing the social body and diminishing its potential for a healthy and productive future. Though fully aware of these potential pitfalls, decadent writers and artists typically neither refuted nor suppressed the association between (the immoderate cultivation of) memory and dream with either antisocial behavior or disease. Just as memory may be a stimulant, so too might it be a narcotic—one often made possible by narcotics themselves, as the protodecadents de Quincey and Baudelaire famously discovered in their experimentation with opium and hashish. Indeed, Proust himself describes memory as a "pharmacy" or "chemical laboratory in which our groping hand may come to rest now on a sedative drug, now on a dangerous potion" (III, 397). Further, memory can feel like an illness, especially in its involuntary mode. When discussing leitmotivic design in Wagner, Marcel is struck by its "reality" as a simulation of memory: Its "insistent, fleeting themes which visit an act recede only to return again and again, and, sometimes distant, drowsy, almost detached, are at other moments, while remaining vague, so pressing and so close, so internal, so organic, so visceral, that they seem like the reprise not so much of a musical motif as of an attack of neuralgia" (III, 156).[70]

To be a brilliant artist at this moment in time was necessarily to suffer nervous disorders, as expressed in the claim that "genius is a neurosis"—an utterance now best known for Nietzsche's sardonic application of it to Wagner when discussing European cultural and artistic decadence.[71] One way the decadents responded to this diagnosis was to transvaluate it in a Nietzschean sense, reversing its polarities to find genius in neurosis. Thus, the decadent neurotic was no longer simply a figure of inertia and sickness but also one of creative and self-creative power. Suffering from various ailments that confined him to his apartment, Proust was a prime historical example of the neurotic genius, and his novel was one of its greatest products. Midway through the novel he places an encomium to his own type in the mouth of Dr. du Boulbon: "Everything we think of as great has come to us from neurotics. It is they and they alone who found religions and create great works of art. . . . We enjoy fine music, beautiful pictures, a thousand exquisite things, but we do not know what they cost those who wrought them in insomnia, tears, spasmodic laughter, urticaria, asthma, epilepsy, a terror of death"—and, in the case of the semiautobiographical *À la recherche,* the neuralgia brought on by involuntary memory (II, 315). We should also not forget that nostalgia was recognized as a bona fide medical condition from the late seventeenth century into the mid-twentieth century.[72]

Even if dwelling on the past were to have negative effects on one's health, it would not have deterred the decadents since the profound psychological knowledge of humanity they sought would have been impossible to achieve without the intense introspection permitted by memory. For Proust, "man" is not only "the creature who cannot escape from himself" but also he "who knows other people only in himself" (III, 459). The infinite resources within us obviate the necessity of looking without to collect and recollect ourselves, as Proust asserts when writing that "there is no need to travel in order to discover [the past] again; we must dig down inwardly to discover it" (II, 89).[73] And yet, as mental activity, memory's self-excavations are not onerous labor but rather allow the rememberer to escape from the "crushing weight of matter to play freely in the fluid spaces of the mind" (III, 50), even if the body is often memory's repository and catalyst.[74] By liberating the self into pure reflection, memory dilates the sense of time by slowing down the "dizzy whirl of daily life" to rescue the distinct colors and qualities of experience from the abysses of habit and oblivion (II, 6).[75] Rather than promoting solipsistic detachment from the world, memory actually expresses a deep devotion to it by attempting, through recollected experience, to preserve it over and against its constant flux. This is the grounding for Proust's observation that, "if our life is vagabond, our memory is sedentary, and though we ourselves rush ceaselessly forward, our recollections, indissolubly bound to the sites which we have left behind us, continue to lead a placid and sequestered existence among them" (III, 1039).[76] By resisting the pull of oblivion, memory joins forces with the imagination to override "those fictitious barriers of death" (III, 539) and, at least for Proust, to stretch toward the twinned promises of happiness and immortality.[77]

The Mnemoanalysis of Music

While the understanding of memory that we have gleaned from Proust's novel may be suggestive for the analysis and interpretation of music, most of its insights require some mediation before we can apply them to these tasks. In other words, we need a methodology that balances the idiomatic qualities of music with the concerns of memory studies. In principle, this methodology should be simple:

After identifying an example of memory in music, we would then pose questions about the operation of memory within it and try to answer them through analysis. Seeking to represent the two disciplines equally, I have compiled a set of questions that address content, timing, transformation, agency, and value. This set offers a rounded view but may be extended, of course, to accommodate the full complexity of these issues. Here, then, is the slate of questions, prefaced by their respective rubrics:

Content: What constitutes present and past?
Timing: When does the past reappear, and how long does it last?
Transformation: How has the past been altered in its reappearance in the present?
Agency: Who or what is remembering the past?
Value: What is the value of the past for the remembering subject?

The value of a methodology depends on its effectiveness, which we usually assess by applying it to individual examples and examining the results. However, to launch into analysis at this point would be premature: While it is clear that these questions address memory, their relation to music still needs to be fleshed out, especially regarding the question of content. One type of content for a musical memory is historical and recognizably belongs to the past, whether it is an entire tonal system or some part thereof, an aspect of rhythm and meter, texture, or instrumentation, a genre, a theme, or the like. A second is contextual and comes from either the past of the piece itself or an earlier movement within the same suite—a compositional device commonly referred to as "cyclic form." A third type arises from the association between a musical moment and a text—an expressive direction, an epigraph, a programmatic scenario, a libretto, lyrics, and so on—which explicitly invites us to interpret that moment in relation to memory.[78]

All three types of content, though clear in themselves and distinct from each other, are vulnerable to critique. The third is relatively straightforward, although in any given example there is no guarantee that the music will either acknowledge or accommodate the thematics of memory in the accompanying text. A question arises upon regarding historical content: If it must belong to the past, how should we deal with pieces that have one foot in the present? An example might be the waltz at the *fin de siècle*, which was a genre in continuous practice from the nineteenth into the twentieth century, as well as a site of nostalgia for a defunct or at least obsolescent culture—a plausible instance of Nora's *lieu de mémoire*. Either we can be content with merely identifying the hybridization of memory and living tradition in such instances of historical ambivalence, or we can attempt to gauge the presence of memory in a specific piece by examining it for marks that betray a sense of distance from the past. Ravel's *Valses nobles et sentimentales* is a good example since it enthusiastically embraces the waltz while still refusing to lose sight of the gap between past and present: Not only does the final waltz, the doleful "Epilogue," belie the presence of the past in the previous seven waltzes, but most of the latter also display the tension between Ravel's modern harmony and traditional form.

When considering the second type of content, we are faced with the dizzying possibility of describing any and all contextual repetitions as memories. To constrain this possibility, we can identify several situations in which we would not confuse the two: When the repeated material still seems to belong to the present (as applies especially well to immediate repetition), when it unambiguously conforms to the dictates of conventional form (as do elements in a binary-form reprise or a sonata-form recapitulation), and, from a phenomenological perspective, when it has been altered so much from its original version as to make it highly unlikely for listeners to recognize it in the past; here, the governing supposition is that music resembles memory more strongly when it actually provokes the listener to remember. Yet these are only rules of thumb and may not apply in certain circumstances—such as a sonata-form movement that is so distant from common practice and heterogeneous in its material that the moment of recapitulation no longer seems routine. Proust actually uses musical terms to describe a similar phenomenon in dreams, whose unpredictability can make ordinary repetition seem extraordinary: "Often it was simply during my sleep that these 'reprises,' these 'da capos' of one's dreams, which turn back several pages of one's memory, several leaves of the calendar at once, made me regress to a painful but remote impression which had long since given place to others but which now became present once more" (III, 549).

The categories of timing and transformation are well suited to music and its analytical methods. Given the precision with which our Cartesian notation charts temporal succession in music, we can refer to measure numbers and beats to answer questions of timing. Nevertheless, the question of timing is always also a question of form since the moment an event occurs within a piece is also the site where the event takes place within its formal design. In more philosophical terms, time unfolds music; music unfolds time; music and time unfold each other.[79] We are also accustomed to answering questions of transformation by breaking music down into its component parameters—pitch, rhythm, tempo, dynamics, articulation, instrumentation, and so on—comparing the parametric array from one example with that of another and then stepping back from these details to make broader aesthetic/stylistic/historical claims about their similarity and difference.

Since agency is often indeterminate and value requires interpretation, these categories are trickier but not impossible to address. Rather than being merely presentist or arbitrary, the interpretation of value is guided by historical accounts (even if they do not achieve consensus) and musical semiotics. Moreover, if we cannot determine an actual subject of memory for a piece of music, we can still speak of a subjectivity realized in and by the mnemonic behavior of that piece. Performers arguably play an important role in this process insofar as successfully enacting memory in an artistic medium would require them to inhabit that memory as if they were actually recollecting its contents and experiencing all of the concomitant emotions.[80] The argument would likely be congenial to Proust: Without personal investment there can be no empathy, and without empathy we would lose touch with the innumerable inflections of time and affect that mark memory's visit.

Analyzing Memory in the Sonatine

As the rest of this book shows, many of Ravel's pieces respond well to mnemoanalysis—the String Quartet, the *Rapsodie espagnole,* the *Valses nobles et sentimentales, Daphnis et Chloé, La valse,* and the Sonata for Violin and Piano, among others—but none demonstrates the effectiveness of this methodology more clearly and concisely than the *Sonatine.*

Content

The *Sonatine* was written in two phases: After composing the first movement in 1903 for a competition that never came to fruition, Ravel completed the second and third movements and published the suite in 1905. As befits the High Classical genre invoked in its title, the *Sonatine* places a sonata form on either side of a "Mouvement de Menuet" (henceforth, "Menuet"). Due to its title and layout, as well as its fairly tonal material and traditional phraseology, the *Sonatine* is often described as neoclassical even though it was composed more than a decade prior to the interwar flourishing of musical Neoclassicism. By giving it the additional designation of a memory piece we are claiming that the relation between past and present in this piece is significant contextually, as well as historically, and thus invites analysis according to the methodology outlined earlier. The more distinct process of recollection in the *Sonatine* is the one involving the contextual past: the primary theme of the first movement, which returns in the second and third movements as an example of cyclic form; example I.5 gives the original statement of this theme, as well as its initial recurrence in each subsequent movement.

Since the contextual past is better addressed by questions of timing and transformation, I focus here instead on the historical past. Through its various associations with eighteenth-century music, the *Sonatine* has the potential to create a shock effect whenever its past breaks into the modernist present. However, as may reflect Ravel's tendencies toward irony and eclecticism, the sound of the eighteenth century at these moments—most acutely enacted at the opening of each

Example I.5 The Cyclic Theme in the First (a), Second (b), and Third (c) Movements of the *Sonatine.*

movement—is not as prominent as one might expect. The first movement begins with an urgent lyricism and rapid accompaniment more similar to a *Lied ohne Worte* by Mendelssohn than sonatinas by Dussek and Clementi;[81] in comparison, the opening phrase of the Menuet displays a stronger debt to the eighteenth century for its rhythm, texture, and articulation but arrives at a modal cadence more reminiscent of Chabrier (e.g., the Overture to *Gwendoline*) than Haydn; aside from the registrally constrained and mechanical textures, the beginning of the finale with its mordant fanfares and modal harmony seems more modern and continues as a quasi-synthesis of the outer movements of Debussy's suite *Pour le piano* (1901), whose succession of "Prélude," "Sarabande," and "Toccata" movements is comparably neoclassical. As a memory piece, the *Sonatine* therefore seems gradually to merge the past into the present as its compositional models become increasingly current.

Timing

Since the question of timing concerns mainly the design of a specific piece, I turn now to the cyclic form of the *Sonatine* and its recurrent theme. We begin with its recurrence in the Menuet (example I.5b), which appears at the midpoint of the movement and occupies six measures, after which it begins to dissipate through repetition. While it may be brief, amounting to a mere 7 percent of the entire movement, it compensates for its lack of quantity with quality, distinguishing itself not only by its status as a cyclic theme but also by its remarkable use of register, harmony, dynamics, rhythm, and texture. This memory is thus a "moment" in the paradoxical sense: short in duration but lasting in impression, due to its extraordinary sound design.[82]

Since issues of timing in music are also matters of form, we should note that the moment of recollection takes place between the climax and the reprise of the Menuet. Independent of both, it is neither the dénouement of the climax nor the retransition to the reprise but rather the "interior" of the Menuet and even of the *Sonatine* as a whole. As an interior, it brings to mind a trio embedded within a minuet.[83] From this perspective the *Menuet antique* (1895) emerges as an important precedent. At the center of the earlier piece Ravel not only places a triolike episode but also uses some of the same musical devices—shifts into a high register and soft dynamics, pedal, metrical dissonance (especially the left-hand hemiola), and motives that cycle back into themselves, as shown in example I.6—to conjure up a similar state of reverie and nostalgia.

Indeed, the moment of recollection in the *Sonatine*'s Menuet seems to represent or reenact psychological interiority, just as its recurrent musical subject brings forth subjectivity in and through the act of memory. The motivic looping (example I.7) that surrounds the recollection evokes interiority through reverberation, thereby making the Menuet into a resonant (mental) space where sounds past and present echo and mingle; the conception of the Menuet as an echo chamber is also a way to interrelate its historical and contextual pasts.

Example I.6 A Moment of Reverie in the Trio of the *Menuet antique*.

Underscoring the pull of memory, the recollection lingers after its moment has passed, with a version of its head motive continuing to flow in an undercurrent beneath the reprise of the opening theme.

In comparison, the timing of the cyclic theme in the finale of the *Sonatine* seems to be simpler to analyze, given its role as the secondary theme within a sonata form. However, on closer review its function is not so clearly defined: While it may behave normally by following the typical midexposition event in minor-key sonata forms—the cadential arrival at the dominant of the relative major—it retains the dominant root from this arrival instead of resolving it into the secondary tonic (here, A major) and thereby confirming the onset of the secondary area. Gently set apart by its tonal irresolution, the initial statement of the cyclic theme plays an oblique role within the finale, suspended between definitive statements of the primary and secondary themes. In this way it recalls not only the cyclic theme in the Menuet but also the melancholic episode in the first movement (example I.8), which mediates between primary and secondary areas in the exposition by deflecting the music away from the relative major and back toward the tonic.[84]

In addition, the cyclic theme in the finale harks back to the recollection in the Menuet through its identity as a formal interior, as well as the motivic reverberation that surrounds and permeates it. These observations about the timing of the cyclic theme in the finale reveal that it is not only a composite but also a second-order memory, a Wordsworthian "after-meditation" recollecting the Menuet's recollection of the cyclic theme.

Example I.7 Motivic Looping as Mnemonic Activity Before (a) and After (b) the Cyclic Theme in the "Menuet" of the *Sonatine.*

a)

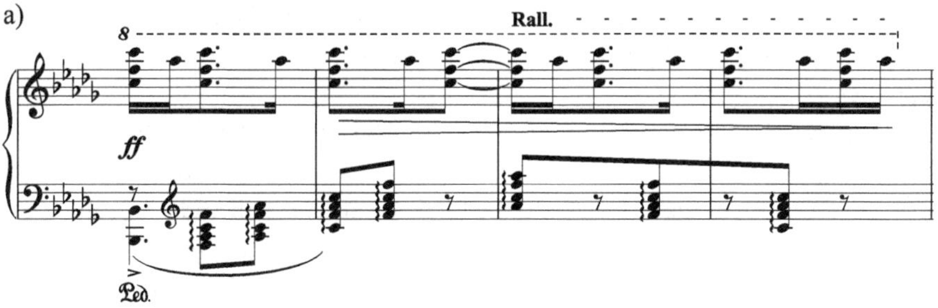

b)

Example I.8 The Melancholic Theme in the Transition of the First Movement of the *Sonatine.*

Transformation

While the question of timing asks when and where the past recurs, the question of transformation asks how it has been altered. Once again, we may pose this question to both the historical and the contextual pasts. With regard to the former, Ravel scholars have most often raised it in discussing the "Forlane" from *Le tombeau de Couperin* (1917) since we can directly compare this piece with the Forlane from François Couperin's *Quatrième concert royal* (1722), which Ravel copied out in 1914 and quite audibly used as a model for his own.[85] Since we do not possess a model for the *Sonatine,* we cannot make a similar comparison.[86] Nevertheless, if we understand one of neoclassicism's intentions to be the rejuvenation of the past, we can observe that tonality seems more effective in the two sonata forms than in the Menuet. Whereas the sonata forms, governed by a tight motivicism, hurtle forth toward pivotal moments of large-scale reprise and resolution in their tonal design, the Menuet is more digressive, meandering from one theme to the next as if the past were a mere pretext for dreamy *flânerie.*[87] As Benjamin once wrote, memory does not always act "as the source but as the Muse," leading the *flâneur* into forgotten byways of the past and making each into a "vertiginous experience."[88]

To assess the transformation of the contextual past in the *Sonatine,* we need only compare the initial statement of the primary theme (example I.5a) with its cyclic recurrence in the Menuet and the finale (examples I.5b and I.5c). The most striking transformation in the Menuet is the theme's refraction into both a superposed melody, which reduces the original from ten beats to six and from piano to pianissimo, and a subposed melody that rhythmically augments and staggers its counterpart above. The effect of this transformation is to highlight the roles of idealization and reflection in memory: The miniaturized, music-box version above idealizes the past, while the version below (marked "piano en dehors et expressif") reviews the past in slow motion as if the remembering subject were ruminating nostalgically upon it. This behavior fits Boym's notion of "reflective nostalgia," which dwells in "longing and loss" and "lingers on ruins, the patina of time and history, in the dreams of another place and another time."[89] Other musical features of this moment—its low pedal point, static harmony, and rolled chords—support this interpretation by creating a still and sensual environment conducive to reverie and reflection. When the theme returns in the finale, it reprises the rapid accompanimental texture it had in the first movement but still bears traces of its transformation in the Menuet, including an elevated register, a rhythmically contracted melody, motivic looping, and prolonged bass tones. At each of its three appearances in the finale, the cyclic theme momentarily inflects the flow of the *perpetuum mobile*, due not only to its asymmetrical meter (5/4) but also to its gradual deceleration from "tranquille" into a more meditative "plus lent."

Agency and Value

Current musicology is well equipped to answer questions of agency and value with respect to the historical past. In the case of the *Sonatine* the agent of memory is Ravel, while the value of its recollected past is the result of multiple factors: the *Sonatine*'s implicit rejection of nineteenth-century Romanticism and its excesses (immoderate expressivity, overblown virtuosity, sprawling forms, rampant chromaticism, etc.), its embrace of contrasting values typically associated with the eighteenth century (moderation, decorum, etiquette, grace, charm, brevity, etc.), a general, nationalistic appreciation for this period as a floruit of authentically French music (especially the music of Lully, Couperin, and Rameau), the composer's personal aesthetics (an identification with dandyism, for example), and a desire to emulate neoclassical essays by his contemporaries (Debussy, Saint-Saëns, et al.), among other possibilities.[90]

It is more challenging for us to answer these questions with respect to the contextual past since its agent of memory is not real but virtual. However, if we view our analytical rubrics as indices for a remembering subject, the profile begins to emerge of a figure who is mired in the aestheticism, solipsism, and melancholy typical of decadence but gradually transcends these attitudes as the *Sonatine* progresses. In the Menuet memory dilates time to offer delectable distraction from the present. An unexpected tritone shift from a chord rooted on B-flat to one on E suggests the mild shock of an involuntary recollection, while the miniaturization, elevation, and rotation of the cyclic theme outline the image of a collector who is holding the past up to the light of memory and turning it slowly, making its amber glow and scintillate. If we interpret the miniature version of the cyclic theme as a synecdoche for the diminutive *Sonatine* as a whole, the historical and contextual pasts converge, along with their respective rememberers: the composer revealed as decadent connoisseur. When the main theme of the Menuet returns a few bars later—restoring convention after its momentary suspension—we feel the subject's nostalgia for the past as if it were our own nostalgia and our own past, bringing to mind Proust's melancholic insights that "the true paradises are the paradises we have lost" and that "the memory of a particular image is but regret for a particular moment" (both I, 462). Nevertheless, as Proust also notes in a display of his own decadent dialectics, the force of oblivion that makes these memories such rare occurrences also preserves their transformative power by protecting them from overexposure.

Memory continues its dynamic transformation of the past—its Proustian "error"—into the finale. However, if memory is felicitous in the Menuet, it is ominous here, with each of the three cyclic recurrences momentarily casting a "cloud" over the otherwise joyous romp.[91] While the Menuet places memory's association with decadence in a positive light, in the finale it becomes more negative. Insofar as the sedentary inwardness of memory appears to threaten the health of this vigorous movement, it recalls Proust's description of Wagner's vague motivic returns as "attacks of neuralgia," as well as his warning that obsessions with the past are potentially perilous for the rememberer. Fortunately, Ravel plots a *retour à la vie* for our suffering protagonist by following these wan recollections with fortissimo restatements of the same theme (example I.9), now harmonized by a quasi-primitivist succession of major triads that descend along an ungapped whole-tone scale in such a striking manner as to recall Glinka's Overture to *Ruslan and Lyudmila* (1842) rather than Debussy, the more usual whole-tonalist.

Thus, the memory narrative linked to the contextual past ultimately dovetails into one linked with the historical past: To cure the West of its civilized decadence Ravel seems to turn to the Russian East, replacing memory's narcotic with a bracing tonic.

In an essay on Ravel, written in 1930 while the composer was still active and productive, Adorno described him as simultaneously "spellbound" by the tradition of tonal music and acutely conscious of its obsolescence; as neoclassical pastiche, torn between belief and disillusionment in the presence of the past, the *Sonatine* is one of the foremost examples of what Adorno calls the "sounding masks" of Ravel.[92] Notwithstanding the brilliance and insightfulness of this interpretation, our mnemoanalysis, which delves into musical and historical details, leads us to a different conclusion. Overtly shaped by memory and history, the *Sonatine* diagnoses and offers a remedy for the decadence of its time—a virtual musical counterpart to

Example I.9 The Vitalist Transformation of the Cyclic Theme in the Finale of the *Sonatine*.

Nietzsche's seminal essay "On the Use and Abuse of History for Life" (1876). In the latter Nietzsche limits an individual's relation to history to three possibilities—"as one who acts and strives, as one who preserves and venerates, and as one who suffers and is in need of liberation"—and gives them the labels "monumental," "antiquarian," and "critical," respectively.[93] At the same time he paints a detailed picture of the cultural decadent, a "pampered idler in the garden of knowledge" who consumes history *en masse* without knowing how to make use of it to perform new deeds in the present.[94] Ravel gives a (self-?)portrait of the contemporary decadent in the Menuet, a *fête galante* whose dalliance with the precious, otiose eighteenth century is not interrupted by but actually culminates in the dreamy digression at its center—a glimpse into the echoing abyss of memory that tempts every decadent. By remembering the past only to leave it behind, the finale seemingly responds to the philosopher's call to act "ahistorically," which flows from the pragmatic wisdom that "all action requires forgetting."[95] Thus, as we move from the Menuet into the finale the decadent subject appears to exchange antiquarian tendencies for critical and monumental attitudes that reorient history toward life. In Adorno's essay, Ravel's music is an impotent remembrance of things past, but in my analysis, it is a deep reflection on interiority that ultimately generates its own future.

Looking Ahead

The following chapters of *Ravel the Decadent* elaborate all of these concerns. Chapter 1 begins the investigation into memory by analyzing thematic cyclicism in Ravel's music, arguing that a gradual shift in his treatment of the return of past material—which becomes increasingly disruptive within the framework of its remembering present—indicates a darkening conception of memory. Chapter 2 turns to a more positive conception of memory as the miraculous reanimation of the past, which surfaces in a number of works. Although the topics of sublimation and desire have already arisen in previous chapters, they receive sustained attention in chapter 3, which discusses the dandy as the embodiment of sublimated desire. Chapter 4 examines the nexus formed by memory, sublimation, and desire in Ravel's music through the dialectic of the idyll and the bacchanal. In chapters 5 and 6 I compare Ravel's two waltz suites according to the different ways they use memory to frame a work and ultimately arrive at an interpretation that upends the common understanding of the prewar *Valses nobles et sentimentales* as an expression of insouciant hedonism and the postwar *La valse* as a purely pessimistic vision of cultural catastrophe. The book concludes with a chapter on one of the quintessential embodiments of memory, sublimation, and desire in French literature, the faun in Mallarmé's "The Afternoon of a Faun." Here, I develop the notion of "faun music" in Ravel: pieces that seem to pay homage to both Mallarmé's poem and Debussy's *Prélude à 'L'après-midi d'un faune'* (1894), which Ravel described as the only "perfect" piece of music ever composed.

1

Thematic Cyclicism and the Ravelian Finale

In 1909 Vincent d'Indy published the second book of his *Cours de composition musicale*, a hefty two-part volume notable not only for its survey of traditional musical genres but also for its emphasis on cyclic form.[1] Conceived as the recurrence of material (usually a motive or a theme) from one piece or movement in a subsequent piece or movement within a single suite,[2] cyclic form, according to d'Indy, reinforces the "*synthetic unity*" of a work, thereby lending it a "monumental character."[3] In tracing the history of cyclic form d'Indy further asserted that it was "transmitted *directly* from Beethoven to César Franck," his esteemed teacher and colleague whose Violin Sonata (1886) is described by d'Indy as the "purest" example of the cyclic sonata.[4]

A century later, we know to take d'Indy's claims with a grain of salt. Although the repertoire of French chamber music and symphonism that he exalts—including works by Franck, Saint-Saëns, de Castillon, Fauré, d'Indy, and Dukas[5]—does indeed play an important role in the history of cyclic form, it is mistaken and chauvinistic of him to exclude from this history the German composers—particularly Mendelssohn, Robert Schumann, and Brahms—who incorporated cyclicism into so many of their pieces.[6] Moreover, the effect of thematic cyclicism may not be solely one of "synthetic unity," as d'Indy asserts, but also disunity; if it is not carefully integrated into its context, the cyclic return that seeks to create global coherence may end up creating local incoherence.[7] The less it meshes with its new context, the more closely it resembles the "decadent detail," which, as remarked in the previous chapter, can disturb the aesthetic effect of a work by drawing more attention to the part than to the whole. Thus, cyclicism may well imbue a piece with "monumental character," as d'Indy argued, but it can also turn it into a decadent ruin.[8]

As I explore in this chapter, thematic cyclicism appears often and to varied effect in the music of Ravel without losing sight of its fundamental ambivalence: its potential both to foster and to undermine a sense of formal coherence.[9] To think through the philosophical issues at stake in this musical phenomenon I turn to the notion of "intermittence" in Proust's *À la recherche du temps perdu*—a novel that he began, coincidentally enough, in the same year d'Indy published his chapter on cyclic form.[10] While the "felicitous moments" at which the past unexpectedly recurs in the present may bring joy to the novel's protagonist and shape to its narrative, their intermittence also bespeaks more melancholic truths—of the ascendancy in human experience of transience over permanence, absence over presence, oblivion over memory, and heteronomy over autonomy.[11] As a musical correlative to intermittence, thematic cyclicism in Ravel brings out the shimmering dialectics of decadence.

The Sense of an Ending

Before I delve into analytical details, it will be helpful to review some basic issues surrounding thematic cyclicism. In adopting this procedure, composers are forced to grapple with many concerns: Which material should be recycled, and where should it recur? What degree of emphasis should it receive in its new context? Should it be a fleeting or more extensive reference? Will it be a literal or varied repetition? Upon encountering thematic cyclicism within a piece of music, listeners are confronted with their own set of questions, closely related to the first: Which part of the musical past is recurring? What is the effect of its recurrence? How smoothly has it been integrated into its new context, and how much has it been transformed during this process? Viewing thematic cyclicism as a memory phenomenon heightens our sensitivity to a third set of concerns: What might it mean to juxtapose this particular past with this particular present? And how does it help to inflect—or even construct—a sense of time within the piece?

All of these issues are indispensable to understanding thematic cyclicism in Ravel, a broad and differentiated practice that appears for the first time in the String Quartet (1902–1903) and for the last time in the Sonata for Violin and Piano (1923–1927; henceforth, the Violin Sonata), while also playing central roles in the *Sonatine*, the *Rapsodie espagnole*, and the Sonata for Violin and Cello (henceforth, the Duo). The simplest instance of cyclicism is the repetition of the same motive at the beginning of different movements. In Ravel, this appears in the use of an arpeggiated major/minor triad as an ostinato to open the first and second movements of the Duo, as shown in example 1.1a; the pizzicato transformation of the motive in the second movement harks back to the String Quartet, whose second movement also begins with a similarly abridged, pizzicato version of a main theme in the first movement (the secondary theme, as shown in example 1.1b)—a parodic gesture not only appropriate to scherzi but also specifically relating the Scherzo of Ravel's String Quartet to the Scherzo of Debussy's, its eminent predecessor.

Example 1.1c occurs in the *Sonatine*, all of whose movements begin with a perfect fourth (or fifth, its equivalent under octave inversion). Made even more remarkable by its rhythmic isolation from the rest of the melody that it initiates, this cyclic motive conjures up the Baroque suite, whose movements often shared a family

Example 1.1 Thematic Cyclicism in Ravel involving the Opening Motives of Suite Movements: the Scherzo of the *Duo* (a), the Scherzo of the String Quartet (b), and the "Menuet" and Finale of the *Sonatine* (c).

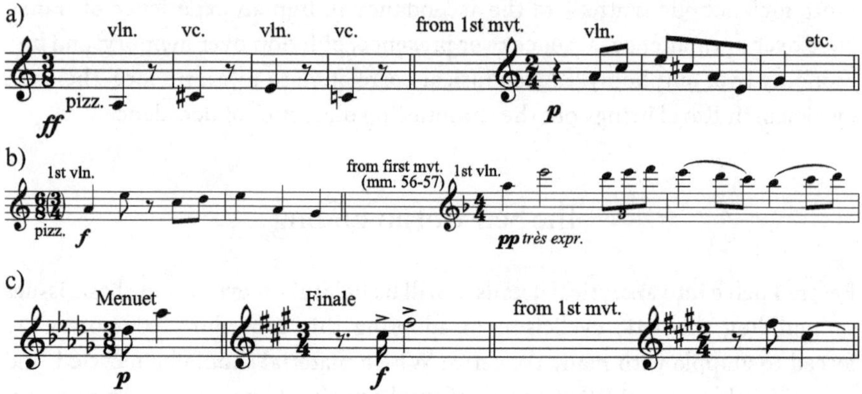

resemblance by beginning with the same motive. However, as we will see, motivic cyclicism is not the only reason for us to associate the *Sonatine* with the *ancien régime*.

In addition to brief motivic repetition at the beginning of movements, Ravel's thematic cyclicism also embraces the wholesale recycling of several previous themes, mainly from the first movement, to provide the bulk of the material for a later movement, usually the finale. Among the five suites in question, three—the String Quartet, the Duo, and the Violin Sonata—have exceptionally cyclical final movements, each of which turns its cyclicism to slightly different advantage. The finale of the String Quartet is a sonata form whose secondary area (mm. 54–85) recalls both of the two main themes of the first movement. This double recollection completes the process of the mutual assimilation of one theme to the other, which began with their opposition in the exposition of the first movement, continued with their tonal reconciliation in the recapitulation, and culminates in their unexpected juxtaposition in the finale, which converts the secondary theme from a melancholy lyricism to a carefree pentatonicism replete with shimmering trills, buoyant pizzicati, and a lilting triple meter (example 1.2).

Ravel has thus fulfilled the traditional criterion for a cyclic theme that requires its reappearance to come as a surprise, without necessarily jolting the listener.[12]

Thematic cyclicism operates similarly in the finale of the Violin Sonata—titled "perpetuum mobile"—but with greater intensity and to different effect. Rather than deemphasizing the finale's dependence on previous movements by placing the cyclic material in its interior, as he did in the String Quartet, Ravel announces it outright, using a brief introduction to show the derivation of the primary theme of the finale from the chirping motive of the first movement. Four more familiar themes soon follow: two from the second movement (R4) and two from the first (R8 and R10), along with some characteristic textures, including the major sevenths/diminished octaves and perfect fifths of the first movement, which sound mainly in the piano. However, in contrast to the String

Example 1.2 The Transformation of the Secondary Theme of the String Quartet from Its Initial Appearance in the First Movement (a; mm. 55–57) to Its Final Appearance in the Last Movement (b; mm. 212–215).

a)

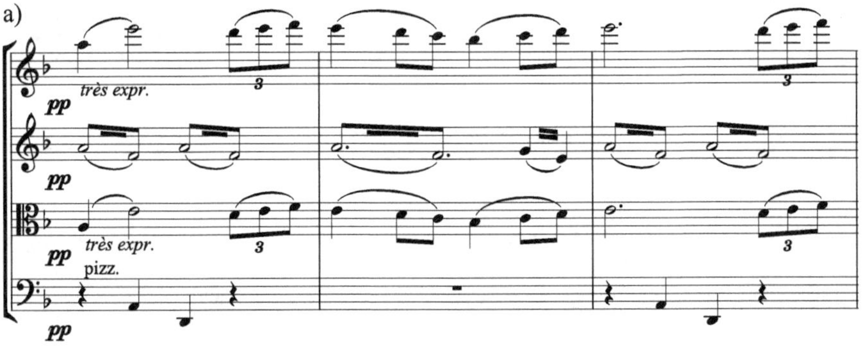

b)

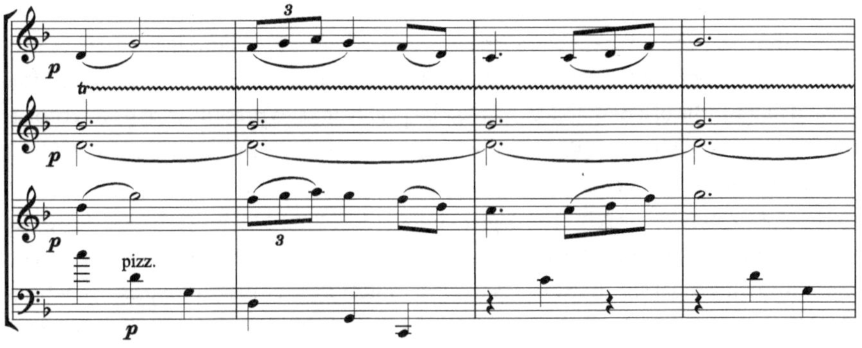

Quartet the mode of recollection here is not gentle reminiscence but rather an active, even voracious appropriation of the past. Previous materials are progressively absorbed into the finale until little remains from the past that has not been consumed in the finale's pyrotechnical bonfire. Indeed, the point at which the violin reaches all the way back to the opening theme of the first movement (R10, shown in example 1.3), subsuming it into an endless stream of sixteenth notes, is the point of no return; every corner of the bucolic world that the theme once sang into being is now in danger of conflagration.

Consequently, the apotheosis of this theme right before the end of the movement (R16) is not a triumphant rebirth but rather its last hurrah—one final, glorious illumination of the beloved past before it goes up in smoke.

The rondo finale of the Duo provides a third possibility for the interrelation of present and past through the technique of thematic cyclicism. In the String Quartet the one accommodates the other: The finale accords a distinct space to cyclic material, while the latter adapts to its new environment without causing any disruption to the sequence of events. The finale of the Violin Sonata, on the other hand, maintains its textural continuity by seizing upon the past with minimal concern for its integrity. The finale of the Duo amalgamates the two. The first episode of this rondo (R5) begins as a relatively faithful recollection of the main secondary theme from the first movement. This image of the past

Example 1.3 The Opening Theme (a) of the First Movement of Ravel's Sonata for Violin and Piano and its "Conflagration" (b) in the Finale.

soon grows unstable, however, and gives way to a related but different cyclic theme drawn from the development of the first movement before abandoning itself to free play in the present. This pattern of entropy recurs in the next episode, albeit in reverse: After several repetitions of a new, folklike tune, the past begins to press its case by interpolating pianissimo statements (R12) of the cyclic ostinato from the first movement. Once established, tensions between present and past reach their climax in the coda.[13] Just as the final statement of the refrain is approaching a fortissimo conclusion to end the whole piece, slashing major sevenths (R24) from the transition of the first movement invade the texture in a fugal stretto whose density of imitation—a musical solipsism, continually looping back into itself—promises to shut out any other material. Not so easily swept aside, rondo themes gradually infiltrate the music and almost succeed in reclaiming it from the cyclic material until another impasse is reached. A second coda (example 1.4) begins afresh with the main rondo theme but soon devolves into the same conflict.

Although the rondo theme seizes the last word in the final two measures of the Duo, it comes so late that it seems to be more an ironic concession to conventions of musical closure than an actual resolution of tensions. No matter. The second coda merely confirms what the finale has already demonstrated—that the past is never quite past in the Duo but keeps vigil at the threshold of the present, ready to rush in at a moment's notice.

The Evolution of Revolution

As we have seen, Ravel often uses thematic cyclicism to address and overcome a perennial difficulty for composers: creating a satisfying finale to a large, multimovement work.[14] In principle this strategy makes good sense since the recollection of themes from earlier movements may help to integrate the finale into the suite as a whole; it also makes sense of the fact that

Example 1.4 The Incursion of the Past in the Second Coda of the Finale of the *Duo.*

the movement most often recollected is the first, not only because it is traditionally the most substantial member of a sonata suite but also because it would benefit the most from being recollected, given its furthest remove from the finale. Among the previous examples, the last movement of the String Quartet realizes these principles best, creating a synopsis of the first movement by integrating its two main themes into a single section and making them easily recognizable. The effect of thematic cyclicism in the other two finales, however, has little to do with either synopsis or integration. In the finale of the Duo, the past returns to besiege the present, whereas the present conjures up the past in the Violin Sonata in order to consume it, dancing jubilantly on its ashes. Thus, during the twenty years that separated the String Quartet from the two other chamber works, Ravel's sense of the possibilities for thematic cyclicism as an art of memory seems to have expanded. Examining and comparing three cyclic works from the first decade of the twentieth century in chronological order—the String Quartet, the *Sonatine*, and the *Rapsodie espagnole*—will help to illuminate this evolution.

Having already discussed the transformed recollections of first-movement themes in the scherzo and the finale of the String Quartet, I turn now to its third and final cyclic aspect: the recurrence, in the slow movement, of a variant of the head motive (mm. 1–2) from the main theme of the first movement. To grasp the effect of this cyclic motive in its new context requires a basic understanding of the latter. The form of the slow third movement is probably best described as an ABA′ elaborated by a ritornello ("x") into a seven-part rondo—xAxBxAx—plus a brief coda. The A section is an aria in G-flat major, sung by the viola and initially divided into four phrases; the aria concludes by folding back upon itself, reprising the first phrase in the last. Due to their tonal, textural, and formal stability, the two A sections contrast not only with the developmental B section but even more strongly with the ritornelli surrounding all three sections—strange, vagrant passages that alternately strike tones of despair, trepidation, and resolve. Given the overt lyricism of the embedded ABA and the melodramatic shifts from one section to the next, we could easily imagine this movement to set an operatic scenario featuring a tender, innocent, but troubled protagonist who sings a paean to a distant beloved while struggling, during the ritornelli, with personal doubts, fears, and tribulations in the present.

Example 1.5 The Cyclic Closing Segment in the Third Movement of Ravel's String Quartet (mm. 19–21).

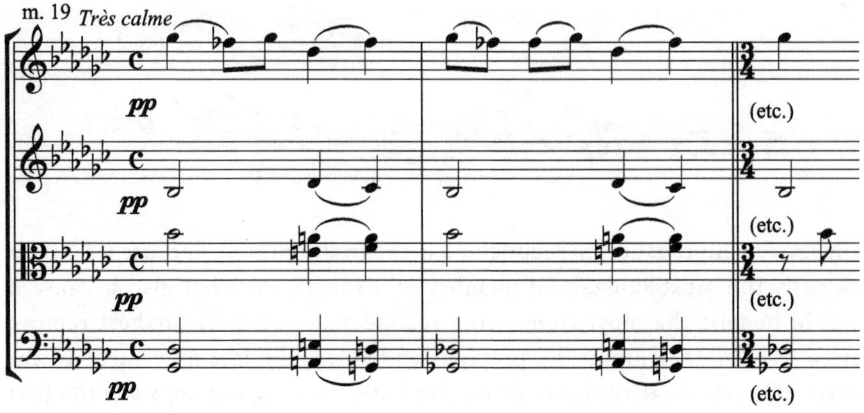

The cyclic motive, shown in example 1.5, plays an important role in the movement. It appears as a closing segment in the A section, which rounds off each of its four phrases by repeating the cadential harmony within a modal progression. Its sostenuto choral texture, soft dynamics, "très calme" expressive marking, quasi-medieval/liturgical modalism, end position in the phrase, and threefold, ritualistic repetition of the local tonic on successive downbeats all evoke prayer or, more specifically, a benediction that looks back upon each phrase and blesses both it and its singer. (A precedent in Ravel for this passage is the "lent et solennel" phrase from the early song, "La ballade de la reine morte d'aimer.") While the cyclic melody typically sounds in the first violin of the String Quartet, it passes to the viola at its final appearance in the movement (mm. 106–108) as if to indicate that the protagonist has finally accepted and internalized the calming message of the prayer. When it appears in the coda (mm. 117–119), its benediction consecrates the entire movement and its implicit dramatic scenario. It is, in fact, at this moment that the third movement most strongly recalls the first insofar as both use the same motive to luxuriate in sentimental reminiscence during their codas—"ruminescence," to borrow a term from Edward Casey.[15] Yet, despite this heady accumulation of memory throughout the movement, at no point do we sense any significant tension between the remembered past and the remembering present. Each benediction blends so seamlessly into the texture and is so complacent in assuming a subordinate role within the overall form that it could just as well have been an original melody. Thus, despite the numerous instances of thematic cyclicism in the String Quartet, at no point do they exploit memory's ability to disrupt ongoing processes in the present.

Thematic cyclicism in the *Sonatine* has several points in common with its use in the String Quartet: The main cyclic material is the opening theme of the first movement, the main site of cyclicism in the suite is the finale, and the main site of cyclicism in the sonata-form finale is its secondary thematic area. Two differences become clear, however, once we place the two finales side by side for comparison. First, the cyclic material in the finale of the *Sonatine* includes only the first theme from the first movement rather than both the first and second themes, as in the finale of the String Quartet. One way to account for this difference is to attribute it to the relative scales of the two pieces: Since the *Sonatine* on the whole is smaller than the String Quartet, its corresponding subsections will likely be smaller as well. However, to my mind, a better way to explain it is to ascribe it to the relation between primary and secondary areas in the respective finales. In the finale of the String Quartet the two areas peacefully coexist, while the primary area in the *Sonatine* finale is so dominant that it allows the secondary area only a brief moment of exposition before its more energetic pace and texture break in and eventually appropriate the cyclic theme at the brilliant climax, as shown in example I.9 of the introduction. Closely related to the first difference, the second involves the relative lack of mediation between the primary and secondary areas in the *Sonatine* finale, with the consequence that its cyclic theme, initially marked "tranquil" and gradually slipping into a slower tempo as it unfolds, is more salient, foreign, and fragmentary within its new context than the corresponding themes in the String Quartet. Even if the frenetic primary material of the *Sonatine* finale—a clear predecessor of the *perpetuum mobile* of the Violin Sonata—ultimately rides roughshod over the cyclic secondary theme, there is nevertheless sufficient friction between the two to create the tension between past and present that was absent from all of the movements of the String Quartet.

What lifts the exploration of memory in the *Sonatine* beyond that in the String Quartet, however, is the middle movement, which I discuss in the previous chapter. In order to understand this movement we must keep two things in mind, neither of which previous commentary on this piece has emphasized. First, Ravel did not label it a minuet but rather a "Mouvement de Menuet," a putative allusion to the classical "Tempo di minuetto," which is probably most familiar from Haydn's music. Second, it is more a Verlainian *fête galante* than a bona fide neoclassical essay—that is, more the product of nineteenth-century French reimaginings of the Italian *commedia dell'arte* than of eighteenth-century Vienna; if the implicit distinction between the Menuet and the Mouvement de Menuet indicates anything here, it is this. Hallmarks of the *fête galante* in this movement include strummed chords, delicate ornaments, and the combination of forthright tonal progressions with magical harmonic turns, especially its two gentle but breathtaking swerves from a tonic D-flat major harmony into a B-flat major ninth (mm. 27–32). The harmonic magic, richly flatted key signature of D-flat major, hushed dynamics, and impassioned outcry at the center of this movement all recall a *locus classicus* for commedia-inspired French music of this period, Debussy's "Clair de lune" from the *Suite bergamasque* and the moonlit serenade of its interior.

As mask, the minuet topic is the first music we encounter in the movement, furnishing the first section (mm. 1–12) of the minuet's ternary form with its crisp, lightly accented melodic motives and sprightly accompaniment. In the second section the mask gradually slips to reveal the longing subject beneath: Dynamics grow more intimate, the tessitura falls, chords relax into arpeggiations, desire-laden suspensions multiply, and *laisser vibrer* slurs introduce a new, dreamy resonance into the texture. By the beginning of the third section (m. 27) the serenade has fully eclipsed the minuet, its legato melody explicitly set into relief (*en dehors*) as it gradually rises four octaves and increases in volume upon approaching the fortissimo climax. At this point we would probably expect either a retransition to the minuet or a new, contrasting section. Instead, memory suspends the form. The following analysis, which overlaps somewhat with its analysis in the previous chapter, should show how this works.

The melody of the recollection in the *Sonatine* (see example I.5b of the introduction) is a transformation of the primary theme of the first movement that compresses and levels out the latter's rhythms while also transposing its second segment down a step. The most striking aspect of this passage may be the mensural canon between the tenor and soprano that plays the cyclic melody simultaneously in two registers at different rates and with different dynamics—a technique with some affinity to the heterophony of Debussy's gamelan-inspired music. The overall effect of this design is to represent memory as a complex scenario within which the upper melody is the thing being remembered: Its uninflected repetition, which cycles the melody back into itself every two measures, lends it the stability of an object, while its high register and pianissimo dynamics—along with its simplification of the original theme—miniaturize it, as if it were being heard at a great distance in space and time. Paradoxically, however, it is an "intimate distance," to borrow a term from Susan Stewart.[16] As previously suggested, the expressive lower version of the cyclic melody is a surrogate for the remembering subject and its inner gaze, which lingers nostalgically on the distant object.

In addition to the complexity of its internal design, this passage stands out among the musical recollections I have already considered for its intricate relation to its environment. On the one hand, the remembered past makes an audible break with the remembering present as the B-flat ninth chord is suddenly replaced by an extended dominant sonority rooted on E; the break is also salient in the score, whose sudden switch to the key signature of the first movement at the exact moment of the recollection makes its provenance unmistakable. On the other hand, ostinati at both ends of the passage, discussed in the previous chapter as the "reverberation of memory"—spreading out from the recollection like concentric rings around the entry of a stone into a pond—smooth out the textural transition from present to past and back again. The introductory ostinato is part of the preceding melodic climax (mm. 35–38), a fortissimo alternation between two notes whose shifted hemiola interlocks with the nonshifted hemiola in the accompaniment below. Instead of moving toward a melodic cadence after its first full hemiola, the alternation repeats, growing slower and quieter until it gives way to the cyclic theme; the technique of disintegrating a phrase immediately prior to introducing a musical recollection recalls Walter Frisch's analysis of the opening of Schubert's String Quartet in G major, D. 887.[17] Just as gradually as we drifted into the recollection, we drift out of it in a retransition whose treble and bass ostinati both use the cyclic head motive to return to the minuet.

If the central passage were not a musical recollection, we would have little reason to consider Ravel's use of the ostinato here as anything other than an elegant way to mediate between contrasting materials. The fact that this passage is a recollection, however, suggests that their melodic drift is also mental drift—the gradual movement of one's attention toward and away from the remembrance of things past. (The ostinati might not simply represent this drift but also promise to induce it in their listeners through their mesmerizing repetitions.) Moreover, given the close resemblance between the introductory ostinato and the tail motive of the original cyclic theme, both of which oscillate between the chordal ninth and seventh of a single harmony, it is also possible to imagine the introductory ostinato as triggering the recollection. This passage additionally involves an ingenious bit of compositional craft that keeps the material more or less the same while rearranging it and assigning it new roles: Comparing example I.5 with example I.7 shows that Ravel streamlines the cyclic theme by snipping off its tail motive, which he then uses in the introductory ostinato to move smoothly into the theme. Sharing their head motives with both the cyclic theme and the primary theme of the minuet, the retransitional ostinati are just as successful as the introductory ostinato, especially insofar as they counteract the latter by accelerating back to the original tempo of the minuet. Two preconditions for memory are stillness and slow time; when the pace begins to quicken, as it does in the retransition, the window for retrospection and reflection begins to close.

Thus, the middle movement of the *Sonatine* projects a detailed phenomenology of memory that surpasses anything we encountered in the String Quartet. The recollection that appears at the heart of this movement is an unexpected, miraculous event. Its precipitating cause is a coincidence between the present and the past—here, the tail motive of the first movement's primary theme reappearing at the climax of the second movement—but it is also the consequence of a gradual increase in intimacy and expressivity as the minuet yields to the serenade. As our moonstruck serenader becomes more expressive of his desires he becomes more receptive to the past, the object of nostalgic desire. Memory helps to satisfy this longing for the past but, insofar as it has sublimated real experience into virtual remembrance, it also fails to do so, thereby perpetuating this desire. The cyclic theme in this movement bears all the marks of nostalgia: Its version in the upper register is simplified, objectified, miniaturized, and idealized while being held at a distance from its lower version, a distance that enables nostalgia by providing the condition for its possibility. Svetlana Boym has told one part of the story with her witty aperçu that "nostalgic love can only survive in a long-distance relationship,"[18] while Susan Stewart has filled in the rest, noting that "the nostalgic is enamored of distance, not of the referent itself."[19] Even though the recollection soon fades, making way for the reprise of the minuet, memory has irrevocably altered the status quo. Relenting prematurely to a tonic cadence, the first section of the recapitulation in the minuet relegates the rest of it to a coda whose slower tempi bespeak the continued influence of the recollection. As there is no end to nostalgia, it is no surprise that the recollection keeps reappearing in the finale and braking the tempo with its doleful retrospection; the alternation between a forward rush and a backward glance in this finale is a prototypical example of the dialectic of memory and oblivion. In the *Rapsodie espagnole,* the third and final station in our trajectory of thematic cyclicism in Ravel, memory broadens to include both the contemplative halt and the mortal thought and even collapses one into the other.

Melancholy Lyricism and the Memento Mori in the *Rapsodie espagnole*

In comparison with the String Quartet and the *Sonatine,* thematic cyclicism in the *Rapsodie espagnole* has a markedly different effect, due mainly to two aspects of the opening "Prélude à la nuit." First, the Prelude does not delineate either melody or form throughout its duration—in direct contrast to the first movements of the String Quartet and the *Sonatine,* both of which launch immediately into strong thematic expositions. Rather, as a piece of "night music" the Prelude devotes its energies to conjuring up and sustaining an appropriately obscure atmosphere. Consequently, when the Prelude resurfaces in the Malagueña and the Feria, it acts more as the bearer of this mysterious affect than of any sharply profiled theme. To the extent that these Prelude fragments resist the compulsion to adapt to their new contexts, they resemble the recollections in the *Sonatine* more than those in the String Quartet. Second, Ravel evokes night in the Prelude by not merely writing atmospheric music but also setting into motion a musical process that follows the contours of a mind lost in nighttime reverie. Recalling the Prelude is therefore to reengage a thought process rather than simply to revive a musical theme.

The core of affect in the Prelude is its ostinato, a descending four-note motive (F-E-D-C♯) in eighth notes, which listeners will most readily identify as a segment of the D harmonic minor scale. The ostinato subdivides into two semitonal sighs (F-E and D-C♯) that become particularly audible when juxtaposed against the quarter-note pulse of the first motive ($R0^{+4}$). Its sighs, minor mode, subdued dynamics, hollow doublings across multiple octaves, and inexorable repetition combine to make the ostinato a central source of melancholic lyricism within the

Prelude—unusual for ostinati, which typically form the background and are more remarkable for their rhythm than their melody. On this point as well, the *Rapsodie espagnole* resembles the *Sonatine* more than the String Quartet, whose second cyclic theme relinquishes its original melancholy upon being recalled in the finale.

While contributing to affect and lyricism in the Prelude, the ostinato also invites us to hear this piece as a process or a segment of a larger process (the "night" and its associated reverie) that extends before and after its sixty-three measures. By describing the Prelude as processual, however, I do not mean to imply that it either lacks form or progresses without a hitch. More than just a haphazard series of themes and textures, the Prelude unfolds according to an ABA'CA'xBxA pattern: a seven-part rondo that pauses twice for cadenzas (at each "x") before reprising the original A refrain. In order to smooth over the seams between sections, Ravel not only continues the ostinato but also models each theme on its predecessors: B (R2) develops the rhythm and neighbor-note motion of A (R1), A' (R3) adopts the initial harmony of A, and C (R4) combines the rhythm of A with the octave leaps of A'.

For the Prelude, thematic and textural continuity are just as important as its tendency to lose energy and dissolve into silence. This entropic behavior is most noticeable immediately before each cadenza, when the piece seems to wind down: The tempo decreases, the register falls, and the texture dwindles to an abbreviated version of the ostinato. This does not mean that the Prelude is wholly inert; rather, it remains suspenseful throughout and even grows livelier during its first half, where each successive theme is more energetic and substantial than the last. However, after reaching the C section—the expressive climax and center of the palindromic rondo—the Prelude begins to regress: Its themes again become pale apparitions that haunt the texture rather than inject vitality into it, bespeaking absence and death rather than presence and life.

Each recollection of the Prelude in subsequent movements is therefore a memento mori that is all the more striking when set into dynamic contexts such as the Malagueña and the Feria. However, instead of bringing out the contrast between the melancholic recollection and its vital new environment, Ravel mitigates it. In the Malagueña, for example, the citation of the Prelude is only the final part of an overarching strategy to rein in the movement's relentlessly accumulating energy. After an introduction that strikes up the dance (RR0-5) the Malagueña launches into its main theme, a stylish *jota*. Immediately after this initial thematic presentation Ravel reduces the tempo and transfers the theme from a forte staccato rendition in a solo trumpet to a pianissimo tenuto version in the strings, as shown in example 1.6.

Like the recollection in the Menuet, this passage is a classic instance of thematic sublimation in Ravel; unlike the former, however, it is a repetition rather than a

Example 1.6 The *Jota* (a; mm. 35–39) and Its Immediate Sublimation (b; mm. 40–46) in the "Malagueña" from the *Rapsodie espagnole.*

recollection since no time elapses between the theme and its sublimated form. Reluctant to leave this sentimental, portamento-rich space, the English horn dolefully echoes the final notes of the main theme before the music reverts to its previous tempo and orchestration.

While building toward a climax the Malagueña is undercut a second time but, with indefatigable quixotic spirit, picks itself up and rebegins. Telescoping the theme from five measures to three and pressing headlong into a vigorous orchestral tutti, it finds its teleology thwarted for a third time and in the cruelest fashion, with the final chord stripped away at the moment the downbeat is about to fall (R12). As in the preceding sublimation, the material that had been presented so dynamically—a cadence involving a triplet embellishment over a harmonic alternation between chords rooted on D♯ and C♯—now reappears radically transformed: The tutti orchestra gives way to a solo English horn, rhythmic stringency to an improvisatory freedom, a romping "animez" to a despondent "assez lent," and a demonstrative forte to an intimate piano. However, as suggested in the parenthetical tempo direction, which asks for the recitative to be taken "a little slower than the Prelude," the instrumental recitative/serenade, as shown in example 1.7a, is mainly a preparation for the cyclic material of example 1.7b.

Example 1.7 The Recitative (a; mm. 70–78) and Recollection (b; mm. 79–83) in the "Malagueña."

At the same moment that the English horn crescendos to an A♭ the Prelude's ostinato and A theme materialize elsewhere in the orchestra in a gesture that sparks several comparisons with the Menuet. First, Ravel uses unexpected harmonies in both pieces to mark the onset of the recollection as a minor miracle; here, the surprise lies in his setting of the A♭/G♯, a local tonic, as a chordal seventh rather than a root. Second, he uses a differentiated texture to impute a complex scenario to memory, one in which an expressive foreground melody in a middle register (played here by the English horn) assumes the role of the remembering subject while the objects of memory remain quiet in the background. Particularly in the Malagueña, which disperses its cyclic material into six octaves of orchestral texture surrounding the English horn, memory becomes a transparent nimbus that radiates out from the mind of its subject, bringing to mind the common trope in visual media that places the face of the rememberer at the center of our vision while surrounding it with a hazy wreath of memories. Finally, in both pieces recollection is an eleventh-hour event whose interruptive quality is heightened by its contrast with not only the music that precedes it but also the music that follows it. The recollection in the Malagueña may not lead into a full-scale recapitulation, as in the Menuet, but it does flow into a coda that briefly reprises the introduction.

The Malagueña thus enacts an agon of active and contemplative impulses that ends with victory for the latter, however provisional it may be. As the final element in this series of contemplative halts, the recollection is also the furthest development of introversion in this movement—a black hole that swallows up the sunburst of activity at the preceding climax. Since the recollection is constrained to a few measures of pianissimo background texture for the English horn, the power it commands here is surprising. One source of this power is its melancholy lyricism, whose plaintiveness is increased by its instrumentation for three solo strings, playing in fragile upper registers. Even more important, however, is its immediate recognizability, a qualitative aspect that has little to do with duration, dynamic volume, or relative prominence. Moreover, from its synthetic design Ravel seems to have known that its ability to be recognized as a memory does not depend on its literal reproduction of the past, for it combines several characteristic features that do not appear simultaneously in the Prelude: the ostinato displaced among one-, two-, and three-stroke registers, the celesta, the augmentation of the ostinato, and a root-position B♭ dominant seventh chord. However, what these features do have in common is that they all appear toward the end of the Prelude: The augmentation precedes both cadenzas in the Prelude and its final cadence; the celesta chimes in between the cadenzas (R7); the B-♭ harmony underpins the second cadenza (R8); and the ostinato registration forms part of the reprise (R9).

The occurrence of the same material at a similar place in both movements suggests that the recollection is not a haphazard event that could have occurred at any point but rather the culmination of a process that gradually assimilates the Malagueña to the Prelude. The comparison of their respective bass lines in example 1.8 reveals that this process began, ironically enough, with the second surge of the main theme (R10): D♯ falls to the C♯ of the English horn recitative, the B♭ of the recollection, and the A of the coda just as the E♭ of the first cadenza in the Prelude fell to the C♯ of its second theme, the B♭ of the second cadenza, and the A of the final refrain.

That the Malagueña aligns itself with the Prelude by adopting the final segment of its middle-ground bass line is not particularly surprising. Not only is this technique more subtle than the wholesale repetition of thematic material, but it also follows from a more widespread tendency in Ravel for bass lines to operate seismographically, as it were (and *pace* similar, well-known musical-metaphorical uses of the term by Varèse and Adorno), varying their contour in order to register the sequence of events in a piece. Even in light of this tendency the Malagueña is still a

Example 1.8 The Middleground Bass-Lines of the "Prelude" (a) and the "Malagueña" (b) from the *Rapsodie espagnole*.

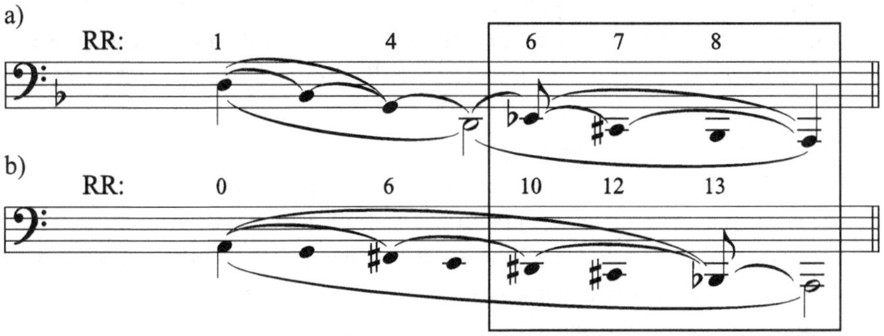

special case since its bass line is equally significant at foreground, middle ground, and background levels. At a foreground level, the bass line is the locus of the main ostinato, which starts on the tonic, leaps up a seventh, and gradually falls back to the tonic. During this stepwise descent it passes through every scale degree except the supertonic. After twenty-eight measures of ostinato, the codetta (R5) to the introduction finally supplies the missing supertonic in the bass line, a Spanish ♭2 variant embedded within a cadential figure; due to the pianississimo dynamic and low register, its debut is somewhat anticlimactic. Instead of remaining obscure, however, this figure becomes a central protagonist in the Malagueña's musical narrative, rounding off the first surge (R9) and being apotheosized in the melody of the climax (R11) before returning to its humble origins in the bass line of the coda (R15).

Although the motive may ultimately fade into oblivion at the end of the piece, it is nevertheless preserved at a background level. This background figure—an A-B♭-A neighboring motion—summarizes the entire Malagueña as an encounter with memory. Here, the B♭ represents the recollection (R13) as the pivotal event, which elaborates the tonic contrapuntally (as neighbor note) and harmonically (as substitute dominant), while also lending the Malagueña its particular drama. Thus, the cadential motive is a skeleton key to the movement as a whole: It calls attention to the musical foreground by participating in its central moments, features an internal B♭ that invites us to anticipate the recollection during the introduction and retrospect upon it during the coda, and frames the recollection as the middle-ground event that penetrates into the background, thereby unifying all three structural levels.

The strong similarity between the Malagueña, the putative scherzo of the suite, and the Feria, its finale, makes the latter into the monumental avatar of the former. In general, the Feria recalls the Malagueña in its bacchanalian tendency to build toward rhythmically vigorous tutti climaxes; in fact, all segments but one in this ABA′ movement are intensifications: both A sections (RR6–11 and 21–26, respectively), the introduction (RR0–6), the retransition (RR18–20), and the coda (RR27–32). While the B section (RR12–18) fails to exemplify this general tendency, it still helps to link the Feria to the Malagueña. Like the final contemplative halt in the latter, it prepares the recollection of the Prelude with lyrical and melancholy solos in the winds—first the English horn, then the clarinet. Since the Feria is the Malagueña writ large, its recollection is more elaborate, so much so that it verges on a synopsis of the Prelude.

There are two gusts of memory during the recollection of the Prelude in the Feria, each of which divides into two phases. The first phase of the initial gust (R15) features a foreshortened version of Theme 2, which is derived from its second statement in the Prelude (R7), while the second phase ("Un peu plus animé") sets a chromatic swell in the strings against two iterations of the Prelude's ostinato in the flute and harp. The second gust (R16) repeats this succession while modifying and extending it in several ways. First, Theme 2 is now louder and richer in instrumentation, ornamentation, and figuration—the result of its synthesis with Theme 3 of the Prelude, which was only barely apparent in the second gust. Next, new materials appear in the second phase: dotted quarter notes and leaping major seconds, stated twice. It is not surprising to encounter these materials here since they originally followed Theme 2 in the Prelude. Nevertheless, we should note for future reference that they occurred only after the first appearance of Theme 2 in the Prelude (R2), whereas the model for Theme 2 in the first gust was its second appearance in the Prelude. In addition to the main intensifying theme of the Feria (R18), which surfaces in the second phase, the Prelude's ostinato no longer sounds primarily in flute and harp but rather in the celesta and three solo strings, where it is distributed among the one-, two-, and three-stroke octaves and harmonized by a B♭ dominant seventh chord, just as it was in the Malagueña.

All of these analytical observations help us to more precisely articulate the conception of memory that governs the *Rapsodie espagnole* and its particular use of thematic cyclicism. The many differences between the recollected materials as they originally appeared in the Prelude and are subsequently remembered in the Feria are indications that memory reshapes the past upon recalling it rather than just reproducing it as it was. The expansion of these materials from one gust to the next generally suggests that remembering is a process by which one only gradually gains access to the past. Moreover, the development of memory can involve its lateral extension farther back in time rather than just an intensive clarification and expansion of its contents, as demonstrated in the second gust by both the increased presence of Theme 3 and the elaboration of Theme 2 by new materials associated with its earlier statement in the Prelude. The interpolation of the dynamic intensifying theme into the second gust—an excellent example of Ravel's art of transition—exposes by contrast the relative stasis and impermanence of this memory and memories in general. Finally, the fact that the ostinato is instrumented and harmonized in the second gust as it was in the Malagueña reveals an abysmal aspect of memory whereby the recollections are themselves recollected.

The Habanera: Misfit or Exemplar?

In this discussion of thematic cyclicism in the *Rapsodie* I have passed over what may be its most remarkable feature: its apparent absence from the Habanera. The most obvious way to justify this absence is to note that the Habanera originally formed part of the *Sites auriculaires* (1895–1897) and thus did not relate organically to the other movements of the *Rapsodie*, which were composed a decade later. This is not a sufficient explanation, however, since Ravel could certainly have introduced some elements from the Prelude into the Habanera to make it fit better into the cyclic suite—so why did he not do this? For one reason, he probably felt that major alterations to the Habanera would have compromised its integrity;[20] instead, the A′ motive (R3) in the Prelude compensates for the lack of retrospection in the Habanera with its triplet-duplet pattern and leaping contour, which anticipate the two ostinati of the Habanera. Moreover, the repetition of the Prelude in all three movements of the suite would likely have seemed heavy-handed and unnecessary to this elegant and economical composer.

The most intriguing explanation, however, is the possibility that the Prelude and the Habanera were already so similar that any literal citation of the former in the latter would have been superfluous. Evoking a state of gentle reverie, both unfold processes in which thematic fragments appear and vanish against a steady ostinato. Bolstered by the Spanish topic they share, the similarity between the two is strong enough to suggest that the Habanera inspired the Prelude. In this scenario, the individual movements would play the same role in the *Rapsodie* as do the thematic fragments in the Habanera, with the dances materializing and dematerializing against the backdrop of the Prelude and its ostinato just as the fragmentary themes appear and vanish against the ostinato of the Habanera.

This idea immediately accounts for the fragility of the Prelude's final cadence—an A-major triad sounded in pianissimo harmonics by the cellos and basses—as well as the composer's direction to proceed immediately ("attacca") into the Malagueña, both of which suggest that the Prelude has an afterlife that continues beyond its final double bar. More significant, though, is the way this new interpretation expands the relationship between the Prelude and the movements in which it reappears: It is no longer simply subordinate to them but also potentially superordinate by encompassing them at a higher level of form—the same level at which thematic cyclicism operates. Previously, I considered the citations of the Prelude in the Malagueña and Feria to be foreign and secondary to their context, but if the Prelude is the canvas for the entire *Rapsodie*, then it is the dances themselves that are foreign and secondary within this extended context. This dual structure is not so much an outright contradiction as it is a double optics. As in the classic visual paradoxes of the rabbit/duck or the old woman/young lady, the two images are copresent but cannot be perceived at the same time. Further, the availability of an image depends on the point of reference we choose as listeners and analysts.

Making the Habanera the model for both the Prelude and the *Rapsodie* gives it a prominence that it has hitherto lacked in discussions of Ravel's music. Possible reasons for this neglect include the fact that the Habanera belongs to an earlier and less mature phase of Ravel's career and is an example of overt exoticism. These reasons seem not to have mattered to the mature Ravel, who saw fit not only to incorporate it into the *Rapsodie* but also to emphasize its importance in print. Instead of passing over the 1895 Habanera as inconsequential juvenilia in his "Autobiographical Sketch" of 1928, Ravel remarks, somewhat mysteriously, that it "contains the germ of several elements which were to predominate in my later compositions."[21] Roland-Manuel, who helped Ravel compose his Sketch and was instrumental in having it published, suggests that the elements to which the composer was referring include its ostinato, harmony, and pedal points, while Arbie Orenstein believes that Ravel was also referring to the topic of Spain and its dance rhythms.[22] To these elements I would add another: its experimental form, which translates the processes of fantasy and memory into musical structures.

The Habanera would undoubtedly become an integral part of Ravel's general Spanish style—think of the quintet finale in *L'heure espagnole*, for example—but there is also evidence that the Ravel of 1895 may have wanted us to understand the Habanera as music specifically from Havana. Drawn from Baudelaire's sonnet "À une dame créole," the original epigraph refers to a "perfumed land caressed by the sun": not just any exotic land, but a tropical island. (Baudelaire's model for this island was La Réunion in the Indian Ocean, which he visited in 1841.) The Creole woman that emerges from this landscape—a "brune enchanteresse" whose "teint est pâle et chaud"[23]—fascinates the poet with her embodiment of contradictions: Hints of racial ambiguity are complemented by her comportment, which is partly savage and partly refined. Markings in the 1895 Habanera suggest that the "dame créole" stepped straight out of Baudelaire's sonnet and into Ravel's music. The "grâce nonchalante" with which Ravel directs the first pianist to play one theme (mm. 19–22) evokes her noble ease, whereas the phrase "en demi-teinte," which forms part of the original expressive marking, "en demi-teinte et d'un rythme las," sounds like a double entendre, calling for a subdued performance appropriate to tropical leisure while simultaneously alluding to her mixed complexion ("teint"). Upon incorporating the Habanera into the *Rapsodie*, however, Ravel suppressed these elements, stifling the homage to Baudelaire and his "dame créole" possibly because it would have been distracting in the new context: He removed the epigraph, replaced "en demi-teinte" with "assez lent," and altered "avec une grâce nonchalante" to "expressif, avec grâce."

The Habanera may never have experienced a second life in the *Rapsodie espagnole* had Debussy not published his own Habanera, "La soirée dans Grenade," the middle movement in the 1903 piano suite *Estampes*. To be sure, the characteristic features of the dance—its trademark rhythm, duple meter, relaxed tempo, and leaping bass—are inevitably going to make one habanera sound like another. However, in light of the numerous additional similarities between the two—the key (F# minor), the expressive markings (with Debussy's invocation of "un rythme nonchalamment gracieux," echoing Ravel's "grâce nonchalante"), the coy swivelings from minor to parallel major, the emphasis on dominant-seventh/augmented-sixth sonorities, especially in guitar-inspired planing progressions, and the dreamlike form in which themes continually phase in and out against a background ostinato on C♯—it is easy to see why Ravel found Debussy's piece derivative of his own; indeed, calling public attention to the fact of his work preceding Debussy's was apparently so important to him that he placed "(1895)" right below the title of the movement in the *Rapsodie*, even though it would reveal the Habanera to be old material, recycled in a new context. Thus, the republication of the Habanera—as well as its prestigious reframing within the *Rapsodie espagnole*, Ravel's first orchestral work—may well have been an attempt to reclaim from Debussy not only the Habanera but also the Spanish topic in general, as James Parakilas has also recently argued;[24] should the notion of "reclaiming" seem too strong, we should bear in mind that Ravel was composing the *Rapsodie* between 1907 and 1908, simultaneous with heightened allegations—launched most directly by Pierre Lalo in his column in *Le temps*—that he was plagiarizing Debussy.[25] This is not to say, of course, that Debussy's contribution did not inflect Ravel's understanding of what was possible. Without "La soirée," would Ravel ever have felt compelled to broaden and deepen the musical exploration of memory and fantasy that he had only begun to broach in the original Habanera?[26] The atmospheric spacing and double cadenza before the final reprise of the "Prélude à la nuit" must owe at least some of their inspiration to "La soirée," whose most striking feature is the "léger et lointain" passage that unexpectedly interrupts the piece twice right before the beginning of the coda. Without Debussy's evening, we might never have experienced Ravel's night.

2

Reanimation and the Primal Scene

According to the previous chapter, the *Sonatine* was a turning point in Ravel's poetics of memory. While memory still appears to be a rational procedure in the finale of the String Quartet, following the dictates of form by supplying appropriate materials at appropriate moments, in the *Sonatine*'s Menuet it is a mysterious, unpredictable event that momentarily suspends the overarching formal process, just as the serenade from which it has arisen momentarily suspends the overarching genre of the minuet. An irrational or involuntary mode of memory appears in the finale of the *Sonatine* as well, whose markedly slower cyclic theme sounds like a suspension of form even though it serves the sonata form as its secondary theme.

One beneficiary of these experiments with memory is the *Rapsodie espagnole,* whose melancholy cyclic themes cut so strongly against the grain of their lively new contexts that they become forbidding reminders of mortality. Another is the *Introduction et allegro,* a septet for harp, string quartet, and winds that Ravel composed in the same year he completed the *Sonatine.* Since the *Introduction* is a single, independent movement, memory does not manifest itself here in thematic cyclicism but appears instead in an introductory formula that sings an elegy to the past before witnessing its miraculous reanimation in the present—a utopian notion exalting recollection as resurrection.[1] As Ravel turned his attention from the *Sonatine* to the *Introduction* he reorganized melancholy and wonder into a sequence that launches a piece rather than interrupting or suspending it. And what launches a piece can relaunch it as well, especially when modified to accommodate its new context, as we will explore later in our discussion of musical "primal scenes."

The *Introduction et Allegro*

The introductory formula of the *Introduction et allegro* is none other than the "Introduction" of its title, a formal segment whose design is as intricate as it is lucid. The three-part structure of the Introduction is organized like a Schoenbergian sentence; although it greatly expands the normative sentence by compounding each segment with multiple themes and increasing the typical length of a sentence from eight measures to twenty-five, I nevertheless take some license and adopt the terminology of the sentence as a convenient way to parse its form. The Introduction divides into a twelve-measure presentation marked "très lent" (very slow) and a slightly longer thirteen-measure continuation that begins "moins lent" (less slow) and accelerates to "modérément animé" (moderately animated) at its midpoint before decelerating into the allegro, which initiates the sonata form. The presentation splits into a compound "basic idea" and its varied repetition, with each lasting six measures, while the continuation embeds smaller-scale sentences that generate momentum and flow. The first six-measure basic idea is shown in example 2.1.

The different tempi not only make audible distinctions between successive sections within the Introduction but also help to shape their affect and meaning. The "very slow" tempo of the presentation, for example, underlines its melancholia by making the melodic leaps upward seem even heavier with longing, the chromatically descending major thirds—a melancholic trope that appears often in Ravel, most notably in the morbid "Le gibet" from *Gaspard de la nuit*—even weightier with pessimism, and the high string theme in three octaves even more searing. The emphasis and continuity the very slow tempo brings to the expression of melancholy in this passage threatens, however, to distract us from another melancholic

Example 2.1 The Opening Phrase of the *Introduction et allegro* with its Fundamental Bass.

aspect: its fragmentary thematic design, which testifies to the failure of the melancholy subject to synthesize experience into a whole.

Fragmentation in this passage includes the division of the presentation into its two basic ideas, as well the articulation of each basic idea into three components: the wind theme in thirds (I1), the high string theme (I2), and the virtuosic harp riff (I3). With its soft, sostenuto, slowly descending doubled thirds, whose rhythmic stagger produces a chain of languorous 7–6 suspensions, I1 seems to allude to the opening of Debussy's "Clair de lune" from the *Suite bergamasque*, thereby providing a mise en scène for the *Introduction et allegro*: the moonlit Italian countryside of the *commedia dell'arte*, a setting already familiar to us from similar allusions in the *Sonatine*'s Menuet. Although I1 will not always sound in the flute and clarinet, it is hard to imagine a mixture of timbres that would more effectively evoke the purity and warmth of moonlight.

Less arioso than I2 and less dramatic than I3, I1 is nevertheless the most important of all three themes. It is the red thread whose harmonic sequence both provides the background for I2 and I3 and stretches across the phrase break to link the two basic ideas. The sequence is a common one—a descending circle of fifths with chordal sevenths and ninths—but is made a little difficult to recognize by the absence of harmonic roots, as well as the distracting influence of I2 and I3, whose interactions with the background pattern slightly distort it. An analysis of the first basic idea, as provided on the bottom staff of example 2.1, will help to illustrate these points. A fundamental bass of E♭, A♭, and D♭ under the first two measures clarifies the first segment of the sequence begun by I1. In the second measure an accented leap in the melody up to a high E♭ anticipates the subsequent entrance of I2 on the same note, an event that inflects the sequence in two ways: The descent to a B♭ in the melody of I2 momentarily introduces a neighboring harmony (an E♭ minor triad), while the leap up to A♭ advances the fundamental bass one more step along the circle of fifths from D♭ to G♭. When I3 enters on the next eighth note, it contributes further to the I1 sequence by moving the fundamental bass now from G♭ to C♭. At the downbeat of measure five, however, I3 suddenly and emphatically exchanges its C♭ dominant ninth chord for another one whose root lies a minor third below.

The harmonic swerve in the middle of I3 has several effects. At a global level, it helps to fulfill a purpose that is typical of introductions: namely, displaying material and foreshadowing events that will recur in the main body of the piece. In this instance I2 will become the primary theme of the allegro, while both the harmony of I3 (minor ninth chords) and its internal interval of transposition (a minor third) point ahead to the intensive use of octatonicism in the development; another reasonable account might point to the contest in the allegro between G♭ major and E♭ minor as primary and secondary key areas, which culminates in a climactic agon between their superimposed dominants just as the sonata form is trying to end ($R27^{+5}$). At a local level, the harmonic exchange in I3 makes a decisive break with the ongoing circle of fifths while also initiating the next circle of fifths with a G♯ fundamental bass that will pass to the C♯ fundamental bass at the onset of the second statement of the basic idea. The latter, in turn, is a wholesale transposition of the first phrase down a whole step, with the single exception that the interval of transposition within its I3 is a tritone, not a minor third. However, since the tritone is another interval of transpositional invariance within the octatonic collection, the reference of I3 to the octatonic development does not suffer disruption. Moreover, the appearance of an E♭ root returns the fundamental bass to its point of departure, which also happens to be the best candidate for a tonic in this passage.

Having analyzed the presentation in detail provides us with a firm basis for its interpretation. Accumulating an additional flat with each step of its harmonic sequence, I1 begins a downward spiral into ever-increasing tonal darkness. A pause in this descent provides an opportunity for the lyrical expression of melancholy in I2. Then I3 enters into the texture to undergird the sequence with the harmonic roots it lacks before abandoning it. After I3 fades away, I1 returns to the harmony of the second measure as if to indicate the ineffectiveness of the intervening incidents, and the same pattern of events cycles through once again.

The sluggish tempo, the fragmented phrase structure, the inexorable descent of I1, the complaint of I2, the outburst of I3, and the monotonous repetition of the basic idea all imbue the presentation with melancholy and despair. It is all the more unexpected and thrilling, therefore, when the continuation brings a fresh sense of hope. The material of the continuation is that of the presentation, now illuminated by the sun rather than the moon. Many characteristics of the opening betray the latent presence of I1, including the melodic leap up to a durationally stressed second beat and the harmonic progression from an E♭ to a D♭ ninth chord on the following downbeat. Here, however, the measures are shorter, the tempo is quicker, the mode of each ninth chord is no longer minor but major, and the main theme in the solo cello is surrounded by an increasingly active accompaniment. In sum, the nocturne of I1 has been transformed into an alborada, a dawn song.

As the sun rises, gradually spreading its warmth, the continuation broadens, accelerates, and crescendos into the climactic "modérément animé," where we encounter an avatar of I3. Just as in the I3 of the presentation, the harp arpeggiates a ninth chord up and down through four or more octaves. Here, however, the motive at the melodic peak of I3 (a 6–5 suspension over the chordal root) is no longer isolated but rather extended and integrated into the main theme in a display of the Introduction's new vitality, which also includes I3's embrace of its dominant function and subsequent resolution into the G♭ tonic at the beginning of the allegro. The latter brings further closure to the Introduction by presenting the final thematic avatar: I2, spare and elegiac during the presentation, is now transfigured into the resplendent main theme of the *Introduction et allegro*.

The sun does not merely illuminate the musical landscape but also brings it to life. The main source of this impression is the stratified texture of the *moins lent*, which is both transparent and complex and thus represents an example of the "simplicité recherchée" that Jules Combarieu identified early on as an essential quality of Ravel's music.[2] This texture is simple insofar as all of the accompanying instruments arpeggiate the same harmony and each accompanying instrument plays an ostinato but is complex insofar as each ostinato has its own distinct figuration. The general pulsation of this texture, which was absent from the presentation, gives the music the feel of a living organism, while the simultaneous multiplicity of different pulse streams within this texture suggests a proliferation of organisms. When further enhanced by flutter tonguing in the winds and the superposition of plucked and bowed strings, the resulting image of the music at *moins lent* is that of a burgeoning microcosm, wondrous to hear and behold.

Animation and Reanimation

In order for the transformation at the midpoint of the Introduction to qualify as an act of memory, it must not simply animate its material but also reanimate it. Before we can determine whether the Introduction does so, however, we must briefly digress from our reading of the *Introduction et allegro* to distinguish animation from reanimation, at least to the extent that they may be understood to participate in such fictional contexts. For our purposes we can define animation as an action that brings life to something that never lived, while reanimation returns life to a being that was once alive (and is now dead or at least dormant);[3] the index of pastness in the latter object—its history of living—is the crucial factor that places reanimation beneath the rubric of memory.

Animation has the remarkable potential to change ontology by giving mobility and even sentience to inert and mindless things. Reanimation works miracles of its own, undoing death and—insofar as death is a consequence of the passage of time—seeming to make the calendar run backward. Thus, when reanimation becomes part of a narrative, it often creates a vertiginous effect that results from the contradiction between two simultaneous tempora: the regressive time of the narrative and the progressive time of narration. As we will see, this special effect, which I describe as "counterchronic," plays an important part in helping us grasp the phenomenon of memory in music.[4]

Boasting prominent examples of animation and reanimation, Ravel's music is a valuable case study for their analysis and interrelation. From an initial survey it seems that one can be easily distinguished from the other and that animation is much more common than reanimation. Closer review, however, throws these findings into doubt. The richest source for such events is Colette's libretto for *L'enfant et les sortilèges*, which includes the animation of many essentially inanimate objects in the child's environment (in addition to their anthropomorphization). Nonetheless, when these objects begin to speak, they call the child's attention more to the past than to the present by reminding him of the roles they played in his life and the debt that he owes them for his happiness during that time. As the emotion elicited from the child shifts from immobilizing fear to a more responsive compassion we encounter entities alive within the child's imagination: most notably, the medieval princess of the fairytale, but also the pastoral creatures of the wallpaper, whose extraordinary colors (cf. the blue dog, amaranthine goat, pink lambs, and green sheep, grazing on a mauve pasture) make explicit their fantastical nature. Moreover, when we take into account the antique music Ravel composed for many of these scenes—the minuet of the armchair and the Louis XV bergère, the fife-and-drum march of the shepherds, and the modal duet between the princess and the flute, for example—it becomes even more difficult for us to assert that they are mere animations in the present that bear no trace of life in the past, whether it be the child's personal past, an imaginary past, the historical past, or some combination thereof.

Composed within a year of the *Introduction et allegro*, the *mélodie* "Noël des jouets" (1905) brings animation and reanimation into a relationship just as tense and complex as that in *L'enfant*. The text of "Noël," which Ravel wrote himself, describes a nativity scene as if it were a tableau vivant that not only inspires a viewer to imagine its animation but also could actually come back to life at any moment; manifold pulsation in the music heightens this impression by suggesting the potential vitality of this scene even before the singer has begun to sing. As the poem nears its conclusion, it is revealed that the toys are, in fact, animated—by their toy mechanisms. When read separately from its accompanying music, this revelation seems to be a purely ironic gesture, a playful subversion of narrative and its tendency to attribute agency to entities that cannot support it. When taken together with its music, however, it loses much of its supposed irony. Rather than making a sharp break with the preceding music—as happens, for example, at the ironic conclusion of "Le cygne," where the noble swan acts like the more humble goose—the song brings it to apotheosis, transposing the main *siciliano* theme from minor into the parallel major, reconciling it with its nemesis, the threatening "Beelzebub" motive, and increasing the tempo from an initial *pas vite* (not fast) to a rousing final allegro. At the same time that the music reaches its apotheosis in the piano the singer arrives at the climactic last word of the poem—"Noël!"—which she sings three times in exultation. Rather than view the animation of toys from an ironic distance that dismisses it, however gently and benevolently, as the self-deception of childish minds, "Noël des jouets" celebrates it without reservation, even adding its joyous whirl to the imagined bustle of the scene.

When compared with these representative examples of animation in Ravel, the opening of the *Introduction et allegro* appears forceful and clear. This is a surprising result since we would expect the opposite to be true—after all, its animation is the only one of these examples to lack an explicit dramatic scenario. This deficit, however, ends up only strengthening the impression of animation in the

Introduction by forcing the piece to rely on music alone to convey meaning. The feature that decisively distinguishes the *Introduction* from these other examples is its division into both an animation and a preface whose relative stasis and melancholy set the dynamism and euphoria of the subsequent animation into relief. As we have also already seen, Ravel uses recognizable musical tropes to associate the first half with night and the second with day, which not only coordinates it with a specific order of time but also opens it up to a hermeneutics of memory.

The linchpin of a memory-based interpretation of the *Introduction et allegro* is the duality of day. When considered as a segment of clock time, the passage from night into day is chronological and oriented toward the future. However, when considered as one cycle in an infinite pattern of natural renewal, it assumes an additional, counterchronic aspect insofar as the dawn of a new day is always potentially a return to a previous state of being. Thus, the cause of the counterchronic narrative effect mentioned earlier is the simultaneity of temporal progression and regression that inheres in the notion of daybreak. This effect produces a sensation similar to striding forward on a walkway that is sliding backward at a faster rate.

If it is the music of the *Introduction* (rather than any accompanying verbal text) that evokes dawn, and if dawn—which involves reanimation, reawakening, and renewal—is the narrative vehicle for memory, then music must provide the ultimate grounding for our interpretation of the *Introduction* as a memory trope. It does so, in part, by forming the presentation and continuation from tonal materials conventionally associated with different historical periods: The chromaticism of the presentation is relatively modern, while the modalism of the continuation is antiquated and even archaic. Ravel's musical time machine has thus transported us back to a primeval, idyllic past; the harp that begins the allegro is the lyre of Orpheus.

Reformulating the Formula

One inheritor of the introductory formula in the *Introduction et allegro* is the single-movement *Concerto pour la main gauche* (Piano Concerto for the Left Hand), whose gradual animation at the beginning also assimilates it to its contemporary, *La valse*, the subject of chapter 6.[5] As the formula appears in the *Concerto*, it recalls in several respects its prior manifestation in the *Introduction*. First, it begins by presenting three themes in quick succession: a pentatonic ostinato, a Baroque overture, and a jazzy melody. Next, it bundles this thematic sequence into the basic idea of a sentence, which it repeats before launching into the continuation, as represented here by the first part of the solo piano cadenza. Finally, the continuation and subsequent music transform these themes into more enlightened versions of themselves: Like I1, the opening ostinato becomes the declamatory alborada at the beginning of the opening piano cadenza, and like I2, the Baroque overture—a marker of antiquity and thus a touchstone of memory—becomes the principal melody of a sonata form; the noble procession of the overture theme in D Lydian reaches back not only to the hymnic sarabande of the "Lever du jour" from *Daphnis et Chloé* but also to any number of dawns in D (the march of the sun across the sky in Haydn's *Creation*, the opening sunrise in Berlioz's *La damnation de Faust*, etc.). The two main differences between these uses of the introductory formula are that reanimation begins sooner in the *Concerto*, underlying the presentation rather than the continuation, and the beginning of the concerto does not accelerate the tempo from *lento* to *allegro*. A later use of it, however, will serve this purpose: The passage that seems to prepare a reprise of the primary sonata form leads instead into the interpolated sonata-form scherzo (R14).

A more complex invocation of this introductory formula is the Prelude to *Ma mère l'oye*. In response to a 1911 commission to transform his 1910 four-hand piano suite into a ballet score for orchestra, Ravel not only wrote a scenario, rearranged the three middle pieces within the suite, and interconnected all five of them with short interludes but also composed two new pieces for the beginning: the "Prelude" and the "Dance of the Spinning Wheel and Scene," which follows immediately from the Prelude and into the piece that initiated the original suite, the "Pavane of the Sleeping Beauty in the Forest." While Ravel may be famous for his skill in adapting old works to new performing contexts (particularly by reinstrumenting them), he was nevertheless loath to tinker with the form and content of compositions he considered fully thought out and finished. How, then, can we explain his apparent willingness to make such significant changes to *Ma mère*? One way to respond to this question is to note that these alterations are not radical but rather reinforce the preexisting design of the suite. Although Ravel reorganized the interior pieces of the suite in 1911, he kept the bookending Pavane and "The Fairy Garden" in place and shaped the dramatic action to strengthen their musical correspondence across the suite's expanse: Just as the C-major sarabande of the Fairy Garden brings modal resolution to the A-minor Pavane, which is a lullaby swaying to and fro once per measure, so, too, does the Sleeping Beauty of the Pavane awaken—simultaneously with the rising of the sun, which reinforces the association among reawakening, reanimation, and memory—and get married in the Fairy Garden, which Ravel expressly dubbed the ballet's "Apothéose."

The main purpose of the new introductory material is to enhance this trajectory. The action of the Dance and Scene provides the Pavane with a backstory about Sleeping Beauty that is largely derived from the Perrault fairy tale—the princess's entry into the room with the spinning wheel, her pricking by the spindle, the cries of alarm from the onlookers, and their recollection of the curse, all of which find representation in the music—while the perpetual whirring of the Dance, as well as its whimsical pizzicati and capricious wind melodies, sets the melancholy stasis of the Pavane into greater relief so that we many better grasp its expressivity and meaning. The Prelude, in turn, anticipates both bookending pieces in its opening measures, which share its meter, tempo, and dynamics with the Pavane and its motive with the Fairy Garden. By transposing into the dominant the motive that will later appear at the C-major climax of the Fairy Garden and lend it the affective qualities of the Pavane, the Prelude not only calls attention to the trajectory between the two preexisting pieces but also creates its own teleology with the Fairy Garden, which tonally resolves the motive and brings it to thematic apotheosis. Despite these dual teleologies, the Prelude does not compete with the Pavane to be the authentic counterpart of the Fairy Garden but rather reinforces its claim as a backward extension of the Pavane that makes the Spinning Wheel Dance anomalous.

For a piece that explicitly addresses dormancy and reanimation and even draws several trajectories between the two to create its large-scale form, the ability of *Ma mère* to be interpreted in terms in memory should come as no surprise. The main site for the performance of memory is the Prelude, which uses the same introductory formula we encountered in the *Introduction et allegro*: a sentencelike structure with a static presentation and dynamic continuation. As before, the basic idea is a phrase that separates into three parts, which here include the Fairy Garden motive, a reveille in a solo horn—sounding its fanfare as if seeking to awaken the dormant past—and a syncopated passage in string harmonics; echoing the main motive in its ghostly timbre, the latter suggests the immense distance in space and time that still separates the present from this legendary past. After a repetition of the basic idea, whose superimposition of its components indicates a desire to accelerate the resurrection of the past, the Prelude launches into a continuation (R1) that seethes with life: Witness the string tremoli, harp glissandi, looping clarinets, and chirping high winds, all playing at twice the speed of the presentation. Although this continuation further emulates the *Introduction* by swelling to a dynamic and textural climax before tapering off, it does not yet culminate in an allegro, as represented here by the Dance of the Spinning Wheel, but instead reverts to the initial material and tempo of the Prelude. Thus, in contrast to the *Introduction*, memory comes tantalizingly close to reanimating the past but fails. However, since the introductory formula comprises only the opening A section of the Prelude's ABA', it will not only have a second chance to reanimate the past as the closing A' section (mm. 35–50) but will also succeed in doing so, at which point the "animez" of the continuation will give way to the allegro of the Dance, and the curtain will be drawn to reveal the spinning wheels and whirling maidens of the fairy-tale world. This reminds us of the observation that Laurence Davies once made about the theater of Jean Anouilh, "whose delicate exploration of a fairy-tale world, brought into being by an eccentric time machine, offers the perfect literary parallel to Ravel's music."[6]

Given this evidence of the introductory formula's continued effectiveness in the Prelude, why does it initially fail? One possible reason is Ravel's desire to have the opening gesture of the Prelude prefigure the cycle of events that will govern the new material as a whole, moving from dormancy in the Prelude to animation in the

Dance and back again to dormancy at the end of the Scene. Another is that it is a consequence of Ravel's attempt to accommodate the slightly different demands of a full-blown Prelude, as opposed to an Introduction of half the length. In projecting the formulaic pattern of failure-failure-success onto a full-blown ternary form, Ravel carves out more time for anticipatory reminiscence, the counterchronic process in the B section, which presents a succession of themes from subsequent members in the suite as if they were being hazily recollected from a distant past: the Pavane (mm. 16–20), "Petit Poucet" (mm. 20–24), "Laideronnette" (mm. 25–35), and "The Conversations between the Beauty and the Beast" (mm. 36–37). The formal design of this musical recollection—a clever take on the potpourri overture—suggests that Ravel either composed or at least planned the Prelude before rearranging the pieces within the suite since this recollection visits them in the order they occurred in the original version for four-hand piano. It also betrays the influence of the "Epilogue" from the *Valses nobles et sentimentales,* a memory piece that Ravel composed several months earlier in 1911. Although we must wait until chapter 5 for an opportunity to examine the Epilogue in detail, we can nevertheless note the Prelude's debt to it in the balance they both achieve between the fragmentation of recollected themes and their smooth integration into their new contexts, as well as the melancholy affect that colors the extent of their recollections.

The third and most intriguing possible reason is that the Prelude is designed, as a "pièce enfantine," to participate in the edification of children by teaching them to appreciate the value of patience and delayed gratification, which Perrault expressly describes in the verse moral to Sleeping Beauty as the lesson to be learned from this story—the story of one who waited a hundred years before finding true love. This insight, in turn, illuminates the Prelude's debt to The Fairy Garden: This ABA′ has an A section that ends in an anticlimax rather than an anticipated climax, a digressive, dreamlike episode for a B section, and an A′ section that attains the climax the A section deferred. As demonstrated in the Prelude, memory is a part of both the delaying of gratification and its fulfillment: When viewing the past as past, it sublimates the desire for this past into a suspended, melancholic reminiscence; when it finally manages to reanimate the past, it fulfills this desire.

The Introduction to *Daphnis et Chloé*

The closest relative of the *Introduction et allegro* is Ravel's music for the ballet *Daphnis et Chloé,* commissioned by Diaghilev's Ballets russes in 1909 and mostly composed (but not orchestrated) between June 1909 and May 1910. That the "Introduction" to *Daphnis* bears a stronger resemblance to the beginning of the *Introduction et allegro* than the corresponding moments of either the *Concerto pour la main gauche* or the orchestral version of *Ma mère l'oye* is not wholly unexpected, given their greater proximity to each other in time. However, there is a significant difference in scenario: Whereas the *Introduction* seems to begin in night, *Daphnis* begins during the daytime, without forsaking the sense of reanimation made possible by the dawn.

Once we are familiar with the introductory formula, its presence in the opening to *Daphnis* is relatively easy to discern. As in the *Introduction*, the Introduction to *Daphnis* is a large-scale, sentencelike structure that divides into a presentation and a continuation. Accompanied by a short preface (R0), the presentation also divides in half, separating into two basic ideas (RR1 and 2, respectively), each of which presents the same sequence of themes while varying them slightly from one iteration to the next. The continuation (RR3–4) then accelerates the tempo and enlivens the texture, building to a climactic apotheosis of themes from the presentation before tapering off to usher in the main movement, the "Danse religieuse." The bass line, which falls an entire octave by whole step across the expanse of the Introduction, smoothes over its internal seams and calls attention to the nature of the Introduction as a gradual musical process.

Although the introductory formula holds these features in common from one piece to the other, its use in *Daphnis* boasts one element that the *Introduction* lacks: a dramatic program, as supplied by the ballet libretto. Mikhail Fokin, the primary choreographer for the Ballets russes in 1909, is responsible for having both selected the eponymous third-century-CE Greek novel by Longus as the literary basis for the ballet and written the first draft of the libretto. However, according to all accounts, subsequent drafts were the result of protracted negotiations between Fokin and Ravel and probably bear further traces of input by others: Diaghilev, Leon Bakst (the set and costume designer for *Daphnis*), Alexander Benois (another designer, who would become a good friend of the composer), Michel D. Calvocoressi (a friend of Ravel's who mediated between him and the Russians), and others.[7] Hammering out a working draft of the libretto in June 1909 was apparently as frustrating and stressful to everyone as it was necessary; from the time that the troupe left Paris at the end of June until their return the following May, at which point Ravel was to have completed the score, the libretto would remain the sole touchstone for their collaborative project.

It was just as well that choreographer and composer worked apart. For one reason, Ravel was not an enthusiastic collaborator (and could hardly communicate with Fokin, who barely knew any French). For another, Fokin wanted Ravel to compose a piece of music that not only disregarded the conventions of ballet music but was also substantial enough to be performed without choreography in a symphony concert, as is often done today with the hour-long score to *Daphnis*. The subtitle that they chose to describe *Daphnis*—a "choreographic symphony"—is a good indication of their original intentions.

Ravel's score for *Daphnis* thus accommodates the action and choreography of the ballet as prescribed by the 1909 libretto, while simultaneously assuming "symphonic" proportions and incorporating structural-rhetorical principles that lend the music a degree of autonomy. The Introduction is an exemplary instance of this tendency toward musical-dramatic synthesis, due largely to its formulaic design: The static first half both presents the main themes and paints the basic pastoral setting, whereas the dynamic second half both generates momentum into the "Danse religieuse" and responds to the initial action onstage by matching its billowing textures and brilliant climax respectively to the gradual assembly of worshippers and their ecstatic hosanna to the gods.[8] It is true, of course, that the first appearance of the introductory formula in Ravel's music preceded the libretto for *Daphnis* by several years, but this does not mean that the Introduction is essentially more symphonic than choreographic. Rather, one could just as easily argue that the libretto for *Daphnis* simply gave Ravel an opportunity to make explicit the scene of reanimation that had always been implicit in the formula. To get a better sense of the coordination between action and music in the Introduction, I now analyze its libretto and score in some detail.

> [Setting:] A meadow at the edge of a sacred wood. At the back, hills. On the right, a grotto, at the entrance to which three Nymphs, carved straight out of the rock, appear in an archaic sculptural style. A little toward the back left, a large boulder vaguely assumes the form of the god Pan. In the background, sheep are grazing. A clear, spring afternoon. At the curtain the stage is empty.
> [Timepoint 1:] Curtain.
> [Timepoint 2:] Young boys and girls enter, carrying baskets of offerings to the nymphs.
> [Timepoint 3:] Little by little the stage fills.
> [Timepoint 4:] The crowd bows down before the temples of the nymphs. The young girls surround the pedestals with garlands.

At the curtain, the stage is devoid of human presence. The first half of the Introduction (whose twenty measures last almost two minutes) gives way at Timepoint 2 to the second half, during which the inhabitants of this ancient Greek pastoral world begin to gather to worship the nymphs, their resident deities. The gesture that brings this action to a head, the crowd's bow before the statues of the nymphs, coincides with the musical climax, which apotheosizes two themes from the first half at the same time: the theme of the nymphs and the theme of invocation. Thus, the two tropes of the second half of the introductory formula both recur here but are marshaled to slightly different dramatic ends: Reanimation appears as repopulation, while daybreak now underscores a pagan celebration of nature in its divinity. This is not the last time that we will encounter the Introduction, for its entire thematic complex—which I later discuss as the "primal scene" of *Daphnis*—returns at cardinal moments in the piece, transformed as necessary to fit its local context. At each successive recurrence of the complex, its dramatic scenario comes closer to realizing the original meaning of its tropes and culminates in the "Lever du jour," which stages daybreak as the reanimation of a world.

NYMPHES and DC

The main musical elements of the Introduction are its three themes, whose first statements are reproduced in example 2.2.

I have labeled these themes according to the nomenclature given to them by program notes published in *Le guide du concert* a day prior to the premiere performance of music from *Daphnis*: the First Symphonic Suite in its debut by Philippe Gaubert and the Orchestre Colonne on April 2, 1911.[9] The Introduction sorts the three themes into two orders: a foreground order that includes both the theme of the Nymphs (NYMPHES) and the love theme of Daphnis and Chloe (DC), and a background order, which includes the motivic-harmonic theme of invocation (APPEL). Although the two orders work in tandem with each other, they organize the Introduction in different ways and thus give rise to different understandings of it as a memory piece.

By arranging its two themes in serial fashion, the foreground order not only forms the basic idea for the Introduction to *Daphnis* but also harks back to the original use of the introductory formula in the *Introduction et allegro*, which similarly concatenates its themes. Throughout *Daphnis* both NYMPHES and DC create a simple correspondence between the music and the action. For example, we hear NYMPHES whenever the nymphs either are invoked or begin to act: During the two scenes of their worship (RR4 and 16), their imprecation by Daphnis for

Example 2.2 The Three Main Themes of *Daphnis et Chloé*: APPEL (a; R0), NYMPHES (b; R1), and APPEL (c; RR1-2).

not having saved Chloe from being kidnapped (R68), their animation during Daphnis's dream (RR70–80), and their final invocation by Daphnis as he pledges his troth to Chloe (R193). In the first half of the Introduction, however, neither theme has yet acquired its specific leitmotivic meaning—which does not mean, of course, that these initial statements are merely "absolute music" and bear no significance whatsoever. Appearing only after the basic décor has come into view, the two themes supplement the setting with their pastoral-erotic associations. NYMPHES in the solo flute evokes a shepherd's sinuous improvisations *en plein air* on a lazy afternoon, while the broad leaps of a fifth, slightly agitated syncopations, and rich harmony of DC in the solo horn gesture toward eros, the pastoral theme par excellence.

The initial basic idea of the Introduction, which pairs one statement of NYMPHES with one statement of DC, engages two modes of memory. The first mode is anamnesis, a Platonic notion that conceives of memory as a double negative—as the forgetting (*an-*) of forgetting (*amnesis*)—and thus imagines discovery in the present as if it were the recovery of a past that is not unwholly unknown to us but merely forgotten, represented here by an idyllic state of nature in which humankind was supposedly once at home; from this perspective, the shepherd's piping in NYMPHES merges back into the landscape as the warbling of birds, a classic example of anamnestic music.[10] More historical than anthropological, the second level prompts us to recall Debussy's *Prelude to "The Afternoon of a Faun"* as a strong predecessor for Ravel's *Daphnis*: In both pieces the flute yields to the horn within a scenario that involves the recollection of nymphs and erotic desire.[11] Even when appearing in the Nocturne rather than the Introduction, the reference of NYMPHES to the opening of the *Prelude* was sufficiently patent to have been remarked upon by one reviewer of the concert premiere of the First Symphonic Suite from *Daphnis*.[12]

On repeating the first basic idea in the second (R2), Ravel raises its internal tensions to a breaking point. In comparison with the themes of the first basic idea, those of the second have a more strident timbre (due to the use of double reeds), are shorter in duration and set farther apart in register, and feature more dissonance. Not only do both themes maintain the presence of mysterious Nature by adopting the exotic "acoustic" scale—which differs from the major scale with its raised-fourth and flattened-seventh scale degrees—but they also extract from the scale a pungent harmonic dissonance: the F half-diminished seventh chord of DC2, which highlights the thematics of desire by reproducing the opening chord of *Tristan und Isolde* at pitch. At a more abstract level, Ravel heightens dissonance within the basic idea by assigning NYMPHES2 and DC2 to scalar tonics (G and D♭, respectively) separated by tritone, the same interval that caused an internal rift at the end of the presentation in the *Introduction et allegro*.

The themes that had been coupled in the basic idea decouple in the continuation, thereby winning the independence they need to acquire their specific meanings within the narrative; when NYMPHES3 sounds at the climax, for example, its identity as a *Gloria in excelsis* to the nymphs is unmistakable. The simple matching of musical signifier to dramatic signified in this thematic apotheosis does not exhaust its significance, however. It is equally important that NYMPHES3 have the identical melody and harmony as NYMPHES2, a repetition whose literalness begs interpretation. When viewed through the lens of memory and reanimation, it indicates that the object has remained the same but that its status has changed: What was distant is now near, and what was past is now present once again. Likely modeled on the crowd's shouts to Yahweh in Florent Schmitt's *Psaume XLVII*, which Ravel described as a "roaring outburst of pagan vitality," the climax of the Introduction is the sound of celebration—of divinity for the dramatis personae but memory for us.[13] Moreover, the trajectory from NYMPHES2 to NYMPHES3 seems to reenact one of memory's paradoxes: its progression *back* into the past, a disorienting slippage that was also palpable in the *Introduction et allegro*.

Like NYMPHES, statements of DC after the first two statements coincide with the appearance of the entities the theme represents. Unlike NYMPHES, however, DC does not participate in the Introduction—unless we were to extend the Introduction beyond its apparent end at the beginning of the "Danse religieuse." After the opening measures, DC next appears in the middle of the "Danse religieuse" (R10), where it sounds twice, once for the debut of each protagonist: first Daphnis with his flock of sheep, then Chloe. Since we have waited so long for the couple to appear, it is only reasonable for us to expect that their debut will be momentous and that they will henceforth remain onstage at least for a while. Neither expectation is fulfilled, however. Daphnis and Chloe appear only at the back of the stage and disappear soon thereafter, breaking off their procession to the altar of the nymphs before they reach it. Further, their associative themes do not ring out in celebration, as did the climactic NYMPHES3, but sound pianissimo in solo winds, recalling the first half of the Introduction rather than the second.

Our suspicion that we have regressed to *Daphnis*'s initial inertia is supported by the musical similarity between the second half of the "Danse religieuse" and the Introduction: DC alternates twice with the primary theme of the "Danse religieuse" before intensifying to a climactic apotheosis of the latter (R14), which is superimposed upon other themes (APPEL and the secondary theme of the "Danse religieuse") in emulation of NYMPHES3. In contrast to the first climax, however, the second climax proceeds immediately to a statement of DC (R15), thereby completing the NYMPHES/DC dyad, which had remained incomplete at the end of the Introduction. The dramatic action that coincides with this statement of DC also represents a moment of completion in various respects: Daphnis and Chloe reappear together rather than separately; they are positioned at the front of the stage rather than the back; they process all the way to the altar and, upon reaching it, prostrate themselves before the nymphs, thus performing a rite of worship that matches the crowd's bow at NYMPHES3.

These analytical details give rise to several insights, all of which flow from the idea that the NYMPHES/DC dyad of the Introduction does not simply disintegrate at the beginning of the continuation but rather is displaced over the entire expanse of the "Introduction et Danse religieuse." If we accept that this dyad is essential to the Introduction and that the Introduction ends only when its essential dyad is completed, then the relation between the two sections is the opposite of what we would suppose: The Introduction does not merely launch the "Danse religieuse" but also encompasses it as an interpolation. The conceptual basis for this interpretation is the rotational theory advanced by James Hepokoski and Warren Darcy, according to which the NYMPHES/DC dyad constitutes a "rotation"—an ordered series of themes that, in the course of being repeated, are subject to various types of alteration, including expansion by interpolating episodes into its interior.[14] In the Introduction to *Daphnis*, the first rotation presents the dyad as the norm, while the second confirms it. The third is the charm, whose dyad is pulled apart to bring forth the "Danse religieuse," a vision of the past made present and animate through an act of the mnemonic imagination.

For a delectable instant—whose fragility is perfectly conveyed by dance, an ephemeral medium that falls so easily into oblivion—the collaboration of memory and fantasy allows us to step into the frame of the past. All too soon, however, the dance ends, and the past recedes once more into the distance. This bittersweet moment of leave-taking is the coda (R16), where the Introduction circles back to its initial stasis, just as the Prelude to *Ma mère* returned to its initial dormancy after the Spinning Wheel Dance and Scene. In the coda the chorus hums the original version of APPEL to express the "gentle emotion" (*émotion douce*) felt by the onstage crowd as it gazes adoringly at Daphnis and Chloe, while the solo violin repeats the original version of NYMPHES to underscore the idyllic pastorality of this scene.

APPEL

Shorter, simpler, and less prominent than either NYMPHES or DC in the texture and narrative of *Daphnis*, APPEL actually plays a more important role than they do. Described by Marcel Marnat as the work's "generative motive,"[15] APPEL is the means by which characters invoke each other, as in the sequence where Chloe calls on the nymphs for help (R66) and the nymphs subsequently call on Pan (R80). Further, it is the building block for several, more elaborate themes (at RR43, 57, 74, and 158), immediately precedes musical themes and sections as if to summon them into existence (*passim*), enacts a Baudelairean/Symbolist *correspondance*—an anamnestic process that circulates between orchestra and wordless chorus to bring nature and humankind (back) into a mysterious, primordial collusion, envoicing the landscape and naturalizing its inhabitants. In addition, it is a siren song indebted to the wordless female chorus of Debussy's "Sirènes" and sounding at a distance, calling out (*appeler*) to listeners to use their mnemonic imagination to recall (*rappeler*) and resuscitate the ancient myth of Daphnis and Chloe.[16] Thus, just as the Introduction takes precedence over the movement it introduces, so, too, is its background material ultimately more significant than its foreground themes. This is not irony for its own sake but rather a consequence of *Daphnis*'s identity as a memory narrative, a genre that is as concerned with the process of recollection as with its product. Moreover, the link between APPEL and memory impels us to conceive of recollection in a different way—as the answering of a call that comes from the outside rather than the fulfillment of an autonomous, internal directive to bring the past to mind. It is the operation of APPEL in the Introduction, in fact, that will inspire us in a later section to generally conceive of memory in *Daphnis* as a Proustian involuntary memory.

It is perhaps only appropriate that APPEL, the generative theme of *Daphnis,* is itself the product of a genealogical process that takes place in its opening six measures. Absent from the other examples of the introductory formula in Ravel, this passage invokes the *creatio ex nihilo* trope in reminiscence of pieces such as Wagner's *Das Rheingold,* Strauss's *Also sprach Zarathustra,* and Debussy's *La mer.* In the first measure, which Ravel added in the course of orchestrating the piano-vocal score, the muted pianississimo double basses play a tonic A1, sustained indefinitely by a fermata and made to quiver by a mysterious tremolo in the timpani. From this generative tone the strings then build an echelon of perfect fifths that loosely simulates the tuning of a lyre or the like in apparent homage to the ancient Greek setting of *Daphnis et Chloé.* The strings enter one at a time in decreasing time intervals that accelerate to the seventh and final member of the cycle: a D♯ 6 in the solo flute, which initiates the first statement of NYMPHES.

Before the cycle reaches the D♯, however, it coalesces into the initial chord of APPEL, inverting the cycle's fifths into fourths around the F♯ 4 that immediately precedes it in the violas and forms the navel-like pitch center of the cycle as a whole. Sounding in the muted horns at the same time that the curtain is being raised, APPEL seems to emanate from the vista itself. Its seductive appeal relies on a mélange of hypnotic and suspenseful effects, the cumulative result of its beckoning dotted rhythms, undulating contour, repetitive chordal pattern (XYXYX), primitivist/futurist quartal sonorities, and tonal irresolution; not only does it begin and end on the nontonic X harmony, but it also undermines each of its X-to-Y resolutions by moving the lowest voice *away* from a member of the tonic A-major harmony (C♯ to B). The succession of APPEL by NYMPHES, which begins immediately after the fifth and final chord of APPEL has been struck, and the use of the latter chord as a basis for the improvisatory melody of NYMPHES both suggest that APPEL is the progenitor of NYMPHES.

After its debut, APPEL continues to conjure up rotational themes while adopting different harmonies and being echoed back and forth between the brass section and the offstage chorus. At the beginning of the continuation it assumes an even larger function in the texture, appearing not only in its normal rhythmic guise but also in fourfold augmentation as the XYXY harmonic pattern that accompanies the repopulation of the stage. Accordingly, at the apex of this passage APPEL receives its own apotheosis: It is sung fortissimo by the full, onstage chorus, it alternates between two stable major triads, and it begins and ends on a tonic harmony while still exercising its ability to invoke rotational themes (the climactic NYMPHES). The expanded role of APPEL in the music of reanimation suggests that it is the conduit between present and past; to follow its seductive siren song does not lead to shipwreck but to a glorious vision of the past regained.

The Primal Scene

As a large-scale work—the most monumental, in fact, that Ravel would ever compose—*Daphnis* conforms to the traditional expectation that a symphony must have sufficient internal variety to maintain audience interest from moment to moment, while also organizing its material in a manner that lends it an overarching sense of coherence. In a seminal essay Lawrence Kramer interprets this duality in *Daphnis* in terms of colonialism: Musical exoticism supplies this internal variety while the "symphonic ideal" administers it, frames it, and sublimates it into an example of Western classical art whose exoticism has been rendered fit (commodified) for easy consumption by his European bourgeois audience. Seemingly inspired by Ravel's description of *Daphnis* as a "choreographic symphony," Kramer's concept of the symphonic ideal encompasses various musical techniques that range from immediate repetition of small motives to long-range leitmotivic recurrence. Ultimately, however, Kramer finds that *Daphnis* fails to do justice to this ideal, asserting that "the surface of the melodic ideas conceals no depth; there is no pressure to integrate the succession of ideas into the perception of a complex, evolving unity."[17]

There is no question that *Daphnis* is a piece of sensuous artifice, ostentatious in its beauty—or, at least, that it invites and rewards such an appreciation. Nevertheless, to the extent that it is also a memory piece—reflecting on its own processes and historicity and repeatedly recollecting itself from the brink of oblivion—it takes on a life of its own and arguably elicits our perception of it as a "complex, evolving unity." The basis for this perception is the systematic use and reuse of the Introduction to *Daphnis* as its primal scene.

"Primal" conveys both the position and the importance of the Introduction among the materials of *Daphnis*: It is the first thing we hear and the template for many of the eighteen numbers that follow. It is a "scene" insofar as it brings diverse musical and dramatic elements into a single configuration and, in so doing, creates specific possibilities for their interrelation and interaction. These elements include the main musical themes, the main dramatic space (the meadow and the sacred grove), and the fundamental dramatic action (the reanimation of the past). To rehearse the Introduction is to revisit this scene.

Coined by James Strachey to translate Freud's *Urszene* into English, the term "primal scene" has a long history predating this discussion, having accrued many connotations on being invoked in numerous contexts, including musicology.[18] In Freudian psychoanalysis the primal scene is an early, formative, and usually traumatic event—whether real or constructed after the fact—in the psychic life of an individual that later recurs in memory and dream to inflect that person's relation to self and to others; the quintessential primal scene is a child's encounter with the parents having sex, which is subsequently overlaid by so-called screen memories.[19] Although the Freudian conception of the primal scene is not identical to ours, the two are nevertheless similar in many respects: Both configure specific actors and actions in a certain space, implicate the viewer as one who identifies with the action rather than viewing it with disinterest (in other words, *we* are the ones who are supposed to respond to APPEL's call to remember), and thrive on their capacity to be endlessly iterated and transformed in memory and fantasy.[20] By staging the infinite production of repetition and difference, the primal scene sublimates selfhood into memory and memory into narrative; each recurrence of the primal scene is a moment for *Daphnis*, as well as its audience, to collect itself by recollecting itself.

The Kiss

Among the various examples of the primal scene in *Daphnis*, the Kiss (RR53–54) is one of the most important and fascinating. The kiss at the center of this scene is Chloe's reward to Daphnis for his victory in the dance contest over his rival, Dorcon. At the moment that we see the couple kiss we hear a statement of DC, whose pianississimo strings, spread over five octaves, convey something of the transcendent beauty of the "radiant couple" (*groupe radieux*) locked in embrace. At the same time, Ravel instructs the chorus to sing quietly with "closed mouths" (*bouches fermées*), thereby imbuing this scene with a hushed intimacy, framing the charmed couple with a "golden nimbus" of sound, as Jankélévitch says, and figuring the sentimental pleasure that this vision affords its viewers.[21] Given the overt eroticism of the kiss, one wonders whether the direction to the singers to keep their mouths closed is not also (literally) a bit of tongue-in-cheek humor that indirectly cautions the osculating dancers against public impropriety.

As the kiss proceeds, we gradually become aware that its statement of DC is not merely an isolated occurrence of the love theme, cited in response to the couple's embrace, but rather forms part of two large-scale structures that stretch back to the beginning of the ballet. The first of these is its rotational design. By the time we arrive at the kiss, we are in the fourth and last rotation of the NYMPHES/DC dyad, which is as easy to hear as it is to see: Both NYMPHES4, which sounded during the coda (R16) of the "Introduction et Danse religieuse," and DC4 of the kiss feature the special timbre of the wordless chorus and coincide with static images of the couple as they are adored by an onlooking crowd. Whereas the third rotation bookended a single, interpolated dance, the fourth bookends several, including the Dance of the Girls and Boys (RR17–28) and the multipart Dance Contest between Daphnis and Dorcon (RR29–52).

We can interpret the vortical form of the NYMPHES/DC rotations in two complementary ways. From one perspective, its progressive expansion expresses the desire to "leave home" (that is, to depart from its rotational material) in quest of new adventures and experiences, as offered by the interpolated episodes. From an opposite point of view, it expresses the quietistic desire to return home and remain at home—a desire that is increasingly frustrated, the more extensive the interpolations become. A dialectical analysis would refuse to privilege one over the other and assert instead that their contradiction is fundamental to understanding the conflictual desire of Ravel's audience. This leads us back to a Kramerian perspective, whereby the double movement of the rotational design expresses the essential ambivalence of tourism, its desire to stay at home while traveling abroad and vice versa. In this case, however, it is preferable to decline the dialectical approach since the second seems to better capture the way desire operates in *Daphnis.*

The rationale for the claim that homecoming is more desirable than leave-taking stems not only from the sense that the rotational themes offer respite from the bustle of the intervening episodes but also from the intuition that each rotation seeks fruition in DC. Although DC is important for refocusing our attention on the eponymous couple of the ballet, it is even more important for representing desire, whether the couple's desire for each other, our desire to witness their desire, or simply desire as such, free of any particular cathexis.

With each successive rotation desire grows more acute: Note the progression from the vague, pastoral evocations of DC1 and the bittersweet *Tristan* chord of DC2 to the spine-tingling *frissons* of DC3 and the full blush of DC4. While each rotation reestablishes desire as a central theme of the ballet, the rotational structure as a whole intensifies it by augmenting not only the musical apparatus for each successive DC but also the time spans that separate one statement from the next. Thus, the widening gyre of the NYMPHES/DC rotations is an instrument of culture that both arouses desire and controls its gratification. The gratification of desire—here, the desire to complete each rotation, rewin DC and its sentimental tableaux, and revel leisurely in the pleasure offered by their sound and spectacle—is spontaneous in the first and second rotations (both of which admit no interpolations) but is increasingly deferred in the third and fourth. The deferral of desire, in turn, has a dual effect on the subject, teaching it to master desire by withstanding ever lengthier periods of privation—the "fort" of Freud's "fort/da" cycle—while also increasing its estimation of the desired object.[22] Absence, after all, makes the heart grow fonder.

The postulate of rotational form in *Daphnis* is thus effective in several ways at once. At one level it is a narrative device that collaborates with the libretto to tell the romantic story of Daphnis and Chloe, approaching the couple from afar in the Introduction—note the "once upon a time" quality of the first two rotations—underscoring their onstage appearance, and culminating in their kiss. At another, it reenacts those civilizing processes that aim to integrate the individual into society by teaching it to master its desires. Moreover, since we are the auditors of these rotations that not only represent desire but also arouse it in us, it is we, rather than simply the characters of the story, who become the ultimate subject of these processes. Directed toward its audience in this way, rotational form in *Daphnis* is a pendant to the novel by Longus, which explicitly seeks to tutor its readers in the ways of love as a post-Ovidian *ars amatoriae*; according to its proem, it is a lesson in Eros that will "cure the [love]sick, comfort the distressed, stir the memory of those who have loved, and educate those who haven't."[23]

Given the prominent role that rotational themes play in the Introduction, it is not surprising that the kiss is also a primal scene. In fact, the two structures dovetail nicely into each other at DC4, which both terminates the cycle of rotations and initiates the cycle of post-Introduction primal scenes. Although the kiss picks up the Introduction only near its midpoint, its emulation of the latter is unmistakable: DC4 gives way to a slightly faster intensification while billowing triplets gradually rise from a low register and peak at a loud, choral APPEL before subsiding. However, in addition to its partial citation of the Introduction, the kiss lacks a foreground theme (like NYMPHES or DC) at its climax. By withholding full emphasis from the climax of the primal scene, this absence indicates that the kiss is an intermediate station that does not bring the plot to a point of fulfillment but rather foreshadows such events. (Their union in the kiss, as we will find out, is only a prelude to their reunion during the Daybreak.) The difference between the respective stage actions of the Introduction and the kiss is even more striking. In the second half of the kiss, the scene loses its animation and population rather than gaining them: "[T]he crowd exits, taking Chloe with them," while Daphnis "remains [alone onstage], immobile, as if in ecstasy." Despite appearances, however, the kiss does not merely negate the primal scene but rather sublates its gesture of animation into a gesture of awakening—of Daphnis's libido—and thereby transfers it from the physical exterior to the psychological interior. If we conceive the primal scene as an effect of the mnemonic imagination, though, then it has always taken place in the mind; the kiss simply makes its site explicit. Further, by relaunching the piece at this moment Ravel stays true to the novel, which treats Chloe's kiss as a Stendhalian *coup de foudre* (lightning strike) that makes him feel reborn: "Daphnis, as though he had been stung, not kissed, immediately looked distressed . . . It was as if he had then, for the first time, acquired eyes, and had been blind before."[24]

The Cardinal Scenes and Their Intercalations

While the kiss is certainly a pivotal moment, the Nocturne (RR70–82) and the Daybreak (RR155–69) supersede it to qualify as the "cardinal scenes" of the ballet, which occur one-third and two-thirds of the way through the work and form the first movements of the First and Second Symphonic Suites from *Daphnis*, respectively. Even though only the Nocturne and the Daybreak stand at the hinges (*cardines*, in Latin) of the triptych, I also count the Introduction as a cardinal scene since it is the original primal scene and introduces its own third of the ballet. Although the three scenes interrelate in complex ways, their kinship is noticeable to even the casual observer; Alberto Mantelli's description of *Daphnis* as representing "the landscape of a mythological Mediterranean through the light veil of a clear spring afternoon, in the silvery light of the moon, and in the shiver of the inchoate dawn" implicitly registers their kinship.[25]

In addition to their association with the basic settings of the ballet, the identity of the cardinal scenes as primal scenes rests on the central role that reanimation plays in each one: In the Introduction, the people of Lesbos repopulate the idyllic landscape; in the Nocturne, the three nymph statues come (back) to life, dance together, and rouse ("ranimer") the unconscious Daphnis within his own dream; in the Daybreak, the landscape itself comes to life with its rushing streams and twittering birds, in addition to the return of the pastoral folk, the actual waking of Daphnis, the reentry of Chloe, and the restoration of the couple. If we include in this series of reanimations the appearance of Pan (R152), whose menacing profile is projected onstage right before the Daybreak, we see that the cardinal scenes realize a spatial hierarchy—the arrangement, in the Introduction, of the worshippers at the front of the stage, the nymph statues in the middle, and the "big boulder vaguely shaped like Pan" toward the back. By reanimating first the worshippers, then the nymphs, and finally Pan, *Daphnis* systematically travels back in time from one order of being to an even more ancient one, thereby following the reverse chronology that we initially discovered in the Introduction and observed to be a hallmark of memory narratives. If Diaghilev had actually accepted the first draft of Fokin's libretto, we would have enjoyed yet another scene of reanimation; as Simon Morrison has recently brought to light, in this draft the Act II curtain rose to "reveal a garden brimming with a superabundance of exotic fruits and flowers, reverently tended by Daphnis" and magically restored to life by the first nymph "with a wave of her hand."[26]

Each cardinal scene features an interpolated dance: the Introduction's "Danse religieuse" (RR5–14), the Nocturne's "Danse lente et mystérieuse" (RR74–79), and, for the Daybreak, an unnamed, triple-time episode that I refer to as the "Danse pastorale" (RR158–166). The purpose of each dance is not merely to extend the reanimation of the past and shape it into a beautiful and rhythmic experience but also to conjure up DC. We have already seen that the "Danse religieuse," which draws its basic syncopation from the love theme, springs up in the middle of the Introduction's third rotation, thereby postponing DC3 in order to better prepare its momentous appearance. The "Danse lente et mystérieuse" also leads toward a statement of DC, which sounds at the moment that the nymphs stop dancing and awaken Daphnis (R79), but arises in the first half of the primal scene rather than the second. Specifically, its main theme, which alternates harmonies in the familiar XYXYX pattern of APPEL, is an improvisatory outgrowth of the Dorian APPEL that underscored DC2. Likewise, the main theme of the "Danse pastorale" draws its opening pitches and rhythms from the quartal APPEL that immediately precedes it in the Daybreak before progressing to the climactic DC of the couple's reunion (R165). Thus, rather than designating these dances "interpolations," it is more apt to call them "intercalations"—from the Latin *calare*, synonymous with the French *appeler*—since APPEL is clearly the source for their main themes. With every intercalation the past is recalled and set into motion as a precondition to attaining DC, the heart that beats at the center of this myth-in-music.

By reconfiguring the elements and relations internal to the primal scene, including its intercalation, each cardinal scene not only helps to tell its particular segment of the plot but also responds to previous primal scenes by revisiting and revising them. At first glance, the Introduction seems to be excluded from such activity since it is the original primal scene and therefore cannot look back to any previous primal scenes. On closer inspection, however, we see that it, too, involves revision, which generates not only the second rotation from the first and the third from the second but also the second half from the first half—a literal revision that makes the past animate and populous before our eyes. An additional aspect of revision in the Introduction is its intercalation, the "Danse religieuse," which is a manifold *mise en abîme* of the entire primal scene.

The "Danse religieuse" emulates the primal scene in three respects. At the broadest level it is an AA′B whose strongest articulation falls between the A′ and the B sections (R10), just as the AA′B of the Introduction is cleft between the second and third rotations. Next, each A section recalls the first half of the primal scene by intensifying toward a choral Dorian APPEL at its climax (RR7^{+4} and 9^{+3}), the gesture that underlay DC2 and firmly linked APPEL to lack and desire. Finally, the B section (RR10–14) resembles both the second half of the primal scene and the primal scene as a whole, as mentioned earlier. The first resemblance is particularly fascinating for its technique of modeling. The B section incorporates the billowing triplets of the Introduction's transformation music in two ways: as a literal citation in the pizzicato first violins of its beginning and in augmentation as a motivic structure—that is, the motivic design of the B section forms an ABABCBCDC (etc.) pattern that is familiar to us from the Introduction's texture of reanimation; example 2.3 shows the original appearance of this reanimatory texture, whose pattern coincides with the *terza rima* rhyme scheme of the *Divine Comedy*, as well as the *pantun*-derived rhyme scheme of poems such

Example 2.3 The Billowing Texture of Reanimation in the "Introduction" (mm. 21–23).

as Baudelaire's "Harmonie du soir," while table 2.1 displays its augmentation in the "Danse religieuse."

The two instances of the transformation music in the "Danse religieuse" have roles to play: The literal citation directs our attention to the augmentation under way, while the augmentation represents the resurrection of the past as a long and arduous task. In case we miss this admittedly obscure link and thus the opportunity to interpret it as such, Ravel makes the toil of memory plain for all to hear: As the B section intensifies toward its massive *réunion de thèmes*—or, better, a massified one since the "Danse religieuse" features the *corps de ballet* as the worshipping masses of Lesbos—it modulates into an almost ponderous march that brings its dancers into lockstep.

By illuminating the memory-based relations that account for both the Introduction and the "Danse religieuse," as well as their interrelation, we have created a new perspective from which to appreciate these two pieces—one that is sorely needed, especially as a foil to previous criticism. In one of the few substantial analyses of *Daphnis* that exist, Riccardo Malipiero decried "the useless verbosity that palpably weighs down the first scene," while even Roland-Manuel—Ravel's student, biographer, and confidant—accused it of "academicism" due to its inordinate length and complexity.[27] As we have seen, however, these features of the "Danse religieuse" should not be understood as compositional defects but rather as means by which the dance performs memory at multiple levels.

Table 2.1 **The Reappearance of the Reanimatory Texture in Augmentation as the Motivic Structure of the Second Half of the "Danse religieuse."**

RR:	*10*			*11*				*12*			*13*		*14*
Theme/ Motive:	DC	DR^1	DC	DR^1	DR^3	DR^1	DR^3	DR^2	DR^3	DR^2	DR^3	DR^2	DR^3/DR^1 (Reprise)
"Rhyme" Scheme:	A	B	A	B	C	B	C	D	C	D	C	D	C/B

Occurring a third of the way through the ballet, the Nocturne revises all three of the preceding primal scenes: the Introduction, the kiss, and the abduction of Chloe (RR61–69). The first half of the Nocturne recalls the Introduction by following APPEL with statements of NYMPHES but transposes both themes from the sunlit landscape of the opening to the dreamscape of the Nocturne by mapping them from a diatonic to an octatonic environment. Moreover, the profusion of NYMPHES in the first half—one for each nymph and then two more during the intercalated "Danse lente et mystérieuse"—supplies in cruel abundance the theme that the abduction had lacked in response to Chloe's desperate pleas for the nymphs' protection; appropriately enough, the theme that Chloe's APPELs tragically invoked during the abduction was the theme of pirates (R66), which coincides with their irruption into the sacred grove and kidnapping of Chloe. Like the Introduction, the second half of the Nocturne (RR81–82) culminates in a theme, PAN, but it sounds not at the apex but at the nadir of the gesture and is obscured rather than illuminated by the atonal, octatonic harmonies. By setting up but not fulfilling the apotheosis of its second half, the Nocturne resembles the kiss but shifts its gesture of near fulfillment from one context to another: from the foreshadowing of sexual consummation to the adumbration of salvation.

Both the kiss and the Nocturne, as well as all the other primal scenes, are fulfilled in the Daybreak, the final cardinal scene and the telos of *Daphnis* as a whole. In comparison to the other primal scenes, which feature thematic apotheosis only in their second half, the Daybreak reaches scintillating climaxes in both halves (RR155–157 and 167–169) and thus reforms the primal scene into an image of unqualified success; should the listener somehow fail to associate these climaxes with the reanimating half of the Introduction, the billowing *terza rima* design of their melodies offers a vital clue. (The downbeats of the bass melody at R155 combine with the on-beat tones of the main ascending melody at R156 to form the familiar ABABCBCDC [etc.] pattern.) The intercalation of the Daybreak, the "Danse pastorale," recalls both previous intercalations: It is an AA′B whose first half refers to "Danse lente et mystérieuse"—an AA′ that ends, here as there, in a Dorian APPEL—and whose identity as a primal scene *mise en abîme* replicates the entire "Danse religieuse." Further, the B section of the "Danse pastorale" (RR164–166) returns to the music of the abduction, only to invert its action and undo its effects. Where we once encountered a terrified Chloe, we now see an "anguished" Daphnis; where we once saw Chloe led off by male pirates and separated from Daphnis, we now see her led in by female shepherds and reunited with Daphnis; where she once threw herself (*se jette*) before the altar of the nymphs, the couple now throw themselves (*se jettent*) into each other's arms. Finally, the DC at the climax of the B section is the apotheosis that we have been anticipating for so long, which coincides with the event that has been withheld for so long, the reunion of the lovers.

It is ironic that the Daybreak is so strongly indebted to the past, given that its twin sunbursts promise to purge all previous scenes from our recollection. As if to preempt this possibility, the Nocturne thrusts its roots deep into memory, passing beyond the upper layers of narrative into the lower strata of ballet history. Fokin's original choreography for the "Danse lente et mystérieuse" conceived of the past archaeologically, as it were, directing the nymphs to move only in profile in a "series of sharply contrasting poses," as if they remained trapped within the two-dimensional surface of ancient Greek vases and friezes;[28] three years later, when he was composing the *Trois poèmes de Stéphane Mallarmé*, Ravel would paraphrase the music of the Nocturne (especially R77) to set the "nymph of the cold ceiling" in "Surgi de la croupe et du bond."

Along with its reveries on ancient Greek dance, the Nocturne recalls a much more recent tradition, the French Romantic ballet of the nineteenth century. Conjured up anew in the Nocturne, the *locus classicus* of this genre was the supernatural scene, most famously represented by the midnight reanimation of the Wilis in *Giselle* and the Ballet of the Nuns in *Robert le diable*. On the one hand, the Nocturne breaks with the aesthetics of Diaghilev's Russian ballet, momentarily turning the spotlight away from the male dancer (here, the sleeping Daphnis) and back toward the female ballerina; after all, the Romantic ballet was an extended "meditation on femininity—its mystique, elusiveness, unattainability, and innumerable avatars."[29] The "unreal lighting" of the Nocturne is the technical aspect of this memory, the contemporary avatar of the eerie gas lighting that was introduced at the Paris Opera in 1827 for the express purpose of creating the moonlit supernatural episodes in Romantic ballet and opera.[30] On the other hand, Fokin had already folded Romantic *ballet blanc* into the repertoire of the Ballets russes, as represented most famously by *Les Sylphides* (1909). Danced to various pieces by Chopin and premiered in Paris simultaneously with Ravel's commission for *Daphnis, Les Sylphides* receives an homage in the Chopinesque music of the Nocturne, whose "Danse lente et mystérieuse" in D-flat major is a close cousin of Chopin's Nocturne, op. 27, no. 2, and Berceuse, op. 57.

The Primal Scene beyond *Daphnis*

The garden scene in *L'enfant et les sortilèges* inevitably springs to mind when searching for primal scenes beyond *Daphnis*, mainly because of its explicit sexuality: In the terms proposed by Richard Langham Smith, it is the "hinge" of this *fantaisie lyrique*, the moment that confirms the full import of sexuality.[31] Confronted by the sight of so many animals in rut, the child can only marvel at how "they love each other," "are happy," and—wholly absorbed in their own affairs—"have forgotten me." However, the failure of the garden scene to reprise any musical material disqualifies it as a primal scene in the broader sense I have been developing. The candidate for primal scene in *L'heure espagnole*, Ravel's other large-scale stage work, fares slightly better in this regard. Similar to its counterpart in *Daphnis*, the candidate for a primal scene in *L'heure* comprises the orchestral Introduction, as well as a two-part rotation that pairs the initial melody with Ramiro's theme (RR0–4). In addition to its appearances at the beginning and toward the end (R118, immediately before the finale), the primal scene returns at cardinal moments (scenes X and XVI) that roughly divide the one-act drama into a triptych like *Daphnis*. The relation between these cardinal scenes is musically and dramatically apparent: Both are monologues by Ramiro, in which he daydreams about replacing Torquemada as the owner of the clock shop and the husband of Concepcion. The final primal scene marks at least the partial fulfillment of this wish, as Torquemada invites Ramiro to stop by his shop each day to be told, by Concepcion, what time it is—namely, the "Spanish hour," the time for adulterous escapades. Thus, Ramiro may not have actually acquired the shop with all of its wondrous instruments, but he has come to possess its most valuable item: the intricate "mechanism that is Woman," as he says during the first cardinal scene. Just as *Daphnis* made DC the telos of its primal rotation, so, too, does *L'heure* valorize Ramiro's theme, thereby realizing the supposed Boccaccian moral of the story, which concludes the final quintet and the opera as a whole: "There is always a moment in the pleasures of love when the muleteer has his day!"

Other than *Daphnis*, it is Ravel's *Introduction et allegro* that relies most heavily on the primal scene as a musical and (implicitly) dramatic device. In both pieces the primal scene is the Introduction, which appears at the beginning of each third of the work; since the *Introduction* is a sonata form, it begins the exposition, the development (R8), and the recapitulation (R18). The primal scene that launches the development of the *Introduction* is relatively weak, just as incapable as the Nocturne—its counterpart in *Daphnis*—to either complete itself or escape octatonic distortion. The third cardinal scene is a cadenza for the harp, which occurs in the immediate aftermath of the climax and downward spiral that brought the development to an end. After taking a few moments to recompose itself, this scene moves through its necessary paces and culminates in a reanimated P1 at the onset of the recapitulation. Nonetheless, the liminal position of the cadenza—caught between the development and the recapitulation and belonging to neither—and its spare instrumentation and ghostly timbre (cf. the harp harmonics) belie the gesture of reanimation. To redeem it requires the entire recapitulation, an effort that comes to fruition in the fortissimo tutti "Animé" coda (R28); the trills (R26) we hear in the winds shortly before we reach the coda are the harbingers of Daybreak—both here and in *Daphnis*.

Texts, Pre-Texts, and Pretexts: Ravel, Longus, and Proust

Having developed our understanding of *Daphnis* and its Introduction by directly engaging the score, we now turn to three ancillary texts, the first of which is Ravel's "Autobiographical Sketch" of 1928. The heart of Ravel's commentary on *Daphnis* in the Sketch reads as follows:

> My intention in writing [*Daphnis*] was to compose a vast musical fresco, less concerned with archaism than with fidelity to the Greece of my dreams, a Greece that rather naturally resembles the one imagined and depicted by French artists of the end of the eighteenth century. The work is constructed symphonically according to a very rigorous tonal plan, by means of a small number of motives whose developments ensure the symphonic homogeneity of the work.[32]

These two sentences concatenate a host of claims, each of which deserves scrutiny; I begin by analyzing the more tangible ones made in the latter sentence. Since Ravel had just referred to *Daphnis* as a "choreographic symphony," it makes sense that he would try to explain the way in which it is symphonic by pointing to its "rigorous tonal plan" and its motivic economy and consistency, all of which combine to produce the overall effect of "homogeneity." Indeed, as we have discovered in our analyses of the Introduction, rotational form, and the primal scene, *Daphnis* has a small set of motives and themes—APPEL, NYMPHES, and DC—that recur at pivotal moments across the expanse of the work. So, too, does *Daphnis* gesture toward tonal coherence by privileging a small, diatonic set of tonal centers, A, B, and D. Nonetheless, it is doubtful that either strategy has the effect of unifying this hour-long, eighteen-movement work since the leading motives recur only intermittently and contribute only marginally to the "tonal plan," shifting shape to fit the local harmonic-scalar region (which is often nondiatonic) and avoiding anything like "development." Thus, to call the work homogeneous and its tonal plan "very rigorous" is misleading, but we need not lay the blame squarely on Ravel's shoulders. The probable source of these claims—redolent of Vincent d'Indy's didacticism and his virile, nationalist poetics of industry, rigor, and purity—is Roland-Manuel, a former student of d'Indy who served as Ravel's scribe for the Sketch. In fact, this passage might even be an example of unconscious self-plagiarism; in his first book on Ravel's music (1914), Roland-Manuel used the same language to assert that the leitmotifs of *L'heure espagnole* "ensure the symphonic homogeneity of the work."[33]

In comparison with the final sentence of the paragraph, the first sounds more like Ravel. The declaration that *Daphnis* evokes "the Greece of my dreams" not only is consistent with his general aesthetics, which prize fantasy over realism, but also supports our description of *Daphnis* and similar works as products of the mnemonic imagination. Here, however, this claim does not stand alone but rather is offered to refute the idea that the score for *Daphnis* was ever (or should ever have been) supposed to sound like authentic ancient Greek music. Although we might think that such a naïve listener is just a straw man, Ravel is actually responding to pressures he felt when collaborating with the Russians. As Lynn Garafola has observed, Fokin's main choreographic ideas for *Daphnis*—"the frieze-like design, profiled stance, and alternation of movement and plastic pose"—were inspired by the gestures that decorated Grecian black- and red-figure vases of the fifth-century BCE.[34] In keeping with his desire for ethnographic authenticity, Fokin apparently asked Ravel to reconstruct ancient Greek music for *Daphnis*, only later settling for "no obvious contradictions and noticeable disagreements [between the music and] the character of the Graeco-Roman art."[35] Nonetheless, Fokin never entirely warmed to Ravel's score, finding it to lack the "virility" that was "necessary for a projection of the world of antiquity."[36] The abduction was a case in point: Whereas Fokin originally wanted the scene to paint a "violent, gruesome picture" that included "the slaying of the shepherds, the abduction of the women, [and] the plunder of the cattle," Ravel opted for an abbreviated episode that minimized the sadistic spectacle.[37]

Leon Bakst, the member of Diaghilev's circle who designed the costumes and sets for *Daphnis*, sided more with Fokin than Ravel in this dispute. In addition to draping the characters in mantles and tunics (the Greek *himation* and *chiton*, respectively) and shoeing their feet with sandals, he placed mandalas on their clothing to express a more exotic and primitivist conception of ancient Greece, one inspired by a trip to Greece that he took in 1907.[38] At the same time that he began work on *Daphnis* in 1909, he published an essay in the journal *World of Art* that he titled "New Paths of Classicism in Art" and in which he echoed Fokin's criticisms of *Daphnis* in more general, historical terms, railing against "the refined, sophisticated, and effete interpretations given Greek art in the eighteenth and nineteenth centuries."[39]

Thus, the association drawn between *Daphnis* and that vision of ancient Greece "imagined and depicted by French artists at the end of the eighteenth century" implicitly acknowledges and rejects the more primitivist approach endorsed by both Fokin and Bakst, while also opening up a valuable perspective on the ballet's aesthetics. With its mythological subject, idyllic setting, and ornamental musical textures it is, indeed, closely affined to eighteenth-century French art—in particular, the rococo stylings of Watteau, Boucher, and Fragonard. Indeed, passages in *French Eighteenth-Century Painters* (1856–1875), the classic account of the French Rococo by the Goncourt brothers that Ravel and Roland-Manuel would surely have known, often sound like descriptions of *Daphnis*: Fragonard's work is portrayed as an "enchanting poem of Desire" inspired by Longus,[40] among others, while the world of Watteau, inventor of the *fête galante*, is suffused with "an eternal indolence" that allows sight and thought to "languish into a vague, vanishing distance," as in the dreamy and erotically charged *L'embarquement pour Cythère*.[41] By comparing *Daphnis* to eighteenth-century French painting Ravel might also have been suggesting that Alexander Benois—who by 1928 had become a good friend—would have been the appropriate set designer for this ballet rather than Bakst; not only did Benois's sensibilities tend toward the eighteenth century, but he was also the author of the libretto for *Le pavilion d'Armide*, a Russian ballet produced in 1909 that was set in eighteenth-century France and featured a scene of reanimation in which a Gobelin tapestry comes to life before our eyes. There is, however, one thing that prevents us from unreservedly endorsing these speculations: the presence of "end" in "at the end of the eighteenth century." Strictly speaking, the end of the eighteenth century in France was the period of the French Revolution, whose stark neoclassicism has little in common with *Daphnis*. Once again, it is possible to explain this incongruity by ascribing it to Roland-Manuel or at least to his influence on Ravel; even though we cannot be sure that he was its source, he nevertheless seems to implicate himself when, in his 1928 monograph on Ravel, he readily compares *Daphnis* to the paintings of Jacques-Louis David.[42]

The impulse to think of *Daphnis* in terms of graphic art may also have come from its literary source, the third-century-CE Greek novel by Longus. At the head of the novel, Longus supplies a proem that accounts for the main story by tracing its origin to a painting the narrator-author happened to encounter on an excursion to Lesbos; the relevant portion of the proem is reproduced here:

> When I was hunting in Lesbos, I saw the most beautiful sight I have ever seen, in a grove that was sacred to the Nymphs: a painting that told a story of love. The grove itself was beautiful—thickly wooded, flowery, well watered; a single spring nourished everything, flowers and trees alike. But the picture was lovelier still, combining great artistic skill with an exciting, romantic subject. Many people were attracted by its fame and came, even from abroad, to pray to the Nymphs and to look at the picture. The picture: women giving birth, others dressing the babies, babies exposed, animals suckling them, shepherds adopting them, young people pledging love, a pirates' raid, an enemy attack—and more, much more, all of it romantic. I gazed in admiration and was seized by a yearning to depict the picture in words.[43]

The similarity between the proem and the ballet's Introduction suggests that the former may have been a model for the latter. In addition to providing the *mise en scène*, both present the grove as a solitary, sacred space before populating it with worshippers. Further, the narrator's gaze in the proem swivels between the nymph statues and the painting of Daphnis and Chloe just as the audience's attention rotates between NYMPHES and DC in the Introduction.

More generally, however, the Introduction resembles the proem insofar as both are pre-texts that give the main story a pretext, both pretexts involve an encounter with the past, and both encounters give way to the reanimation of this past. In the proem, the central artifact from the past is the painting, which the narrator brings to narrative life in an act of ekphrasis; defined in the proem itself as the narrator's desire to "depict the picture in words," ekphrasis is a rhetorical device that draws much of its power from its ability to animate the inanimate. Neither the painting nor the hunter appears as such in the Introduction, but that does not mean that they go wholly unrepresented in the ballet. Rather, the cycle of images in the painting, which is supposed to portray the main stations of the mythic tale, is displaced across the "vast fresco" of *Daphnis* to form a series of dramatic tableaux, including Daphnis and Chloe praying to the nymphs (R16), their first kiss (R53), the captive Chloe in despair (R139), the reunion of the lovers (R165), and their betrothal (R193).[44] The hunter, gazing admiringly at the painting of the myth, finds his surrogate in a series of audiences arranged in concentric semicircles around the couple in the ballet: the diegetic crowd; the semidiegetic, quasi-Greek chorus; and the actual audience. Of the three, however, it is we who relate most closely to the hunter since it is ultimately our mnemonic imagination—accessing memory in a collective, anamnestic mode—that revives the past.

Among literary pre-texts whose pretext is memory, the best known is the "Overture" to Proust's memoir-novel, *À la recherche du temps perdu,* which he began to write in the same year (1909) Ravel began to compose *Daphnis*. The Overture falls into two parts, each of which accesses the past differently. In the first part the narrator, Marcel, recalls his childhood in Combray by means of "voluntary memory," which Proust once described in an interview with *Le temps* as belonging "above all to the intelligence and the eyes" and offering only "untruthful aspects of the past."[45] The second part features the renowned "madeleine" scene, in which the narrator is inspired to search for times past after tasting a tea-soaked cake such as he had not eaten in years. After several failed attempts by Marcel to locate the origin of this experience in the past, the recollection begins to slowly rise to the surface of his consciousness, creating an "echo of great spaces traversed."[46] When it finally bursts forth, it seems to resurrect Combray rather than merely recollecting it:

> As in the game wherein the Japanese amuse themselves by filling a porcelain bowl with water and steeping in it little pieces of paper which until then are without character or form, but, the moment they become wet, stretch and twist and take on color and distinctive shape, become flowers or houses or people, solid and recognizable, so in that moment all the flowers in our garden and in M. Swann's park, and the water lilies on the Vivonne and the good folk of the village and their little dwellings and the parish church and the whole of Combray and its surroundings, taking shape and solidity, sprang into being, town and gardens alike, from my cup of tea.[47]

While the first part of the Overture involves only voluntary memory, the second engages both voluntary memory—as demonstrated in Marcel's fruitless efforts to force the recollection to mind—and involuntary memory, which brings the past to life in a miraculous *moment bienheureux* (felicitous moment).

Proust's Overture arguably provides the best way to understand Ravel's Introduction to *Daphnis*—namely, as a *moment bienheureux*. Before we begin to connect the dots, however, let us pause to ask how we might account for this coincidence. Since Ravel and Proust were neither friends nor friendly acquaintances, we can hardly imagine that they would have shared their work with one another, especially when that work, in 1909, was only in its incipient stages. It is possible, however, that Proust's Overture could have been partially inspired by a performance of the *Introduction et allegro*, whose reanimating Introduction, as we have seen, is the putative model for the Introduction to *Daphnis*; in fact, at least one Proust scholar has noted the similarity between two septets: Ravel's and Vinteuil's, whose performance forms another *moment bienheureux* for Marcel.

The difficulty involved in determining a cause for this affinity does not make it any less striking, of course. In the first half of the Introduction the past is a *vision lointaine*—distant, dormant, and entangled in the thematic looping of NYMPHES/DC, as if it were butting up against the limitations of "voluntary memory"—whereas the second half revises this vision, wresting it from the "intelligence and the eyes," restoring to it live bodies, and endowing it with overwhelming sonic presence. As the billowing texture, replete with echoing motives, leads us up to the crest of this *moment bienheureux* we can even imagine that we hear memory traverse the "great spaces" that separate one era from another.

Wedded to the primal scene as its most glorious possibility, the *moment bienheureux* operates in *Daphnis* as it does in Proust's novel, launching the main narrative and appearing thereafter in diminished capacity before arriving in a fantastic display to conclude the expansive work; the triple climaxes of the Daybreak correspond nicely to what Roger Shattuck has called "a great sunburst of memory" in the seventh and final installation of Proust's novel, *Le temps retrouvé*.[48] Given the overarching importance of the primal scene to the large-scale coherence of *Daphnis*, what Walter Benjamin said about *À la recherche* may apply just as well to Ravel's "choreographic symphony": "[O]nly the *actus purus* of recollection itself, not the author or the plot, constitutes the unity of the text."[49]

3

Dandy, Interrupted

During the past century of critical discourse on Maurice Ravel and his music, the concept of sublimation—which includes but does not limit itself to explicit citations of the term—has figured significantly in evaluations of the composer's life, his compositions, and their interrelation. Commentary with an aesthetic focus most often invokes the concept to articulate a perceived "elevation to a higher state or plane of existence" or even a "transmutation into something higher, purer, or more sublime," while biographical commentary engages the concept's psychoanalytic sense: "the refining of instinctual energy, especially that of the sexual impulse, and its manifestation in ways that are socially more acceptable."[1]

In appealing to the latter definition, biographers are usually rationalizing Ravel's apparent lack of a sex life—part of the phenomenon known during the composer's lifetime as his "sexual enigma"—by proposing that his libido was sublimated into the production of his artworks.[2] However, the multivalence of the concept of sublimation, which is implicated in a variety of discourses, including the geological, the chemical, the alchemical, the magical, the religious, the poietic, and even the ethical, has allowed its use in Ravel criticism to proliferate well beyond psychobiography. Under the rubric of sublimation, scholars have discussed topics such as the role of the mechanical in his dramatic output, musical representations of class-historical membership, orchestrational techniques and effects, relations between his ballet music and its choreography, and stylistic shifts that mark his development as a composer.[3]

In this chapter I braid together many of these strands of discourse in a discussion of the dandy, the elegant and cultured figure who, as Baudelaire asserted, "aspires to be *sublime* without interruption."[4] Appearing in fiction by authors such as Balzac, Barbey d'Aurevilly, Stendhal, Huysmans, Wilde, Proust, and Nabokov and theorized at length in two famous French literary essays of the mid-nineteenth century, Barbey d'Aurevilly's *On Dandyism and George Brummell* (1845) and Baudelaire's "The Painter of Modern Life" (1863), the dandy was recognized for an elegance in dress and comportment that often involved androgyny and narcissistic self-adoration, an aristocratic demeanor that shunned vulgarity and demonstrations of passion, and an independence of character that manifested itself in behavior ranging from apathetic nonchalance to scathing derision, noble stoicism to fierce antisociality, and impish playfulness to forbidding chilliness. From this repertoire of behaviors the dandy dynamically fashioned his persona; as Barbey says, the dandy is an artist whose artwork is "his life itself."[5]

Personal reminiscences and biographical accounts of Ravel consistently affirm his dandyism. A lifelong connoisseur of Baudelaire, Ravel would undoubtedly have been familiar with the poet's comments on the dandy in the *Journaux intimes*, "The Painter of Modern Life," and elsewhere. Moreover, it is certain that he knew and cherished Barbey d'Aurevilly's *Du Dandysme*: According to Ricardo Viñes's private journal, the twenty-two-year-old Ravel lent him a copy of this book on May 8, 1897.[6]

In an effort to bring the man and his music into a more intimate relation, some critics have proposed that certain compositions by Ravel can be fruitfully understood as self-portrayals of the artist as dandy. Referring to the first song from the cycle *Histoires naturelles* (1907), Theo Hirsbrunner has suggested that "the peacock with its dandyist behavior is nothing other than the allegory of an artist of the *fin de siècle* who, caught up in his own wishful fantasies, was frequently encountered at that time in Paris."[7] Benjamin Ivry goes even further than Hirsbrunner by identifying Ravel with both the swan and the peacock in that cycle and calling attention to the closet knowledge about the composer that such an interpretation seems to suggest. Both birds are described by Ivry as "aloof and disdainful of others, showing but never offering themselves. Ravel may have intended a self-portrait in the peacock, who cries 'Leon, Leon' [his absent bride], surely not coincidentally, the name of Ravel's beloved friend, Fargue."[8]

Rather than dismissing Ivry's implicitly gay reading of "The Peacock" as unfounded or tendentious, it is more profitable to recognize that discussions of the (male) dandy almost inevitably prompt the question of his sexuality, and for good reason: Not only was the category of "homosexual" coalescing at about the same time as the emergence of the dandy, but his sublimity also implicates him in a history of strategies designed to cope with sexual desire in repressive cultural contexts.[9] These points notwithstanding, to discuss Ravel's sexuality remains a difficult and contentious matter—and not merely because of the apparent absence of information about his intimate relationships. In fact, the issues involved here are strikingly similar to those that have swirled even more contentiously about Handel, as are the solutions that Ravel's biographers have come up with to deal with this question; the ladyfriend trap, the mother alibi, the sexless and celibate syndrome, and the aesthetic fallacy—the primary means of rationalizing and refuting potential evidence of homosexuality in Handel's life, as labeled and discussed by Gary Thomas—have all played important roles in Ravel biography as well.[10] While the association of dandyism with sublimation seems to position it beneath the rubric of the aesthetic fallacy (in sum: "I have sacrificed my personal life to my art"), its "scattered field of reference" has allowed it to slip through the disciplinary clutches of heteronormative discourse, both in Ravel's time and our own.[11] Here I do not use the notion of dandyism to deliver a verdict on Ravel's sexuality but rather allow the dandy to maintain his fullness as a queer figure whose embodied opposition to contemporary bourgeois norms extends to his sexuality regardless of whether this opposition be a counterproposal (of homosexuality) or a dismissal (i.e., that the issue of sexuality cannot be resolved in any current categories).

As we are beginning to see, the issues surrounding this phenomenon are quite rich—richer than scholarship has generally suggested hitherto. Dandyism is neither an inert fact of Ravel's personal life nor a simple pretext that allows us to treat particular musical-dramatic characterizations in his work as self-caricature nor a means by which we may declare him once and for all to have been gay. Rather, it is a comprehensive and queer orientation toward the world that installs sublimation at the center of an individual's life, investing it with supreme value as a means by which the individual may negotiate the demands that it, others, and culture at large make upon its appearance and behavior. Thus, investigating dandyism in Ravel's music promises to shed light upon sublimity as both a guiding poetic principle and a means of interrelating the artist and his art.

The composition by Ravel that is best suited for this investigation is *Daphnis et Chloé*. In his essay "Consuming the Exotic: Ravel's *Daphnis and Chloe*," Lawrence Kramer locates sublimation in both the work's elevation of commercial exoticism to the status of high art and its implementation of various compositional strategies to organize and control a motley group of exotic themes, motives, and textures.[12] Like Kramer, I am also interested in assessing the specific means by which beauty is produced in *Daphnis*, particularly the beauty that the dandy cultivates in his person; unlike Kramer, I invoke sublimation more explicitly as a psychoanalytic concept that can be applied directly to the behavior of the characters in the ballet.

Sublimation is featured throughout the ballet as the psychic means by which raw sexual desire is modulated to produce beautiful gestures of courtship and as the musical process by which noise is transformed into serenade. In the first third of this ballet both procedures of sublimation not only outline Daphnis's character in general but also lend him the profile of a dandy. The centerpiece of this analysis is the "Light and Graceful Dance of Daphnis," a solo number in which a trio of figures—Ravel, Daphnis, and the dandy—join hands in a round of displaced identities. Before I focus upon the Dance of Daphnis, however, I first examine its point of origin in a passage that I henceforth refer to as the "volte-face" and which begins with a "brusque gesture" by our protagonist.

Desire and Its Sublimation in the *Volte-Face*

At R29 Daphnis performs a "geste brusque" to separate Chloe from his rival, Dorcon, just as the latter is going to kiss her, as shown in example 3.1.

This gesture is contextually marked in at least two respects: It is one of the first acts performed by an individual acting independently rather than as part of a group, and it is also the first display of violence in a narrative that has hitherto presented only gentle and fluid acts of dance, prayer, and courtship.

With this gesture Daphnis vents the feelings of jealousy that had accrued within him during the previous "Dance of the Young Girls and Boys" (RR17–28).[13] His jealousy is an effect of an underlying sexual desire that the naïve protagonist understands imperfectly, if at all. In the literary source for the libretto, Daphnis and Chloe have been constant companions since infancy.[14] Upon awakening to their sexual desire for each other—and to sexuality altogether—they are disturbed and dumbfounded by it.

Well attuned to the novel, the ballet only gradually sexualizes their relationship. Daphnis and Chloe make their debut (R10) as individuals, which underplays their status as a couple; when they eventually appear as a couple (R15), their act of religious devotion diverts attention away from the more personal aspects of their relationship; during the subsequent episode, the "Dance of the Young Girls and Boys," they begin at last to experience desire for each other—but only indirectly, in the form of jealousy. Daphnis's "geste brusque" unveils sexual desire as the truth that, underlying the whole scenario, can no longer be suppressed.

As example 3.2 shows, the "geste brusque" participates in a rough transition between two formal sections that incorporates two moments of disruption: the shift from the three measures of "Beaucoup moins vif" to the three measures of "Vif", and then a shift back from "Vif" to "Moins vif."[15] The latter reversal coincides with Daphnis's *volte-face* as he turns away from Dorcon to "approach Chloe tenderly."

Example 3.1 Daphnis's "Geste brusque."

The music of the *volte-face* represents the dramatic action by pivoting from the "geste brusque" to the "waltz theme," an expansive serenade sung by the solo first violin. Roland-Manuel, Vladimir Jankélévitch, and Deborah Mawer are among those to have proposed that we assign the waltz theme to Chloe.[16] However, in my study of *Daphnis* I have noted that only the middle two of its six separate appearances (RR29–30, 51–52, 64–65, 131–140, 164, 204–205) are associated exclusively with Chloe, while the other four involve the couple. Thus, we might better understand the waltz phrase to be a secondary love theme; the primary love theme (DC) that frames the ballet (RR1 and 209) seems to operate at a greater remove from the dramatic action. Indeed, it is quite natural for a waltz theme to represent the desire that binds a couple in love, given the sexual threat that this dance held during its history.[17]

The *volte-face*, which encompasses both the "geste brusque" and the waltz theme, might at first glance seem merely to be the farcical agon that occurs when men jostle for a woman's attention. The comedic aspect of this moment is not only undeniable but also has precedent in *L'heure espagnole*. Realizing that Concepcion, the female protagonist of this comic opera, does not favor him, the pompous and portly Don Inigo decides to exchange his "imposing and severe appearance" for a lighter and more appealing persona (scene IX). Simultaneous with this decision, the music transposes its material from one genre to another, transforming a ponderous overture into a light waltz in a gesture that is quite similar to the *volte-face*; one commentator has even described the product of this motivic transformation—the waltz—as revealing the *figure* of Inigo's sexual desire, a multivalent French term that we may understand as either his "face" or his whole person as a

Example 3.2 Daphnis's *Volte-face*.

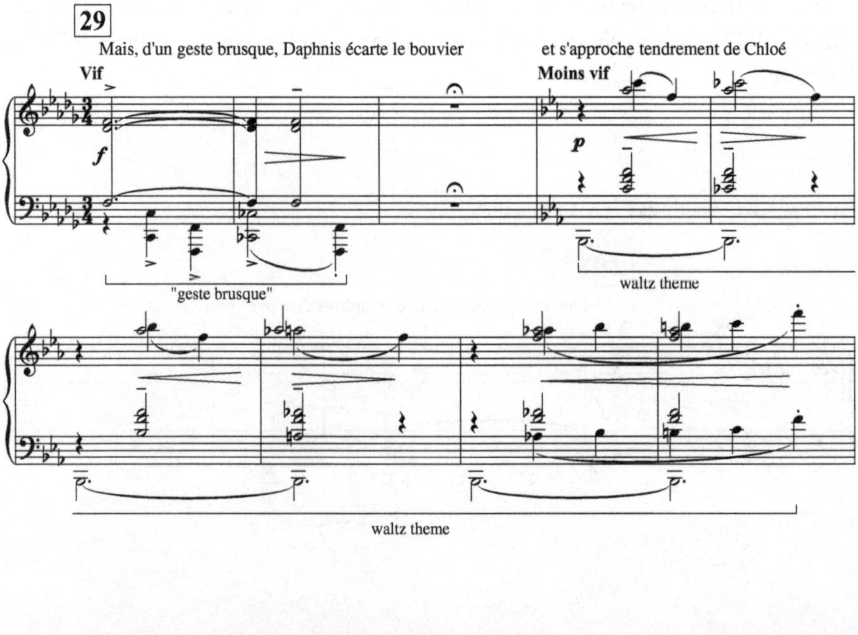

"figure" for desire within this sex-obsessed romp.[18] Nonetheless, insofar as the *volte-face* plays a central role in Daphnis's complex psychological development in the ballet, its comedic aspect cannot aspire to a status beyond that of a fragile veneer.

Both elements of contrast and continuity between the "geste brusque" and the waltz theme in *Daphnis* lend far-reaching significance to the *volte-face*, which, on the basis of its musical gesture alone, is quite startling: Upon hearing the violent and discordant musical "geste brusque," who would have anticipated its sudden translation into a waltz? Moreover, while it is common in Western classical music to find thematic wholes dissolving into motivic fragmentation, it is less common to find a fragment succeeded by its whole. The conspicuous strangeness of this passage requires interpretation.

I propose that this surprising transformation is best understood to represent the sublimation of sexual desire.[19] Sublimation, in this context, refers specifically to the Freudian "vicissitude of the instinct" or "destiny of drive" (the two standard English translations of the original German *Triebschicksal*).[20] Across the measure of rest that separates the "geste brusque" from the waltz theme, Daphnis's sexual desire undergoes a transformation whose effect is simultaneously visible, legible, and audible. At the level of dramatic action sexual aggression gives way to a gentle "tenderness" (*tendresse*), and lustful physicality is refined into the stylized courtliness of the waltz.[21]

One might object to this interpretation on the grounds that, in the "geste brusque," Daphnis's desire is not expressed directly toward its object, Chloe, but rather as aggression toward the potential obstacle to its satisfaction, Dorcon. In answering this objection, I would mention again that the "geste brusque" vents the jealousy felt by Daphnis during the immediately preceding "Dance of the Young Girls and Boys" and further point to its musical genesis from a motive that the libretto explicitly associates with jealousy (cf. the alto flute's syncopated repeated tone at RR20^{+8} and 25^{+7}).[22] Freudian psychoanalysis, on the other hand, would account for this displacement of both object and affect as a typical example of sadism, in which aggression "cannot be conceived of at all without envisaging its fusion with sexuality."[23]

In sublimating the music of the "geste brusque," the waltz theme turns it inside out. The snarling instrumentation of the "geste brusque" cedes to the waltz's abyssally capacious texture, projecting the melody up three octaves into the first violin solo, which, like a daring funambulist, capers vertiginously above a low B♭ in the contrabasses. The catapulting of the "geste brusque" melody up three octaves across the grand pause (R29) is even more striking, preceded by a three-octave fall (RR28^{+9}–29^{+4}).[24] Further, the melody is not reinforced by a doubling at the octave below, as in the "geste brusque," but rather is shadowed intermittently two octaves below by a solo cello. The dynamics shift from an accented forte to piano "espressif," and the upper strings, muted and stroked on the fingerboard (*sur la touche*), implore gently.

These transformations in gesture, language, and music all bespeak the process of sublimation, which refines musical-dramatic behavior across the grand pause and increases its aesthetic and cultural value in progressing from fragment to phrase, cacophony to euphony, percussion to song, brutality to tenderness, and violence to dance. Even the shift in tempo across the measure of rest sublimates: The "Vif" or "vital" expression of the sexual instinct in the "geste brusque" is audibly suppressed in transition to the "*Moins* vif"—or "*less* vital"—waltz theme.

The comparative adverb "moins" suggests that sublimation in the *volte-face* has not eliminated sexual desire but rather only lessened its expressive force. This statement is not necessarily a contradiction in terms as several scholars have claimed, including Mary Ann Doane. Viewing sublimation as a process of complete and irreversible desexualization, Doane interprets various attempts by psychoanalytic theorists to resexualize this concept as indications of its untenability.[25] Doane's understanding of sublimation seems to me unnecessarily restrictive, however, especially in light of the notion of partial sublimation in Freud's *Three Essays*, in which he proposes that sublimation need neither eradicate the expression of sexuality nor permanently suppress the sexual instinct.[26] More recently, in his 1959–1960 seminar on ethics Jacques Lacan also warned against the equation of sublimation with desexualization and asserted that the former "does not on all occasions necessarily follow the path of the sublime. The change of object doesn't necessarily make the sexual object disappear—far from it; the sexual object acknowledged as such may come to light in sublimation."[27] To my ear, the systolic and diastolic rhythms in each two-measure subphrase of the sublimated waltz theme—as emphasized by dynamic swells, chordal pulsation in the accompaniment, tenuto articulation, and Ravel's specific bowings—keep the physical body and its lusts in mind by transforming the music into a *corps sonore*.

The Dance Contest and the "Danse grotesque de Dorcon"

In the wake of the *volte-face*, the ballet stages a dance contest between Daphnis and Dorcon so that they may properly resolve their claims to Chloe's affections.[28] The *volte-face* and its ensuing material are consequently absorbed into the contest as the refrain (A) of its rondolike structure (ABA'CA"). Simultaneous with its subsumption into this structure, the *volte-face* is also projected on a larger scale: Just as the elegant waltz theme succeeded the violent "geste brusque" in the *volte-face*, so, too, does the "Light and Graceful Dance of Daphnis" follow the "Grotesque Dance of Dorcon."

This fascinating pair of dances and its isomorphic relation to the *volte-face* have received short shrift, perhaps due to its apparent conventionality. In a review of the ballet's 1912 premiere performance in Paris, Gaston Carraud cited the Dance Contest in criticizing the overall ballet scenario: "The libretto of *Daphnis et Chloé* is surprisingly poor and banal. One would believe it to have been made for the Opera and the *Prix de Rome*. We even see a dance contest—this supreme cliché of the genre!—whose prize is a kiss from Chloe."[29] While dance contests may indeed have become commonplace in ballet by 1912, the role of the Dance Contest in the work's ongoing narrative of male sexual desire and its sublimation lends it a contextual value that transcends mere cliché.

In the pursuit of this value, however, we should not disregard the pointed reversal of characterization that occurs here: Dorcon's suavity in his attempted kiss is transferred to Daphnis in his light and graceful dance, and Daphnis's violence in the "geste brusque" is transferred to Dorcon in his grotesque dance. This chiasmus ostensibly dissociates Daphnis from unseemly expressions of desire while ascribing them to Dorcon, who is consequently treated as a scapegoat and driven off by the jeering crowd.

The "Danse grotesque" is, accordingly, a brutish piece whose harshness of tone is mitigated by the dance's overall *buffo* character. The allusion to *opera buffa* spectacle is precise: In the libretto that Ravel's audience would have held in their hands (Durand plate number 8434), the role of Dorcon is described as "1er danseur bouffe." Possibly taking a cue from the libretto, the critic Émile Vuillermoz acknowledged the generic aspect of Dorcon's dance in his review of Adolf Bolm's *création du rôle*: "Bolm triumphed in a boldly designed *buffo* dance in which he demonstrated a truly heroic rhythmic precision."[30] Heroic in dance, perhaps, but not in dress: As shown in figure 3.1, which was taken shortly before the 1912 premiere, Bolm's Dorcon was more cave dweller than cowherd.

The stomping bass and guttural noises of the three bassoons at the beginning of Theme 1 limn Dorcon's physical (and presumed vocal) traits. In addition, the bizarre succession of triads—E♯, F♯, G/g, G♯/g♯, A♯, b—over an E dominant pedal at the opening of the "Danse grotesque" is a musical correlative to the "awkward gestures of the cowherd" (*gestes gauches du bouvier*) that Dorcon produces in attempting to perform within a genre unsuited to him. As the dance unfolds, Ravel constantly broadens the range of musical techniques available to convey Dorcon's *gaucherie*. Salient instances of intensive dissonance include chromatic clustering around the root in the climactic chords of the second theme (R34) and widespread incongruity between the bass and accompanying harmonic structures. Examples of extensive dissonance include botched harmonic arrivals at the end of phrases and chromatic slippage in the bass line. Adding insult to injury, Ravel follows the first successful harmonic arrival at the A-major tonic (R39) with a glissando in the trombones that reels drunkenly between B-minor and B♭-major triads.

Articulation, dynamics, rhythm, meter, and instrumentation complement harmony in outlining Dorcon's crudeness as a dancer and an individual. Percussive

Figure 3.1 Adolf Bolm as a Troglodyte Dorcon in the 1912 Premiere of *Daphnis*.

accentuation and sudden, violent outbursts pervade the musical texture, generally recalling the uncontrolled rages of *buffo* basses in opera (Osmin, for example) and specifically bringing to mind Daphnis's earlier "geste brusque." A trace of the marking "lourdement rythmé," which originally stood at the head of the dance in the 1910 piano score, appears in "Pesant" (R40), at which point the "crowd imitates ironically the cowherd's ungainly gestures."

Thoughts of furious Osmins lead quite naturally to the recognition of the "Danse grotesque" as a piece of Turkish janissary music. Although it is removed by more than a century from its heyday in the repertory of Gluck, Haydn, Mozart, and Beethoven, Ravel's "Danse grotesque" nevertheless fulfills a similar Orientalist purpose of caricaturing the Other; as Mary Hunter has explained for the eighteenth century, the *alla turca* style represents Turkish music "as a deficient or messy version of European music rather than as a phenomenon with its own terms of explication and reference."[31] Once one opens one's eyes to the *alla turca* element in this dance, the identifying characteristics become glaringly apparent: simple duple meter; a janissary instrumentation featuring bass, military, and snare drums, tambourines, cymbals, a triangle, and a wind band; melodic turns ($R32^{+5-6}$); sudden shifts in mode (R34); various uses of the stereotypical short-short-long *usul* rhythm; and a conspicuously repetitive thematic design. (The "War Dance" in part 2 of *Daphnis*, which is an implicit ode to nineteenth-century Russian music [Glinka, Musorgsky, Balakirev, et al.], also draws on these elements.) At one level, the "Danse grotesque" is a bit of campy, musical-historical kitsch that allows Ravel to represent Dorcon's masculinity as ridiculous, thereby rendering him quite obviously unsuitable to be paired with the delicate Chloe. At another, it is potentially a piece of musical invective that is aimed at a specific Other, thereby implicating the Dance Contest in a political situation contemporary to the ballet's composition, as we will soon explore.

The "Danse légère et gracieuse de Daphnis"

Within the *volte-face* formed by the Dance Contest, the "Light and Graceful Dance of Daphnis" corresponds to the second of the two original terms;[32] thus, to move from Dorcon's dance to Daphnis's dance can be understood as a progression from an unsublimated to a sublimated representation of the self-in-desire.[33] This musical, dramatic, and choreographic progression simultaneously engages other binarisms of character by shifting from the awkward to the graceful, the ugly to the beautiful, and the primitive to the civilized.

While Fokin's original choreography may be lost, qualities of sound and gesture in Ravel's music make the diametrical contrast between dances and dancers immediately apparent. As the "Danse grotesque" gives way to the "Danse légère," so, too, does a growling bass yield to elevated melodic undulation, tortured chromaticism to effortless diatonicism, and percussive outbursts to mellifluous serenade. Further, while Dorcon is unable to end the "Danse grotesque" on his own terms—his prerogative rudely overridden by the mocking crowd—Daphnis offers not only a coda but also a pair of additional ornamental gestures (the trill and glissando of $R50^{+8-11}$) that manifest a certain self-mastery in his ability to lend closure to his performance.

We need not wait until the conclusion of the Dance Contest to determine its victor since the adjectives "grotesque" and "graceful" alone make sufficiently clear who will win. No matter: the fascination of the contest depends most strongly on the Dance of Daphnis. In forty-seven finely wrought measures, Ravel not only paints a portrait of Daphnis as dandy—the highly cultured figure that, as Baudelaire asserted, aspires to be "sublime without interruption"—but also shatters the dandy's typical self-composure by exposing him to the rending force of erotic desire. Tracking the psychological vicissitudes of the dandy-in-love, the Dance of Daphnis oscillates between a celebration and a critique of sublimation.

The presence of an autobiographical element in this dance raises the stakes for our analysis even higher. Ravel's identification with Daphnis through the notion of dandyism, as well as his disidentification with Dorcon's Turkish music as the unskilled craft of his enemies, invites us to interpret the Dance Contest as an aesthetic and tendentious reenactment of Parisian musical politics circa 1910, pitting the bungling exoticism of Vincent d'Indy's Société Nationale versus the iridescent art of Ravel and his newly formed Société Musicale Indépendante. From these considerations the Dance of Daphnis emerges as an aesthetic manifesto, drafted by the composer at the height of his artistic productivity and incorporated as a centerpiece into his most prestigious work thus far—prestigious not only for its symphonic proportions but also for its status as one of the first ballet scores that Diaghilev commissioned from a Western composer for his Ballets russes.

Aspiring toward the Waltz

The musical face that Daphnis turns toward us in the opening measures of the A section in this ABA′ form could hardly contrast more strongly with Dorcon's: Unlike the trio of bassoons that began Dorcon's dance, the wind trio in example 3.3 is elevated in register and eschews chromaticism, drawing its triads exclusively from a hexachordal subset of the diatonic scale, the one that excludes the leading tone.

While the low tessitura of Dorcon's bassoons bespeaks a barbarous masculinity, the higher tessitura of Daphnis's flutes projects a youthful androgyny. In addition, the rhythmic homogeneity and undulation of the melody, the choral facture of the flute trio, the compound meter, and the leisurely tempo all recall the genre of the barcarolle, as Jankélévitch has noted.[34]

Example 3.3 The Opening of the "Dance of Daphnis."

To the extent that this music is meant to seduce, appearing as it does within a ritual of courtship, it offers a Baudelairean "invitation to the voyage," promising "luxe, calme et volupté" in a musical phrase whose periodic recurrence correlates it to the poem's well-known refrain. However, the listener would be hard pressed to discern a note of importunity in this seduction; rather, as courtier, Daphnis seems to place *himself* on display as a beautiful presence to be desired and courted. In fact, it was this apparent contradiction—a courtier playing "hard to get"—that first turned my attention to this piece, and it was Ravel's "L'indifférent," the third song from the cycle *Shéhérazade* (1903), that assured me that there was, indeed, something to investigate more deeply here. The "indifferent" character in Tristan Klingsor's poem is a beautiful, exotic androgyne whose momentary encounter with a first-person, presumably male narrator provokes the latter's admiration and desire. It is easy to imagine the first sentence of the poem applied to the Daphnis of the "Danse légère": "Your eyes are gentle like those of a girl, / Young stranger, / And the delicate curve / Of your beautiful face shadowed by down / Has an even more seductive line."[35] To convey the auratic beauty of the innocent androgyne, as well as the euphoria of the desiring subject, Ravel chooses materials very similar to those that begin Daphnis's dance: a slow, quiet, diatonic barcarolle in compound duple meter that exudes luxury, repose, and pleasure.

The impulse in Baudelaire and Ravel to marry nature and art under the banner of hedonism is fundamental to *Daphnis et Chloé* and its thematics of sublimation; its strong presence here indicates the importance of Daphnis's characterization to the aesthetic profile of the entire artwork while simultaneously incorporating the "Danse légère" into a network of internal relations. In particular, the beginning of this dance recalls the beginning of the ballet. Melodic emphasis upon the fifth scale degree and the rising bass figure in example 3.3 create an openness of sound and an organicism of gesture that also appeared as effects of the quasi-acoustic series of ascending perfect fifths in the ballet's initial measures.

Both in Daphnis's dance and at the beginning of *Daphnis* the sounds and gestures of nature have been stylized in a manner reminiscent of Art Nouveau in France at the end of the nineteenth century. As Debora Silverman has explained, this revival of the rococo "glorified nature as its subject and fashioned all the elements of interior space into animated, undulating, and asymmetrical forms derived from the flowing trellises of plants and the scroll and serpentine fan shapes of grottoes and shells."[36] In example 3.3 the bass overtone figure climbs upward on the notated page like ivy to fold its tendril into the melodic superstratum. Repeated at the beginning of each phrase in the two A sections, these overtone gestures culminate at the fourth and final instance (R49), where the trombones present the first ten elements of the harmonic series in order. Here, the dialectic of nature and art hits fever pitch: The furthest exploration of the natural overtone series within the dance, reinforced by harmonics in the flutes, is coextensive with the desire to move among the upper partials, its more refined members.[37]

The APPEL motive, discussed at length in the previous chapter, also contributes to this web of relations. APPEL is a stepwise alternation between two trichords that has its debut in the horns of the ballet's sixth measure and subsequently appears throughout the entire work; although the three-voice undulation of the flutes does not incorporate the dotted rhythm of APPEL, the influence of the latter upon the F major/G minor triadic successions is no less palpable. By recognizing APPEL's presence in this passage—a beckoning choral gesture reminiscent of Debussy's "Sirènes," as we previously noted—we add further support to our description of the dance's opening as both a barcarolle and a musical seduction: a siren song that, by definition, sounds at a distance and awakens our desire to overcome that distance.

Subtler but more significant than these genealogies is the relationship of these measures to the waltz theme from the *volte-face*. To perceive this relationship we must attend to aspects of the music that are less readily apparent to the analytical eye than themes and gestures: the registral distribution of tones within certain chords and the distribution of these chords across the four phrases of the two A sections. Example 3.4 juxtaposes the initial sonority for the waltz theme (4a) with the initial sonorities for each of the four phrases in the dance's A sections as they occur chronologically (4b–e).

While 4b already evokes the waltz theme well, 4e is an exact match. Further, the series of phrase openings outlines a teleology: 4c transforms the F triad of 4b from major to minor and raises it to its goal register, 4d places the upper triad into a major ninth chord (lacking a chordal third), and 4e transposes this chord into its proper register and pitch level.

Insofar as this teleology binds together both A sections and the A sections are representative of the dance as a whole, the entire "Danse légère" can be summed up as an emulation of the waltz theme, which gradually draws closer to its sublime ideal.[38] The wit of this compositional gesture lies in its reflexive allusion: Advancing gently toward its object of desire, the dance courts the waltz theme just as Daphnis previously courted Chloe to it. This analysis thus bears out the initial proposition that the Dance Contest is the *volte-face* writ large: The "Danse

Example 3.4 The Gradual Approximation of the Waltz Theme by the Opening Sonorities of the Four A-Section Phrases in the "Dance of Daphnis."

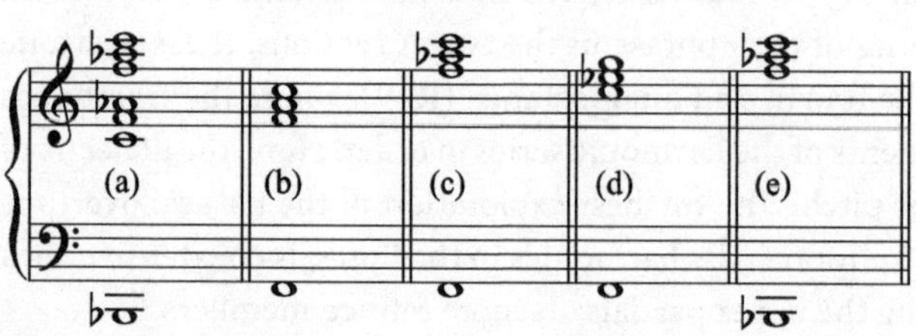

grotesque" corresponds to the "geste brusque," the "Danse légère" corresponds to the waltz theme, and the operation that transforms the expression of desire from the first to the second dance is sublimation.

Daphnis as Dandy

The dance's emulation of the waltz theme figures Daphnis's aspiration toward a sublimity of self, which itself coincides with the dandy's quintessential aim to be "sublime without interruption."[39] Dandyism in the Dance of Daphnis is first evident in the adjectives "light" and "graceful," which appear in its title. While these descriptors may render explicit the contrast between the two competitors and their respective dances, it also projects feminine qualities onto Daphnis, elevating him beyond the mere youth of Longus's novel to become one of Barbey's dandy-androgynes.[40] At first glance one might also suppose that this couplet of "light and graceful" verges on hendiadys, but this is not necessarily so: The French adjective "léger" may mean not merely "light" but also "frivolous," which brings to mind Baudelaire's claim that the dandy exemplifies a socially contrarian "gravity in frivolity" by embodying a decorative and nonutilitarian way of life.[41] Dancing above the pedestrian world of utility and duality, Ravel's Daphnis resembles Nietzsche's Zarathustra, likewise a daring funambulist; how distantly related, in fact, is the shepherd's crook, which Nijinsky used in the premiere,[42] to the dandy's walking cane or Zarathustra's balancing pole?

The musical persona of the dandy—a being of apparently pure and perfect exteriority—speaks to us from the A sections of the dance: from its façade rather than its interior. The "ancient repose" that the strange and wonderful apparition of Barbey's dandy reintroduces into "the bosom of modern anxieties" appears in the barcarolle topic of the first few measures, as well as the archaic purity of its voice leading;[43] the fleet arpeggios that interrupt each A phrase at its midpoint set into further relief the basic equanimity of this music, which resumes after the interruptions as if nothing had occurred. Then, when the music resumes in the second half of the phrase ($R43^{+4-6}$), the texture becomes even more recognizably antique: a Renaissance fauxbourdon replete with parallel 6/3 chords, a slightly decorative melody, and a triple-metrical feel.

Involving the dandy in our analysis of the "Danse légère" also enhances our understanding of overtone gestures in the bass. The Art Nouveau–inspired mixture of nature and artifice in these gestures is representative for the dandy, whom Baudelaire at one point describes as a "sublime deformation of nature"[44] and whose prerogative has otherwise been expressed as an attempt to "overcome the conflict between nature and culture."[45] Moreover, the slow ascent of brass instruments from their registral depths—akin to awakening from a state of dormancy—captures the dancing Daphnis in his identity as a dandyist "Hero of idle elegance" who brings his body into motion just as Apollo plays a prelude upon his lyre.[46] Moreover, the rising bass does not merely figure the gradual overcoming of physical inertia (note the relatively long duration of the incipient tone) but rather sublates the body in the full threefold sense of the Hegelian dialectical *Aufhebung*, elevating, negating, and preserving the corporeal in a musical incorporeality. As Wanda Klee has noted, this musical and masterful performance of the body is a hallmark of the dandy: "The overemphasis of the corporeal through clothing and posture serves to negate the body as an end-in-itself. . . . The body is at best, therefore, a skillfully employed instrument upon which the dandy knows how to play virtuosically."[47] The complex interaction of body and music in the opening bass gesture of the "Danse légère" is yet another way in which the dance emulates and tropes upon its ancestral *volte-face*, which also invokes sublation in transforming the somatically driven "geste brusque" into the ideally conceived waltz theme.

The contradiction that the double arpeggios introduce into the A phrases is equally characteristic of the dandy, whose caprices help him to maintain his independence from behavioral norms and expectations. In more specific terms, these sudden and disruptive gestures musically instantiate the techniques of "l'imprévu" (the unforeseen) and "l'inattendu" (the unexpected) that the dandy cultivates in his conversation, conduct, and attire.[48] Here, the illocutionary force of "l'imprévu" derives not only from its rupturing of musical texture but also from its palpable displacement of tonal trajectory, diverting the opening A-section phrase from F major to A♭ major, the second from F minor to G major, the third from B♭ major to A♭ major, and the fourth from E♭ major to D♭ major, all of which involve a key change of at least two accidentals. Ravel compounds the element of surprise by repeating each arpeggio after its harmony has been resolved and its textural ebullience quelled, thereby intensifying the effect from merely amusing to disconcertingly mordant.

While these arpeggios may raise listeners' eyebrows, they are nonetheless subtly prepared in multiple musical dimensions. For example, in the melody of the first A-section phrase, a leap from C5 to F5 in the second measure helps to mitigate the startling effect of the subsequent octave leap from C5 up to C6; likewise, the appearance of the D half-diminished seventh chord in the second measure is initially enigmatic—its questioning quality heightened by an agogic accent—but it may be accounted for, in retrospect, as an applied leading-tone sonority (viiø7/V) that enables modulation into A♭ major; moreover, the arpeggios in the third and fourth measures can be heard as rhythmically contracted but registrally expanded versions of the opening bass ascent.

The relation between the bass ascent and the arpeggios continues the dance's dialogue between music and the dancing body. According to Calvocoressi, Ravel composed these arpeggios in homage to the spectacular leaps of Nijinsky, who, as Diaghilev's *premier danseur* at the moment of the ballet's commission in 1909, was slated to dance the role of Daphnis at the premiere.[49] If, in the initial measures of the dance, Daphnis resembles the dandy in Baudelaire's description of him as an "idle Hercules," he suddenly draws upon his reserves of strength midphrase and springs into action, reminding us that the dandy's idleness and nonchalance can be a dissembling ruse carefully designed to augment the effect of his eventual and impertinent *éclat*.[50]

Who better than Nijinsky to play both androgyne and strong man? Catching sight of him once in a dressing room, Calvocoressi noted that "although his muscles were on the big side, his body suggested that of a Greek athlete, reposeful as well as strong . . . It had none of the almost feminine grace which he so often showed when appearing in stage costume—in *Armide*, for instance, and later in *Le Spectre de la Rose*"—curiously enough, the two ballets in which Nijinsky was known to show off his miraculous sideways leaps.[51] This perspective from one of Ravel's closest associates deserves our attention, for it is likely that Ravel's musical portrayal of Daphnis was influenced by an overall sense of Nijinsky similar to Calvocoressi's, not just a narrower appreciation of his ability to leap sideways. Nijinsky's perceived androgyny would have strengthened Daphnis's characterization as a dandy. According to Charles Batson, "Nijinsky was not 'ordinarily' masculine, but neither was he feminine: his performances, acted out on and with his flesh, point to some combination of two genders that reveal themselves not to be mutually exclusive."[52] The affiliation between Nijinsky and dandyism is further supported by Deborah Mawer's description of him as "emotionally detached," a quality also reminiscent of the characteristically impassive dandy.[53]

Just as the arpeggios and leaps stir up a musical discourse in danger of congelation (as Roland Barthes would say), so, too, does impertinence enliven the dandy's persona and bring its complex of behavioral elements into mutual complementation. In order to explicate the role that impertinence plays in the dandy's autopoetics, Barbey devises a genealogical scheme in playful allusion to Hesiod, Apollodorus, and other ancient mythologists:

> Daughter of Lightness and Aplomb . . . Impertinence is also the sister of Grace, with which it has to remain united. Both render each other more beautiful through their mutual contrast. Without Impertinence wouldn't Grace resemble a too dull blonde, and without Grace, wouldn't Impertinence be a too piquant brunette? So that they remain what they are separately, it is advisable to mix them together."[54]

Gathering together lightness, grace, aplomb, and impertinence in the space of only six measures, each of the four A phrases in Daphnis's dance, represents the dandy in his identity as an exacting epicure of the self; the crystalline tones of the *jeu de timbres* that characteristically crown the end of each phrase—as well as the celesta riff introducing the dance as a whole—bespeak these qualities with perfect concision.

Ravel as Dandy

Given the central role that self-reflection plays in dandyism—requiring, as Baudelaire asserted, that the dandy maintain his uninterrupted sublimity by "living and sleeping in front of a mirror"[55]—it follows naturally that the creators of fictional dandies and the theorists of dandyism have often been dandies themselves who have transformed their art into another reflecting surface. Solely responsible for tailoring Daphnis's musical character to the contours of the dandy, Ravel is no exception to this phenomenon. Confirmation of Ravel's personal dandyism, which appears throughout biographical accounts of the composer, is well represented by the following statement by Roland-Manuel: "The Ravel who wears sideburns and sacrifices discreetly but assiduously to the demands of fashion successfully fits the type of the Baudelairean dandy: elegant coldness and horror of triviality and of all emotional outpourings."[56] Even at age fifty-two he remained the stylish and impertinent dandy, as evident in Olin Downes's 1927 encounter with Ravel in Paris:

> His dress was exceedingly plain, fastidious, exotic. And now he sat in a very charming garden known to a few, fussing with his food, sampling a Ravelian liqueur, saying the most monstrous things, in phrases that cut so swiftly that seconds flew by before the full and awful import of the words sank into a slower brain.[57]

Characteristic posturings of the dandy also suffuse Ravel's written correspondence, which demonstrates a consistent inclination toward esoteric allusion and evasive circumlocution. Two letters by Ravel illustrate these tendencies effectively, the first of which is the earliest that appears in the collection edited by Arbie Orenstein. Writing to Madame René de Saint-Marceaux on August 28, 1898, Ravel refers to himself as both "the little symbolist" (*symbolard*) and a present-day Alcibiades.[58] Not only are both references uttered from a position of ironic remove from the self that is customary to the dandy, but the latter identification is even explicit in its association with dandyism: Together with Caesar and Catiline, the Athenian general Alcibiades is one of the ancient-historical dandies cited by Baudelaire in "The Painter of Modern Life."[59]

The second letter, addressed on June 12, 1906, to Maurice Delage, contains a moment of self-deprecation that articulates in dandyist terms an awareness of his own penchant for writerly esotericism: "The bosom of the Naiads, where I go each morning to imbibe some conceptual forces for the day, has been unable to refresh me: understand by that image, whose elegance surpasses its simplicity, that I often visit the Grande Jatte baths, which are not far from my home."[60] The self-deprecation here is of a piece with Ravel's self-description as a *symbolard*, whose outright neologism is just as conspicuous as its pejorative suffix.

It is only appropriate that dandyism, which seeks to transform life into art, should play such a central role in the music of this composer who provocatively proclaimed art to be "the supreme imposture" and delighted in feats of pure originality.[61] Calvocoressi is once again a useful resource on this point, having emphasized Ravel's concern with "points of originality in idiom and texture. When calling attention to some beautiful thing, he would often wind up with 'No one had ever done that before, you know!'"[62] The valorization of originality is a defining mark of the dandy; when attempting to explain the passion that fueled dandyism, Baudelaire proposed that "it is above all the burning need to make an originality of oneself."[63] That the dandy draws upon pastiche in his quest for originality is a paradox that suits him to a tee.

The Interrupted Dandy and the Return of the Repressed

Ruffling feathers with his provocative utterances and air of superiority, the dandy has been a lightning rod of critique ever since he came into being. If, for the dandy, to be is to seem, for his critics this can be a mere dissembling that often leads them to ask, what he is trying to hide? Those who have viewed the dandy in relation to his social-economic situation have proposed that an abiding fear of obsolescence, coupled with a desire for self-preservation, may have compelled him to cultivate an impregnable façade in order to stave off quasi-aristocratic *déclassement* in an increasingly democratic, capitalist, and bourgeois society. Deborah Houk has made this point clearly and perhaps even sympathetically: "Viewed in the context of his loss of power in the public sphere, the dandy's project of constructing his self as an impenetrable outer shell represents a defensive reaction to a very real social threat."[64] Although Daphnis is only a fictional character drawn from an ancient Greek romance, the music composed for him may nevertheless bear the traces of Ravel's contemporary understanding of the dandy and his plight. As early as 1909, when Ravel began work on *Daphnis*, the dandy had become a potential object of nostalgia: Two years earlier, Marcel Boulenger had lamented that "the dandies are no more," attributing their extinction to a world "too vast, too congested, and too dispersed for an undisputed supremacy to be established."[65]

While the delicate texture of the A-section phrases may help to indicate the dandy's fragility, for many critics his greatest threat is himself. Having described dandies as quasi-religious figures that are at once "the priests and the victims" of their stringent regimen of self-surveillance, Baudelaire was just as aware as Irving Wohlfarth that the repressive self-containment of the dandy was self-destructive and knew just as well as Emilien Carassus that "eros is the passion that most threatens [the dandy's] impassive rule."[66] In the Dance of Daphnis, repressed desire erupts to produce the turbulent B section.

How can we reconcile the hypothesis of a sublimation of desire with one of repression without risking contradiction? An orthodox understanding of Freud does not seem to admit the simultaneous operation of these two destinies of drive, as confirmed by Volney Gay's assertion that "repression prevents sublimation, is its opposite, because it 'drags down' actions and thoughts associated with the forbidden topic into the unconscious."[67] Without straying too far from Freudian hermeneutics, I propose that a solution to this conundrum was articulated earlier in the notion of a partial sublimation of libidinal impulses, which can be further supplemented by the idea that every destiny of drive must be dynamically maintained rather than established once and for all.[68] Nonetheless, we should not imagine that the two destinies of drive are supposed to coexist peacefully but rather that repression stands in a critical relation to sublimation, raising doubt as to whether the nonlibidinal aesthetic self is only an aesthetic fallacy (to reinvoke the terms of Gary Thomas's analysis).

The potential for Eros to interrupt the dandy's sublimity leads us to revisit the initial thesis that prompted our analysis of the Dance Contest: namely, that the latter composes out the *volte-face* by expanding the "geste brusque" into Dorcon's "Danse grotesque" and the waltz theme into Daphnis's "Danse légère." In the *volte-face* the waltz theme reflects an "ego ideal," Freud's term for a model image of selfhood that is assembled from cultural norms and "possessed of every perfection that is of value" to the subject.[69] The dandy's narcissistic obsession with his ideal image jibes nicely with Baudelaire's mandate that he "live and sleep in front of a mirror." Thus, the "aspiration toward the waltz" that we discerned in the succession of A phrases in the "Danse légère" represents Daphnis's attempt to emulate his ego ideal—an asymptotic approach toward sublimity that Jessica Feldman has described as characteristic of the Baudelairean dandy: "The dandy . . . is one distant from the ideal, but who is nevertheless moving toward it."[70] As mentioned earlier, Daphnis, Ravel, and the dandy join in a Matisse-like round dance insofar as this perfectionist attitude toward the self is echoed in remarks that Ravel once made upon his own poetics: "My objective . . . is technical perfection. I can strive unceasingly toward this end since I am certain never to attain it. The important thing is to draw ever closer to it."[71]

If the sublimation of desire helps to elevate the dandy toward his lofty ego ideal, the psychic strategy of repression threatens to lose control over the repressed contents and send this Icarus plummeting back toward the earth. The particular notion of repression involved here, as well as the strategies for its musical representation, can be elucidated through three secondary sources. First, in his essay on narcissism, Freud explains the occasion for repression as one in which libidinal impulses "come into conflict with the subject's cultural and ethical ideas."[72] Second, in a widely disseminated chapter from *Feminine Endings* Susan McClary has described how the outer sections of ABA structures have been used by composers to contain or "frame" material that is deemed threatening to cultural status quo, especially representations of madness and the feminine.[73] Third, Robert Fink has extended McClary's idea of the musical frame to instantiate not only the containment of the feminine by the masculine (and all relevant binarisms) but also "the internal contradictions of a sexuality turned neurotically against itself," as in the psychic mechanism of repression.[74]

If the B section represents the return of repressed desire in all its immoderate excess, the A sections represent the repressive frame that brackets the B section in three senses: framing, parenthesizing, and marginalizing it to the point of erasure. When the third A phrase (R48) resumes its aspiration toward the waltz, it is as if the frenzied B section had never occurred; making pointed reference to the measure of rest that separated the "geste brusque" from the waltz theme, the grand pause between the B and A′ sections seems to symbolize the impasse that cleaves the dandy's psyche in two. In contrast to the waltz theme in the *volte-face*, the Dance of Daphnis does not simply attempt to produce the sublime self but rather critiques, through the palpable intrusion of Eros, the phenomenon of sublimation in its alleged purity and durability.

A Premonition of Erotic Interruption

While the repressed libido may completely shatter the prevailing texture and mood at the beginning of the B section, its presence can be felt earlier as well—as early as the first two measures of the piece, where metrical and harmonic discontinuities intimate that not all is "luxe, calme et volupté" in the dandy's dominion. By separating the emblematic texture of the A section into its seven component rhythmic layers, table 3.1 not only reveals a discrepancy between the apparent simplicity and actual complexity of the musical facture but also lays bare a specific clustering of metrical and submetrical "grouping dissonances."

The term *grouping dissonance* is drawn from Harald Krebs's *Fantasy Pieces* (1999), in which he defines it as "the association of at least two interpretive layers whose cardinalities are not multiples/factors of each other," labeling it with a "'G' followed by a ratio of the cardinalities involved."[75] For example, in this notational scheme a "five-against-three" within a 3/4 measure would be designated as "G5/3; unit = quarter." In our analytical excerpt, the hemiola is the primary type of grouping dissonance, arising threefold from the simultaneity of Layers 2 and 3 (a G6/4; unit = eighth), Layers 4 and 5 (a G3/2; unit = eighth), and Layers 6 and 7 (a G3/2; unit = sixteenth note). Insofar as both the discrepancy and the clustering of metrical dissonances are involved in representing Daphnis's character here, they bespeak an interiority that belies the dandy's placid countenance. Eros is superheating Daphnis; at the slightest disturbance, desire will erupt.

Upon approaching the midpoint of the phrase, the music gradually becomes entangled in various melodic, harmonic, and metrical complications. The repetition of the F-major tonic triad on the second eighth note of measure two interpolates a stutter into the treble texture that halts the melodic undulation, aborts the smooth

Table 3.1 **Segmenting the Emblematic Subphrase of the "Dance of Daphnis" into its Component Pulse Layers**

Layer #:	*Pulses in Passage/ Attacks per Pulse:*	*Duration of Pulse:*	*Pulse Articulated by:*
1	1/12	dotted whole	the complete two-measure *Gestalt*
2	2/6	dotted half	the initial F-c-f bass-melodic motive
3	3/4	half	the sinusoidal contour in the treble
4	4/3	dotted quarter	the large-scale c^2-d^2-c^2 melodic motive
5	6/2	quarter	the recurrence of the tonic triad in the treble
6	8/1.5	dotted eighth	the bass
7	12/1	eighth	the treble

continuation of Layer 3, and displaces Layer 5 by an eighth note, thereby shifting the hemiola into a syncopated position within the bar—which, in turn, introduces yet another level of metrical dissonance, the Krebsian D2+1 (unit = eighth).[76] This dissonance is a "displacement dissonance," which results from "the association of layers of equivalent cardinality in a nonaligned manner"; the first number denotes the cardinality of the layers, and the second the units by which it has been displaced. My determination here of a D2+1 is slightly speculative since the layer against which the D2+1 of measure 2 is displaced is not literally present in the texture but rather is virtually extended from the hemiolic Layer 5 of measure 1 (where the three quarter-note pulses of Layer 5 dissonate metrically against the two dotted-quarter-note pulses [beats] of Layer 4). This speculative maneuver has precedent in Krebs's system, however, and can probably be subsumed under his category of "subliminal dissonance," which he defines as "dissonance formed by the interaction of at least one explicitly stated interpretive layer and at least one conflicting layer that is only implied (by the context and by the notation)."[77]

My analysis must become a bit more detailed to register the subtle harmonic changes in measure two that follow in the wake of these metrical shifts. When the G minor triad that the stutter had displaced arrives an eighth note later, it is marked by its deferral: An F5, the highest melodic tone so far, is superimposed upon the triad, transforming it into a minor seventh chord, the first harmonic dissonance in the subphrase. If we interpret the superimposed F5 as tonal residue from the tonic stutter, then the G-minor triad appears to respond to the tonic in kind, inflecting the subsequent F-major triad's mode to minor and subposing its own residual tone (D4) to form the half-diminished seventh chord that ends the emblematic subphrase.

This point of relative harmonic obscurity is also a moment of relative semiotic clarity in which the bass and treble gesture toward Eros as the invisible genius behind these disruptions in musical flow. Within the ballet, the half-diminished seventh chord harmonizes Daphnis and Chloe's primary love theme, the central leitmotif whose eleven integral statements over the course of the work help to articulate its overall musical-dramatic narrative. Beyond the ballet, of course, the chord is conventionally recognizable as a transposed version of the harmony that Wagner uses to symbolize the bond of the lovers in *Tristan und Isolde*. Ravel had already made explicit the primary love theme's debt to *Tristan* in the Introduction to the ballet (R2^{+5-6}), whose statement of the theme reproduces the prototypical version of the *Tristan* chord in such a way as to suggest that the whole romance is born from an arch-Romantic *Sehnsucht* (longing).[78] Immediately after having sounded the chord, the Introduction comes alive, building to a massive climax as the empty stage starts to fill with both the dance troupe and the members of the hitherto invisible chorus. So, too, in the "Danse légère" does the chord of desire spark a vital response: the previously discussed leaps, understood here as unexpected displays of wit that allow the dandy to remaster his desire and thereby regain control over his musical-choreographic performance.

Musical Erotics in the Interior of the "Danse légère"

Through a rift in the dandy's sublime façade Daphnis's repressed libido returns with a vengeance at the opening of the B section, his Baudelairean "latent fire" now a firework whose scintillating parabola is traced in the opening measure by a sudden fortissimo harp glissando upward and followed by the slower registral descent in pizzicato strings and flutes; rapid flutter tonguing in the flutes extends the opening's passionate energy by adding a lambent quality to the melody. Passing into the second bar, the music changes fourfold: The fleet melody of measure one gives way to plangent sighs in a muted solo trumpet, harmonic support is transferred from horns to strings and harp, an F-minor triad cedes to the alternation of major ninth chords rooted on A and E♭, and the meter switches from compound triple to compound duple. The opening two measures, in their juxtaposition, exemplify the characteristics of the B section as a whole: melodic discontinuity, harmonic incongruity, orchestrational promiscuity, and metrical inconsistency.

These two measures portray the dandy in a moment of crisis as he slips into a dangerous psychic state; delving further into Baudelaire's notions of subjectivity, we may describe the transition from the A section to the B section as reflecting a shift from the "centralization" of the self to its "vaporization."[79] According to the poet, the dandy doggedly maintains the first in order to ward off the second, which Wohlfarth has explained as indicating the "evaporation and dissipation of the self,"[80] while Bernard Howells has defined it more broadly: "any kind of 'jouissance' in which consciousness is dispersed into its objects: sexual desire, reverie, memory and anticipation, religious feeling, political enthusiasm, identification with the life of the crowd and the city, or with complex rhythmic movement."[81] Among these objects, however, sexual desire usually has pride of place in Baudelaire's writings.

> Eros once again limb-loosener whirls me
> sweetbitter, impossible to fight off, creature stealing up.[82]

Long prized for its pungent insight into the nature of desire, Sapphic Fragment 130 encapsulates several aspects of erotic experience conjured up by the B material in the "Danse légère": The suddenness with which it erupts captures Eros in its predatory surprise and violence; its unabated freneticism bespeaks the "loosening" and whirling of dancing limbs; melodic-harmonic sighing and swooning (R45)—whose rhythm makes yet another reference to *Tristan*, this time to a motive that I have labeled in example 3.5 as "Leiden im Sehnen" ("suffering in desire")[83]—expresses the pleasurable pain of eros, its "sweetbitterness"; the resurgence of B material in the coda (R50) shows that Eros has "once again" stormed the ramparts of the dandy's psyche in a return of the repressed.

In both sections, the image of the passionate body finds acute reflection in arpeggiated textures, as the sudden leaps of the A phrase give way to the rolling

Example 3.5 The Opening Measures of the B Section of the "Dance of Daphnis."

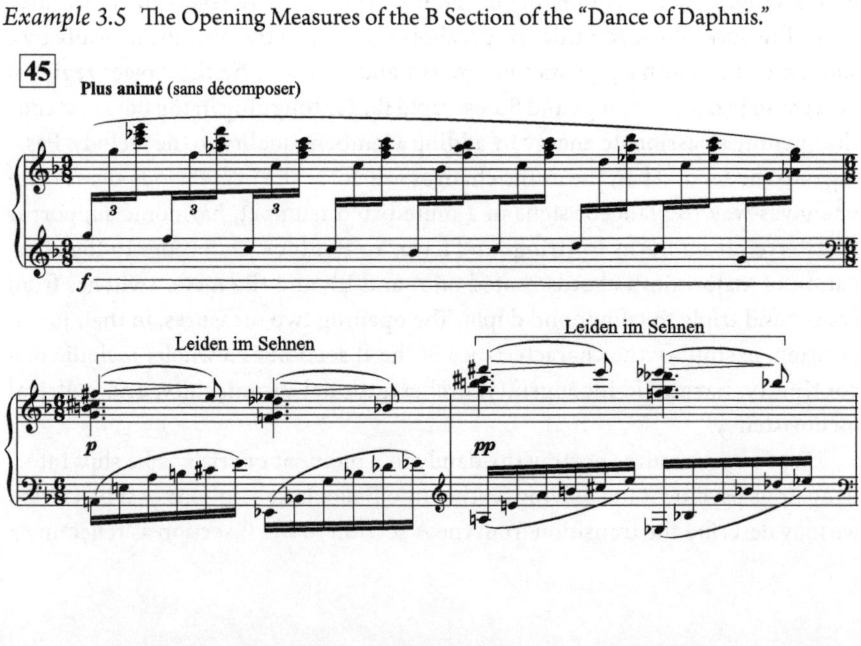

arpeggios of the B section. Associations between the arpeggio and the body already form part of our music-metaphorical language, in which the arpeggio is often described as "fleshing out" a texture and, perhaps in a more choreographic vein, "supporting" a solo melody. Running the gamut between the flayed Marsyas of Greek mythology, the suffering Christ, and the Romantic protagonist as Aeolian harp,[84] associations between the arpeggio and the passionate body have historically featured the harp (or lyre or cithara) as a mediating figure that represents the body under performance by external dominating forces; Ravel's sole assignment of the arpeggio to the harp in the B section, as well as its featured position as accompaniment to the "Leiden im Sehnen" motive, reinforces this association.

Together with our interpretation of the B section as an expression of the libido unleashed and the incorporation of upbeat rhythms into its musical design, Ravel's unusual parenthetical marking at the head of the B section "sans décomposer"—loosely translated as a direction for the musicians to gallop through this stretch without breaking stride[85]—brings to mind a passage from *The Ego and the Id,* in which Freud suggests that:

> In its relation to the id [the ego] is like a man on horseback who has to hold in check the superior strength of the horse. . . . Often a rider, if he is not to be parted from his horse, is obliged to guide it where it wants to go; so in the same way the ego is in the habit of transforming the id's will into action as it if were its own.[86]

Before this precipitous journey draws both rider and beast spiraling down into the abyss (R47), they endure a series of shocks and blows rendered by the textural shifts at each barline (RR45–46). At R47, however, the metrical whipping administered by the shifting barline[87] gives way to a more consistent beating by a sequence of minor ninth chords rooted upon the nodes of the octatonic collection $OCT_{0,1}$.[88]

The second return of the repressed (R50) initiates another musical adventure that is just as harrowing as the B section but traverses a different tonal landscape and enjoys a firmer sense of arrival. It begins with a tonic harmony compromised by an E♭ and a G♭ that extend the F-major triad into a minor-ninth chord familiar from the B section, thereby using harmony to collapse together the rhetorical functions of large-scale cadence (of the A′ section) and continuation (of the B section). Next, a complete D♭ acoustic scale leads into a G♭ acoustic scale before the latter yields to the tonic in an altered descending circle-of-fifths progression. If, as shown in the last row of table 3.2, we measure degrees of tonal shading by the number of flats in each collection, we may chart a progression from "dark" (three flats) to "darker" (five flats), "darkest" (six flats), and then to the "brilliantly light" space of the flatless F-Lydian hexachord; the pairing between the latter two collections is reinforced by their aggregate complementarity: Between the two, every note in the chromatic scale is represented once, and only C is represented twice.

According symbolic significance to these black-key/white-key relations, which Ravel's music elsewhere invites us to do,[89] we may understand the passionate subject in this coda once again to undergo a harsh trial at the hands of Eros, suffering the most severe torments before—in a miraculous turn of events—reemerging unscathed.

A Dialectics of the Dandy

The coda glides by so lightly and gracefully that we might feel compelled to reevaluate the B section as a mere pantomime of erotic passion and its effects: All along, it seems, the dandy was in perfect control of himself. Or perhaps the sentiments expressed in the B section were sincere but ephemeral—passing, like any other fancy that he might entertain. The suddenness of such apparent recovery from the afflictions of Eros brings to mind the *volte-face* that the dandy Swann performs at the end of the first section of Proust's novel, having finally awakened from his nightmarish obsession with the courtesan Odette. Looking back upon this period, Swann expresses surprise over his behavior in a single, blackly humored phrase whose blunt indifference gives it a particular salience for those readers who have just witnessed his sufferings and self-mortifications for 150

Table 3.2 **The Tonal Design of the Coda to the "Dance of Daphnis."**

Character:	*nonsublimated*			*sublimated*		
Measures:	1.5 – 2	2 – 3.5	3.5 – 7.5	7.5 – 8	8 – 9	10 – 11
Content:	B-section material			Cadence	Trill	Fall
Scalar Collection:	(OCT0,2)	D-flat acoustic {DbEbFGAbBbCb}	G-flat acoustic {GbAbBbCDbEbFb}	F major	F Pentatonic and Lydian hexachord	
Harmonic Function:	Tonic (compromised)	The Dominant of...	the altered Dominant of...	the Tonic		
Tonal Palette:	Dark...	Darker...	Darkest...	Brilliantly Light		

pages: "To think that I've wasted years of my life, that I wished to die, that I had my greatest love for a woman who didn't please me, who wasn't my type!"[90]

To endorse this interpretation, however, would force us to turn a deaf ear to the dialectical dimension of the coda. The trill between F major and G major triads in the codetta may refer summarily back to the opening measures of the first A phrase, which featured a leisurely alternation between tonic and minor supertonic triads, but it also recalls the much earlier tremolo between tonic and major supertonic triads in the Introduction's ecstatic apotheosis of APPEL (appearing predominantly in the violins, harps, and clarinets of $R4^{+4-9}$). In fact, the codetta as a whole springs from a topos of ecstasy: Following a tremolo between major tonic and supertonic chords with a quick downward pentatonic riff strongly resembles the climactic final measures of Debussy's *L'île joyeuse* (1905), albeit at a considerable diminution of scale.[91]

The suggestion of ecstasy within the sublimely poised codetta complements a hint of sublimity within the otherwise ecstatic B section. As table 3.3 shows, sentential design operates at two levels of form in the B section: A fifteen-measure-long sentence (S) divides into a three-measure-long basic idea (BI), its slightly varied repetition (BI′), and a nine-measure-long continuation (C), while the continuation is itself a smaller-scale sentence (s) that builds to the climactic onset of the octatonic spiral before subsequently subsiding and trailing off into silence. The lower appendages to table 3.3 mark out concealed references to two musical emblems for Daphnis's sublime self: the gentle melodic cadence that ends the A phrases, and the waltz theme. Modally mapped from a diatonic onto an octatonic scale, the phrase cadence of A is easier to identify in its new guise than the waltz theme, which has undergone not only melodic, harmonic, and rhythmic distortion but also dismemberment into its three two-measure subsets. In Baudelaire's terms, the concentrated self is here demonstrably vaporized; in Nietzsche's, the Apollonian individual has been torn apart, delivered up to a Dionysian dismembering.[92] Singing

Table 3.3 **Diamonds in the mud: Sublime Material Embedded in the B Section of the "Dance of Daphnis."**

Reh./m.:	45/1	2	3	4	5	6	46/1	2	3	4	47/1	2	3	4	5
Phrase Elements:	S														
	BI			BI′			C (s)								
							bi		bi′		c				
Motives:	a	b	b	a	b′	b′	c	c′	c	c′	c motive in sequence			rising motive	grand pause

⥣ Cadence of A phrase

waltz theme

Liebesmotive, the first two *membra disiecta* (RR45^{+2-3} and 45^{+5-6}) pay homage to the desire that has disfigured the sublime Orphic body almost beyond recognition.

Dandy contra d'Indy

To the extent that we wish to view this dance as the composer's musical self-portrait, its conflicted subjectivity leads us to question any commentary that has presented Ravel's dandyism as a source of stable and unproblematic personal identity. Indeed, it is hardly a coincidence that the B section reaches out toward a *Tristan*-indebted semiotics to give voice to passionate suffering. Deeply moved by an orchestral performance on November 1, 1896, of the Prelude to Wagner's music drama, Ricardo Viñes was unexpectedly touched on the hand by his companion Ravel, who had apparently noticed his friend's reaction and sympathized with it, confessing that " 'It's always like that, every time that I hear it.' " As Viñes relates in his diary, at this moment "Ravel, who appears so cold and cynical, the super eccentric decadent, was trembling convulsively and crying like a child—but deeply, since his sobs escaped only in fits and starts (*par à-coups*)."[93] Nowhere else in biographical commentary on Maurice Ravel do we find so clear an image of the dandy, interrupted in his sublimity.

Considering the "Danse légère" in its negative narrative role—that is, as opposed to the "Danse grotesque"—returns us to our initial perspective upon the contest as a large-scale projection of the dichotomous *volte-face*. Moreover, if we may understand their opposition to establish a contrast between "good" and "bad" music, as the dramatic scenario invites us to do, then the contest must convey some sense of Ravel's musical and aesthetic values. In fact, once we situate Daphnis's dance within both the ballet and his compositional career, it attains the status of an artistic manifesto. Shortly before Ravel received the commission for this ballet in 1909, he complained to his friend Cipa Godebski about the "rotten musicians" of the Société Nationale, who, according to the composer,

> can't even orchestrate so they fill in the gaps with "Turkish music." Craftsmanship is replaced by fugal diversions, and themes from *Pelléas* make up for the lack of inspiration. And all of this makes a noise! from the gong, tambourine, military drum, glockenspiel, and cymbals, used at random.[94]

As is well known, Ravel's discontent with the administration and the aesthetic priorities of Vincent d'Indy's Société Nationale (SN) inspired him to found a rival concert society, the Société Musicale Indépendante (SMI), whose first concert took place on April 20, 1910, in the Salle Érard in Paris. As demonstrated in this debut, which featured Ravel's *Ma mère l'oye*, Debussy's *D'un cahier d'esquisses*, and

Fauré's *Chanson d'Eve*, the SMI embraced a lighter musical aesthetic than the SN, presenting the work of "a less organized group of young, free-spirited people" who "strove to perceive [their natural instinct's] slightest external manifestations profoundly, and with more subtlety."[95] The parallelism between the Dance Contest in *Daphnis* and the musical politics that coincided with its composition should now be clear: As the only instance of Turkish music that Ravel ever wrote, the "Danse grotesque" mercilessly caricatures the "rotten musicians" of the SN. Just as the SMI arose to challenge the preexisting SN, so, too, does the "Danse légère" succeed the "Danse grotesque" to exemplify a more attractive counterideal. Calvocoressi's testimony that Ravel began composition of *Daphnis* with the music for the "Danse légère" suggests that he may have identified with the dance and its protagonist.[96]

While we may never know whether d'Indy ever grasped the covert polemics in the Dance Contest, during the period of *Daphnis*'s composition he was formulating a musical-political critique of his own in the opera *La légende de Saint-Christophe*, composed between 1903 and 1915.[97] Here he mocks the Impressionists in terms resembling those in which Ravel lambasted his group in the "Danse grotesque"—as the producers of formless, arbitrarily designed, garishly exoticized rubbish. When a visual image of the guild of "False Artists" is presented in *La légende*—the foremost members bearing a gray standard emblazoned with the Latin word "Pigritia" (Sloth)—some carry "shapeless blocks of stone," others "canvasses spotted with various colors," and a third group "bizarre oriental instruments that they don't even seem able to play," all of them chanting the following:

> Instigators (*Fauteurs*) of a rare and tenuous art,
> We make fashion and follow it.
> Let everything be lowered to our height (*taille*).
> Down with enthusiasm! Down with Ideal Art!
> No more rules, no more studies,
> Let's make it small, let's make it original.[98]

Martin Cooper has described the music of the False Artists as "a parody, fairly nondescript, of 'modern' cacophony" and adds that "it would not be difficult to understand it—especially in conjunction with 'faisons petit'—as a hit at Ravel."[99]

As shown in example 3.6a, percussion, offbeat outbursts, and tone clusters are just as important in the music of the False Artists as in the "Danse grotesque" for representing poorly crafted cacophony and bungled exoticism. (Note especially the use of the bass drum, military drum, tambourine, and cymbals to similar purpose in the two pieces.)

Despite these musical coincidences, however, d'Indy's caricature differs fundamentally from Ravel's: The hypermasculine Dorcon cannot be confused with the effeminate False Artists, whose music sounds mainly in an upper register, is

Example 3.6 The Music of the "False Artists" in d'Indy's *La légende de Saint-Christophe.*

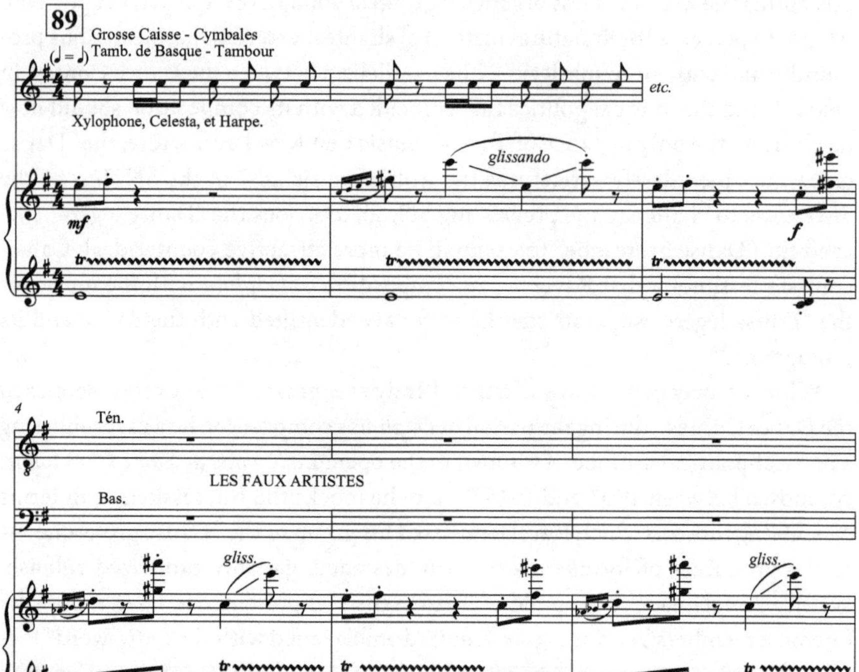

adorned with high trills and tremoli, and is garnished with capricious ornamentation and swooping glissandi. In example 3.6b the *coup de grâce*—with an emphasis upon "grâce"—occurs simultaneously with the line that Cooper singles out as most clearly directed at Ravel, at which point we hear quasi-Baroque dotted rhythms that debouch into a succession of added-note sonorities reminiscent of the *Histoires naturelles* and the *Valses nobles et sentimentales*. If Ravel slandered

Example 3.6 (Continued)

(b) R90.6-91.1

d'Indy and his ilk as Turkish brutes in *Daphnis*, d'Indy reviles Ravel and his artistic kin in *La légende* as effete dandies pursuing originality through the most frivolous of means.

Dandyism beyond *Daphnis*

If one wished to articulate a more general phenomenon of musical dandyism in Ravel's oeuvre, grace, caprice, irony, paradox, and pastiche—all of which help to unify Ravel's otherwise variegate repertory—would undoubtedly figure significantly as stylistic determinants.[100] Current research on Ravel invites the theorization of musical dandyism just as readily as earlier commentary by Roland-Manuel and Jankélévitch, who introduced the now widely accepted, dandy-related notions of "imposture" and "masks" more than seventy years ago. More recently, Thomas Kabisch, author of the entry on Ravel in the second edition of *Musik in Geschichte und Gegenwart*, has placed dandyism at the center of reception history for this composer, claiming that "problems of understanding between Ravel and subsequent generations generally stem from the fact that he, in both his life and his music, followed the Baudelairean model of the dandy, whose modernity and anti-bourgeois impulse were no longer immediately comprehensible after World War I, at the very latest."[101] Although the phrase "subsequent generations" is most likely supposed to refer to members of the postwar European avant-garde (Les Six and Boulez, for example), what intrigues me in this claim is the potential impact that a clear and comprehensive theory of Ravel's dandyism would have upon the current reception of this composer, which is still unsettled and would benefit from attempts to air and resolve these "problems of understanding." My efforts here to theorize dandyism in the "Danse légère" seek to contribute to such a rapprochement.

Any resonance between Ravel's musical dandyism and camp could offer a new and illuminating perspective on his artistic achievements and thus a fresh way to think about its relevance to our time, especially as queer art. Immediately, however, we must confront a question that affords no easy answer: What is camp? Having recently compiled a massive anthology and bibliography of camp, Fabio Cleto speaks well to this issue:

> Tentatively approached as *sensibility, taste,* or *style,* reconceptualised as *aesthetic* or *cultural economy,* and later asserted/reclaimed as *(queer) discourse,* camp hasn't lost its relentless power to frustrate all efforts to pinpoint it down to stability, and all the "old" questions remain to some extent unsettled: about how camp might be defined and historicised, about its relation—be it ontological or happenstantial—to homosexuality (is it an exclusively gay cultural mode of representation, or what? if so, how subversive is it and how much does it comply, or has it historically complied, with the compulsory heterosexual, and both gyno- and homophobic, dominant structures of interpellation?), where and in what forms it can be traced, and about its relation to postmodern epistemology and theories of textuality/subjectivity.[102]

These enormous issues notwithstanding, an obvious (albeit controversial) starting point for such inquiry might be Susan Sontag's 1961 essay "Notes on Camp." After having described camp at length in dandyist terms—as decoration, artifice, style, play, being as seeming, Baudelairean "gravity in frivolity," androgyny, archaeophilia, eighteenth-century rococo and Art Nouveau—Sontag finally declares camp to be "the modern dandyism."[103] According to Sontag, the main distinction between the original dandy and his modern counterpart is the latter's ability to delight in vulgarity and mass culture instead of despising and repudiating them.

Although "vulgar" might ultimately be too strong to describe any aspect of Ravel's meticulous art, several potentially campy examples of a departure from highbrow aesthetics immediately come to mind: the colloquial declamation of French in the *Histoires naturelles,* the moment-by-moment mimicry of stage action in the operas and ballets, and the wholehearted embrace of pastiche throughout.

In addition, in his essay on *Daphnis* Lawrence Kramer entertains the possibility that the ballet, with its commodified artifice, was designed for mass consumption—an appreciation, in other words, of "modern dandyism" in Ravel that awaits a more general application to his repertory. However, the campiest aspect of these tendencies might be the apparent exuberance with which Ravel engages in them; one need only recall the loud, fast, and flamboyantly dissonant opening to the *Valses nobles et sentimentales* to reexperience this overflowing joy.

Lacking the time and space necessary to flesh out these macroscopic possibilities, however, I instead track the dandy's footprints in Ravel's oeuvre so that we may fit the image of Daphnis as dandy into a fuller context. It can hardly be coincidence that several examples—*Jeux d'eau* (1901), the setting of Tristan Klingsor's poems in *Shéhérazade* (1903; cf. the discussion of "L'indifférent" given earlier), *Miroirs* (1905), and the *Valses nobles* (1911)—are associated with the Apaches, the group of mainly male artists to which Ravel belonged and which met regularly from the turn of the century up to World War I, forming a greenhouse for the communal fostering of refined aesthetic sensibilities.[104] Before a single note of the *Valses nobles et sentimentales* sounds, its allegiance to dandyism is already evident in the epigraph from Henri de Régnier that Ravel pinned to the work's lapel: "the delicious pleasure of a useless occupation," which unmistakably recalls Baudelaire's categorical imperative of the dandy not to reduce life to a "repugnant *utility*" but rather to take pleasure blatantly and flagrantly in uselessness.[105] *Jeux d'eau* (1901), the other work by Ravel to feature an epigraph by Régnier—"the river god laughing at the water that tickles him"—exhibits a dandyist flair for textural differentiation and frequent, unexpected transformation rivaled only by "Noctuelles." A fleet-fingered study in musical volatility and even coquetterie, this quasi-prelude to the piano set *Miroirs* (1905) assumes as its proper register a relatively high range that it leaves frequently to indulge in cadenzas that cascade up and down the piano; sudden changes in meter and texture demonstrate the dandy's penchant for *l'imprévu* in a manner that recalls Daphnis's leaps in the "Danse légère."[106] Since each piece in *Miroirs* is dedicated to a member of the Apaches, it is reasonable to suppose that the moths fluttering about in the prose poem by Léon-Paul Fargue from which "Noctuelles" drew its title represented, at least for Ravel, the like-minded members of this homosocial group and their late-night conviviality.[107]

The more specific issues of the dandy's sublimity and its "interruption" arise in a series of three pieces—"Le paon" from *Histoires naturelles*, "Les entretiens de la Belle et de la Bête" from *Ma mère l'oye*, and "Placet futile" from *Trois poèmes de Stéphane Mallarmé*—that share with the "Danse légère" several characteristics: Each is in F major, draws upon that key's historical connotations of pastorality and eros, sets a dramatic scenario that is concerned with courtship, and features a musical process that interrelates a primary, dandified material cast in a precious, static, and antiquated style and a secondary "interruptive" material, whose chromaticism and dynamism differentiate it from the primary material.

As a member of the scandal-causing *Histoires naturelles*, "Le paon" helps to fulfill the cycle's twin dandyist aims to find gravity in the frivolous and frivolity in the serious: Framing a rustic scene within the urbane genre of the *mélodie* (and the Baroque instrumental genre of the pompous overture) realizes the former, while the depiction of the peacock's desperation realizes the latter.[108] The critical-parodic impulse here ostensibly derives from Renard's poetry, which illuminates cracks in the façade of the beautiful by laying bare the self-delusion that buoys up the peacock's pride.

Just as the peacock abandons its self-composure to cry out for its fiancé(e), so, too, does the music—as the mirror before which these dandies "live and sleep"—deviate from its established patterns to register the interruption of his sublimity; the shrieks of "Léon! Léon!" at the midpoint of the song are violent and tragic, replacing the peacock's Don Inigo-like persona as a self-important buffoon with that of the abandoned lover.[109] The return of the peacock's impassivity after its disruption is perhaps even more disturbing than the disruption itself. Once interrupted, sublimity, like innocence, can never be fully restored to its pristine state; likewise, elements of the reprise subsequent to measure forty-one are subtly dislodged from their original pitch levels.

Unlike "Le paon," "Les entretiens de la Belle et de la Bête" initially distributes the sublime and nonsublime between two characters before it maps them onto the Beast-turned-handsome-prince; "Les entretiens" thus incorporates the structures of both the Dance Contest and the "Danse légère." Its musical-dramatic form can be divided into four sections that reduce the children's tale to its essential elements: the presentation of the two characters (mm. 1–68), two bouts of pleading by the Beast and resistance by the Beauty, which culminate in crises (mm. 69–105 and 106–145), the Beast's transformation into a handsome prince as an ultimate solution to these crises (mm. 146–158), and a "happily ever after" codetta.[110] It might seem as if "Les entretiens" lacked a dandy-androgyne altogether if one did not actually hear the music that Ravel composed to represent the Beast's sublime transformation into a male Beauty. The contrast made by transposing the contrabassoon's original theme up five octaves into the solo violin (using harmonics to begin on a stratospheric F7) is even more exaggerated than that in the related *volte-face* in *Daphnis*, thereby making the prince's melody sound unnaturally, almost grotesquely "beautiful"—it does not represent a musical persona that we would associate with any male character (except, perhaps, for a castrato). On the one hand, the codetta of "Les entretiens," like that of the "Danse légère," reinforces the moral of the story by recapitulating it in small: The momentary incursion of a black-key altered dominant (a G♭/F♯ dominant seventh) recalls the libidinally charged, beastly episode of the story proper, while the dominant's resolution reassures us that the unseemly threat has indeed been dispelled. On the other hand, lingering memories of the Beast's transformation seem to admonish us to be careful about what we wish for, else these musical genetics present us with an unclassifiable member of the third sex—a prince more "beautiful" than Beauty herself.

As in both "Les entretiens" and the *volte-face*, the assignment of specific themes to distinct registers is crucially important for Ravel's setting of Mallarmé's "Placet futile." The song begins with an instrumental prelude that is structured as a pantomime between an amorous abbot and the princess he adores. A capricious motive relatively high in the winds evokes her presence, while an inversion of this motive set low in the first violin marks his. The lack of dynamic or expressive inflection in her motive bespeaks a cool indifference, whereas the warmth of his motive (given dynamic shape and played on the G string, "expressif" and "très ralenti") communicates ardent desire. After this exchange is repeated once, the singer enters with the abbot's petition for her affectionate attention. In light of the hyperbolic preciosity of the petition, which culminates in the abbot's request to be named the "shepherd of [her] smiles," we may say that the abbot treads the same fine line that Daphnis trod between dependent courtier and independent dandy.

The music of "Placet futile" cleaves closely to Mallarmé's sonnet, its thematic material dividing into halves between the second quatrain and the first tercet and subdividing further to distinguish the individual quatrains and tercets in each pair. While registering the poem's natural division into two or even four segments, Ravel nevertheless manages to embed a tripartite scheme into the two quatrains whose ABA′ divisions align exactly with the first three rehearsal numbers.[111] Similar to the "Danse légère," this scheme allows Ravel to represent the dandy in his contrasting states of composure (the A sections) and emotional dissolution (the B section). The emotion that radiates from lines five and six—the lines set by the musically fluent B section—is a bitter jealousy, legible in the sense of the text and audible in its phonology ("Comme je ne suis pas ton bichon embarbé, / Ni la pastille, ni du rouge, ni jeux mièvres"). The music for these lines does not adopt the caustic, reproachful tone of the text, however, but rather surges up and down pitch space in small durations, counterpointing the princess motive against the rising motive that first appeared in the first violin of measure seven. While the former enters in stretto as the plaything of a jealous mind, the latter is enlarged to a symmetrical sighing gesture—the "petition" in all its glorious hope and despair—that crescendos and decrescendos over two measures.

Thus, we may add "Placet futile" to the group of pieces by Ravel that represent the dandy in both his sublimity and its interruption. In addition, the coordination of the musical interruption with the dandy's expression of jealousy is reminiscent of the link between jealousy and desire that we established in the opening discussion of the "geste brusque" in *Daphnis*. Here, however, the importance of "Placet futile" exceeds these points by speaking to the situation of the artist between desire and its sublimation into art and the role that the imagined muse plays in sustaining both.[112] Of equal significance to the magnification of desire's symbol in the B section is the ambitus of its swell, which seeks to overcome the registral distance separating the princess's tessitura from the abbot's. The rise and inevitable fall of the petitioning sigh recalls the white fountain's parabola toward and away from the azure ideal in

"Soupir," the first poem of Ravel's Mallarmé set. In both contexts, the feminine figures invoked—the "calm sister," the princess—stand in for the artist's muse, whose presence (and degree of distance) drives the production of art; if the petition were ever to be granted, desire would cease, as would the art that it helps to generate.

In his 1907 setting of Verlaine's "Sur l'herbe," Ravel treats the figure of the abbot more whimsically, as befits the character's distracted, flirtatious conversation in the poem. In Mallarmé/Ravel's solitary scene, however, the abbot commands attention not simply because he is richly dandified but also because he represents the decadent artist who is oscillating between the poles of desire and its sublimation. At this point in our discussion, we progress from "dandyism beyond *Daphnis*" to "*Daphnis* beyond dandyism." Mallarmé's representation of the artist as a flutist in the penultimate line of "Placet futile," as well as Ravel's incorporation of a musical pantomime in the instrumental introduction, brings to mind one of the classic representations of desire and its sublimation: the myth of Pan and Syrinx as performed in the Pantomime from *Daphnis*, which is one of the subjects of discussion in the final chapter of this book.[113]

Mirrors of Ink and Sound

Our broader consideration of musical dandyism in Ravel originated in the analysis of the *volte-face* in *Daphnis et Chloé*, the moment at which Daphnis shoves Dorcon aside before turning tenderly to Chloe. This musical-dramatic sequence is as provocative as it is brief, projecting upon Daphnis a psychological complexity that he previously lacked. At first glance, the subsequent Dance Contest seems to eliminate this complexity by dissociating violent expressions of sexual desire from Daphnis and ascribing them instead to Dorcon. A more sensitive musical analysis, however, suggests that the "Light and Graceful Dance of Daphnis" does not disregard the psychological implications of the *volte-face* but rather incorporates them in a more refined manner. The framing sections of this dance instantiate the dandy as the personification of sublimated desire, while the contrasting interior section represents the Baudelairean "interruption" of this sublimity. The extremity of this contrast has compelled us to reconsider the psychic processes under representation to have not merely sublimated but also repressed these libidinal contents, which erupt forth with a virulence typical of a Freudian "return of the repressed." Finally, we have traced the thread that sublimation, interruption, and the dandy combine to form in his work, while also pursuing the political and autobiographical implications of the Dance Contest that inhere in comments made by Ravel and Viñes.

The most direct way to extend these findings is to continue developing our inchoate notion of musical dandyism. In addition to a consideration of camp in Ravel as modern dandyism, one could also investigate the contribution that the specific figure of the dandy has made to modernist Western European music. The best-known representation of the dandy in this repertoire is probably Schoenberg's "Der Dandy," the third song from *Pierrot lunaire* (1912). Most recently, Jennifer Goltz has isolated various details in this piece that help to characterize the dandy in his vanity, effeminacy, and inconstancy: a high instrumental tessitura, volatile and ornamental textures, and dramatic shifts in dynamics, declamation, and register.[114] Equally significant for our concerns, however, are the associations that both poet and composer make among Pierrot, sublimation, and the dandy. Schoenberg first invokes the special timbre of harmonics in the piano to literally tone-paint the "sublime style" in which Pierrot powders his face at the end of the song. This timbre notably reappears in "Rote Messe" to accompany the same harmony (a minor-major seventh chord) in a song whose spectacle of rent vestments and a torn-out heart is a gory interruption of the dandy's sublimity.

Another explicit contribution to the musical representation of the dandy is "The Three Distinguished Waltzes of a Jaded Dandy" (*Les trois valses distinguées du précieux dégoûté*), composed by Erik Satie in 1914. Given the extravagant appearance of the dandy, as well as the excessive attention that he is thought to lavish upon his appearance, most portraits of the dandy, whether literary or musical, are simultaneously caricatures of this creature in his narcissism. Thus, it is only natural for scholars to have understood Satie's set as a parody, especially since he named each waltz after an aspect of the dandy that he would presumably fetishize: his waist, his monocle, and his legs. Satie's first biographer, Pierre-Daniel Templier, suggested in 1932 that Satie was aiming solely at Ravel in his parody of the dandy, but it is probably more profitable to imagine, as Steven Whiting has recently suggested, that Satie was caricaturing himself as well.[115] Indeed, the excessive accoutrement of the music with verbal texts of various sorts—the near-alexandrine of the set's title, the individual titles and choice literary epigraphs for each waltz, the running narrative of the dandy's actions and thoughts, and the directions for the pianist—is reminiscent of Barbey's conspicuous footnoting of *Du dandysme* some sixty years before, an ornamental treatment of the text that he declared to be a signature gesture of the literary dandy. This is not the place to provide a thorough analysis of either the music of *Les trois valses* or its relation to the accompanying texts, but I can nevertheless mention a few points of overlap with the "Danse légère"—particularly in Waltz I—that help to support my interpretation of the latter as a representation of dandyism: a precious reference to fifteenth-century music in the "air" that the dandy hums to himself; a Baudelairean attitude of leisure in the tempo, meter, motivic repetition, and diatonicism of the waltz; a disruption of this leisure by skewed, provocative harmonizations of the opening melody; and subtler indications of psychological strain in subsequent textural discontinuities.

The reference to the *gommeur*—the eccentric character in *fin-de-siècle* Parisian cabaret—at the end of Satie's first waltz opens up yet another path for future research: the relation of the dandy to a set of satellite figures that include not only Pierrot and the eccentric but also the trickster and the androgyne. For anyone who has studied the music of this historical moment, this motley crew would probably bring Debussy more swiftly to mind than any other composer, especially in light of his musical sketches of General Lavine, Pierrot, Pickwick, Puck, and Saint Sebastian.[116] Indeed, once we realize how closely related the dandy is to these and other figures, the similarity of the opening of *Les trois valses* to Debussy's "Minstrels" (mediated through the eccentric) and "Danseuses de Delphes" (mediated perhaps through the gymnopedic androgyne) is so striking that one wonders why such a connection has not yet—at least to my knowledge—been mentioned and explored in print.

The force that holds these figures in orbit around the dandy might not, in fact, simply be a similarity in character but also a shared potential for self-portraiture. I am using this term in two senses: as a representation that is merely secondary to the authorial self and as a representation that actually constitutes this self. While the first form of self-portraiture is easily grasped, the second is more complex. A book that can help us clarify the second concept is Michel Beaujour's *Poetics of the Literary Self-Portrait*. According to Beaujour, in response to the basic question that autobiography poses to its authors—"Who am I?"—the self-portraitist typically replies, " 'I am this appearance'; I am, for instance, my 'styles,' my 'writing,' my 'text'; or even, more radically, I am style, writing, text."[117]

In applying the Beaujourian notion of self-portraiture to Ravel, I wish only to offer an alternative to the more common model of autobiography, whereby the textual self refers to a primary, nontextual self. Exclusion of the latter would needlessly dissolve the valuable links that we forged between the Dance Contest and contemporary musical politics, as well as threaten to lead us back into Thomas's aesthetic fallacy and once again compel us to commit the crime of relegating queer sexuality to the domain of the imaginary and impersonal instead of the real and personal. However, the alternative of Beaujourian self-portraiture is no less valuable insofar as it highlights the dandy's greatest aspiration as an autobiographer: the transformation of the self into art through an act of sublimation that redefines the textual self as the primary self and the nontextual as the secondary. The continual possibility to fashion and refashion the self that this reversal offers—a possibility limited only by the imagination of the self-portraitist—inspires the production of a potentially disorienting autobiographical text that suspends dichotomies such as true/untrue and authentic/inauthentic. Considering the thrall in which these dichotomies have often held Ravel reception over the past century, a theorization of self-portraiture in his music might help us at last to escape these eddies of discourse and develop more productive ways to interrelate the man and his music—including, most prominently, dandyism, a life philosophy that aspires toward the pure fictionality of self regardless of the artistic media into which it is transposed. For Ravel, the mirror in which he saw himself—the mirror before which, as Baudelaire says, the dandy lives and sleeps—was, to adopt and extend the original title from Beaujour's book, a mirror of ink and sound.

4

Idylls and Bacchanals

As previously mentioned, a style-historical label most commonly applied to Ravel is neoclassicism. Despite the seeming anachronism of associating works such as the String Quartet (1903) and the *Sonatine* (1905) with a movement that flourished between the two World Wars, this interpretation has endured.[1] One of its primary supports is the perception that Ravel approached music as mechanism and formulated a rationalist and constructivist poetics to produce schematic forms and quasi-automated textures. Epitomized in Stravinsky's famous comparison of Ravel to a Swiss clock- or watchmaker (*horloger*), the assertion of his tendency to treat musical composition as mechanical engineering forms part, as Deborah Mawer has noted, of "a neoclassical aesthetic founded on abstraction, manipulation, and reconstruction," as well as tradition and craft.[2]

Recent scholarship has begun to think more deeply about these issues: Carolyn Abbate has proposed that we imagine *Le tombeau* as an uncanny hybrid of man and machine, reanimated from within by the hands of revenants,[3] while Steven Huebner has invoked Bergson, who identified the basis for comedy in rigid, mechanical action, to better explain the humor in *L'heure espagnole*.[4] Mawer has also contributed to a critique of the neoclassical understanding of mechanism in Ravel by building on Derrick Puffett's notion of the "ostinato machine," pointing to both its "destructive potential"—the machine run amok—and its collusion with the body to produce "dance-machines."[5]

In this chapter I bring further attention to the humanity of the mechanical in Ravel by associating it with a bacchanalian element and coupling this element with the idyll to produce a decadent dialectic involving memory, sublimation, and desire. The bacchanalian features of Ravel's music, which are displayed most prominently in his finales, place mechanism in a vital, sensual, and embodied context that extends the demonic virtuosity of Paganini, Liszt, and their successors to reach new levels of energy expenditure (to invoke Bataille). At the opposite pole lies the idyll, which counterbalances the bacchanal by sublimating desire and cultivating memory in its pastoral sanctuary.[6] The idyll/bacchanal dialectic can be profitably understood as another instance of decadence's perennial decay, mobilizing and undermining boundaries between the human and the machine, the individual and the mass, the primitive and the civilized, memory and oblivion, and life and death.

In the previous chapter I identified three moments that represent distinct stages in the development and expression of desire in *Daphnis et Chloé*: the incipient stirrings of desire as jealousy in the "Dance of the Young Girls and Boys," its violent outburst and immediate sublimation in the *volte-face*, and its elaboration in the Dance Contest, which pits the crude "Danse grotesque" against the sophisticated "Danse légère et gracieuse." The element common to all three moments is the adolescent Daphnis, who—before our eyes and ears—quickly learns to recognize and master his desire for Chloe.

In order to complete our survey of desire in *Daphnis*, we must examine three further episodes: the "Danse guerrière" (War Dance), the Daybreak, and the Bacchanale. Although one set of episodes may seem to have little to do with the other, there is, in fact, substantial continuity between them. The War Dance, which features the lustful, drunken pirates, amounts to an expanded version of Dorcon's "Danse grotesque": Both represent desire in its unmediated expression, use a primitivist aesthetic to capture this mode of desire, and realize it musically with pervasive dissonance, noisy textures, harsh accentuation, and sudden, percussive gestures.[7] Likewise, the Daybreak adopts the lightness, grace, and sublimity of Daphnis's Dance, while projecting these qualities onto a grander scale. Thus, the War Dance and the Daybreak, which respectively introduce parts two and three of the ballet, reprise the Dance Contest in its representation of desire. Contrary to the claims made by Ravel (and probably also Roland-Manuel) in the "Autobiographical Sketch," the large-scale coherence of *Daphnis* does not result only from its leitmotivic structure and tonal design but equally from its sustained involvement with topics such as desire and its sublimation; across the expanse of the "choreographic symphony" we witness the gradual magnification of this dichotomy, with the *volte-face* giving rise to the Dance Contest, and the Dance Contest to the War Dance/Daybreak pair.

Discontinuity between the two sets, on the other hand, arises from the reduced presence of Daphnis, whose desire is not a common element among the members of the latter set. Of the three movements only the Daybreak involves Daphnis, who reunites with Chloe in the interior of the movement. By rejoining the separated couple and folding their reunion into a general expression of joy in nature, the Daybreak concludes not only the romance proper but also the ongoing struggle in *Daphnis* to situate desire and imagine the terms of its fulfillment. If the pastoral scenes in part one of the ballet represent desire as gentle and innocent, and the pirate scenes in part two (including the War Dance) show it to be overtly sexual and even violent, the Daybreak synthesizes the two to produce a vision of desire that is both sublimely beautiful and frankly erotic. Like any true dialectic, however, the struggle between the idyll and the bacchanal is not over, as the massive Bacchanale threatens to override and supplant the equally imposing Daybreak as a conclusion to *Daphnis* and its narrative of desire. As we will see, the Bacchanale gained the power to mount this challenge only after Diaghilev and his associates compelled Ravel to recompose it; the original version of 1910 was more idyllic than the final 1912 version and only half its size.

The War Dance

The War Dance—together with its avatar, the Bacchanale—is first and foremost an homage to the Ballets russes and the Russian cultural traditions they represented. As a vehicle for dance, it showcased the novel and defining feature of the troupe, its virtuosic male dancers, while also referring to a specific choreographer and number: Fokin's choreography for Borodin's "Polovtsian Dances," which became an instant classic at its debut in 1909, the same time that Diaghilev approached Ravel about *Daphnis*. Thus, when the pirates appear at the beginning of the War Dance, "running hither and thither" with their booty, they reprise the moment that the Russians burst onto the stages of Paris in all their rough-hewn Eastern glory. Although the score for the War Dance is clearly indebted to a "Scythian" strain of Russian music with its unbridled verve and slashing dissonances, it also recalls another number that Fokin choreographed for the 1909 season: Glinka's "Lesghinka" (from *Ruslan and Lyudmila*), which formed part of the ballet *Le festin*.[8]

These external references notwithstanding, the War Dance plays an important role in the narrative of *Daphnis*. As the opening number for part two of the ballet, it introduces the pirates and the world they inhabit, which contrast diametrically with the pastoral denizens and idyllic environment of parts one and three. The audible basis for this contrast stems mainly from the War Dance's exploration of desire as a raw, physical, masculine lust, which is more suited to the bacchanal than the idyll. The medium for this exploration in *Daphnis*-as-text is the music rather than the libretto, which does not prescribe any specific action for the pirates until they collapse in drunken exhaustion at the end of the dance.[9] Nevertheless, much of the music is strongly suggestive of specific choreography, as the descriptions in table 4.1 indicate.

As shown in row two of table 4.1, the War Dance divides into two rotations, each of which cycles once through alpha (α) and beta (β) material. In the first rotation alpha material falls into three subrotations, whose themes unfold in the following order: stomping ostinato (R92), toccata (R93), galop (R94), whip gestures (RR94^{+5-7}), leaping ostinato (R95), and brass fanfare (R96). The central element within this thematic array is the galop, which, parodically distorted, bursts forth from the opening toccata to seize a climactic registral, orchestrational, and dynamic plateau.[10] In addition, the opening sequence of ostinato-toccata-galop harks back to the "Danse grotesque," the predecessor of the War Dance. As noted parenthetically in column two,

Table 4.1 **The Musical Design of the "War Dance" (RR92-130) in Daphnis et Chloé**

Rehearsal:	*92*	*104*	*122*	*126*
Section:	Rotation One		Rotation Two	
Subsection:	3 α Subrotations	6 β Subrotations	1 α Subrotation	1 β Subrotation
Content (in order):	stomping ostinato; toccata; galop; whip gestures; leaping ostinato; brass fanfare (NB: The pirate theme replaces the latter two in the third subrotation.)	exotic ostinato; exotic theme; pirate ostinato; pirate theme	stomping ostinato; toccata; leaping ostinato; pirate theme	exotic ostinato + choral war whoops; exotic theme; pirate theme + pirate ostinato

the third and final alpha subrotation (R101^{+5}–R103) is a hybrid of alpha and beta material that combines modified versions of the toccata and galop with the pirate theme. This hybrid subrotation appears twice in the War Dance, each time enabling a smooth transition between the two halves of each large rotation.

Simpler in content, the beta subrotation comprises the sequence of exotic ostinato (R104), exotic theme (R105), pirate ostinato (R107), and pirate theme (RR107^{+5-8}). While the thematic material is more varied in the alpha subrotation, the beta subrotation harbors greater internal tension by staging an agon between its two principal melodies, the exotic theme and the pirate theme. As if to prepare for the agon, the two themes and their introductory ostinati are strongly contrasted: The exotic theme is played softly by a high wind instrument in a texturally transparent 6/8 meter, while the pirate theme is ushered in by a gruff, stomping ostinato in 2/4 meter and sounded forte by brass instruments. The two themes confront each other once each subrotation, with the serrated fanfares of the pirate theme disrupting the beautiful, swirling surface created by the exotic theme.

The thematic agon is the focal point of the representation of sexual desire in the War Dance. Register, instrumentation, and meter invite us to hear and conceptualize the thematic opposition in terms of gender, with the sinuous, "feminine," exotic theme inciting the "masculine" pirate theme to a state of activity and arousal. Thus, in each beta subrotation we alternate between a feminized musical image and the eruption of male desire as provoked by the image. Although this scenario is common to exotic narratives and their veil dances, Ravel might once again have been paying homage to a specific Ballets russes number from the 1909 season: Fokin's choreography for *Cléopâtre*, whose eponymous heroine drives her slave crazy with desire.[11]

This interpretation builds upon the dramatic contextualizations of the pirate theme and its ostinato that appear outside of the movement. Prior to the War Dance, the pirate theme debuts (R62) to the flight of women across the stage as the pirates follow in hot pursuit. Shortly thereafter the pirate theme (R66), borne aloft on a textural and dynamic wave, overrides Chloe's invocation of the nymphs at the moment that the pirates break into the sacred grove and abduct her. Subsequent to the War Dance Chloe attempts twice to flee (R135 and R139) but is foiled both times by the pirates, who catch her and bring her back "with violence" to a shred of the stomping ostinato. In all four instances, statements of the pirate ostinato and theme accompany the onstage manifestation of violent male desire for women.

The War Dance places great emphasis upon the pirate theme and its concomitant topic of desire by situating it as the telos for four internested trajectories: Within each of the final nine subrotations it is the last to appear; within each alpha and beta subsection, it is stated in full rather than in motivic abbreviation; both large rotations culminate in its extended canonic treatment; and its final arrival marks the endpoint and climax of the entire dance. The goal of every level of form in War Dance, the pirate theme represents desire in its inexorability.

The Daybreak

The notion that the Daybreak sublimates the desire expressed in the War Dance in an overarching *volte-face* may seem, at first glance, to ring false in several respects: Unlike the paired elements of previous *volte-faces,* they do not immediately succeed each other, belong to the same local scenario, or share thematic material. These differences notwithstanding, the two movements bear many points of comparison. As mentioned earlier, the dances begin parts two and three of the ballet. Further, they present the respective settings of the two parts in their essential contrast, with the nighttime vision of the rocky seashore opposing the daytime view of verdant meadows—one populated by belligerent pirates and the other by peace-loving shepherds. As music, they share the same symphonic breadth and bear similar structures, which can be interrelated through the idea of sublimation. Both dances feature an ostinato that initiates each movement and remains fundamental to it throughout its duration; thus, in moving through the turn of this *volte-face* we can imagine the stomping ostinato of the War Dance (R92) to modulate into the shimmering whirl of the famous Daybreak ostinato (R155). Likewise, sublimation can also interrelate the textural and dynamic ascents that begin the two dances, transforming the chromatic and spasmodic toccata of the War Dance into the pentatonic and unbroken ascent of the Daybreak. While the impetuous War Dance proceeds immediately from the toccata into the galop, the Daybreak waits until the register descends and the climax subsides before beginning its main waltzlike theme.

As the Daybreak unfolds, the sublime composure of its melody is broken three times: twice by the flute music of shepherds (R159 and R160) and the third time (R163) by the *Tristan* chord, which is associated with DC, the main love theme of the ballet, and is cited verbatim from the ballet's Introduction. While the shepherd's music is a gentle interpolation into the melody of the Daybreak, the *Tristan* chord breaks with this melody in a direct, unsublimated annunciation of desire that coincides with the awakening of Daphnis, the primary subject of desire. If the Daybreak is the monumental avatar of the Dance of Daphnis, then this caesura corresponds to the interruption of the dandy in the latter's interior; in fact, during the caesura we witness the dandified Daphnis in complete disarray, "anguished" over the loss of Chloe and desperate to find her. Since he learned of her abduction right before he fainted, it makes sense that his search takes place to a reprise of the music that accompanied the abduction (R66). Here, however, the thematic apotheosis that caps this music does not involve the pirate theme, as it did originally, but rather the love theme of Daphnis and Chloe, which sets their ecstatic reunion (R165). The exchange of the love theme for the pirate theme does several things: It confirms that the inhabitants of the pastoral world have indeed superseded the pirates and thus also that the idyllic Daybreak has supplanted the bacchanalian War Dance; it also demonstrates that desire has been restored to the protagonists, where it properly resides, and thereby brings the romance to its *lieta fine*.

The Daybreak is not complete, however, until it reiterates its musical frame. The initial frame (RR155–157) performs and celebrates the daybreak itself, while the second (RR167–169)—which follows so quickly on the heels of the climactic reunion as to become its reverberation—is a quintessential moment of "pathetic fallacy" that involves nature in its celebration of the protagonists, their reunion, and their love for each other; in contrast to the climax of the initial frame, the much more brilliant climax of the closing frame (R168) features the invisible chorus, which envoices nature by singing APPEL in its original form: as quartal harmonies separated by a whole step, ancient and pure in their immaculate pentatonicism. As if this fortissimo conglomeration of voices and tutti orchestra were not sufficient to convey the magnificence and importance of this moment, Ravel made it even more splendid by adding ornamental cascades on the two harps, the celesta, and the *jeu de timbres*. On the one hand, this moment forms the apogee in *Daphnis* of both the idyll and the sublimation that generates it; on the other hand, as maximally sensual music it is the ultimate expression of desire and its gratification. Thus, the Daybreak sublimates desire while also purging sublimation of that repressive element that had still haunted the Dance of Daphnis. In this way it fulfills an aim that Herbert Marcuse, among other critical theorists, once set for art: to heal the division between eros and civilization.[12]

A Second Return of the Repressed

At the beginning of this chapter I noted that, among the members of the second group of desire-related pieces in *Daphnis,* only the Daybreak incorporated Daphnis's desire, which had been the common thread linking the members of the first group. Although this judgment is correct, it does not tell the whole story. Aspects of the libretto, together with the psychoanalytic perspective that we have been developing over the last two chapters, invite us to interpret the pirates' behavior in part two as a representation of Daphnis's desire for Chloe: a second and more virulent return of the repressed that follows the interior episode in the Dance of Daphnis. In fact, according to this interpretation all of the characters in part two —the pirates, Chloe, Pan, and his supernatural cohort—are elements within an extended Dream of Daphnis that both express and censor his more violent sexual fantasies. This interpretation not only accounts for inconsistencies in the libretto but also adds depth to *Daphnis* in various ways: Part two would no longer be a merely diverting spectacle but rather a substantive scenario that penetrates further into desire by locating it simultaneously in the exterior behavior of collectives and the interior drama of individual psyches—an endeavor friendly to the author of both *The Interpretation of Dreams* and *Group Psychology and the Analysis of the Ego.*

This interpretation responds to a basic discontinuity in the libretto between the natural outer sections of the ballet and its supernatural middle section, which includes the Nocturne and choral Threnody, as well as part two proper. The supernatural section begins with the animation of the nymph statues and ends with the appearance of Pan and his minions; neither the nymphs nor Pan nor his cohort appear elsewhere in the ballet. Internal continuity in this section sets its discontinuity with the outer sections into further relief: All of the events transpire under unnatural light, whether the "unreal light" of the Nocturne, the "violent" illumination of the pirates' torches, or the "little fires" of Pan's minions; in addition, the invocation of Pan at the end of the Nocturne is the action that calls forth the god's appearance at the end of this middle section, thereby rounding off its dramatic narrative.

The moment of recognition (R166) during the reunion in the Daybreak both acknowledges the problem of discontinuity and tenders a solution. The libretto for this moment reads as follows: "Daphnis notices Chloe's crown. His dream was a prophetic vision: the intervention of Pan is manifest." For the first time in the ballet the Nocturne is described as a dream episode. This information clarifies a few previously obscure details: The unreal light of the Nocturne can now be understood to signify the transformation of landscape into dreamscape; the animation of the nymph statues does not suddenly introduce magic into a hitherto nonmagical reality but rather takes place solely within Daphnis's fantasy; he is not actually roused twice from sleep but only once, at the beginning of the Dawn scene (R163).

The interpretive benefits that stem from the revelation of the animation scene as a dream episode threaten, however, to distract us from the ambiguity of voice and perspective in these lines. We are not, in fact, obliged to read the second and third sentences as statements of objective truth but may alternatively understand them as conclusions, in free indirect speech, that Daphnis draws from observing Chloe's crown. Once we divest these statements of their absolute authority, their problems are more salient. For example, it is incorrect to describe the dream as a "prophetic vision" since Daphnis does not passively foresee Pan's intervention but rather actively invokes it through prayer. The causal relation between invocation and intervention is even clearer in the corresponding scene in the Greek novel, which resembles the ballet version except in one aspect: Daphnis prays for the god's assistance in reality, not in a dream.

This divergence of the ballet libretto from its literary source raises the question of whether, once applied to the invocation of Pan, the transplantation of events from reality to dream would also govern the god's intervention and all contingent actions—the War Dance, Chloe's dance, and her attempted rape by Bryaxis. In other words, does the "dream" to which the libretto refers encompass not merely the opening scene of the middle section but rather its entirety?

Three aspects of the musical-dramatic design say "yes." First, since the initial dream episode does not actually end with the dreamer's awakening, it is unclear whether it ends at all. Next, the choral movement, a threnody for Chloe that is sung in utter darkness, follows immediately upon the dream episode, leads smoothly into the War Dance, and may be understood both to extend the dream and merge it into the War Dance. Finally, an unconscious Daphnis, who is described as lying in exactly the same position in which he collapsed right before the Nocturne began, brackets the entire middle section of the ballet as if his dream comprised it all.[13]

The hypothesis that the middle section represents the Dream of Daphnis increases in plausibility to the extent that the actions and actors of this section fit neatly into a psychosexual narrative. Cavorting about in a drunken, chaotic orgy, the pirates figure Daphnis's liberated sexual drives; the acceleration of the dance at its coda and the resulting collapse of the pirates combine to illustrate an orgasmic release of sexual energy.[14] Their leader, Bryaxis, who appears only at the end of the War Dance, is a surrogate Daphnis who does not sublimate his desire but rather takes pleasure in subjecting Chloe to his will instead of courting her as Daphnis did.

The resemblance between Bryaxis and Daphnis becomes even stronger once we note their shared position of desire and power. As a spectator of female dance during Chloe's "Danse suppliante," Bryaxis recalls Daphnis at three separate moments: when he is recumbent before the veil dance by the seductress Lyceion in part one, Chloe's dance as Syrinx in part three, and possibly even the nymphs' "slow and mysterious" dance in the Nocturne.[15] Bryaxis's attempt to rape Chloe at the end of her dance, however, exceeds the behavior permissible for Daphnis, thereby expressing the violent sexuality that Daphnis displayed in the "geste brusque." The rape is abruptly halted by the figure of Pan, who, as a Freudian dream censor, counters violence with violence; the pirates scatter as Daphnis's sexual fantasy is called to an end.

As with Bryaxis and Dorcon, Pan is also legible as a surrogate Daphnis: In both the novel and the ballet, the pantomime episode introduces the myth of Pan and Syrinx as a model for the relationship between Daphnis and Chloe; moreover, as a god of both war and peace, Pan recalls Daphnis in his stark duality of character as exemplified in the original *volte-face*. The mutual surrogacy of Pan and Bryaxis suggests, therefore, that their confrontation in the Dream of Daphnis plays out an internal conflict within the protagonist's psyche.

The Daybreak reverses the action of the middle section as if to cast it into oblivion. The light is natural and plentiful, and the landscape is no longer a jagged coastline but rather a grassy pasture filled with natural entities (birds and rushing water) instead of supernatural ones (satyrs and flashing fire). Musical and nurturing shepherds replace violent pirates both generally and specifically insofar as a group of shepherdesses rather than pirates introduces Chloe. Unshackled, Chloe now does not attempt to flee the male who desires her (Bryaxis) but instead rushes ecstatically into his arms (Daphnis).

The Two Versions of the Bacchanale

Commissioned by Diaghilev in June 1909, *Daphnis* was apparently intended for the 1910 May–June season of the Ballets russes in Paris. Working hard to meet this deadline, Ravel finished the complete piano-vocal score on May 1, 1910, and simultaneously sent a letter about contract negotiations to M. D. Calvocoressi, his liaison with the Russian troupe. The premiere had to be postponed, however, ostensibly because Ravel had not completed the orchestration and the Bacchanale was unsatisfactory; judging purely from the result, Diaghilev seems to have wanted a more extensive and orgiastic finale, a formula that was successful for the Russians in other exoticist ballets, including *Cléopâtre* (1909) and *Schéhérazade* (1910). Disappointed but resigned, Ravel returned to the drawing board. He eventually produced a finale that satisfied Diaghilev, but it took him two years to do so. During this time Fokin's star fell within the company as Nijinsky's rose. Since *Daphnis* had been Fokin's pet project from the start, it suffered neglect as well: It was granted only a few rehearsals, shunted to the end of the 1912 season, and performed only twice during its premiere in Paris.

Ravel made no bones about the fact that he was forced to recompose the Bacchanale, discussing it privately with his friends and publicly in his "Autobiographical Sketch." Since he was notorious for destroying his sketches and other preliminary compositional material, no one ever expected to have an opportunity to compare the original version of the Bacchanale with its published version of 1912—until Jacques Chailley stumbled across the printer's proofs for the 1910 piano-vocal score in a Parisian bookstore in the 1960s.[16] A few years later, Arbie Orenstein called attention to an additional copy of the proofs that Ravel's publisher, Durand, had deposited in the Library of Congress for the purpose of copyright. The comparisons that Chailley and Orenstein made between the two versions are useful overviews that rightly single out the Bacchanale as the main point of difference but do not provide many details to flesh it out. In the context of our interpretation, however, these details are crucial: They seem to give the last word to the Bacchanale rather than the Daybreak, thereby shifting emphasis from the sublimation of desire to its raw, unsublimated expression and imputing to *Daphnis* a different meaning.

Comparison between the two Bacchanales begins with the simple observation that the 1912 version (henceforth, "Y") is longer than the 1910 version (henceforth, "X"). Since meter varies within each version, as well as between them, the most reliable way to measure this difference is by quarter-note pulse: Y (676 pulses) is almost one and one half times longer than X (463 pulses). The greater length of Y

Table 4.2 **Comparing the Two Bacchanales by the Length of their Individual Sections. (Under "Location" for the 1912 piano-vocal score, rehearsal/measure numbers from the orchestral score replace page/system/measure numbers, since the full orchestral score is more readily available.)**

1910 (Original) Version of the Bacchanale				*1912 (Revised) Version of the Bacchanale*			
Section	Subsection	Location	Pulses	Pulses	Location	Subsection	Section
Transition	n/a	91/1/1	52	54	193	n/a	Transition
A	Intro	92/2/2	57	56	196	Intro	A
	Main Part	93/3/3	114	134	198/4	Main Part	
B	D&C	96/2/3	48	40	204/2	D&C	B
	Darion	97/3/1	45	60	206	Dorcon	
	-	-	-	45	209	DC	
A′	Intro	98/2/1	54	100	210	Intro	A′
	Main Part	99/3/2	93	187	214	Main Part	

results from Ravel's alteration of existing material from X, as well as his interpolation of new material into it.

As table 4.2 demonstrates, both Bacchanales are ABA′ forms, prefaced by a transition that leads from the betrothal and final embrace of Daphnis and Chloe (RR193–195) into the Bacchanale. Sounding in the clarinets and violas, the initial statement of the introductory theme (R196) coincides with the marking "joyeux tumulte" in the libretto, which neatly encapsulates the action and affect of the Bacchanale; the theme itself declares at the outset its general debt to Russian music by making an unmistakable reference to Rimsky-Korsakov's *Schéhérazade*.[17]

The mirror layout of table 4.2 helps us to locate inequities between the corresponding sections of X and Y and, in turn, leads us to identify the differences in content that generate them. The first major inequity lies between the main parts of the A section, which has twenty additional pulses in Y. The cause for this added length is a new, secondary theme for tutti orchestra (R203). It adopts the motivic structure of the primary theme—aabb, where "b" features quick chromatic runs—but uses this template for an ecstatic, fortissimo breakthrough, whose ascending chromatic major thirds invert the main lament of the Threnody for Chloe. In addition to deriving the secondary theme from previous materials, Ravel heralds its debut by inserting into the Introduction a new motive ($R196^{+4}$) that is closely related to the theme. Greater than this inequity is the one that lies between the A′ sections, whose Introduction and Main Part in Y are twice the size of their counterparts in X. In both versions the bounding sections follow a simple gestalt, beginning quietly and intensifying gradually toward the climax at its end. However, whereas the A′ section in X is comparable in length and intensity to its A section, the A′ section in Y is much longer, more energetic, and more complex. In short, the revised Bacchanale takes itself more seriously as a bacchanal. The A′ section in X states the introductory theme once and the primary theme three times before ushering in an idyllic, albeit rapturous coda that features the original quartal APPEL in an A Lydian environment. In contrast, the A′ section in Y begins with a motley grouping of materials that, although it accumulates gradually, barely keeps chaos at bay: Stated four times (rather than once), the introductory theme mingles freely with fragments from the secondary theme while the chorus enters out of nowhere ($R212^{+3}$) to sing the lament that the secondary theme had inverted. In addition, as soon as we reach a modicum of stability with two statements of the primary theme (RR214 and 215), the chorus and tutti orchestra let forth a series of barbaric yawps. Equivalent to the Bacchic "Euhoe!" these cries initiate octatonic wedges that pump more energy into the music with each quarter-note pulse, like massive bellows. When we finally reach the coda of Y (R221), which reduces the secondary theme to a shuddering tremolo, not a shred of X's idyll remains.

By focusing on the bounding sections of the Bacchanale, we have passed over what might be its most significant addition: the soaring statement of DC (R209) that Ravel added to the B section, thereby extending it by half its length. In X, the B section is little more than a concession to convention, setting aside time for the main dancers—those playing the roles of Daphnis, Chloe, and Dorcon ("Darion," in an earlier draft of the libretto)—to bound back onstage to the final hurrahs of the audience. The addition of DC, however, transforms the retrospectivism of the B section from conventional behavior into a compelling gesture. If we conceive of this full citation of DC as intrinsic to the Bacchanale, it becomes an act of conscience whereby the movement atones for having interrupted DC during the Final Embrace (R195) and thus continues the nostalgia that the previous moment expressed for the adorable couple and the captivating story of their romance. However, if we refuse to attribute conscience and memory to a bacchanal, which typically shuns reflection on the past to embrace pure action in the present, then the resurgence of DC is the swan song of the Daybreak, which presses into its nemesis with the force of a rebuttal. In fact, there is musical evidence that Ravel might have wanted us to understand it in just this way: Not only does DC receive the same, special harmonization it had during the Reunion within the Daybreak (that is, a major ninth chord instead of the usual half-diminished seventh chord), but it also occupies the same position, sounding in both cases at the end of the B section within an overall ABA′. Moreover, to interpret this thematic reminiscence as the inbreaking of the idyll into the bacchanal lends even more significance to the subsequent A′ section, which asserts the claims of the Bacchanale—toward chaos, abandon, and pure, unreflective expenditure of energy—even more strongly than it did before.

One difference between the two versions that does not show up in table 4.2 is the one that commentators have noted most often: the shift from triple meter (3/4 or 9/8) to an additive duple meter (5/4). Ravel undoubtedly introduced this change in response to criticism by Diaghilev and his group that the Bacchanale needed to seem less idyllic and more primitive. Nevertheless, it is not as novel and transformative as some have wished to believe. To make this change Ravel lopped off the first beat of every second measure and merged the two measures into one. Moreover, the use of additive meter is not a Stravinskyan innovation that Ravel simply appropriated from models such as the "General Rejoicing" in 7/4 at the end of *The Firebird* (1910). In fact, by 1910 the use of additive meter was common practice for Ravel: It appeared fifteen years earlier in his *Sites auriculaires* (1895), whose "Entre Cloches" is predominantly set in 10/8 (an additive quadruple or triple meter: 3+3+2+2 or 3+3+4); it was a feature of his finales before the Russians came to Paris, as demonstrated in the String Quartet (1903) and the *Sonatine* (1905), and it formed part of the 1910 version of *Daphnis*, surfacing in the 7/4 "Dance of the Young Girls and Boys" from part one, which, like the Bacchanale, is also a lively dance for the *corps de ballet*.

The Orchestral Manuscript of the Bacchanale

In the absence of detailed personal testimony about the compositional process behind *Daphnis*, the best source for understanding it is the manuscript of the full orchestral score, which the composer signed and dated. The manuscript, in residence at the Harry Ransom Center at the University of Texas–Austin, is a massive and complex artifact that boasts 186 numbered pages of forty-stave paper with numerous markings by multiple hands, complete and incomplete erasures, pages pasted together, scratched-out measures and sides of pages, sketchings, marginal corrections, double and conflicting paginations, directions by editors and composers, and doodling. Given that the Bacchanale gave Ravel a great headache, it should come as no surprise that it is the most troubled site in the manuscript.

The manuscript Bacchanale occupies twenty-eight manuscript pages, excluding two unpaginated verso sides. A cursory overview detects signs of haste, undoubtedly due to efforts to meet pressing deadlines: Note the unruled bar lines amid the ruled ones, as well as the editorial direction ("urgent") on the upper margin of its first page, which testifies to its completion close to a printing deadline. As mentioned earlier, in the right margin of the last page, 186v, Ravel gave April 5, 1912, as the date of his completion of both the finale and the entire manuscript.

Table 4.3 **Characteristics of the Full-Score Manuscript Finale for Daphnis**

	G / L	Side	Paper		Ink		Phase	
First Envoi	159 / 1	r	M		db		1	
	160 / 2	v	M		db		1	
	161 / 3	r		P		lb		2
	162 / 4	v		P		lb		2
	163 / 5	r	M		db		1	
	164 / 6	v	M		db		1	
Second Envoi	165 / 1	r		P		lb		2
	166 / 2	v		P		lb		2
	167 / 3	r		P		lb		2
	168 / 4	v		P		lb		2
	169 / 5	r	M		db		1	
	— / —	v	M		db		1	
	170 / 6	r		P	db	lb	1	2
	171 / 7	v		P		lb		2
	172 / 8	r		P		lb		2
	— / —	v		P		lb		2
	173–186 / 9–22 (end)	(etc.)		P		lb		2

Key:
- G / L = global / local pagination
- r = recto; v = verso
- M = Munich paper; P = Paris paper
- db = dark brown ink; lb = light brown ink

Unfortunately, we do not know many facts about the process of recomposition and orchestration that intervened between May 1, 1910, the day he completed the original piano-vocal score of *Daphnis,* and April 5, 1912. For example, we do not know with certainty when he might first have drafted the orchestration of any finale material, how that first draft sounded, which parts of it remain in the manuscript, when he initiated and halted work on subsequent drafts, and how the recomposition of the finale overlapped with its orchestration. Not all is lost, though. A close inspection of material traces in the manuscript, as well as the comparison of these traces with those found in other manuscripts from the same period, will cast light into some of the darker corners of this history.

Table 4.3 lays out the main features of the manuscript finale—its pagination, paper, and ink—while simultaneously marshaling these features to generate two analyses of the finale: as a poetic process in two phases and as an editorial process in two envois. Entries in the leftmost column "G / L" indicate that each page in the finale has two page numbers for the *first time* in the entire manuscript: a local number (L) that situates it within an envoi to Durand and a global number (G) that was added later and situates it within the manuscript as a whole. (Countering chronology, I have placed the global number before the local in table 4.3 to facilitate reference.) The vertical curly brackets on either side of table 4.3 divide the manuscript into two envois; their placement on the left side emphasizes their derivation from the local page numbers, while their placement on the right side shows that the envois do not coincide with the phases of Ravel's work on the finale.

The two rightmost columns of table 4.3 divide Ravel's work on the finale into two phases that distinguish themselves materially in the manuscript by their respective paper and ink, as well as by the ruling of bar lines, which I have not included in the table. In general, pages inscribed during Phase 1 have dark brown ink on paper of Munich provenance with ruled bar lines, whereas pages inscribed during Phase 2 have light brown ink on paper of Parisian provenance with unruled bar lines. The sole exception, 170r, belongs to both phases, due to its combination of the two types on ink on Paris paper with ruled bar lines. As shown in the table, however, work during Phase 2 did not proceed smoothly from work during Phase 1 but rather involved its revision; every "2" that occurs in the rightmost column before 169r presumably replaced a previous page inscribed during Phase 1. The impetus for Phase 2 was a new compositional idea whose realization required Ravel to adjust not only the orchestration but also the music of passages in the finale written prior to his having this idea. Material traces in the manuscript allow us to specify this idea and situate it within Ravel's overarching effort to complete the finale. The following reconstructive narrative identifies the idea, explains the role of the two unpaginated sides (169v and 172v), interrelates the two phases, and correlates them with the manuscript's division into two envois. One of the most intriguing and novel discoveries here is an intermediate draft of the finale, part of whose content is deducible from the manuscript.

Sometime after the Ballets russes found fault with the original 1910 finale, Ravel drafted a new version of it that he partially orchestrated during Phase 1, notating the score in dark brown ink on Munich paper with ruled bar lines. Since he seems to have orchestrated only the A section (RR193–203) during this phase, only this section allows us to differentiate the original version from the intermediate draft. The most salient changes to the original draft include the aforementioned metrical shift to 5/4 and the chromaticization of the modal-diatonic sixteenth-note runs that ended the original A section; the waltz theme of Daphnis and Chloe at the beginning of the B section, which does not actually appear in the 1910 version, was probably also added during Phase 1, having been notated in dark brown ink on 170r, the side whose pitches were inscribed during both phases—half of them in Phase 1 and the other half in Phase 2.

Phase 2 was precipitated by Ravel's "eureka" for the finale, the fortissimo secondary theme (R203). This idea proved useful to Ravel in another respect as well. His decision to replace the modal-diatonic runs at the end of the A section deprived him of his original ending, which had featured these runs. To solve this problem he made use of the new secondary theme, streamlining its rhythm and repeating it many times to create the rousing coda of the Bacchanale (R221). This would also preserve the formal parallelism in the original draft, which used the same melody to round off both the A and A′ sections of the finale.

As we have seen, the incorporation of the new secondary theme added a relatively small amount of music, ultimately amounting to only a single page. Nonetheless, it compelled Ravel to make numerous material changes to the manuscript, which are displayed in table 4.4.

According to the information entered into the "Phase 1" row of table 4.4, the intermediate draft of the finale comprised six folios and eleven inscribed sides. During Phase 2, Ravel inserted the anticipatory, *sotto voce* version of the new secondary theme into the second folio ($161^a/62^a$), which necessitated the wholesale replacement of

Table 4.4 **Phase 2 Alterations to the Phase 1 Manuscript Finale**

	Folios:						
Phase 1:	$159^a/60^a$	$161^a/62^a$	$163^a/64^a$	$165^a/66^a$		$167^a/68^a$	169^a
Phase 2 Alterations to Phase 1 Material:	none	Replace	none	Replace	⇑ Insert	Flip ($168^a/67^a$); Strike (168^a/~~67^a~~); Renumber	Renumber (as 170)
Results of Phase 2:	$159^a/60^a$	$161^b/62^b$	$163^a/64^a$	$165^b/66^b$	$167^b/68^b$	169^b/~~67^a~~	$170^a/71$

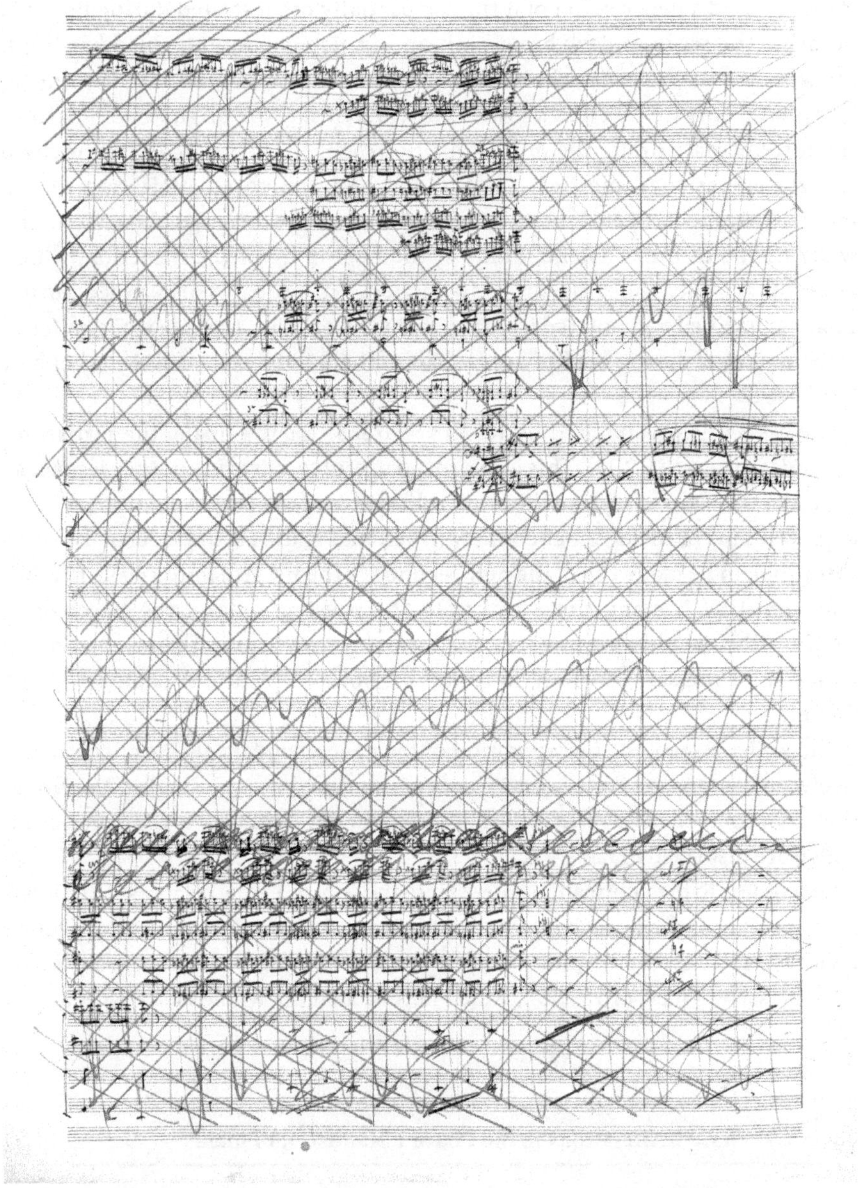

Figure 4.1 The Rejected Ending of the A-Section of the Bacchanale for *Daphnis*. Used by permission of the Harry Ransom Humanities Research Center at the University of Texas at Austin.

this folio in the manuscript. Now that he had finally worked out a firm plan for the finale as a whole, he locally paginated the first three folios in graphite pencil as pages 1–6 and sent them off as his first envoi—a sop to Cerberus, whom we may suppose to be his editor at Durand, Lucien Garban. Garban then added global pagination in blue crayon, wrote "urgent" at the top of the first page, and forwarded the envoi to the printers.

After replacing the fourth folio ($161^a/62^a$), Ravel inserted one that contained all of the material for the climactic appearance of the new idea ($167^b/68^b$; see the "⇑" in table 4.4). Pressed for time, he decided not to rewrite the next folio but rather salvage it for its second side, whose music—a transition between the A and B sections of the finale—was still usable. In addition to ripping the page out of its binding, which left a ragged edge, he flipped it once around its vertical axis and scratched out the previous ending to the first section on 167^a. However, as often happens in the course of history, what was trash to Ravel has become treasure to us. Reproduced in example 4.1, page 167^a, which the composer rejected as the ending for the first section in the Phase 1 manuscript finale, is now the centerpiece of our reconstructed intermediate draft of the finale.

The insertion of one folio and the alteration of a second had consequences for the organization of the manuscript. Even though Ravel did not actually number pages at this stage, 168^a had now effectively become 169^b, and 169^a had become 170^a. After finishing the orchestration of 170^a, he persevered to the end of the finale, signed and dated its completion to April 5, 1912, and—presumably heaving a big sigh of relief—sent it off to Durand as his second envoi. Although there is local pagination here as well, extending from pages 1 to 23, its orthography and inscription in blue crayon do not indicate Ravel's hand.

As mentioned previously, we do not have enough hard evidence to lay out an exact chronology for Phases 1 and 2 of the finale's recomposition and orchestration. Nonetheless, material traces in the orchestral manuscripts for *Ma mère l'oye* and the *Valses nobles et sentimentales*, which were produced within the same time span as the revised finale for *Daphnis*, provide potentially valuable points of orientation. As with *Daphnis*, Ravel was orchestrating both *Ma mère* and the *Valses* for their production as ballets, with the premiere of *Ma mère* taking place on January 29, 1912, and the *Valses nobles* (renamed as the ballet *Adélaïde, ou le langage des fleurs*) on April 22, 1912. Since the same dark brown ink is the medium of notation in both *Ma mère* and Phase 1 of Ravel's work on the *Daphnis* finale, it is reasonable to think that both were inscribed in late 1911. Moreover, since the same light brown ink is the medium of notation in both the *Valses nobles* (orchestrated during a two-week period in March 1912) and Phase 2 of Ravel's work on the *Daphnis* finale, it is also reasonable to assume that both were inscribed in spring 1912. In fact, the unruled bar lines that characterize the *Valses nobles* and Phase 2 of the *Daphnis* finale bespeak a similar degree of haste, suggesting that Ravel might have taken up Phase 2 in late March 1912, immediately after having finished the slightly more pressing task of the *Valses nobles* orchestration.

The Dialectic of the Idyll and the Bacchanal

Throughout this chapter I have taken license in referring to the finale of *Daphnis* as a Bacchanale since it appears in the score only as a "Danse générale," the generic designation for a ballet number that involves the entire *corps*. However, when revelers "dressed in Bacchic costume" stream across the stage at the beginning of the dance, we are in no doubt as to what we are witnessing. Due to a strong affinity between the finale and the War Dance on the basis of their music, as well as their action—which, in the case of the War Dance, involves an increase in activity until the pirates finally collapse in drunken exhaustion—I have considered the War Dance to be at least bacchanalian, if not an outright bacchanal.

All of which raises the question, what exactly is bacchanalian about the Bacchanale and the War Dance? From these two examples we can extrapolate a number of hallmark characteristics. In general, the music is aggressive, belligerent (in the etymological sense of "warlike"), primitivist, elemental, relentless, frenzied, heterogeneous, borderline chaotic, eruptive, and ecstatic. Specific compositional features include a lively tempo, swift, chromatic melodies, brash and discordant harmonies, sharp and widespread accentuation, quivering textures (trills, tremolos, and drumrolls), driving percussion, a continuous pulse stream in small rhythmic divisions, and long-range intensifications that lead to massive climaxes. In Ravel's music, however, a bacchanal is just as important for what it is not: an idyll. Ravel does not simply juxtapose the two genres but rather sets them into a dialectic, which means that the one cannot be understood without the other and that the one implies the presence of the other whether or not the other is actually present. Moreover, as the members of a dialectic, the idyll and the bacchanal embody poles of experience, complementary ways of doing and being. Since they are both potentially memory genres, their dialectic is also mnemonic: The idyll is passéist, likes to "ruminesce" at leisure and sublimate desire into a beautiful, static vision, while the bacchanal is oblivious to or at least unsentimental toward the past and finds its participants mobilized by raw, unsublimated desire.

We have already seen how this dialectic informs *Daphnis*, as reflected in multiple dichotomies: the bipolar behavior of the Dance of Daphnis, with its composed exterior and hemorrhagic interior, the opposition between the Religious Dance of part one and the War Dance of part two, and the hybridized Daybreak and Bacchanale, where the former is an idyll crackling with libidinous energy and the latter a bacchanal with a nostalgic conscience. The dialectic is not confined to *Daphnis*, however, but is remarkable in Ravel's entire oeuvre, surfacing most often in finales that either remain content to foreground idyllic moments against a bacchanalian background or work toward a synthesis of the two. One example that immediately comes to mind is the "Final" of the *Trio* (1914). Its primary theme is perfectly idyllic, evoking the nascent dawn with pianissimo harmonics and tremoli in the strings, as well as pentatonicism and open fifths in the piano. Gradually the sonata-form exposition intensifies toward its secondary theme (R4), which is an unmistakable descendant of the secondary theme in the Bacchanale and even anticipates Messiaen's moments of ecstasy with blazing fortissimo fanfares in the piano and sustained trills in the violin and cello; although the primary theme returns fortissimo in the coda and is made responsible for tonal closure, the ecstatic secondary theme has the last say, overriding any gestures toward synthesis.

Other instances of this dialectic include almost all of the finales mentioned in chapter 1. The last movement of the String Quartet begins as a bacchanal, but the extended, peaceful recollections of its secondary thematic area help to tame it. In contrast, the finale of the *Sonatine*, whose primary melody is a clear precursor of the primary melody of the Bacchanale, is incorrigibly bacchanalian; the internal moments of thematic recollection, which are just as sweet as those in the String Quartet finale but slightly more melancholic, amount to little more than speed bumps on its path toward Dionysian self-annihilation.[18] The "perpetuum mobile" movement of the Violin Sonata is an equally inexorable bacchanal that emulates the Bacchanale by allowing the idyllic primary theme of the first movement of the sonata to ring out in full glory right before it launches into its conclusion, just as DC sounded in the Bacchanale right before it began its final intensification. The two gestures in the finale of the Violin Sonata conjure up a Faustian scenario—undoubtedly filtered through settings by Berlioz, Liszt, and Gounod—wherein Mephistopheles strikes up his fiddle to spur on the revelers on Walpurgis Night while Faust, who is just about to be snatched away to hell, recollects his one "beautiful moment" of happiness and fulfillment.

The most systematically designed example of the dialectic between the idyll and the bacchanal, however, is the *Introduction et allegro*, which I discuss at length in chapter 2. When the primary theme of this sonata-form movement first appears in the solo harp at the beginning of the Allegro, it is an idyllic, pastoral music that seems to flow straight from Orpheus's lyre. As the development proceeds, however, it transforms this theme into its bacchanalian other, which appears at the climax of its intensification (R16). The recapitulation then reprises the development to a different end, eventually synthesizing the idyllic and bacchanalian versions of the theme in an ecstatic coda-performance (R28) that, like the Daybreak, simultaneously reconciles these poles of experience and celebrates their reunion.

5

Epilogism in the *Valses nobles et sentimentales*

The eighth and final waltz of the *Valses nobles et sentimentales*, designated by Ravel as its "Epilogue," frames the previous seven by both succeeding them and incorporating them as thematic fragments. However, rather than passing over them in a sentimental review, the Epilogue involves them in a melancholic musical process that inflects and is inflected by them in many ways. Here, as much as anywhere else in Ravel's music, thematic recollection is not simply the transposition of musical material from a past to a present context but rather a means to substantiate and shape a larger process of remembering. Although many pieces by Ravel thematize memory in their musical structures, as we have seen, the Epilogue is unlike any other. Replete with dozens of thematic recollections that appear at unexpected moments in unpredictable ways, it is a unique and especially rich demonstration of a poetics of memory.

A Little Night Music

The tendency to evaluate the historical valence of a piece by assessing its harmonic language—particularly its degree of dissonance and reliance on techniques of chromaticism—has undoubtedly helped focus attention in secondary literature about the *Valses* almost exclusively on Waltz I and its cacophonous opening.[1] In order to shift attention to the presence of memory in the *Valses*, I dwell instead on its Epilogue—the eighth and final waltz, of which Ravel was apparently very proud, according to his student Manuel Rosenthal. To realize the Epilogue properly, according to Rosenthal, is an art: the performer must carefully and meaningfully allow the motives "to return one above the other and vanish."[2]

Before we enter into the specific design of the Epilogue, however, we should first examine the interpretive context that Ravel provided for the *Valses*: the libretto he wrote for its 1912 production as the ballet *Adélaïde, ou le langage des fleurs.*[3] The scenario describes a soirée at the home of the courtesan Adélaïde in Paris of 1820.[4] A love triangle between the coquettish Adélaïde and two of her suitors, the passionate Lorédan and the arrogant Duke, plays out in the course of the first seven waltzes. The Epilogue begins with the retirement of the guests, including the Duke, whose rejection by Adélaïde leaves only Lorédan remaining at her side. Although the music predates the libretto, it nonetheless accommodates the latter fairly well. For example, one can easily imagine the reappearance and disappearance of previously heard musical themes at the beginning of the Epilogue as representing the mingling and leave-taking of the guests at the end of Adélaïde's soirée.[5]

A more striking correlation between music and libretto is their shared reference to the night. The slow tempo of the Epilogue, its soft dynamics and muting (indicated by the frequent indication of "sourdine" in the piano score), extended pedal points, registral breadth, transparency of texture, and alternation between expected motivic repetition and new material are all generic and recognizable traits of "night music," a characteristic that typically goes unremarked in appraisals of the piece. This is not the first time that Ravel wrote night music; the two most important precedents to the Epilogue in this respect are the "Prélude à la nuit" from the *Rapsodie espagnole*, composed between 1907 and 1908, and the "Nocturne" from *Daphnis et Chloé*, largely composed between 1909 and 1910. At first glance, it might seem as if these two precedents differ fundamentally from the Epilogue, having been conceived from the outset as orchestral movements, whereas Ravel orchestrated the *Valses* only after having received the commission for *Adélaïde*.[6] However, as Roy Howat has noted from his vantage point as both a musicologist and an experienced performer of this repertoire, the piano texture for the *Valses* implicitly points to a fuller sonic realization and requires "a high degree of operatic and orchestral voicing, well beyond what a [piano] score can indicate."[7] Hallmarks of musical nocturnalism common to the Prelude, the Nocturne, and the Epilogue in their orchestral settings include the use of division, harmonics, and glissandi in the strings and the incorporation of soft trills and tremolos throughout.

The cultivation of special effects in the Epilogue has motivated several scholars to search for precedents outside of Ravel's music. Seizing upon the notion of mystery, Vladimir Jankélévitch has adduced two pieces by Debussy, "Pour la danseuse aux crotales" and his setting of Mallarmé's "Placet futile."[8] Others have suggested music by Robert Schumann, a proposal compelling in several respects. His deep engagement with the music of Schubert makes Schumann a natural candidate for mediating historically between Schubert and Ravel, both composers of *Valses nobles et sentimentales.*[9] Next, the inclusion of a postlude that is liminal to the set—standing both inside and outside it—is a specialty of Schumann's, as Charles Rosen has noted in *Dichterliebe* and the *Davidsbündlertänze.*[10] Finally, the Epilogue is akin to specific works by Schumann, as some have remarked (albeit incidentally). While Benjamin

Ivry finds similarity between the Epilogue and the enigmatic *Der Vogel als Prophet* from the *Waldszenen*, op. 82,[11] Jean-Christophe Branger's association of the Epilogue with the finale of *Papillons* is potentially more appropriate and revelatory.[12]

Like Ravel's *Valses*, Schumann's *Papillons* is a suite of dances for solo piano, bearing an apparent debt to the Schubertian waltz and featuring a finale that uses thematic recollection and fragmentation to frame the entire set.[13] As the finale unfolds, its identity as a piece of night music gradually emerges through its hushed dynamics, sound effects—specifically, of bells tolling the midnight hour—widely spaced registration, and sustained pitches, including pedal points. The similarities between the two sets and their respective finales might stem from a coincidence between their dramatic scenarios, both of which illustrate an evening at a ball that involves a love triangle and ends with the departure of guests. However, they might also have resulted from Ravel's attempt in the *Valses* to pay homage to Schumann. Not only was Schumann's music widely appreciated in France during Ravel's lifetime,[14] but knowledge of his association of *Papillons* with the masked-ball conclusion to Jean Paul's novel *Flegeljahre* had also been disseminated since the publication of the composer's *Jugendbriefe* in 1885 and their translation into French the following year.[15] Although it is probably impossible to prove that Ravel intended the *Valses* as an homage to Schumann and his *Papillons* (and possibly also the *Davidsbündlertänze*, whose concluding gestures of thematic return and night waltz are split between the final two numbers), the possibility that Schumann represented a model for Ravel as a composer should be easy to imagine, considering the latter's investment in quintessentially Schumannian topics such as dance, coquetry, masks, musical ciphers, humor, childhood, and nostalgia. A comparison of their music and aesthetics is a potentially intriguing study that—like many on Ravel—remains to be written.

When better to illuminate the workings of memory than by the light of the moon?[16] Like dreaming, recollection has often been conceived as the mind's turn away from external stimuli and inward upon itself, a process well suited to the relative calm of the night. In Ravel's time, Henri Bergson made this movement of the mind a condition of possibility for what he called *la mémoire pure*, whose reflective nature contrasts with our reflex-oriented "habit memory," which uses mnemonic reserves to act and react unthinkingly in the present. In his classic study *Matière et mémoire* (1896) Bergson asserted that, in order for us to make full use of our *mémoire pure*, "we must be able to withdraw ourselves from the action of the moment, we must have the power to value the useless, we must have the will to dream."[17] Before a single note sounds, the *Valses* has already fulfilled the first two of Bergson's criteria. In the original Durand publication of the *Valses*, beside the title that proclaims its debt to the nineteenth-century genre of the waltz (Criterion One as an escape into history) we find an epigraph by Henri de Régnier exalting the "delicious and ever-new pleasure of a *useless* activity" (Criterion Two; emphasis mine). Criterion Three, the "will to dream," becomes manifest at the other end of the *Valses* in the *musique nocturne* of the Epilogue. We can glean a further sense of the potential reciprocity and symbiosis between memory and night in Bergsonian thought from a passage by Jankélévitch, one of Bergson's students: "[A]s night gradually descends upon us, memory gradually rises up again within us like a prayer."[18] Night, then, may not descend all at once upon the Epilogue but rather spreads its wings as gradually as the flow of memories increases and broadens, with both reaching their fullest extent in the penultimate phrase. Whether memory resounds simply and innocently as a "prayer," however, is more doubtful here, given both the profane vitality of the waltz and its rather drastic fragmentation in the Epilogue.

Rationales for the Irrational

On the evidence of this fragmentation, the Epilogue's past can no longer be recalled in one uninterrupted act but rather only in fits and starts—or, perhaps, in fits and restarts since the end of each bout of thematic recollection loops back to the same motive and phrase structure at the beginning of the next phrase.[19] By mapping out the thematic content of each phrase in the Epilogue and presenting the contents in tabular form for easy comparison, example 5.1 provides a valuable synoptic perspective that faithfully reproduces the idiosyncratic proportions of this piece while also charting the equally unusual fluctuation of its contents.

Before we begin to analyze the information represented in example 5.1, we must first understand its symbols. In the upper-left corner, "P1 (1–8)" means "Phrase 1, measures 1–8"; surveying all of column 1, we note that the Epilogue's 74 measures divide into six phrases, P1–P6. With the exception of the initial 4 measures for each phrase, whose content allows them to be reduced to a single column, each cell represents a single measure in the Epilogue. Each measure, in turn, contains thematic material from the following three types: a Roman numeral, which represents a citation from the corresponding waltz (but not a harmony!), "~," a part of the main theme of the Epilogue, and "0," which indicates an absence of melody; the division slash (/) is used when two material types appear together in the same measure.[20] At first glance, it might seem that example 5.1 is

Example 5.1 Phrase Structure, Length, and Content in the "Epilogue" (Waltz VIII) of the *Valses nobles et sentimentales.*

	4-bar presentation	continuation												
P1 (1-8)	~	~	~/IV	IV	IV									
P2 (9-20)	~	~	~	~	~/IV	IV	IV	IV	IV					
P3 (21-8)	~	VI	VI	VI	0									
P4 (29-45)	~	~	~	~	~/IV	IV	IV	IV	IV	IV′	IV′	I	I	0
P5 (46-61)	~	VI	VII	VII/VI	VI	VI	III	III	III	III	III/IV	I	I	
P6 (62-74)	~	0	0	II	II	II	II	0	0	0				

overly literal in its representation of form and content in the Epilogue. However, this literalism provides a proportionally accurate overview of the whole and allows its contents to be easily parsed.

The jagged right edge of example 5.1 and its motley dispersal of symbols indicate a variety in length and content among the six phrases of the Epilogue. As shown by the brackets in example 5.1, every phrase can be parsed into a "presentation" and a "continuation," the two halves of a Schoenbergian "sentence," in which an initial presentation of a so-called basic idea and its repetition is followed by a continuation that extends this material in some way.[21] A brief survey of the columns reveals that the six presentations are uniform in their length and motivic content, whereas the six continuations are pluriform as a whole and individually unique. The boundary between uniform presentation and pluriform continuation was important enough to Ravel that he directed pianists to use the soft pedal ("sourdine") to demarcate it in performance. Example 5.2 reproduces the first phrase of the Epilogue to show this typical midphrase demarcation.

Since each continuation relies mainly on thematic recollection and since these processes of recollection produce unpredictable results, it may be most fitting to describe the operative memory here as "involuntary memory." Although we have previously discussed involuntary memory, a brief review will be helpful. This term, as well as the phenomenon it signifies, is most strongly associated with the writings of Marcel Proust, one of Ravel's contemporaries and author of the best-known and most exhaustive literary treatment of memory, *À la recherche du temps perdu*. In the context of this work, involuntary memory is best explained through the dichotomy it forms with voluntary memory: Voluntary memory is a faculty of the conscious intellect, controllable but unilluminating in its results, while involuntary memory is an unconscious faculty that brings the past suddenly and vividly to life but cannot be summoned at will.[22] Proust devotes the introductory section

Example 5.2 Phrase 1 (P1, mm. 1–8) of the "Epilogue."

of his novel to the illustration of this dichotomy, describing the narrator Marcel's childhood at Combray first from the standpoint of voluntary memory, then from that of involuntary memory. Nighttime acts of voluntary memory repeatedly conjure up the evening he was separated from his mother, whereas a chance encounter in the daytime with some materials from his childhood—the famous madeleine soaked in lime-blossom tea—stimulates his involuntary memory to fully resurrect the past and lend it an immediacy that voluntary memory never could.

This incident of involuntary memory does not merely show us how important the past is to Proust's narrator but also sets up and launches the main part of the novel. Situated at the end of a narrative, involuntary memory in Ravel's Epilogue is no less unexpected in its behavior but nonetheless serves an opposite rhetorical purpose by drawing the work to a quiet close rather than beginning it with a bang. The Epilogue's embedding of thematic recollection within a quiet conclusion recalls not only the finale of *Papillons* but also the ending for the first movement of Robert Schumann's *Fantasie*, op. 17, which features a musical quotation from Beethoven's *An die ferne Geliebte*. Charles Rosen invokes the same mnemonic phenomenon to describe this moment, remarking how "the phrase of Beethoven is made to seem like an involuntary memory, not consciously recalled but inevitably produced by the music we have just heard."[23]

Another bridge between these two musical examples of involuntary memory is an imaginary scenario prompted by the flowing textures of the music itself: the image of Ravel freely improvising at the keyboard and occasionally being surprised by the turns that the music has happened to take under his fingers. Although this scenario may not correspond to Ravel's actual compositional process, it is nonetheless an important heuristic that answers, at least provisionally, the question of who the subject of memory might be here, while also giving memory a corporeal dimension. Although the topic of the body continues to be neglected in the humanistic field of memory studies, it was central to Proust's notion of involuntary memory, which was typically triggered by the physical reexperiencing of distinct sensations from the past—a taste, a smell, a sound, and even a stumble.

Within the scenario of improvisation I am proposing for the Epilogue, the main memory triggers are the hand's sense of touch and its registral position on the keyboard. When the right hand eventually wanders down into the middle register at the ends of P1, P2, P4, and P5, it recalls previous music belonging to that register (Waltz IV) and plays it as if it had a mind and memory of its own. Likewise, when it wanders up into a high register on the back of Waltz VI, as shown in example 5.3, it begins to rehearse the swaying strains of Waltz III, which was remarkable for having sustained the highest tessitura of all waltzes in the set.

In fact, there is good reason to speculate that it is not only register that sparks the recollection of Waltz III. Before the citation begins, the right hand plays two major thirds—A♭5-C6 and E♭6-G6—that will end up bracketing the pitch spans of the lower and upper halves of the melody's main motive. Although the

Example 5.3 The Passage Between Citations of Waltzes VI and III in P5 (mm. 52–55).

second third lies higher and comes later than the first, it is the first third that receives dynamic emphasis. While one might wish to account for these somewhat counterintuitive dynamics by describing them as a mere repetition of the previous ascent, when applied to this passage they serve a different purpose, laying clear stress on the first third as a memory trigger that motivates the hand's subsequent recollection. In my own experience as a performer of this piece, this is by far the most compelling way to make sense of these unusual dynamics, as well as the subsequent imperative "Cédez"—a direction to heed memory's sudden call—which coincides with the brief decrescendo. However, in order to realize fully the imaginative scenario that I am proposing here, performers should try to maintain the illusion that the moment precipitating the Waltz III recollection is a musical-muscular event that happens involuntarily rather than pressing forward willfully into it as if the notated dynamic swell were urging them to identify with it and "express" its impulse.

At such moments of apparent subjection to the dictates of involuntary memory, the performer's profile blends into that of the automaton whose presence Carolyn Abbate has asserted to be fundamental to an understanding of Ravel's aesthetics.[24] There is even a trace of this in Ravel's own 1913 recording of the Epilogue, whose sudden shifts in tempo and affect from one waltz fragment to the next suggest that the composer wished us to regard the pianist performing the Epilogue as the plaything of involuntary memory.[25] But can we make such an assertion without succumbing to contradiction? How, indeed, can one behave like an automaton while simultaneously being susceptible to a deep experience of memory? Bergson's *Matière et mémoire* helps us work through this apparent difficulty. As evident from the title, one of the book's main purposes was to address both materialist and idealist notions of memory instead of treating each in isolation. Bergson maintains that the physical action of habit memory and the mental reflection of pure memory represent extremes of consciousness between which individuals continually oscillate in the course of daily life. At one moment, habit memory might guide them smoothly through the routines of the day; at another, it might trigger an association with a long-forgotten experience, thereby diverting their attention suddenly inward toward some deeper level of memory. The same possibilities are arguably in play in the Epilogue: The improvising hand ranges comfortably up and down the keyboard, happening now and then upon a familiar space and reacting with a musical gesture previously associated with that space. However, these physical deflections toward embodied memory, which are relatively unconscious events, may greatly move the mind and stir the emotions of the remembering subject. Without the verbal testimony of Proust's novel and the like, the only trace of the impressions these memories make upon the rememberer is the affective design of the music, which we will soon investigate in depth.

The Epilogue offsets the inconsistency of involuntary memory by some more consistent musical behaviors, most notably the recurrence of Waltz IV. While it is hard to say with any certainty why Waltz IV should appear as often as it does—apart from the preceding rationale that links musical memory to bodily memory—the libretto for *Adélaïde* suggests a psychological rationale that associates this waltz with happier times and the desire to recollect them.[26] Without recourse to spoken dialogue, the members of the love triangle communicate with each other through the "language of flowers" as mentioned in the ballet's secondary title, a convention that assigns individual floral species a symbolic meaning within the ritual of courtship. Near the beginning of the Epilogue Adélaïde offers the lovesick Lorédan a poppy (*un cocquelicot*), whose symbolism of oblivion encourages him to forget their brief dalliance. However, he refuses this suggestion and leaves, returning later to prove the depth and sincerity of his love by prostrating himself before her and threatening to commit suicide. Lorédan's will to remember and stay true to his passion provides another way to rationalize thematic recollection in the Epilogue—specifically, the frequent citation of Waltz IV, the same waltz during which he and Adélaïde first danced together and demonstrated their mutual affection. (In a handwritten manuscript of the libretto the composer designated Waltz IV a "pas de deux" for Adélaïde and Lorédan.[27])

Unfortunately, Waltz IV cannot sustain its buoyant infatuation for long and collapses into Waltz I the last two times it is quoted in the Epilogue (at the ends of P4 and P5, measures 43 and 60, respectively). Indeed, one might even say that the Waltz I fragments quash the hopes tendered by the Waltz IV fragments: Not only have their formerly vigorous leaps, culled from the opening measures of the *Valses*, now been reduced to anemic shudderings, but they also truncate the flow of musical memory in P4 and P5 to bring both abruptly to an end. Serving as Adélaïde's poppies to Lorédan's passionate Waltz IVs, the Waltz I fragments are also akin to the responses of the second "ghost" (*spectre*) to the questions and exclamations of the first in Verlaine's "Colloque sentimental," which is best known for its setting by Debussy as the final *mélodie* in the second book of his *Fêtes galantes* (1904).[28] As we will see in the next section, the "colloque sentimental" between the spectral fragments of Waltzes IV and I in the Epilogue is only one among other musical manifestations in this piece of an equivocation between hope and despair.

An additional and equally significant thematic exchange with Waltz IV in the Epilogue involves Waltz VI. Referring to example 5.1 will help us sort through their alternation, which operates mostly between phrases. For instance, P1 ends with a citation of Waltz IV, as does P2. Next, P3 diverges from the two previous phrases by citing Waltz VI. Then, P4 reverts to the Waltz IV recollection of P1 and P2 and even appends a second. Next, P5 emphasizes Waltz VI, like P3 did, but also incorporates Waltz IV near its end. Finally, P6, the last phrase, cites neither, thereby confirming the end of any further exchange between the two.

The alternation between Waltzes IV and VI lends a dynamic element to the Epilogue that offsets its more static qualities of tempo, rhythm, and dynamics: It inaugurates a dialogue between consecutive phrases at the level of theme, injects contrast into this exchange, with the rising contour of Waltz VI opposing the falling contour of Waltz IV, and intensifies it in the middle of the piece, while holding the initial and final phrases above the fray, so to speak. Insofar as P5 (measures 46–61) is the only phrase to include citations from both waltzes, it emerges once again as a centerpiece for the activity of memory in the Epilogue. It should come as little surprise that we keep returning to P5 as a main site of interest since it contains material from all of the waltzes except for II and V. Thus, P5 is the frame within the framing Epilogue, a second-order *mis en abîme* of the *Valses,* whose microcosmic status is important not only for its quantity of citations but also for the distinct affective quality of each.

A final aspect of the Waltz IV/VI alternation is the degree to which the Waltz VI citation in P3 refreshes the act of involuntary memory. The exclusive and repeated enactment of involuntary memory through Waltz IV in P1, P2, and P4 threatens to diminish its effect of unpredictability and surprise. The more we come to expect Waltz IV, the more it becomes habitual for both performer and listener, evoking a merely sentimental pleasure rather than the arresting enthrallment that involuntary memory is supposed to inspire.[29] Ravel seems to have been acutely aware of this danger, which he tantalizingly courts in the first half of the Epilogue, only to dispel it in the second with some well-chosen musical-mnemonic techniques.

A Dialectics of Memory in P1

For Rosen, the main fascination of the Beethoven quotation in Robert Schumann's *Fantasie* is the way Schumann makes it seem as if the thematic recollection were a foreign object, as well as the natural consequence of antecedent thematic activity—a citation both within and without scare quotes. I propose that we understand this paradox to manifest an inherent doubleness in memory, whereby a recollection is the offspring of both the *recollected past* and the *recollecting present.* By itself, this idea is nothing new, for we often conceive of memory as a liaison between two tempora, with the past as the content and memory as the faculty that retrieves it in and

Example 5.4 A Stratified Representation of P1 (mm. 1–8).

for the present. However, rather than understanding memory in such a rigid, instrumental dichotomy, I suggest that we focus our attention on the way it brings its tempora to act upon each other in a fluid, dialectical process. Memory phenomena in Ravel's shape-shifting Epilogue respond well to this approach, as can be demonstrated in an extended analysis of P1, which will allow us to come to terms with its musical elements and their configuration before proceeding to more hermeneutic reflections. Despite the apparently simple design of P1, at least in relation to the other five phrases, its analysis is rather complex and will help articulate the basic conditions under which memory seems to be operating in this piece.

As previously mentioned, P1 is an eight-measure sentence that divides into a four-measure presentation and a four-measure continuation. Each half phrase also divides in half, with the presentation splitting into a basic idea and its varied repetition, while the continuation follows its own motive with a citation of Waltz IV. Thus, P1 is stratified into three layers, as shown in example 5.4. In the presentation, the lower layer contains a relatively slow single-voice progression (mainly of roots), the middle layer a more active series of triads, and the upper layer swift ornamental gestures. From this distribution of materials we can derive two principles that organize the texture: a quasi-acoustic principle that places fundamentals below and upper partials above, and a related rhythmic principle that increases activity as the register ascends. The Epilogue's sympathy for acoustic materials becomes ever more apparent as the piece unfolds: Note, for example, the use of the acoustic scale in the continuations of P2 and P4, as well as the acoustic tonics that end P4 and P6.

Counterbalancing these stabilizing structures are more dynamic musical behaviors, including the expansion and contraction of individual layers, the migration of material between layers, and the transformation of material within layers. In addition, the harmonic relationships among the layers are in constant flux. Several of these possibilities come into play in P1 when the presentation passes into the continuation, as is evident in example 5.4: The bass begins to move between two different octaves, the triads rise from the middle to the upper layer before descending once again, the middle layer expands to accommodate the citation of Waltz IV, and the ornamental gestures of the upper layer disappear.

Example 5.5 The Sequence Underlying P1 (mm. 1–8).

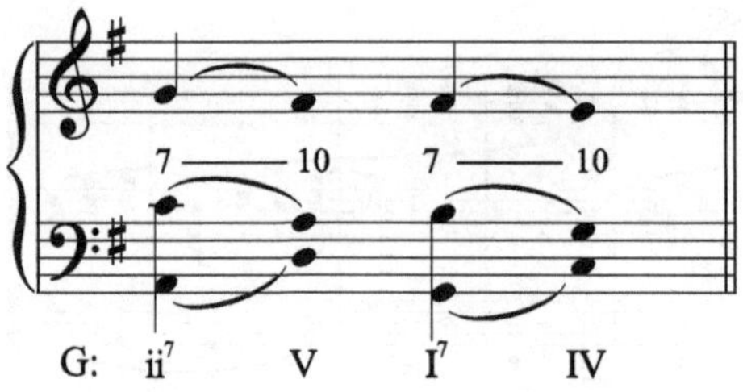

Example 5.6 Suspensions and Altered Dominants in P1 (mm. 1–8).

The coherence of P1 across its segmented expanse is primarily an effect of its underlying circle of fifths, which I have extracted and reduced in example 5.5. The most salient aspect of this sequence is the fact that it coasts beyond the G major tonic to end up at the subdominant. If we look back at example 5.4, we will see that Ravel places the entrance of the tonic bass in the lowest register and at the downbeat of the continuation, where it sounds alone. Nevertheless, he withholds dynamic emphasis from it and directs the pianist to mute it ("sourdine") upon striking it pianissimo and refrain from using the full resonance ("3 cordes") of the instrument until reaching the subdominant, whose arrival coincides with both the dynamic climax and the citation of Waltz IV.

Example 5.6 shows how harmony is coordinated between the lower and middle layers. As you can see by this series of suspensions, the triadic progression of the middle layer lags behind the bass line of the lower layer. Example 5.6 also points out a special dissonant sonority—a ♯7♯5 chord—that propels the sequence from dominant to tonic and subsequently reinterprets the tonic *as* a dominant. The two arrows below the staff point out this chord, which first occurs in slightly expanded form (with an additional ♯8) in the opening measure of Waltz I, as shown in example 5.7a. The first measure of example 5.7b reconstructs the voice-leading technique that governs this progression: All of the notes of the upper structure are treated as leading notes, ascending by semitone to resolve from dominant to tonic. The second measure of example 5.7b isolates the two dominant-tonic progressions from P1 that use this altered dominant. Here I follow Brian Hyer's example of a

Rameauian approach to tonal analysis by using the functional labels of "DOM"(inant) and "TON"(ic) instead of Roman numerals.[30]

Approaching Ravel's music from a Rameauian perspective may seem anachronistic, but there are at least three good reasons to do so here. First, a listener is more likely to follow the circle of fifths in the bass and hear local chordal functions rather than immediately and definitively identify the key of P1 as G major, especially after it concludes on C. Second, Rameau's interest in the dynamic role that dissonances play in impelling one chord into another is well suited to the sequential flow of P1. Third, a Rameauian viewpoint will also be helpful in making sense of the stacked-third verticalities that result from textural stratification. Ravel, whose personal collection of scores by Rameau seems to indicate an esteem for the latter, would probably not have been displeased by this approach.[31] Nonetheless, it goes without saying that Ravel's tonal idiom is not Rameau's; to take the example of the *Valses*, tonics can sound like either subdominants (compare Ravel's use of Rameau's "l'accord de la sixte ajoutée") or dominant sevenths (the acoustic tonic seventh), and dominant sevenths need further alteration and extension to maintain the effect of dissonance.

The other main source of coherence in P1 is its basic idea, which features three triads: C major, B major, and A minor. If the third of the triad on B were a D♮, we would consider it as only an inconspicuous passing chord between the two triadic subsets of the A minor seventh harmony. The D♯ is an unexpected detail that

Example 5.7a The Opening Measure of Waltz I.

a)

Example 5.7b Dominant-Tonic Progressions in Waltz I (mm. 1–2) and the "Epilogue" (mm. 4–8).

b)

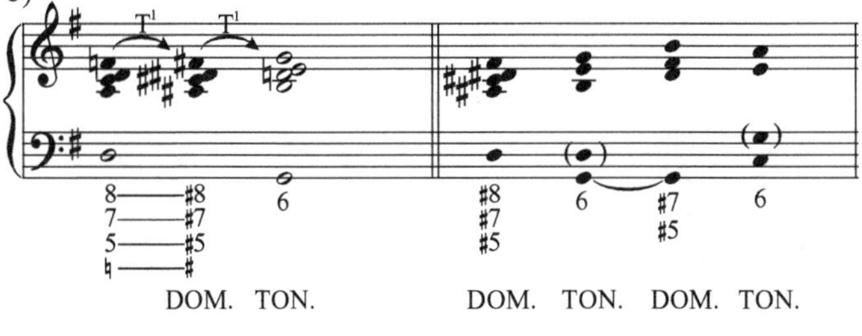

commands our aural attention and suggests P1 to be in E minor, not G major. However, when the bass finally moves, it gestures toward G major, thereby inaugurating a tonal equivocation between the relative major and minor that will continue to the end of the phrase and includes the pitting of E minor against G major in measure 6, as well as A minor versus C major in measure 8. The conclusion of P1 at the chordal pairing of C major and A minor should sound as if P1 had gone astray, but, for some reason, it does not. Rather, it sounds as if we have come full circle, returning to the opening measures in P1—which we have, at least harmonically. The basic idea oscillates between the same two triads—C major and A minor—that are superposed in measure 8. Further, as example 5.8 demonstrates, the final two measures of P1 simply reconfigure the three harmonies of the basic idea: chords T, U, and V.

The marking "expressif et en dehors" (expressive and prominent) in measure 1 calls attention to the basic idea's melody, whose pitch contour and distance from the bass further connect the presentation with the continuation. As noted in example 5.9, we can hear the continuation motive as condensing the melody of the presentation, while simultaneously reorganizing its intervals with the bass into new patterns. Especially notable is the similarity between the continuation motive and the subsequent citation of Waltz IV. If composers wanted to call attention to a thematic recollection, we might assume that they would create a background context against which the recollection would stand out in vivid relief, thereby clearly distinguishing musical past from present. This is not what Ravel does here, however. As we can see from the musical example (which admittedly levels out the rhythm of the waltz citation and slightly abbreviates it), the continuation motive is virtually identical to the waltz citation in intervallic contour. From example 5.9

Example 5.8 The Reconfiguration of the Three Basic-Idea Triads at the End of P1 (mm. 1–8).

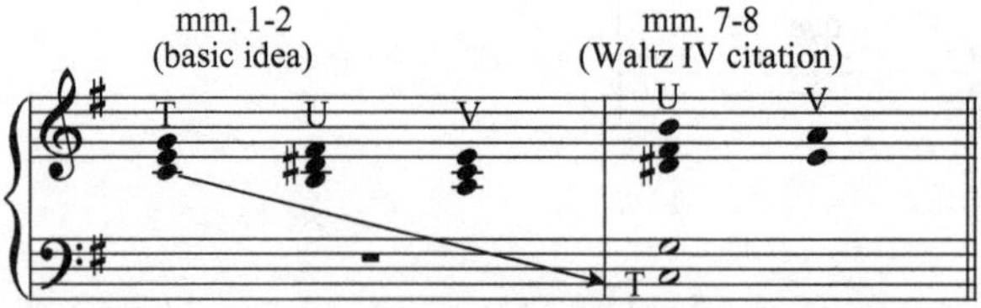

Example 5.9 Motivic Continuity in P1 (mm. 1–8).

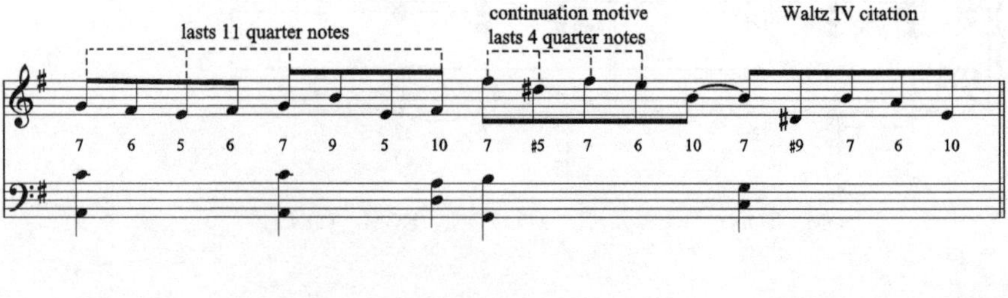

it is clear that the dialectic of past and present in memory is beginning to take musical form.

Thematic recollection in the continuation is reminiscent of not only the distant past of Waltz IV but also the recent past of the presentation in P1. The chord of the middle layer that initiates the citation is the first-inversion B major triad that appeared in measure 3. This triad, in turn, is a registral rearrangement of the root-position B major triad at the corresponding place in measure 1. By inverting this triad, Ravel transfers its root from bass to treble, causing the middle layer to touch the lower boundary of the upper layer for the first time and thereby raising the issue of boundary demarcation.

The middle layer, with its sinusoidal course, is the most active layer of all three in the presentation, but its pitch-space ambitus is conspicuously constrained to a major ninth between A3 and B4, which also belong to the pitch classes of the lower and upper layers, respectively. In example 5.10a I suggest that we think of these two boundary notes again from a Rameauian standpoint as "subposed" and "superposed" thirds around the initial C major triad of the basic idea. The bass descent in the basic idea to the subposed A3 may receive strong emphasis, but the melodic leap up to B4 is also quite salient for its disruption of an established pattern. In example 5.10a I use arrows and stems to highlight the three moments in which the basic idea touches its boundaries, while in example 5.10b I propose a more radical way to conceive the middle layer as mediating—literally and figuratively—between its two bounding layers: Every time the basic idea sounds either triadic subset of the A minor seventh chord, it directs our attention to the A pedal in the lower layer, whereas the B major triads direct our attention to the B octaves in the upper layer. According to this rationale, the tonal allegiance of the middle

Example 5.10a Boundaries for the Basic Idea in P1 (mm. 1–4).

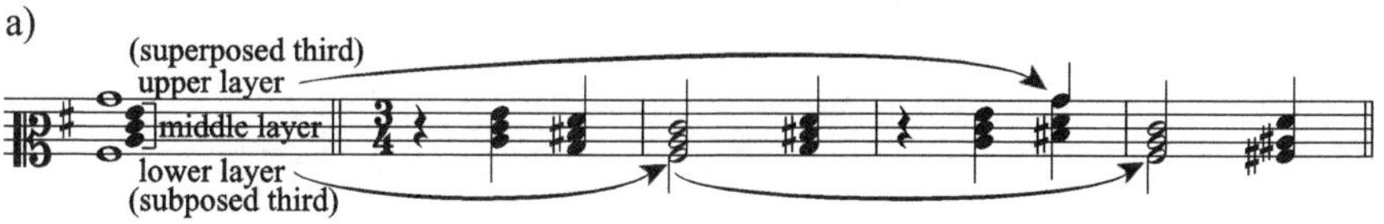

Example 5.10b Tonal Mediation of the Bounding Layers by the Basic Idea in P1 (mm. 1–4).

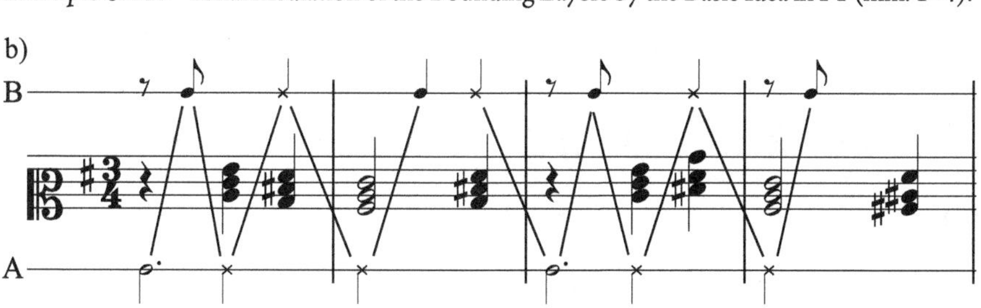

layer switches with almost every chord of the presentation and on almost every beat, thereby revealing dynamism in a texture that might otherwise seem quite static.

Having analyzed P1 in detail, we can now tender its interpretation in terms of memory, an approach we derive from thematic recollection in P1 and throughout the Epilogue. From this standpoint, musical structures and processes in the Epilogue reenact mental structures and processes. The stratified texture separates the mind into different registers of thought and emotion, while the dynamic properties of expansion, contraction, migration, and transformation, which govern these musical registers, figure the mixture and continual modulation of that thought and emotion. The acoustical mimicry of this stratified texture also has a place in our interpretation as a characteristic that assimilates the structure of the mind to some natural, elemental hierarchy, wherein the heavier affects rest at the bottom while the lighter affects rise to the top. The basic idea, which is both subject and subjectivity, vacillates in the first half of P1 between the melancholic brooding of the bass and the sanguine scintillations of the treble, just as it will participate throughout P1 in a tonal equivocation between relative minors and majors.

Example 5.11 A Succession of Sighs in P1 (mm. 1–8).

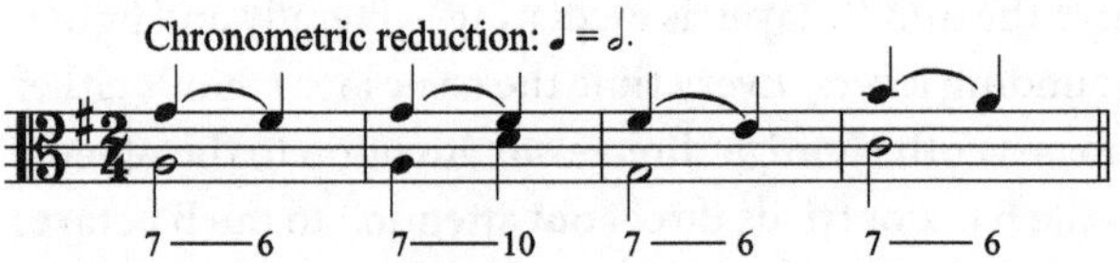

Example 5.12 A Possible Model (First System) from Waltz IV (mm. 1–4) for the Waltz IV "Premonition" in P1 (Second System, mm. 5-6).

The subjectivity of the Epilogue that we come upon off-tonic—in midreflection, as it were—is generally more melancholic than sanguine, however; witness the series of sighs outlined by the melody of P1 and reproduced in example 5.11, and recall the despondent sluggishness of the middle-layer suspensions against the bass. From the pervasive fragmentation and disordering of preceding waltzes in the Epilogue, the source of this melancholy would seem to be the loss and irrecoverability of a desirable past. It is a hopelessness that gives hope, insofar as brooding over the absence of the past may fuel a longing to make it present once again, if only in recollection.

For memory to work in its redemptive, involuntary mode, however, the mind must be primed for it. The emulation of acoustic resonance in the Epilogue is one aspect of this priming, to the extent that it imbues the music with an attitude of passivity and vulnerability, thereby opening it up to the occasion of memory as a visitation from without. Only when the mind is in this suggestible state, as it is in P1, can it receive a premonition of memory's visit, as well as the visit itself. The two measures preceding the citation of Waltz IV act as just such a premonition, beginning in a muted pianissimo with mysterious upper harmonies that gradually float back down into the middle register, where remembering then takes place. Having first identified it as an interior fragment from Waltz IV, we might then recognize the premonition as the opening gesture of Waltz IV, which likewise floats down against a broadly arpeggiating bass. Example 5.12 superposes the premonition (above) and its putative model (below) to facilitate their comparison.

Retrospecting further toward the beginning of P1, we will find an even earlier preparation for this memory: the sparking B of the upper octaves, an ember of hope that gradually begins to smolder in the melodic and harmonic Bs of the middle layer before flaring up at the initial B triad of the thematic recollection.[32] There seems to be little cause for hope, however, since the harmonic complex of the basic idea, which is most involved in representing this melancholic subjectivity in the present, is also the harmonic complex of the memory. The existential wisdom that we may derive from the conjunction of cyclicism and brooding melancholy in P1—that memory offers only fleeting and illusory redemption from our inescapable confinement in the here and now—can be counterbalanced by a more dialectical wisdom that memory is as much an effect of the present as it is an effect of the past, as I proposed earlier and revisit once more later on. Accordingly, the thematic recollection of Waltz IV is not transposed directly and mechanically into the Epilogue. Rather, it has been transformed to accommodate an ongoing P1, just as P1 has been shaped to accommodate it—so seamlessly, in fact, that we may not even recognize it as a memory until it has nearly passed us by. Thus, in the opening phrase of the Epilogue to the *Valses* Ravel performs the sleight of hand that so impressed Rosen in Schumann's *Fantasie*, making involuntary memory appear to simultaneously suspend and extend ongoing mental-musical processes.

Resistance and Compliance

Having analyzed P1 in detail, we can now pass more quickly over the subsequent phrases. The guiding impulse of P2 (measures 9–20) is to secure the tonic from which memory deflected P1. A renewed sense of purpose is audible in its presentation, where the opening ninth chord on A is major, louder, and more thickly scored than the ninth that began P1. Fate, however, has other plans for P2. At the onset of the continuation (measure 13), the dynamics drop precipitously, the bass falls a minor third, and the harmony shifts to a strange sonority. (It will eventually function as a dominant in B major, but we do not know that yet.) At the bottom of a two-octave descent (measure 16) the melody launches into the same recollection of Waltz IV as P1, only more extensive. And just as this recollection diverted P1 from the tonic, so, too, does it convey P2 to a cadence in the remote key of B major, or III♯.

Example 5.13a An Analytical Reduction of P2 (mm. 9–20).

Example 5.13b An Analytical Reduction of P3 (mm. 21–28).

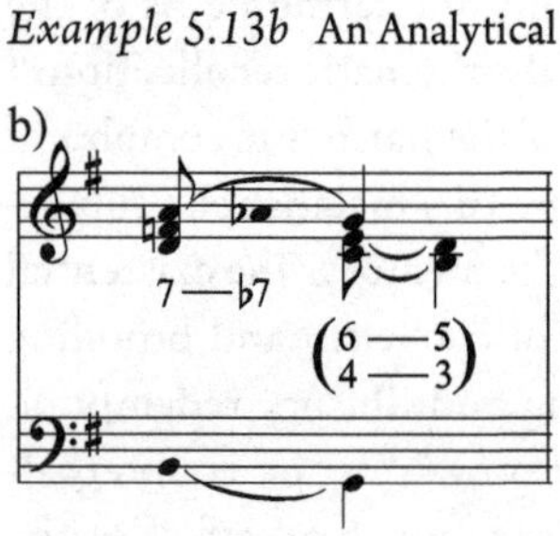

Example 5.13c An Analytical Reduction of P4 (mm. 29–45).

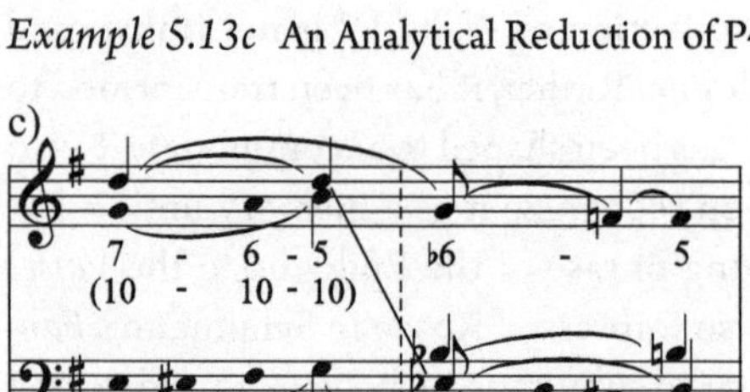

The contrapuntal reduction of P2 in example 5.13a shows the compounding of this irony at a further level. At this level, P2 has indeed succeeded in transforming the linear-intervallic pattern associated with the basic idea into a cadential formula, but it is a Pyrrhic victory since the cadence is tonally quite distant from the tonic. To the extent that P2 sought to avoid further distraction by involuntary memory, it does not succeed.

The other tonal reductions of example 5.13 show how P3 (measures 21–28) and P4 (measures 29–45) recast the behavior of P2, with each striving but failing to right what went tonally astray in the previous phrase. As is evident in example 5.13b, P3 sets the 7-6-5 intervallic progression of the basic idea and reaches a G-rooted harmony, but its local function is dominant, not tonic. In example 5.13c, we see how P4 coordinates a 7-6-5 intervallic progression with a bass ascent to cadence in G major in what seems a satisfactory end for itself, as well as the Epilogue. However, at the next downbeat memory scotches this ending with its most unsettling intervention so far, one that destabilizes the preceding cadence. As shown in example 5.13c, motion into an inner voice and a 5-6 exchange transform the cadential G major triad into an acoustic tonic with its characteristic lowered seventh.

However, perhaps we have let the priorities of conventional tonal analysis mislead our understanding of this moment. Perhaps this intervention is more continuous with than discontinuous from the preceding music. Both are, after all, citations of the same waltz, whose succession could simply be explained through the cognitive phenomenon of "memory chaining," whereby one recollection involuntarily causes another. Ironically, the shared origin of these two separate recollections of Waltz IV only ends up increasing the effect of discontinuity between them. As previously noted, the first citation of Waltz IV in P4 (measures 36–40) marks the third time we have heard it in the Epilogue; each time it reappears, its aura of pastness and strangeness decreases. However, the second citation of Waltz IV in P4 (measures 41–42) reverses this trend, restoring to it and the general phenomenon of thematic recollection the power they originally had to inflect the Epilogue's musical discourse. This renewal of discursive power derives, in part, from the relative position and function of the two citations within Waltz IV: The first comes from an interior phrase of the waltz, while the second is modeled on its opening phrase, previously excerpted in example 5.9. Thus, when we move from the first to the second citation we regress temporally within the memory itself, slipping from the past to the past's past. With the direction "pianississimo très lointain" (very, very soft and at a great distance) Ravel seems to wish to make audible this further wrinkling of time.[33]

Realizing itself powerless to either resist or control involuntary memory's intrusions after the disorienting phrase extension of P4 (measures 41–45), the mind henceforth surrenders itself to them and goes with their flow. Consequently, P5 (measures 46–61) releases a stream of thematic recollections that begins immediately at the onset of its continuation and unfolds across two textural waves, while the bass line prolongs a tonic pedal point for the rest of the piece. Now that the bass line

Example 5.14 Motivic Design in the Bass Line of the "Epilogue."

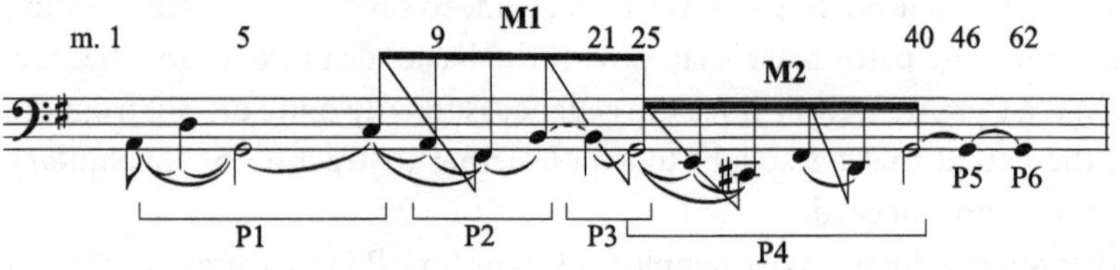

is no longer active, its role in staging tonal dialogue among phrases—and even asserting its tonal will against the arbitrary inflections of involuntary memory—becomes retrospectively apparent, as shown in example 5.14.

Example 5.14 lays out the bass line of the Epilogue, uses numbered brackets to divide the line according to the individual phrases, diagrams tonal relations within the line, stems and beams notes together to articulate motives, and labels the two motivic statements as M1 and M2, following their chronological order. So far, we have examined and compared phrases mainly as discrete entities. Now, however, motivic structure in the bass line invites us to group them together. For instance, M1 spans P2 and P3, ostensibly seeking to resolve the dominant tritone of P2 into the major third of P3, as shown in the diagram by Schenkerian unfoldings. Since the G arrival at the end of P3 functions locally as a half cadence, M1 fails in its tonal purpose. Then M2 attempts to remedy this situation by repeating and altering M1 so as to correct it. The compositional strategy behind M2 is cunning: Since the fifth and final note of M1 set a dominant harmony, M2 begins a perfect fourth below M1 so that *its* fifth note will become the dominant scale degree in G. Then M2 receives a sixth note, G, which resolves its dominant. When the second citation of Waltz IV melts the harmony above this G into an acoustic tonic, however, M2 turns out to have fared little better than M1.

Hope, Despair, and Time's Arrow

The general affect of the Epilogue, as noted earlier, is a gentle melancholy that transforms its gestures of recollection into expressions of nostalgia and regret. The main vehicle for this melancholy is the basic idea—both subject and subjectivity—that begins every phrase. The drooping inertia characteristic of melancholy finds the same musical correlatives in every version of the basic idea: a slow tempo, a dark, prolonged harmony (except, perhaps, for the major ninths of P2), and a soft but expressive melody that sighs over a low and inert bass. Although Ravel does not actually use the term *mélancolique* in the Epilogue, he nevertheless directs the pianist to play the reprise of P1 (measure 62) "même mouvement un peu *plus* las," thereby making explicit the melancholic lassitude that has governed the piece from its beginning.[34]

Example 5.15 Waltzing Between Memory and Melancholy in the "Epilogue."

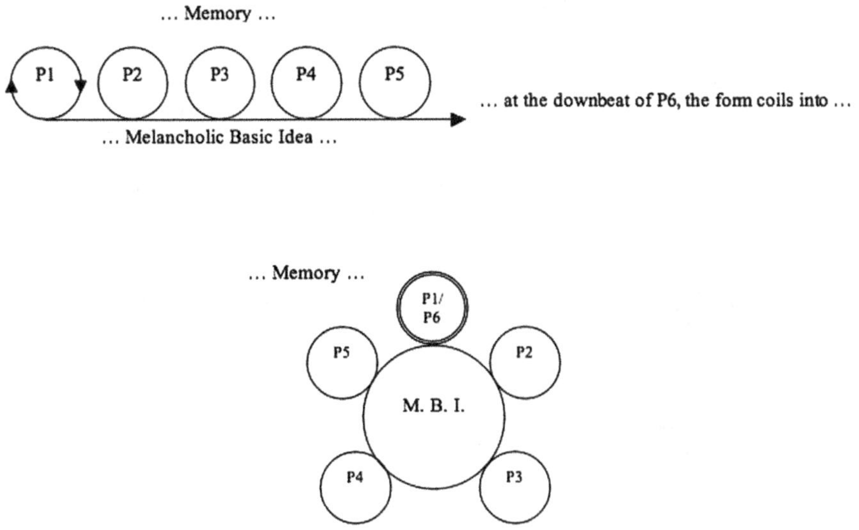

Yoked to the basic idea, the affect of melancholy comes to participate in formal processes. As shown in the upper diagram of example 5.15, each phrase in the Epilogue begins with the melancholic basic idea—situated, on the diagram, at the points where each circle intersects with the horizontal axis—before swinging away from this motive during the continuation to dally in thematic recollection, as represented by movement in the open space above; the lateral displacement of each circle along the x axis indicates that the basic idea does not remain invariant over time but rather metamorphoses from phrase to phrase, adapting to their tonal spaces. The unexpected reprise of P1 in P6, however, terminates this potentially infinite production of repetition and difference and thus, all at once, transforms our understanding of the overall form from linear to cyclical, as shown in the lower diagram of example 5.15.[35]

The lower diagram makes graphically clear a recursive structure that arises at the moment of transformation: the completion of a large-scale return that echoes the smaller-scale returns of the individual phrases. As an aspect of musical design, this nesting of circles is satisfyingly elegant. Moreover, it reveals another aspect of memory in the Epilogue: it remembers the waltz by musically simulating its dance pattern. In other words, the phrase design inscribes smaller circles inside a bigger circle, similar to a waltzing couple as they whirl along the circumference of a ballroom, thereby transferring choreography from the dancer's legs and feet to the pianist's arms and hands. The Epilogue is only the spectral memory of a waltz, however, and in this waltzlike recollection of the Waltz, the nostalgic subject

Example 5.16 The Melancholic Reprise in the "Pantomime" (RR172–175) of *Daphnis.*

dances alone—as if anticipating the widowed Dragonfly in the "Valse lente américaine" of *L'enfant et les sortilèges.*

The recursion in example 5.15 also conveys melancholy's inescapability. Hope for a situation that will bring an end to a state of melancholy arises each time a phrase swings out into the memory space of its continuation but dissolves again as the music swings back toward the basic idea to begin the next phrase. (The bookending chords of P1's basic idea make it a prime example of such closed circuitry.) The continual mutation of the basic idea from phrase to phrase keeps alive the possibility of change—until P6, that is, when the melancholic point of departure pulls back on the music and recasts the basic idea into its original form. At both levels of form, reversion to the basic idea figures the melancholy subject returning to present consciousness of itself and its pitiable condition, which was only momentarily alleviated by memory's flights into the past. While there may be no musical precedent for this recursive cyclical structure in Ravel's music, there is a literary one, the poem "Si morne!" [How Sad!] by Émile Verhaeren, which Ravel set for voice and piano in 1898 under the additional heading *déformation morale* [moral or mental derangement].[36] After opening with the exclamation "Always to fold back upon oneself, how sad!" (*Se replier toujours, sur soi-même, si morne!*), Verhaeren's melancholic lament about melancholy ends as it began, invoking in its final lines the *ennui* that "folds back upon itself at night." A melancholic bit of musical nocturnalism that folds back upon itself at two levels of form—or "deformation"—the Epilogue appears to be the belated, successful realization of the poem that had fascinated Ravel more than a decade earlier, when he was still a fledgling composer.

Due to the intimate association between melancholy and the basic idea in the Epilogue, the large-scale reprise at P6 consolidates affect, as well as form, broadcasting melancholy strongly by decelerating to an even wearier tempo and doubling the lamenting middle layer in the upper layer. A precedent for this melancholic reprise within Ravel's oeuvre may be found in a passage in *Daphnis et Chloé* that he had composed less than a year before: the Pantomime, in which the central couple acts out the roles of Pan and Syrinx in the Greek myth of metamorphosis. The brief allusion to the Pantomime in this chapter anticipates its more elaborate discussion in the conclusion to this book.

The Pantomime proper lasts eighteen measures and forms an ABA′ that prepares the subsequent Dance of Syrinx by modulating to the dominant. During the Pantomime, Chloe's appearance as the nymph Syrinx prompts Daphnis-as-Pan to declare his love (Section A), whose rejection inspires a second, more pressing entreaty by him before she finally flees, disappearing into a bank of reeds (Section B). The moment of reprise (Section A′) finds Pan alone and "in despair" (*désespéré*)—a state of mind similar to Lorédan, who is "sad unto death" (*triste à mourir*) upon returning to Adélaïde's salon during the Epilogue.[37] Whereas Lorédan's despair motivates him to pull out a pistol and threaten to shoot himself in the head in a manner reminiscent of Goethe's Werther, Pan's despair inspires him to pull up some reeds, form a panpipe from them (as in the Ovidian myth), and play a "melancholic tune" (*un air mélancolique*). Like the reprise in the Epilogue, the reprise in the Pantomime amplifies the initial melodic motive by thickening its texture, elevating its register, and augmenting its dynamics, which combine to bring out its latent character as something we might call a "heaved sigh," a characteristic Ravelian trope whose descending interval is greater than a step.[38] Unlike its precedent in *Daphnis*, however, the reprise in the Epilogue occurs within a formal scheme that is more complex and innovative than the Pantomime's ABA′, one that proceeds phrase by phrase in search of lost time and mixes repetition with a more extensive process of through-composition.

The effect of any reprise, of course, depends not only on how it sounds but also when and where it is heard. It is only fitting that the melancholic reprise of P6 follows the Waltz I fragments that terminate the memory flow for both P4 and P5. More bitterly ironic, however, is the fact that P6 should follow P5, the phrase that finally managed to break through the psychic resistances of the remembering subject to explore most fully the accidental inflections of involuntary memory. In so doing, it held out the greatest promise of not only resurrecting the past in memory but also experiencing, through memory, the true depth and character of *la vie intérieure* (the life lived within). To think of P5 in these terms is to align it with Bergsonian *durée*—usually translated as "duration," for lack of a better term—in which the objects of consciousness are no longer conceived as discrete elements, juxtaposed in homogeneous space, but rather as "penetrating" each other in a continuous production of heterogeneity and qualitative difference. Since music can readily be viewed as a modulatory flow wherein each part not only enlarges the whole but also transforms it into something different, it is not surprising that

Bergson frequently upheld music as an instance of *durée* in our everyday life.[39] The following paragraph from Bergson's groundbreaking doctoral thesis, *Essai sur les données immédiates de la conscience* (1889), will further help to situate this notion within his thought:

> Therefore, in fact, there would be two different selves (*moi*), of which one would be, as it were, the external projection of the other, its spatial and so to speak social representation. We attain the former [i.e., the interior self] by deep reflection, which makes us grasp our internal states as if they were living beings, ceaselessly developing, states impervious to measurement that penetrate each other and whose succession in *durée* has nothing in common with juxtaposition in homogeneous space. But those moments when we grasp ourselves again in this way are rare, which is why we are rarely free. Most of the time we live outside ourselves, seeing of our true self only its colorless phantom, the shadow that pure *durée* projects into homogeneous space. Thus, our existence unfolds in space rather than in time: we live for the external world rather than for ourselves; we speak rather than think; we are "acted upon" rather than acting ourselves. To act freely is to reclaim the true self, to place oneself once again into pure *durée*.[40]

One does not need to be intimately familiar with the development of Bergson's thought to hear echoes in this passage of what we already know about his next monograph, *Matière et mémoire*. In the *Essai* he divides the self into mutually exclusive halves, attributing to one the capacity to fulfill the practical demands of social life and to the other the ability to experience—anew, at every moment—the depth and quality of its existence. The dichotomy in *Matière et mémoire* between nonreflective habit memory and reflective pure memory is thus the progeny of this earlier dichotomy of selfhood and is equally critical—perhaps along the lines of Rousseau's distinction between *l'amour de soi* and *l'amour-propre*—of the tendency of socialization to alienate individuals from themselves.

By linking *Matière et mémoire* to the *Essai*, I am suggesting that the elaborate, intensely memorious continuation of P5 (measures 50–61) is akin to Bergsonian *durée*. As in the presentations of all the other phrases of the Epilogue, the first four measures of P5 constrain the musical-mnemonic subject within predetermined parameters of motive and meter; melancholy is not only the affect under repetition here but also the reaction against such repetition. The subsequent continuation, however, swings far out and into the recesses of memory (to reinvoke the circular loops of example 5.15), reveling in the unpredictability and heterogeneity of its recollections. In Bergson's terms, this stream of memories displays a "confused multiplicity" in the way the individual recollections "penetrate" each other without assimilating, for, as Suzanne Guerlac has remarked, each moment in *durée* is "radically discontinuous from the next, even though it flows out of one and into another."[41] From this perspective, then, quantity expresses quality. The pianissimo of the Waltz VII fragment (measure 51) is not simply quieter than the piano of the Waltz VI fragment in the previous measure but rather marks it as wholly other, with the two occurring in separate universes, as it were—a distinction that could make all the difference to performers' understanding of the piece, if they had not in fact already intuited it. So, too, is it insufficient to describe the subsequent citation of Waltz VI (measures 52–54) as simply the repetition of its previous citation under specific rhythmic, tonal, and textural operations. Instead, it may be preferable to view it as a unique occurrence that musically substantializes the activity of *durée* in memory—or, even better, of memory as *durée*.

To approach thematic recollection from this viewpoint raises a difficult but important question—a question, in fact, that Bergsonian thought wishes to make both difficult and important for us to answer: How does time relate to memory? One plausible response is that time as we conceive of it in daily life—a thing subject to incremental and equal division, which Bergson referred to as "spatialized time"—is effectively excluded from an experience of such a profound, interior phenomenon as *la mémoire pure*.[42] Jankélévitch, once again, beautifully transposes this possibility into memory's terms: "[T]he time of dreamy nostalgia and poetic *flânerie* is no longer divided up by an agenda, nor articulated into successive segments: it is a time without schedule or calendar, a diffluent and invertebrate time whose metronomic divisions blend together and lose all rigor."[43] If we were the editors of the Epilogue, and we wished to represent it in this way, we might consider replacing the standardized rhythmic and metrical notation of the phrasal continuations—the measure lines and durations—with alternative notation that would better indicate its nonmeasured, momentary quality, thereby representing it as a sort of free "postluding" (a complement to the historical practice of *Präludieren*). This editorial experiment would not only help realize our imaginative scenario of the composer improvising at the keyboard but also liberate those motives and patterns that were obscured by and ran counter to the triple meter of the waltz: the five-beat continuation motive of P1, P2, and P4, the duple-time phenomenon of Waltz VI in P3, the nested hemiolas of the second Waltz IV fragment in P4, and the 4/4 accompanimental pattern under Waltz I in P4, not to mention all the metrical eddies in the continuation of P5. As attractive as this immersive, even oceanic, conception of time might be in some respects, however, it neglects other pertinent and important issues.

A common way to interrelate time and memory is think of the latter instrumentally—that is, as a means to import the past into the present. Though it is only natural for us to feel the predomination of the past in this transaction between temporalities, the role played by the present itself is at least equally important: It is, after all, the only time in which we are able to remember. A further consideration is the way the unidirectionality of time ensures not only the impossibility of making the past present but also the certainty of a future in which both past and present can be recalled, among other actions. The articulation of this dilemma, as well as the existential ambivalence that results from it, is one of the signal contributions of Jankélévitch's *L'irréversible et la nostalgie*, which can profitably be read as both a critical development of Bergsonian thought and a valuable supplement to memory studies *avant la lettre*, given the relatively little effort this field has devoted to theorizing the role of the future in memory. According to his argument, the irreversibility of time breeds melancholy and despair about the incontrovertible pastness of the past (*la prétérition*) but also hope about the endless production of the future (*la futurition*) as an opportunity not only to reexperience the past in memory but to experience it in a new way as well. At one point Jankélévitch brings all three temporalities together in a moment of conceptual synthesis by describing how "the experience of the past, which is, after all, an experience in the present, itself takes part in the production of the future; our attempt to conjure up 'anew' the ghost of a former experience actually results in a new experience."[44]

Thus, the openness toward the past that we witness in the continuation of P5 is also an openness toward the future and the new experiences in memory it will bring. This helps to explain the central role of the Waltz VI fragments (measures 50 and 52–54), which, with their ascending contour and mounting dynamics, initiate textural waves that not only clear a path for the thematic arrivals of Waltzes VII and III at their crests but also seem to anticipate them. Yet there is no denying the melancholic consciousness of *la prétérition* in P5, whose presence ultimately overwhelms any optimism associated with *la futurition*. Compare, for example, the two thematic arrivals with their original statements. In its proper milieu, the Waltz VII passage excerpted in P5 was climactic and performed by the tutti orchestra. However, upon reappearing here (measures 51–52), it is presented by a pianissimo quartet of first violins, whose delicate sound is made uncanny by ethereal harmonics and fingerboard glissandi in the accompanying strings. In addition, the melancholic subject is unable to sustain the memory of Waltz III (measures 55–59), which slows down after its motivic presentation and falls silent for a beat—or, rather "chokes up," *beklemmt*, as in Beethoven's op. 130 Cavatina—before it can continue pianississimo and at an even slower tempo, ultimately trailing off instead of bringing the phrase to its expected conclusion. The sudden subsequent citation of an energetic Waltz IV (measures 59–60) is a final flame of hope that is soon extinguished in the blackness of despair that ends P5—a "grand sommeil noir," to invoke the depressive poem by Verlaine that Ravel set some fifteen years earlier. The reprise at P6 is, without a doubt, the great tragic gesture of the Epilogue, especially coming after P5's breakthrough into memory, *durée*, and hope-filled *futurition*, but it is not a wholly unexpected turn of events, given the persistence of melancholy from P1 to P5.

Mon fin est mon commencement

The source of melancholy in the Epilogue that subtends its every measure is the knot that binds together the desire to make the past present and whole again with the knowledge that this is impossible. From a melancholic point of view, the fragmentation, distortion, and disordering of the waltzes when they reappear in the Epilogue are traces of memory's failure to preserve the past intact. At a broader historical level, they are the effects of an oblivion that, at the end of the long nineteenth century, was in the process of transforming the waltz from a cultural monument into a ruin. Or—since the notion of ruins would likely bring to mind the blasted landscapes of Caspar David Friedrich more readily than musical genres—it might be better to describe the waltz as a *lieu de mémoire* [site of memory].

The concept of the *lieu de mémoire* stems from Pierre Nora's historiography of modernism, in which he describes the transition into modern life at the end of the French nineteenth century as a gradual loss of social bonds, a process as much reflected in as caused by the simultaneous decline of collective memory and the rise of a secular, administered society. *Lieux* are those entities that the cultural imagination values for their association with the disappearing past, as well as their continued relevance to the present, for their ability to "stop time" and "block the work of forgetting," as well as their capacity for sustaining "an endless recycling of their meaning and an unpredictable proliferation of their ramifications"—both excellent ways to grasp the uses to which Ravel puts the waltz in his *Valses.*[45] However, any constructive characteristics of the *lieu* are ultimately subordinate to its enveloping sense of historical loss—or, rather, of history as loss. As he explains the concept further from his vantage point as a historiographer:

> Our interest in *lieux de mémoire* where memory crystallizes and secretes itself has occurred at a particular historical moment, a turning point where consciousness of a break with the past is bound up with the sense that memory has been torn—but torn in such a way as to pose the problem of the embodiment of memory in certain sites where a sense of historical continuity persists. There are *lieux de mémoire,* sites of memory, because there are no longer *milieux de mémoire,* real environments of memory.[46]

If the first seven waltzes with their variety and exuberance manage to sustain the illusion that the waltz is still a living tradition, the Epilogue shatters this illusion by breaking these waltzes into fragments, thereby revealing the genre at the end of the long nineteenth century to have become a mere *lieu de mémoire.*

While the consciousness of historical loss permeates the presentation of P6 in both form and affect, the continuation—the Epilogue's last word—is not as clearly melancholic. As the instances of "0" back in example 5.1 indicate, the continuation of P6 (measures 66–74) is unique among previous continuations for beginning without a melody. By the second "0" measure, the prolonged absence of melody begins to suggest that melancholy's nihilism has shut down any further efforts by the mind to recollect the past, voluntarily or no. However, at the upbeat to the third measure the low D unexpectedly introduces one final melody: the lyrical theme of Waltz II. Ravel enhances its twilit quality by transposing it down an octave from its original statement and assigning it in the orchestral version to the lowest part of the clarinet's dusky chalumeau register. More apparition than revenant, this thematic recollection exits as it entered, returning to its incipit note before disappearing back into the background silence from which it mysteriously emerged.

At first hearing, the dolorous quotation of Waltz II seems to sing the swan song of the waltz as a lyrical expression of its beauty-in-obsolescence.[47] If, in the *Valses*, as Marcel Marnat has asserted, Ravel "bids adieu to the waltz as he bid adieu to the serenade, the minuet, the pavane, and the whole assortment of classical dances that had become sonorous symbols of our civilisation," the final melody is the perfect gesture of valediction.[48] After further thought, however, it can also be imagined to challenge the entire melancholic perspective of the Epilogue. A single note in this melody—the fifth, which is an F instead of an E—indicates its derivation from the reprise of Waltz II (measures 41–44) rather than the exposition (measures 9–12). This minute difference shifts the relationship between the Epilogue and Waltz II into a different light. By aligning them according to their internal reprises, the thematic recollection of Waltz II suggests a bona fide affinity with the Epilogue rather than the more arbitrary relation that involuntary memory has established between it and the previous waltz citations.[49] This hypothesis stands up to scrutiny: Both are *valses lentes*, both begin with similar motives, and both feature octave grace notes in the treble, an ornamental gesture that does not appear elsewhere in the set. A rationale behind Ravel's having saved the recollection of Waltz II for the final measures of the Epilogue is gradually taking form: When the final waltz turns to Waltz II, it is not merely showing its continued dependence on external thematic sources but rather comes into its own.[50] Given the internal ordering of the *Valses*, Waltz II is more than an alter ego for the Epilogue—it is its origin, hidden until now.

A return to origins at the end of a work is a specific, radical example of the narrative phenomenon that Gérard Genette has called "anachrony" and which I mentioned previously as "counterchronic" behavior in chapter 2. In an anachronic narrative the time of the narrative moves in contrast to the chronology of the narrated story, flashing occasionally forward in "prolepsis" but more often backward in "analepsis," whose counterchronology frequently forms part of a recollection performed by either the narrator or a character in the story. A gradual counterchronic trajectory is a feature of Ravel's Epilogue, as well as the first movement of Schumann's *Fantasie,* which ends with the Beethoven quotation from *An die ferne Geliebte,* which, as Rosen has argued, sounds like the source of the themes preceding it and is implicitly the impetus for its creation insofar as Schumann's movement performs an homage to a "distant beloved" who is also the artist's muse.

By revealing its origin the Epilogue appropriates it, thereby lessening the alienation of the one from the other and the melancholy felt in response to this alienation. The familial relation between the Epilogue and the waltzes it frames suggests that neither their difference nor the temporal difference they represent—that which separates the present from the past—is absolute. Once again, we need not simply consider the past as something absent from the present but rather can see the two in active, ongoing negotiation with each other. Recall the dialectical interaction we observed between the waltz fragments and their context in the Epilogue: Their alteration may be understood to represent not only inevitable ruination in the present but also creative transformation. Proust's narrator voices this insight into memory when he, correcting himself, exclaims, "Seek? More than that: create."[51]

Thus, at one level the Epilogue expresses what Richard Terdiman has called the "memory crisis" of modernism—an acute, melancholic awareness of its incapacity to reproduce the past.[52] At another, the Epilogue articulates and embraces the fact that *the past is always already a construction of the present.* Emulating both memory and the Epilogue, our analysis has also proceeded counterchronically and arrived at a final insight that is a precondition for understanding the *Valses nobles et sentimentales* as a whole.

6

Dynamism in *La valse*

By coupling the *Valses nobles et sentimentales* (1911) with *La valse* (1920) in the final chapters of this book, my intent is not to compare them according to their respective treatments of the waltz but rather to focus on other phenomena that may, at first glance, seem peripheral but are centrally important to both pieces: the sections that frame the main waltz suite in each piece and the role that memory plays in each one. In both the *Valses nobles* and *La valse,* musical frames seem to represent the waltz as an object distant in memory, an artifact that is available to the present only upon being recalled from the past. Varied attempts in these frames to recollect the waltz achieve varied results: Whereas the end frame (Epilogue) of the *Valses nobles* can recall the previous waltzes only as fragments, the opening frame of *La valse* gradually assembles waltz fragments into complete phrases. Within our interpretive scenario this musical difference reflects a difference in memory, whose success in making the fragmentary past whole and present (virtually, at least) is just as remarkable at the beginning of *La valse* as is its failure at the end of the *Valses nobles.* Although additional factors mitigate and subtly vary this opposition, it nonetheless defines the basic relation between the two pieces. Moreover, it also affects the way we understand the relation between each piece and its historical situation. Usually the two pieces are thought to mirror their historical circumstances, with the flamboyantly retrospective *Valses nobles* embodying the prewar hedonism of the so-called banquet years in Paris and the violence of *La valse* replaying the catastrophic effects of the Great War on Old Europe and its cultural heritage. Careful study of the role of memory in the frames for each piece, however, leads to a reversal of these long-standing associations. At the conclusion of this chapter, we should find it more fitting to claim it is the *Valses nobles* that mourns the irreversible loss of the past and *La valse* that celebrates its miraculous recovery.

La valse and the *Valses nobles*

As two waltz suites written by the same composer within a decade of each other, it is only natural to conceive of *La valse* and the *Valses nobles* as a pair, and many have done so, albeit for various reasons and to varying effect.[1] Some have found the two waltz suites to be more similar than dissimilar, connected as they are by a sense of melancholy and a "feeling of valediction";[2] George Balanchine's combination of the two into a single ballet production is perhaps the most striking, though implicit assertion of their compatibility as a pair.[3] Ravel, however, would probably not have encouraged any attempt to assimilate the two since, among other possible reasons, it would have called attention to a potentially unseemly moment of repetition in his oeuvre. In an October 1931 interview Ravel addressed this general phenomenon, cautioning composers not to develop musical personas that are "immediately recognizable and stylized in unchanging formulas" but recommending instead that they "isolate" themselves from their previous work and "completely 'forget' a work once it is finished."[4] Notwithstanding the general value of artistic innovation and its specific presence in Ravel's oeuvre, any listener would be hard pressed to completely forget the *Valses nobles* when listening to *La valse*, especially at the points of marked resemblance between the two. Compare, for example, the climactic arrivals in Waltz VII (mm. 51–66) of the *Valses nobles* with similar moments in *La valse* (RR16–17), as well as Waltz IV in the former and an interior waltz (RR18–25) in the latter.[5]

Claims of difference seem nevertheless to have prevailed over perceptions of similarity in comparisons of this pair, due largely to the stark contrast between their respective historical situations. A notable advocate of this viewpoint is Vladimir Jankélévitch, who heard a "change in tone" from one to the other as testament to the war that divided the "old Europe" of the *Valses nobles* from the "new Europe" of *La valse*. According to Jankélévitch, Ravel's experience of the war as both a citizen and a soldier caused him to abandon his identity in the *Valses nobles* as a "dilettante in search of 'useless activities' " and produce instead a "single and unique *Valse*, a great and tragic *Valse* that is, all alone and at once, noble and sentimental—but seriously, this time."[6]

In another commentary on *La valse*—probably the best known of all, even though it was made by a cultural historian rather than a musicologist—Carl Schorske found *La valse* so unique and powerful in its relation to history that he had no need for the *Valses nobles* as a foil. For Schorske, *La valse* reenacted not only the "violent death of the nineteenth-century world" but also the fate of the individual in the midst of this societal upheaval.[7] In his interpretive scheme for *La valse*, individuals in society are represented by musical themes that coalesce into a coherent whole in the first part of the piece but fly apart in the second; for Schorske, the musical transition registers the disintegration of bourgeois liberal culture in Western Europe at the end of the long nineteenth century, as well as the concurrent transformation of well-socialized "rational man" to poorly socialized "psychological man . . . not merely a rational animal, but a creature of feeling and instinct."[8] Although Schorske's reading lacks musical detail, does not compare Ravel's two waltz suites, and is intended to introduce a history of the Austrian rather than the French *fin de siècle*, it nonetheless proves to be a valuable resource for our memory-based analysis and interpretation of *La valse*.

As mentioned in the introduction to this chapter, *La valse* and the *Valses nobles* complement each other according to the notion of memory. Both use musical frames as memory tropes, and in both instances, the objects of memory are waltzes whose fragmentation and unmediated juxtaposition indicate this memory to be in a state of crisis. While these similarities establish a firm basis for comparison, there are nonetheless two main differences between the respective uses of frames in the two pieces. First, *La valse* has not one but two frames that bookend a central waltz suite. Second, the frames of *La valse* are more energetic than the melancholic Epilogue of the *Valses nobles*. As we will see, music analysis, historical contextualization, and hermeneutics can be combined to lend a complex significance to these simple differences in form and affect: The opening frame of *La valse* rejoices in memory's redemption of the past, whereas its closing frame adopts a more ambivalent relation to memory by reiterating the redemptive gestures of the opening frame while simultaneously obliterating past materials in an ecstatic rout. When Schorske described in *La valse* the gradual metamorphosis of its "sweeping rhythm" into "compulsive" and "frenzied" behavior, he was undoubtedly sensing the same qualitative shift where memory switches from a constructive to a destructive mode—or, better yet, a "deconstructive" mode since it is at this moment that memory is most clearly interwoven with oblivion and the present with the past in an aggressive act of dialectics that challenges the stability of both dichotomies.[9] Before we proceed to these reflections, however, we must first acquaint ourselves with several basic elements of *La valse*: the form, the ballet scenario, and two of its most important musicological analyses whose contradiction expresses the dialectical aspect of this piece.

La valse and Its Scenario

The 756 measures of *La valse* form an ABA', as shown in row 1 of table 6.1.[10] In row 2 I have divided each frame into two "phases"; in both cases, the second phase reinitiates and redirects the growth processes of the first. In the opening frame, the waltz fragments of the first phase prepare the inchoate waltz suite of the second phase, while in the closing frame, the first wave of waltzes yields to a second, which begins at a faster tempo and ultimately attains an even more shattering climax than the first.[11]

Rows 3 to 5 go beyond the notes to coordinate the form and content of *La valse* with three different programs it has been thought to project. The source for Interpretation 1 is the ballet scenario that Ravel composed and had his editor publish together with the score for what he called a "choreographic poem":

> Bright spells within thick, whirling clouds allow momentary glimpses of waltzing couples. The clouds disperse little by little, revealing (at A [R9]) a vast hall filled by a whirling mass of people.
>
> The stage is gradually illuminated. The light of the chandeliers bursts forth at the fortissimo (B [R17]).
>
> An imperial Court, about 1855.[12]

As the table indicates, the "whirling of clouds" and their intermittent clearing take place during Phase 1 of the opening frame, and the partial to full illumination of the ballroom maps exactly onto Phase 2, whose boundaries are marked by Ravel's rehearsal letters A and B. The composer's scenario thus provides a coherent dramatic context for a unified stretch of music, during which whirling (*tourbillonnant*, in Ravel's French) masses of clouds are displaced by similarly whirling (*tournoyant*) masses of people. As a partial scenario, however, it fails to interpret the most challenging aspect of *La valse*: the closing frame with its broad and complex reprise of almost all of the previous material.

In contrast, interpretations by Hermann Danuser and George Benjamin encompass the entirety of the piece and divide it into four stages, as shown in the bottom two rows of table 6.1.[13] Although Benjamin was seemingly unaware of Danuser's earlier analysis when he published his own, the two readings are nonetheless strikingly similar in their use of organicist metaphor, probably because the opening frame is so clearly modeled on what is often called a *creatio ex nihilo* trope.[14] Leading from birth to maturity and then to death by "destruction," the

Table 6.1 **Form and Content in *La valse.***

Formal Divisions:	*A—Opening Frame (RR1-17)*		*B—Waltz Suite (RR18-53)*	*A′—Closing Frame (RR54-end)*	
Formal Subdivisions:	Phase 1 (RR1-8)	Phase 2 (RR9-17)	(none)	Phase 1 (RR54–75)	Phase 2 (RR76-end)
Interpretation 1 (M. Ravel)	"whirling clouds" + "bright spells"	partial to full illumination of hall and crowd	(no further commentary in official ballet scenario)		
Interpretation 2 (H. Danuser)	"Genesis"		"Flourishing"	"Triumph"; "Destruction" ↕	
Interpretation 3 (G. Benjamin)	"Birth"		"Life"	"Decay"; "Destruction"	

two readings dissociate at the penultimate stage, as highlighted in the table. The section under dispute is the closing frame, which initially signifies "triumph" for Danuser but "decay" for Benjamin. Rather than choosing one interpretation over the other, I propose that the two are equally valid as responses to the complex affect of the closing frame, which is both tragic and ecstatic—"Dionysian" in the Nietzschean sense of the term. Further, I argue that the affect and internal design of both frames can profitably be conceived under the rubric of memory. Some analysis will now help us to flesh out these two propositions.

Re-membering the Waltz

The opening frame of *La valse* remembers the waltz in two senses, not only recollecting it but also piecing it together from its musical components. This process of assembly and growth places multiple musical parameters in continual development over the span of the framing section and involves phenomena such as a rise in tessitura, an accumulation of orchestral layers, an increase in dynamics, and a consolidation of phrase structure, which transforms thematic fragments into metrically and tonally coherent phrases. While this process is relatively smooth, it can nonetheless be divided into six stages, as shown in table 6.2.

The first four stages take place in quick succession during the opening measures of Phase 1, as displayed in example 6.1. The addition of a new orchestral layer marks each of the four initial stages. Starting at the bottom of example 6.1, we begin with a rhythmically and melodically undifferentiated tremolo in the first two divisions of the contrabasses. In measure five the third division of the contrabasses enters, articulating the meter with pizzicato crochet attacks and introducing a subtle syncopation on the second beat through an agogic accent. In measure nine, the first harp and the timpani appear together to flesh out the previously unmarked third beat, while simultaneously introducing the octave interval in both harmony and melody (that is, when heard as an extending "echo" of layer two's low F). Finally, at R1 the bassoons present a waltz fragment that synthesizes the three preceding stages, incorporating the minor third of layer one, the rhythm of layer two, and the octave transposition of layer three. The consistent stagger of

Table 6.2 **Re-membering the Waltz in Six Stages**

Opening Frame					
Phase 1			Phase 2		
Stage 1	Stage 2	Stage 3	Stage 4	Stage 5	Stage 6
R1^{-11} (m.1)	R1^{-7}	R1^{-3}	R1^{+1}	R9^{+1}	R17^{+1}

Example 6.1 The First Four Stages of Musical Re-membering in *La valse*.

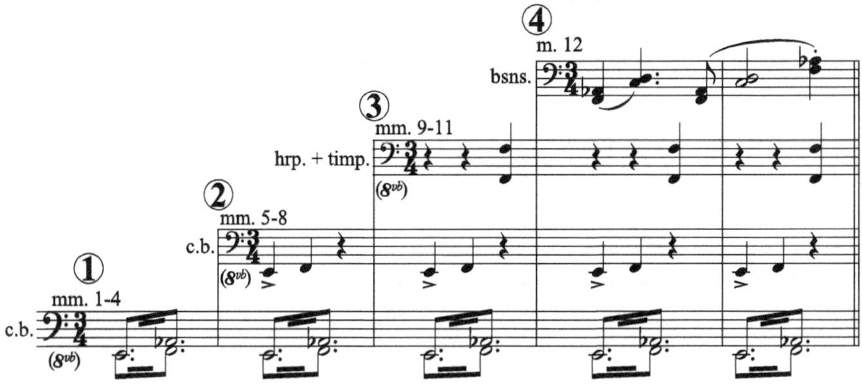

each layer's entry by three or four measures underlines the systematic nature of this formative process.

The final two stages occur during Phase 2 and correspond to Ravel's rehearsal letters A and B. Stage 5 maintains the overall continuity of this process by transforming material from the previous stage. The music of rehearsal A converts the waltz fragment from Stage 4 into a complete and elegant phrase by elevating its melodic register, diatonicizing its harmony, expanding its rhythm, relaxing its accompanimental texture, and adding violas to make its instrumentation more songful. In addition, the repetition of the waltz fragment in Stage 4 now becomes a consequent phrase within a parallel continuous period of sixteen measures.

Before we can proceed to the final stage, however, Ravel introduces a newly textured passage that supplies the consequent phrase at the end of the second period (R12). Immediately thereafter, Ravel reorients the introduction by recalling a second waltz fragment from Stage 4 (R6), now transformed in a manner similar to the first waltz fragment. As this theme develops, it leads smoothly into the tutti fortissimo phrase of rehearsal B, which represents the culminating stage of the musical-mnemonic process in the opening frame: the point at which the musical past has become whole and present.

As the opening frame passes into the waltz suite, the full orchestra suddenly thins to a fraction of its previous size, sounding a delicate and insouciant piano melody in the oboe against a discreet accompanimental texture in the winds and strings. Not until this moment of relaxation do we realize, in retrospect, how much time and energy were expended in getting to the waltz suite. One scholar has even tried to summarize the opening frame by citing the Latin phrase *per aspera ad astra* (through adversity to the stars), thereby expressing not only the teleology of this musical process and the astral splendor of its telos (recall Ravel's description of rehearsal B as the moment the light of the chandeliers "bursts forth") but also the asperity of its demands.[15] The arduousness of memory work, here and elsewhere, tells us that it is more than the simple retrieval of stored information: It is also an active struggle against an ever-present oblivion that constantly threatens to make the past inaccessible to memory. Various writers have used different metaphors to capture the effect of forgetting on our efforts to remember: For Bergson and Proust, it is the difficulty involved in ascending the "the slope of our past";[16] for Walter Benjamin, the burdensome weight of memory's catch in the sea of consciousness;[17] and for Ravel, the overclouding of memory's vantage point on the past. The Epilogue of the *Valses nobles* also invokes oblivion as the precondition for the activity of memory within its bounds and the cause for the fragmentation of its waltz recollections. Nonetheless, the sustained intensification in the opening frame of *La valse* makes oblivion even clearer as the force to which memory is a heroic counterforce, rowing against the tide of time to win back the past for the present.

Dismembering the Waltz

The sudden reprise of the opening measures terminates the waltz suite abruptly, thereby awakening us from our reverie on this idyllic past and tearing us from its "homogeneous, bourgeois soundworld."[18] Although the end of the waltz suite may seem unexpected, it is foreshadowed a few measures earlier in the passage reproduced as example 6.2.

The grand waltz (R46) begins to gesture toward an energetic conclusion in the manner of Ravel's more ebullient Spanish pieces, such as "Alborada del gracioso" from *Miroirs* and the "Feria" from the *Rapsodie espagnole.* The tempo, dynamics, and instrumental density all increase, while the motives undergo a rhythmic stretto, their durations contracting from four measures to two, from two to one, and from one measure to two beats. The climax presaged by these events is then deferred by the interpolation of a new waltz at rehearsal 50.[19] It is exquisite and delicate—almost excessively so, as the high wind tessitura is matched by an equally high string accompaniment replete with pizzicatos, trills, and quasi-falsetto harmonics and further ornamented by the *jeu de timbres.* The new and pressing awareness that the waltz suite is living on borrowed time creeps into the music, reminding us that the past is present only in memory and constantly threatens to slip back into oblivion; it

Example 6.2 The Stretto of Motive 16 in the Waltz Suite of *La valse.*

can hardly be coincidental that Balanchine introduced at this moment the figure of Death, bringer of oblivion, in his 1951 production of *La valse*.[20] Soon thereafter the edifice of the waltz suite comes crashing down, prompting the music to begin anew.

In listening to *La valse*, it is relatively easy to perceive points of large-scale formal articulation but much more difficult to keep track of the ensuing sequences of themes and motives. The reprise (R54) offers the best example of this discrepancy: The return of the distinctive opening measures can hardly be missed, while the subsequent motivic-thematic succession of the closing frame is lengthy and complicated. The closing frame—which Deborah Mawer, grappling with its role within the overall form, as well as its internal complexities, has alternately called a "grossly distended final section" and a "recapitulation-cum-coda"—clearly revisits previous materials but does not do so in a transparent manner.[21] A motivic-thematic analysis of *La valse* will help to clarify both the structure of the closing frame and its relation to the two preceding sections, the opening frame and the waltz suite.[22]

Table 6.3 **Motivic-Thematic Design in *La valse*.**

A & B			
Section:	Begins:	Lasts:	Motive #:
A (Opening Frame, Phase 1)	R1	9mm	1
	R3	8mm	1
	R4	4mm	2
	R5	5mm	3
	R6	6mm	4
	R7	7mm	5
	R8	9mm	6
(Phase 2)	R9	30mm	1′
	R12	7mm	7
	R13	24mm	4 (+ 6′)
	R16	17mm	8 (5′)
B (Waltz Suite)	R18	32mm	9
	R22	32mm	10
	R26	32mm	11
	R30	32mm	12
	R34	16mm	13
	R36	40mm	14
	R41	40mm	15
	R46	32mm	16
	R50	36mm	17 (7′)

	A′ (Partial Reprise of B in A)			
	Motive #:	Lasts:	Begins:	Section:
	1	7mm	R54	A′ (Closing Frame, Phase 1)
	5	9mm	R55	
	3	9mm	R57	
	4	5mm	R58	
	5	8mm	R59	
	18	12mm	R60	
5	5	9mm	R62	
	14	20mm	R63	
	5	4mm	R66	
	13	4mm	R67	
	5	9mm	R68	
	5 + 13	18mm	R69	
	12	22mm	R73	
	15	60mm	R76	(Phase 2)
	16	16mm	R85	
	8	4mm	R88	
	E1	6mm	R89	
	8	4mm	R90	
	E1	6mm	R91	
	8	3mm	R93	
	E2	6mm	$R93^{+4}$	
8	8	18mm	R94	
	9	2mm	R96	
	8	7mm	R97	
	E3	18mm	$R97^{+8}$	
	8	4mm	R100	
	E4	10mm	$R100^{+5}$	
	(8)	2mm	$R101^{+8}$	

Table 6.3 divides into a left side, which tabulates the motivic content of the opening frame and the waltz suite, and a right side, which is devoted exclusively to the long and highly segmented closing frame. To allow the reader to compare content more easily, the two sides have been placed in mirror formation.

As we can see from the left side, Phase 1 of the opening frame has a rather simple motivic-thematic design, with new material irrupting into the texture every four to nine measures. In contrast, Phase 2 returns several times to previous material, including Motives 1 and 4; the latter is particularly important, integrating Motive 6 into a complete phrase and setting up Motive 8 as a more stable version of Motive 5, as indicated in the table by the parentheses. Motive 7, the only one that seems to belong exclusively to Phase 2, is ironically the most out of place. It forms the "digression" that interrupts not only the phrase structure of Motive 1′, as discussed earlier, but also the teleology that is gradually replacing the short fragmentary phrases of Phase 1 with the longer, complete phrases of Phase 2. Reflecting its role in suspending teleological progression, it also resurfaces under slight alteration as Motive 17 (the "exquisite and delicate" waltz theme mentioned previously) to defer the end of the waltz suite, as indicated by the parenthetical 7′ in the bottom right corner of the table.

The closing frame is primarily a reprise of the opening frame. The vertical brackets in table 6.3 help to clarify the interrelation of the two frames through the correspondence of their phases: Just as Phase 1 of the closing frame features a motive (5) from Phase 1 of the opening frame, so, too, does Phase 2 of the former focus on a motive (8) from Phase 2 of the latter. Further, Motive 8 represents the overall telos and climax for the closing frame, just as it did for the opening frame. At a more detailed level of content, the closing frame borrows techniques of phrase fragmentation, juxtaposition, and interruption from the opening frame (especially its first phase) and extends them throughout its three-hundred-odd measures. Accordingly, both frames have the same average motivic length of approximately eleven measures.

The secondary aspect of reprise in the closing frame is the partial return of the waltz suite. The first theme from the suite to appear is Motive 14, which enters obliquely halfway through Phase 1. Referring to table 6.3, we see that the closing frame reprises the opening frame from its beginning and proceeds in order through its sequence of motives. Motive 5 interrupts this progression early on to form a second, competing narrative strand but is assimilated into the first when the two strands converge (R59). However, at the moment that Motive 5 becomes part of the primary strand, a new secondary strand is born. Alternating with Motive 5, this strand begins with a new theme, Motive 18, and then progresses in retrograde through several motives of the waltz suite—perhaps in emulation of memory's counterchronic processes—passing through Motive 14 before arriving at Motive 13, whose counterpoint with Motive 5 indicates a second convergence of the two strands. As if in celebration, the music erupts in a tutti fortissimo apotheosis of the previously demure Motive 12, thereby reaching the end of Phase 1.

By initially presenting two long stretches of motives from the waltz suite in their original order, Phase 2 seems to confirm the ascendancy of the waltz suite over the opening frame. Aspects of the score challenge this conclusion, however. Together with various chromatic techniques—a gradually ascending ostinato and bass line, as well as a progression of harmonies under grotesque distortion from an expected sequence of diatonic tonics, dominants, and subdominants—the extension of Motive 15 by an additional twenty measures disfigures this waltz into an uncanny double of its original version. In its uncontrolled excess Motive 15 neither leads into Motive 16 nor cadences on its own but rather only increases its whirling until it nearly annihilates itself. In fact, *La valse* might have ended here had Motive 16 not granted it a temporary reprieve. Nonetheless, the return to normalcy implied in the initial tempo for Motive 16 ("Mouvement du début") is all too brief; the stretto that hastened Motive 15 to its end recurs at "Pressez" (R86), thereby sealing the fate of Motive 16, as well as the waltz suite reprise.

In the wake of the waltz suite's aborted attempts at a full reprise, Motive 8 reasserts the primacy of the relation between the two frames, forming the climactic endpoint for both and interrelating their phases in a similar way. As we have seen, Phase 2 of the opening frame redeems various materials of Phase 1 by transforming them from chromatic to diatonic and from fragments into wholes. Along these lines, Motive 8 can also be considered to redeem Motive 5 by sharing the latter's rhythmic profile (a hemiola, shifted forward by one beat) and occupying approximately the same relative position within its phase but boasting an expanded phrase length and a more triumphant affect. In recalling both motives from the opening frame, the closing frame keeps their relationship largely intact. Motives 5 and 8 still play a central role in their respective phases, as shown by the vertical brackets in table 6.3. However, while Motive 5 ultimately loses its contest with materials from the waltz suite, yielding to Motive 12 at the end of Phase 1, Motive 8 has the last word—an utterance, however, that teeters on the brink of coherence. Interrupted six times over the course of its ninety measures, Motive 8 in the closing frame is conspicuous for lacking the stability it enjoyed in the opening frame.

In both the opening and closing frames, the fates of Motive 8 and memory are intertwined. The opening frame remembered the past in six stages, gradually overcoming the forces of oblivion in Phase 1 that kept the past fragmentary until it finally attains Motive 8 at the end of Phase 2 as an image of the past made present and whole. Although the closing frame assumes the opening frame as its model, it either cannot or will not quell the destructive tendencies of forgetting. Consequently, the materials in Phase 2 undergo the same fragmentation as those in Phase 1; Motive 8—the formerly inviolate image of memory's redemption of the past—is now rent into tatters.

As in the Epilogue of the *Valses nobles*, the fragmentation of the waltz in the final measures of *La valse* reminds us that the past was present only in memory, not in reality. Unlike the Epilogue, however, this truth is accompanied in *La valse* not by melancholy but by joy. The solution to this conundrum lies in Nietzsche's idea of the Dionysian, and the vehicle for the Dionysian in *La valse* is the musical-choreographic genre of the Bacchanale.

La valse as Bacchanale

The primary historical link between *La valse* and the Bacchanale is Ravel's association with Diaghilev's Ballets russes. Although Ravel first conceived of this project around 1906, a few years before the Russian Ballet took Paris by storm, he gradually reconceived it as a "choreographic poem" composed especially for the troupe. (Note, too, its dedication to the Russian Misia Sert, who, along with Calvocoressi, was a principal liaison between Ravel and Diaghilev.) Unfortunately, when Ravel auditioned the piece for Diaghilev in Sert's apartment in early 1920, the impresario rejected it with the infamous declaration that it was not suited for a ballet but was rather the "portrait" or "painting" of a ballet.[23] The rejection must have stung Ravel even more acutely than critics have imagined hitherto, insofar as he had already anticipated and accommodated the company's preference for bacchanalian endings by incorporating one into *La valse*. While Diaghilev certainly exploited the Bacchanale as a formula for finales, it was Mikhail Fokin, the company's first choreographer, who introduced it into the Russian Ballet's repertory. Lynn Garafola locates its original use in *La vigne* (1906), in which "the tipplers and the wines they tippled came together for a final Bacchic rout. This ending, a variation on the traditional coda, became the prototype of the frenzied, freewheeling crowds that sent shudders of excitement through Fokin's prewar audiences."[24]

If Diaghilev's Russian Ballet historically links *La valse* to the Bacchanale, *Daphnis et Chloé*, with its bacchanalian finale, links them musically. As discussed in previous chapters, before Ravel composed *La valse* he had gained firsthand experience with the Bacchanale through his collaboration with Fokin on *Daphnis et Chloé*. Ravel responded to criticism by the Russians of a first draft by transforming the finale from a rather short movement to a more elaborate and raucous Bacchanale.

The finale of *Daphnis* resembles *La valse* so strongly that we can reasonably consider the former to have been the model for the latter. Each piece is an ABA′ whose reprise begins at its midpoint. Frenetic looping and alternation of themes (A) lead to an initial climax and usher in a more leisurely thematic succession (B) before being recapitulated (A′). A battery of percussion at the moment of reprise provides added impetus for a final intensification, which stacks orchestral layer upon layer until it reaches a climactic plateau. After the plateau has endured multiple interruptions and interpolations, a foreshortened main theme bursts forth to bring the piece to a shattering end. Throughout, the texture is saturated by musical tropes of primal energy, massive movement, and sexual desire: chromatic surges, dynamic swells, and wavelike contours of various proportions, all of which are germane to the Bacchanale.

One conclusion we can draw from this resemblance concerns the genesis of *La valse*. Since the composition of *La valse* seems to have gained momentum only after Ravel had completed *Daphnis et Chloé* and was consequently able to reconceive *La valse* as a second Diaghilev production, we have good reason to speculate that the time and effort he spent revising the Bacchanale between 1910 and 1912 gave him the ideas and impetus he needed to complete *La valse*, one of his long-standing projects.

More important, however, the strong resemblance between the finale of *Daphnis* and *La valse* supports our tentative categorization of the latter as a Bacchanale. This is a significant insight, especially since listeners and scholars have long considered *La valse* as little more than a pastiche of the Straussian orchestral waltz. Who could blame them, after all? Neither the libretto nor the score refers explicitly to bacchanalian behavior; in fact, the opening tempo is marked "dans le mouvement d'une valse viennoise." While the label "Bacchanale" also does not appear in the finale of *Daphnis*, its libretto nonetheless makes its identity clear. It begins with "a group of girls dressed up like Bacchants" who run across the stage. Only after a group of boys appears on stage in lustful pursuit of the girls does the Bacchanale properly get under way, as marked in the libretto by the phrase "joyeux tumulte," in which the notion of *joie* denotes bacchanalian *jouissance* as much as the more mundane *plaisir* (to borrow Roland Barthes's well-known dichotomy). It is clear, then, that we are meant to understand the finale of *Daphnis* as a Bacchanale from its beginning, but when does *La valse* seem to make the transition from civilized dance to primitive revelry?

I propose that this transition occurs at the onset of the closing frame. I am not alone in perceiving a qualitative shift at this point; as we have already seen, Schorske and Benjamin understand this formal seam to mark a transition from integration to disintegration and from life to decay, respectively. In addition, Marcel Marnat finds the closing frame to "place into question" everything that previously transpired,[25] while Tobias Plebuch senses an exchange of "aestheticism" for "realism."[26] For these four authors the reprise of the first half of *La valse* in the second half strips the former of its pretensions, stabilities, and certainties—an act of critique whose violence and subversion mesh well with a conventional understanding of the Bacchanale.[27] It is less obvious, however, how our interpretation of the closing frame as a Bacchanale will interact with the overriding hermeneutics of memory in this chapter. To address this question, I now turn to Nietzsche's notion of the Dionysian, as laid out in his monograph, *The Birth of Tragedy out of the Spirit of Music* (1872).

As is well known, in this text the young philologist Nietzsche introduces the Dionysian as the counterpart of the Apollonian, which—in whatever cultural form it may appear—represents beauty, form, individual identity, moderation, and self-knowledge, as well as more fragile entities like visual appearance, illusion, and dreams. The Dionysian, on the other hand, is associated with instinct, immediacy, vitality, corporeality, the masses, formlessness, tragedy, ecstasy, intoxication, waves, floods, and excess. As one might guess from these two lists, this dichotomy flows naturally into issues of memory, whereby the Apollonian delights as much in preserving the past as the Dionysian obliterates it and all its attendant obligations in order to live fully in the present. However—and this is Nietzsche's fundamental point—despite its recognition of history as a tragic dance of death, the Dionysian does not withdraw into mourning and melancholy but rather celebrates destruction as a principle and consequence of life. Endowed with Dionysian wisdom:

> We are really for a brief moment primordial being itself, feeling its raging desire for existence and joy in existence; the struggle, the pain, the destruction of phenomena, now appear necessary to us, in view of the excess of countless forms of existence which force and push one another into life, in view of the exuberant fertility of the universal will. We are pierced by the maddening sting of these pains just when we have become, as it were, one with the infinite primordial joy in existence, and when we anticipate, in Dionysian ecstasy, the indestructibility and eternity of this joy. In spite of fear and pity, we are the happy living beings, not as individuals, but as the one living being, with whose creative joy we are united.[28]

Thus, when viewed from the standpoint of Nietzschean aesthetics, the transition from waltz to Bacchanale in *La valse* is best described as a movement from the Apollonian to the Dionysian. In the opening frame, a deficient present is redeemed by an Apollonian strategy: the gradual recreation of the glorious past in memory. Ravel's program for this section further assimilates it to the Apollonian; just as Nietzsche attributes "the image world of dreams" to the latter as its characteristic realm, so, too, does Ravel describe the reemergence of the past as a visual phenomenon.[29] Next, the waltz suite elaborates this aesthetic with an orderly procession of symmetrically phrased themes. In the closing frame, however, Ravel reprises previous material only to expose them to the forces of rapture and oblivion: Whereas the waltz was joyfully *re-membered* in the opening frame, here it is tragically *dismembered*—tragically in the Dionysian sense, however, one that celebrates life in all its destructive fury.

Our Dionysian interpretation of the closing frame not only enhances our own understanding of *La valse* but also resonates with several aspects of its historical reception. It retroactively provides a firm aesthetic basis for the numerous concert reviews of the piece that have associated its ecstatic gestures with visions of orgies and debauchery,[30] as well as Schorske's claim that "Ravel celebrates [rather than mourns] the destruction of the world of the waltz" in this piece, whose "frenzied" conclusion paints a quintessential portrait of the *fin-de-siècle* "psychological man," the servant of his "instinct" rather than his reason.[31] In addition, it resolves the discrepancy between Danuser's "triumph" and Benjamin's "decay" as adequate descriptors of the closing frame. If we view the closing frame as a Bacchanale rich in Dionysian wisdom, we do not actually have to choose between the two affects, for both are equally important and bound up with each other.

The most important commentary on *La valse* illuminated by this discussion, however, is Ravel's own. In an interview with André Révész published on May 1, 1924, in *ABC de Madrid*, the composer remarked that:

> Some people have seen in this piece the expression of a tragic affair; some have said that it represented the end of the Second Empire, others said that it was postwar Vienna. They are wrong. Certainly, *La valse* is tragic, but in the Greek sense: it is a fatal spinning around, the expression of vertigo and of the voluptuousness of the dance to the point of paroxysm.[32]

In light of this description of *La valse* as a Dionysian phenomenon, it is tempting to adduce it as proof that we have successfully recovered the composer's intentions, at least as far as the Bacchanale is concerned. Recent scholarship, however, has cast doubt upon the ability of Ravel's commentary on *La valse* to reveal anything about his original conception of the piece. After patiently reviewing this commentary and its circumstances, Deborah Mawer concludes that the piece was, for the composer, "about nothing more than the Viennese waltz itself" and that statements such as the one given earlier reflect Ravel's impulse to accommodate journalistic desire for interpretive scenarios rather than his intent to speak the truth about his intentions for the piece itself.[33] I agree with Mawer's basic skepticism toward naively taking composers' comments on their own work at face value, as well as her implicit appeal for interpretive restraint. Nevertheless, I feel that Ravel's description of *La valse* as tragic "in the Greek sense" fits our carefully constructed argument about its bacchanalian and Dionysian elements too well for us to dismiss it as either random coincidence, authorial whimsy, or red herring. I also do not think that Ravel was merely accommodating the press when he insisted, in a private letter to the choreographer of the world premiere of *La valse* in 1926, that it "must be considered as a sort of tragedy (I mean that in the Greek sense, naturally, and I do not require that one disembowels oneself)."[34] Even when Ravel does not explicitly liken *La valse* to Greek tragedy, he still inscribes it beneath a Dionysian rubric—take, for example, his remark in an interview published in *De Telegraaf* on September 30, 1922, in which he depicts

La valse as "a dancing, whirling, almost hallucinatory ecstasy, an increasingly passionate and exhausting whirlwind of dancers, who are overcome and exhilarated by nothing but 'the waltz.' "[35] Given the rich cultural history of the waltz, as well as its infinite adaptability to all sorts of musical idioms and dramatic contexts, to reduce *La valse* to "nothing but 'the waltz' " actually opens it up to a world of possibilities.

I suggested earlier that Ravel was able to complete *La valse* only after having worked through the idea of the Bacchanale during his revision of the *Daphnis* finale. This does not mean, however, that his reconceptualization of *La valse* as a Bacchanale was wholly different from and incompatible with its original conception—on the contrary. His first documented reference to *La valse* appears in a February 7, 1906, letter to Jean Marnold, in which he not only revealed his plan to write a "grand waltz" but also justified it by confessing his "deep sympathy for these wonderful rhythms" and "the *joie de vivre* expressed by the dance."[36] It is only natural for us to pass over this common French phrase without a second thought, but its context here gives it a special charge. First of all, *joie* will eventually seed the "joyeux tumulte" of the Bacchanale in *Daphnis* and, by extension, *La valse*. Second, Ravel uses this expression in writing to a person for whom "joy in living" might have extraordinary significance as a tenet of philosophical vitalism. Music critic for the *Mercure de France*, Jean Marnold (1859–1935) was not simply one of Ravel's friends but had also coauthored a few years earlier (c. 1900) the first French translation of the *Birth of Tragedy*, which was all the more prominent for having appeared as volume 1 of Nietzsche's *Œuvres complètes*.[37] Who would have grasped *joie de vivre*—or, in the philosopher's hyperbolic terms, the "infinite primordial joy in existence"—in its full Dionysian potential better than Marnold?

In Retrospect

Ravel's two waltz suites—the *Valses nobles et sentimentales* and *La valse*—are substantial and complex enough to support a variety of analytical approaches. In these two case studies I chose to focus on the music framing the waltz suites rather than the suites themselves. On the one hand, the frames provided a meaningful context for the object being framed; in both pieces, their fragmentation and defamiliarization of the waltz revealed its historical contingency and fragility. On the other hand, the frames were also treated as worthwhile ends in themselves, exemplary reenactments of remembering-in-music, whose analysis can lead to diverse insights, particularly into dialectical aspects of memory—the inextricable entwinement of remembering and forgetting, past and present, and so on. The diversity of these insights results, in part, from the unique perspectives on memory and the waltz that each frame adopts: The Epilogue of the *Valses nobles* mourns

Example 6.3 The "Backward Glance" in *La valse.*

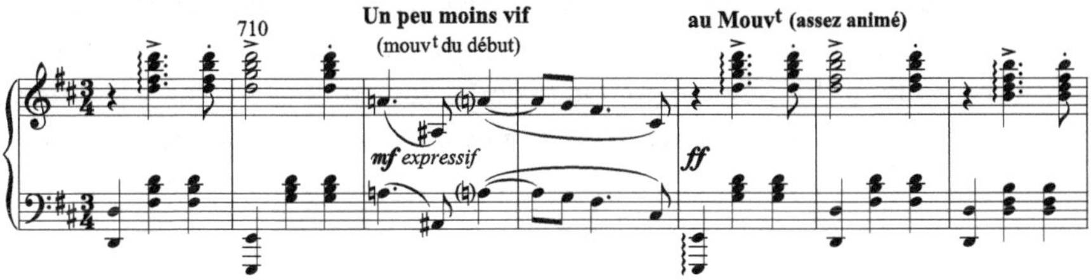

the loss and ruination of the past represented by the waltz, the opening frame of *La valse* rejoices in its virtual revivification in memory, and the closing frame remembers it once more only to ecstatically dismember it in a bacchanalian frenzy. Following Nietzsche further, we might even say that memory in Ravel is not only a melancholy art but also a gay science.

I conclude by discussing a detail that we have so far overlooked: the brief hiatus of activity at the end of *La valse,* which we may call its "backward glance" and which sets the dialectics of memory into striking relief while also recalling the Final Embrace from the end of *Daphnis,* as discussed in the Introduction.

In example 6.3 the tutti fortissimo orchestra is suddenly and briefly suspended, allowing a small ensemble of winds and strings to play two measures of Motive 9—the delicate and insouciant waltz that originally opened the interior suite—before it picks up where it left off and drives toward the shattering conclusion of the piece.[38] Since Motive 8 directly precedes Motive 9, Ravel is simply allowing the A section to pass once again into the B section; the irony, of course, is that the great contrast between the two materials renders this formal plausibility implausible.

As with many moments of irony, the backward glance can make us laugh as easily as cry. From the standpoint of the Dionysian reveler, this retrospective swivel is only a brief, trifling, and perhaps even amusing distraction from the destructive ecstasies of oblivion. For the Apollonian individual, however—one filled with reverence and longing for the past—it evokes intense nostalgia and melancholy, expressing as it does the drastic truth that dreamy reminiscence has no place in a brutal reality. Ravel would have been highly sensitive to this issue at this point in his life since the period in which he composed *La valse* coincided with a period of mourning for his beloved mother, Marie Delouart, who died on January 5, 1917, while Ravel was still a soldier at the front. Writing to Madame Casella from his mountain refuge in Lapras in the winter of 1919–1920, Ravel confessed that "I think about her every day, or rather every minute. Especially now that I've started to work again [on *La valse*] and think back to those happy moments when I left her. . . . Naturally, I am not doing so well but I am slogging away [*je turbine*]."[39]

Here, as elsewhere in his correspondence, Ravel takes advantage of a pun: In colloquial French the verb *turbiner* means "to work hard," but its literal sense is to move like a turbine—to spin fast and mechanically, like the dancers in *La valse*. Thus, the waltz of this "choreographic poem"—sometimes graceful, sometimes frenetic—also engraves an image of the composer, who keeps his pen in constant motion for fear that a pause may cause his mind to revert to the past and know, in a backward glance reminiscent of Orpheus himself, what he has irretrievably lost.

Conclusion: In the Footsteps of the Faun

In the course of this book, we have encountered a motley band of decadent figures: the melancholic Pierrot of the *commedia dell'arte,* the lustful Abbot of the *fête galante,* the neurotic des Esseintes of Huysmans's *À rebours,* the precious dandies of Baudelaire and Barbey d'Aurevilly, the androgynous male protagonist of *Daphnis et Chloé,* the nostalgic subject of the *Valses nobles,* and the Dionysian reveler of *La valse,* among others. The one, however, that best embodies memory, sublimation, and desire is the faun of Mallarmé's eclogue, "L'après-midi d'un faune" (1876). As we follow in the footsteps of the faun in this final chapter, tracking his path through Mallarmé, Debussy, and Ravel, we open up one more perspective on the importance of these three topics for the music and literature of this period. In addition, by ending our investigations at a point of departure—Debussy's *Prélude à "L'après-midi d'un faune"* (1894), which was exemplary for Ravel at the beginning of his career as a composer—we are emulating memory in its *cancrizans* ability to progress by regression, to move forward by moving backward in time. This instance of performativity should not surprise us too much: It is a time-honored characteristic of writing on decadence to become decadent itself, absorbing the qualities of its object of study in another instance of the perennial decay of boundaries.[1]

Ces nymphes, je les veux perpétuer.

The centrality to Mallarme's poem of memory, sublimation, and desire is apparent from the beginning. The famous opening statement of the poem—"These nymphs, I want to perpetuate them"—manifests the faun's desire by an outright declaration of intent ("je les veux") and a rhetorical emphasis placed on its object: The word "nymphes" is forefronted, set apart from the rest of the line by a comma, underlined by the demonstrative adjective "ces," and reiterated in the pronoun "les."[2] Lest we suppose that we can reduce the faun to his bestial half and view him as merely an animal in heat, Mallarmé ends the line by qualifying the faun's desire as a will to "perpetuate" the nymphs.[3] Whatever this phrase might mean, it exceeds the simple idea of ravishing them, as becomes clear upon comparing this line with its varied appearance in the two previous versions of the poem. In the original version, titled "Monologue d'un faune" (1865), the first line portrays the faun's desire in its pure lust; right after two nymphs slip from his embrace, he raises himself up from the ground and proclaims, "J'avais des nymphes!"[4] [I had some nymphs!]. It is in the second version of the poem, the "Improvisation d'un faune" (1875), that the first line is fundamentally altered; its only semantic difference from the final version is the faun's wish to "astonish" (*émerveiller*) rather than perpetuate the nymphs.[5] The final version of the first line thus enriches the characterization of the faun by counterposing his desire with its sublimation, contrasting the vertical intensity of the former with the horizontal "perpetuation" of the latter, which displaces the expression and gratification of desire into rituals of courtship, acts of memory and fantasy, and artistic creation, all of which play a role in the poem. This juxtaposition captures the faun in his hybridity as a volatile contradiction of man and animal, mind and body, reflection and instinct, enmeshing him in decadent dialectics, just as Robert Greer Cohn noted when describing Mallarmé's faun as "a son of late civilization, a *homo duplex* torn between extreme opposites."[6]

> *Ces nymphes, je les veux perpétuer.*
>
> *Si clair,*
> *Leur incarnat léger, qu'il voltige dans l'air*
> *Assoupi de sommeils touffus.*
>
> *Aimai-je un rêve?*

Situated at the end of the line, "perpétuer" fades off into the white of the page (the Mallarméan *blanc*) just as the stressed open vowel at its end resounds beyond the punctuating period, both of which seem to evoke the faun's mental perpetuation of the nymphs through what I have been calling "ruminescence." The verb does not end the twelve-syllable alexandrine, however, which allows the end of the first semantic unit ("perpétuer") to dovetail into the beginning of the second ("Si clair,"), thereby asserting the flow of thought against the regulative structure of the verse. The second blank space, which separates the second sentence from the third—"Aimai-je un rêve?" [Did I love a dream?]—operates more negatively than the first by registering the doubt that has crept into the faun's ruminescence and forestalled it.[7] The faun now stands before his basic predicament, which is commonly identified as his uncertainty whether the encounter with the nymphs was real or imaginary. Although this description is valid, it is more appropriate for our purposes to frame the predicament by the general philosophical problem it raises: the indeterminable position of memory between past and present, reproduction and representation, recollection and imagination, truth and falsehood, and related dichotomies—in other words, its dialectics.

Memory in "L'après-midi" is of such a quality and an importance that it reaches beyond mere content to give form to the 110-line poem; each attempt by the faun to remember the past—at "Réfléchissons . . ." [Let's think back; line 8], "O bords siciliens d'un calme marécage / . . . CONTEZ" [O Sicilian shores of a calm marsh / . . . TELL; lines 23–25), and "O nymphes, regonflons des SOUVENIRS divers" [O nymphs, let us reinflate various MEMORIES; line 62]—promises to renew the poem but is repeatedly frustrated by the dialectics of memory. Just as the faun is settling into his reflections during the *blanc* that follows "Réfléchissons . . .," the troubling overlap between memory and imagination rears up to disrupt his reverie, prompting him to ask himself "ou si les femmes dont tu gloses / figurent un souhait de tes sens fabuleux!" (or whether the women you are glossing / represent a wish of your fabulous senses! [lines 9–10]).[8] As this train of thought comes to an end, the faun attempts once more to recollect the encounter but now with more focus and urgency, as evident in his melodramatic appeal to the "Sicilian shores" and an array of new typographies: majuscules for the imperative "CONTEZ," as well as quotation marks and italics to highlight the narrated memory. For a second time, his effort to remember is derailed by the possibility that the nymphs were merely projections of his sexual desire. After an abortive attempt to sublimate this desire into art by improvising on his panpipes (lines 42–51), he finally confronts and accepts memory's dialectic with fantasy. No longer will he allow himself to be stymied by his conscience, which demands that he definitively distinguish between "true" memories and "false" imaginations, but instead begins to spin forth an extended narrative of his encounter with the nymphs, however fictional it might be. He likens this act of the mnemonic imagination to reinflating a bunch of grapes (with the poet's inspiring breath, that is) after having sucked them dry of their juice, then holding them up to the sun and peering through their "luminous skins" until evening falls—a perfect image of ruminescence.[9] From our vantage point, the particular interest of this conceit lies in its decadent dialectics: a heady mélange of both idyllic reflection and bacchanalian inebriation, memory and oblivion, a desire both sublimated and desublimated by its transformation into artful narrative; as presaged by the unusual locution of "reinflating" memories, as well as the typographical inflation of the word "souvenirs" [memories] by majuscules, his narration of sexual dalliance ends up arousing him once more to his "primal fervor, / erect and alone" (lines 35–36) and even provokes ecstatic verbal ejaculations—"Je t'adore, courroux des vierges . . ." [I adore you, wrath of virgins . . .] (lines 75–81)—that interrupt the recollection at its midpoint.[10]

Memory, sublimation, and desire inform "L'après-midi" so strongly that their ability to interrelate Mallarmé's poem and Debussy's tone poem should come as little surprise.[11] In the poem, as well as the Ovidian myth of Pan and Syrinx, on which the poem is ultimately based, the faun's panpipes are not only his *vade mecum* but also his *alter ego*—his better half, which translates his rude desires into

Example C.1 The Opening Theme of Debussy's *Prélude à "L'Après-midi d'un faune"* (mm. 1-4). Arrangement for solo piano by Ladislas Kun. Used by Permission of Edward B. Marks Music Corporation.

elegant melody.[12] Thus, when we hear the solo flute theme of example C.1, which begins the *Prélude à "L'après-midi d'un faune,"* it is perfectly reasonable that we imagine it as not merely the sound of the solitary faun, improvising on his pipes as he wakes up from his nap, but rather a musical surrogate for the faun himself. Although this theme eventually passes to other instruments (m. 31) and is transformed with every iteration, it is nevertheless the red thread that binds together the entire piece—often described as a series of variations on the opening theme—just as the faun's presence unifies the somewhat disjunct narrative of the poem.[13] If the faun theme is the "sonore, vaine et monotone ligne" (line 51) of the flute melody into which he tries to sublimate his sexual desires and thereby "perpetuate" the nymphs in musical reminiscence, and if the entire piece is the elaboration of this theme, then the *Prélude* as a whole represents the sublimation of desire into music, a possibility that accounts neatly for its seemingly infinite lyricism, not to mention its remarkable continuity of theme, texture, and tempo.[14]

Within the overall continuity of the *Prélude* three moments of relative discontinuity stand out, attracting attention and provoking interpretation. One of these is the unmediated juxtaposition of two contrasting statements of the faun theme, which happens twice in a row toward the end of the piece (mm. 79–93); example C.2 reproduces the first of these juxtapositions. Whereas the first part presents the theme in its original tempo and with noble lyricism, the second shatters the sustained line with a battery of syncopations and articulations and shifts into a livelier tempo. Each composite phrase conjures up a dialectical image of the faun, torn between composure and abandon, due to not only the internal juxtapositions but also the fact that the second thematic statement yields both times to scampering textures that seem to paint the nymphs fleeing before him and his lust (mm. 85 and 91–92).

A second moment is the horn call (m. 5) that follows the opening statement of the faun theme and appears in example C.3. It makes sense for commentators to have interpreted it as the musical correlative to "Aimai-je un rêve?": Just as the question interrupts the faun's reminiscence, so, too, does the horn call contrast with the faun theme in melody, harmony, and instrumentation, introduce the

Example C.2 A Portrait of the Faun in the *Prélude,* Torn between Composure and Abandon (mm. 79-85). Arrangement for solo piano by Ladislas Kun. Used by Permission of Edward B. Marks Music Corporation.

only measure of silence in the whole piece—akin to the *blanc* that follows the question in the poem—and precipitate the end of the first phrase. I would go even further to suggest that the call is not merely the nagging of doubt but also an invitation to memory and desire that provides the piece with impetus and purpose, just as the question did for the poem. Regarding desire, the snapped

Example C.3 The Opening Horn Call in the *Prélude* (mm. 4–5). Arrangement for solo piano by Ladislas Kun. Used by Permission of Edward B. Marks Music Corporation.

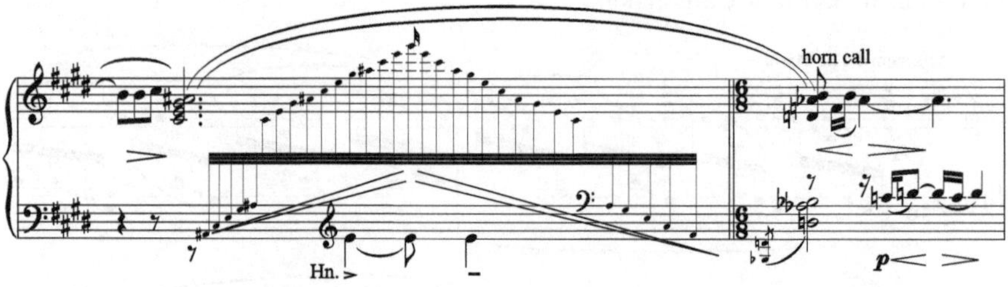

Example C.4 The Transformed and Amplified Statement of the Horn Call in the Second Phrase of the *Prélude* (mm. 17-20). Arrangement for solo piano by Ladislas Kun. Used by Permission of Edward B. Marks Music Corporation.

rhythm, hooked contour, and undular secondary motive of the call lend it a beckoning quality similar to the seductive melodies of Debussy's "Sirènes," while the rich harmony and timbre of its accompaniment heighten the sensuality of its appeal; when the call returns in the subsequent phrase (mm. 17–20, reproduced in example C.4), its amplified instrumentation and surging, *Tristan*-esque dynamics only strengthen its association with desire. Regarding memory, the horn's timbre and its subsequent echoing in the opening phrase make it seem to come from a distant point in time or space.[15] Likewise, its increased sonority in the second phrase, as well as its partial assimilation to the faun theme by means of its altered contour, suggests that it is becoming more present to mind as the faun continues to rouse himself from sleep.

The third moment of relative discontinuity is the interior section in D♭ major (mm. 55–78), which brings our interpretation of memory, sublimation, and desire in the *Prélude* to a head. Although its main melody is literally new, it is often analyzed as another transformation of the faun theme. Once again, I would

Example C.5 The Interior Melody of the *Prélude* as a Synthesis of the Faun Theme and the Horn Call (mm. 55-58). Arrangement for solo piano by Ladislas Kun. Used by Permission of Edward B. Marks Music Corporation.

go further to assert that it synthesizes both the faun theme and the call, combining the pitches, contour, and sostenuto lyricism of the former with the pitches and flat-key area of the latter, as shown in example C.5. Simultaneously a point of arrival, a point of departure, and a midpoint, it plays the same role in the *Prélude* that the line "O nymphs, let's reinflate our MEMORIES" did in the poem.[16] In fact, it may well paint that exact line: The apparent melodic allusion to the Chopin Nocturne in D♭ major, op. 27, no. 2, makes it a memory, both themes are conspicuously "inflated" to form the new cantilena—as is the faun theme's characteristic C♯, which, respelled as D♭, now appears in the bass as the head of the abbreviated theme and as the tonic for the entire section—and the section reconciles opposing themes, just as the third bout of recollection in the poem reconciled two binarisms: memory and fantasy, and the subject and remembered/imagined object of desire, fused now into the first-person plural of "let us reinflate."[17] In retrospect, the repeated return to the faun theme in the *Prélude,* which culminates in the episode in D♭ major, may correlate to the repeated effort by the faun to remember, which culminates in the "SOUVENIRS" episode.[18]

For Ravel, Debussy's *Prélude* was the pinnacle of modern French music and possibly of the Western classical-music tradition as a whole. He often testified to its value in public interviews and private conversations: At one time, he declared it to be "the unique miracle in all of music,"[19] while at another, he referred to it as "the only score ever written that is absolutely perfect";[20] one reporter even noted that, when Ravel began to discuss the *Prélude,* the composer suddenly became "pensive, his gaze lost in a sort of vision," and "said very simply that his dearest wish would be to be able to die gently lulled in [its] tender and voluptuous embrace."[21] Although Ravel never published a detailed analysis of the piece, he nevertheless made a few remarks that help to explain his esteem for it. In an essay written sometime after 1913, he described Debussy's "symphonic poem" as "supple, undulating, gently tinted, and of unprecedented fluidity."[22] Elsewhere, he rounded out this assessment by observing that the *Prélude* is "intensely rich in musical matter,"[23] thereby eluding any attempt to understand "how it had been built up."[24]

Example C.6 The *Prélude*-like Accompaniment for Gonsalve's "Le Jardin des Heures" in *L'heure espagnole,* Scene IV.

It should come as no surprise that Ravel, who viewed perfection as a leading goal of composition, should make both musical and verbal homages to Debussy's "perfect" piece.[25] His most direct acknowledgement of the *Prélude* is his 1910 transcription of it for piano four hands, while a close second is its parody in the music he wrote for Gonsalve, the poet-suitor in *L'heure espagnole,* whose serenades are accompanied by *Prélude*-like textures such as the one for "Le jardin des heures," shown in example C.6.[26]

Other, less explicit homages are no less compelling. One is *Shéhérazade* (1903), the early song cycle in which Ravel himself identified "Debussy's influence, at least spiritual":[27] Note, in particular, the undular barcarolle of "Asie," the alternately melancholic and capricious flute arabesques of "La flûte enchantée," and the sensual ruminescence of the E-major "L'indifférent"—by far the most Debussyan of the three and not only because Ravel dedicated it to his future wife, still "Madame Sigismond Bardac."[28]

As can be surmised from Ravel's description of the *Prélude* as "supple, undulating," and "of unprecedented fluidity," an even more significant, albeit indirect and possibly unintentional homage (if such a notion is not too oxymoronic) is his series of water pieces for piano, especially *Jeux d'eau* (1901) and "Ondine" from *Gaspard de la nuit* (1908).[29] Ravel's cursory remark that *Jeux d'eau* is "based on two themes, like the first movement of a sonata,"[30] is misleading since, like Debussy's *Prélude,* it is more invested in continuously unfolding and proliferating new themes and textures than demonstrating bithematicism or articulating sonata form.[31] The strongest principle of form in *Jeux d'eau* is its cycle of sublimation-desublimation-resublimation, which begins in a gentle idyll, intensifies toward a bacchanalian climax at its midpoint (mm. 38–50), and gradually reestablishes the idyll as it draws to a close (mm. 80–83). This cycle also governs "Ondine," whose architecture is as fluid as the watery palace in the eponymous poem by Aloysius Bertrand. Like the *Prélude,* "Ondine" draws its inspiration from a mythological figure (the water nymph) that combines the human and the natural in a way that is both seductive and threatening. In addition, it transforms its opening melody (mm. 2–4) so gradually throughout the piece as to make it impossible, on simple audition, to determine "how it was

Table C.1 **Palindromic Ordering in the Thematic Design of "Ondine."**

								developmental interior										
Theme:	v	1a	1b	1a'	1c	1d	2	1a	3	1a	3	2	3	2	1d	1a'	1b	v
Measure:	0	2	10	14	16	22	32	42	45	47	50	52	57	66	72	80	84	89
Palindromic Module:	1	2	3	4		5	6		7		7		7	6	5	4	3	1

built up." Moreover, as shown in table C.1, the thematic design of "Ondine" is loosely but noticeably palindromic—even more than *Jeux d'eau*, which bows to convention in reprising its opening measures shortly after its interior climax—and thereby further resembles the *Prélude*, which Arthur Wenk has convincingly analyzed as a palindrome.[32]

While Ravel may have created a host of homages to the *Prélude*, the opportunity to pay homage to both Mallarmé's poem and Debussy's music arose only when he was commissioned to compose the score for *Daphnis et Chloé*. In the ancient Greek novel by Longus, Daphnis and Chloe thank Pan for saving her from her abductors by reenacting the myth of Pan and Syrinx, the Ovidian myth of metamorphosis, which provided a strong point of reference for Mallarmé's poem. Longus recounts the myth as follows:

> Pan started to chase her, intending to use violence. Syrinx ran away from Pan and his violence. When she got tired in her running, she hid among some reeds and vanished completely into a marsh. Pan angrily cut down the reeds, but he couldn't find the girl. When he understood what she had suffered, he invented the Panpipes: he blew into the reeds, after fastening together reeds of unequal length because their love had been ill matched.[33]

In the process of transforming the novel into a ballet, Fokin and Ravel incorporated the reenactment of the myth as a pantomime/pas de deux and situated it between the couple's reunion in the Daybreak and betrothal at the beginning of the Bacchanale.[34] The Pantomime reproduces the myth as told in the novel and diverges from it only when Pan begins to play his melancholy tune in memory of Syrinx, at which moment Chloe reappears in the ballet—but not in the novel—to "figure, by her dance, the accents of the flute." As the flute solo gradually becomes more frenzied and reaches a climax, Chloe spins in a "death spiral" (*tournoiement de mort*) and collapses in exhaustion. Attempts by Daphnis to revive her lead to a resplendent coda, which ends the scene on a celebratory note. Both musically and dramatically the Pantomime forms an ABA', where A is the Encounter between Pan and Syrinx, B is Pan's Reminiscence, and A' is Chloe's Resuscitation by Daphnis.

As one might predict, the main site of homage is Pan's Reminiscence, which divides into a slow first half (RR176–179) and a fast second half (RR180–187). During the first half, Pan sublimates his frustrated libido into an improvisation on his panpipes, whose "melancholy" quality expresses his regret over losing Syrinx. During the second half, the sublimation deteriorates back into lust as he reimagines his pursuit of her. Her collapse at the end of this pursuit is ostensibly a metaphor for the result of his violence toward her, as represented figuratively in the myth when Pan "angrily" cuts down the reeds into which she had been transformed. This also points to the importance of the myth, which provides an etiology not merely of the flute, as Roland-Manuel and Jankélévitch have noted, but rather of music as the unstable sublimation of violent (male) sexual desire.[35] On the one hand, this insight gives a more sinister resonance to those lines in Mallarmé's poem, where the faun describes, with the seeming innocence of an artist, how he cut down the "hollow reeds tamed / By talent" (lines 26–27). On the other, it invests the myth, and the Pantomime along with it, with the power to illustrate the Benjaminian maxim that every cultural artifact—here, music, most of all—is also a testament of barbarity.[36]

Ravel's homage to Debussy in Pan's Reminiscence, though modest, is easy to identify. As indicated in example C.7, the most salient gesture is the melody's stepwise descent in triplets, which recalls the "flowing motif" of the *Prélude*.[37] Others include the "expressive et supple" opening scalar ascent to the supertonic, reminding us of not only the opening measures of "La flûte de Pan" from Debussy's *Chansons de Bilitis* (example C.8) but also the subtle shading of harmony throughout the Reminiscence, which brings to mind the "gentle tinting" of the *Prélude*. When compared to Pan's Reminiscence, however, the allusion to the *Prélude* at the beginning of *Daphnis* is relatively stronger, placing a theme for the solo flute (NYMPHES) after one for the solo horn (DC) in fine pastoral fashion. One possible reason that the allusion to Debussy is more subtle in the Pantomime than we might have expected is that Ravel did not need to make more than a slight nod to acknowledge his predecessor. Another is that Ravel saw himself in competition with Debussy—and possibly also Mallarmé—for the more powerful rendering of this archetypal scenario; more overt and extensive allusions to Debussy would have threatened to both detract and distract from its originality. During the season of its premiere performance in 1912, *Daphnis* lost to the *Prélude* in its claim for attention, with Nijinsky's shocking "two-dimensional" choreography for Debussy's piece completely overshadowing *Daphnis* with its comparatively tame choreography by Fokin.[38]

The Pantomime is not simply an allusion to "L'après-midi" since the myth of Pan and Syrinx was already part of the literary source for *Daphnis et Chloé*. Nonetheless, when we consider the context of its reception—a society for whom Mallarmé's poem, not to mention Debussy's *Prélude*, had already become a modern masterpiece of French art—it is hard to imagine that the Pantomime would not have made a member of this society automatically think of "L'après-midi" and that Ravel would not have realized this as well and responded to it in his music; even in a brief reference to this scene Roland-Manuel felt compelled to explicitly quote

Example C.7 The Opening to "Pan's Reminiscence" from *Daphnis* (R176).

Example C.8 The Opening to "La flûte de Pan" from Debussy's *Chansons de Bilitis* (mm. 1–2).

"L'après-midi" by describing the interior episode as the " 'long solo' " (line 45) of Pan's flute.[39]

As a putative response to its two illustrious forebears, the Pantomime renders the central themes of Mallarmé's poem more clearly and emphatically than Debussy's *Prélude*. Like the poem, the Pantomime highlights memory and imagination by making the mind the primary arena of activity, as can easily be felt in the juxtaposition between the brief physical Encounter (18 mm.) and the lengthier and more elaborate Reminiscence (77 mm.). The gesture of sublimation in Pan's Reminiscence is also more acute: Whereas Debussy's flute peaks around C6, Ravel's flute exceeds this pitch height several times and even hovers about a G♯6 for the first three measures, thereby placing the following key lines from Mallarmé's poem into greater relief: "And to make, as *high* as love modulates, / A sonorous, vain, and monotone line, / Distilled from banal thought of back / Or pure thigh, pursued by my inner glances" (lines 48–51).[40] Moreover, the Pantomime's clear separation between the encounter and its recollection enables Ravel to articulate the mnemonic act in a way the *Prélude* does not: Note the

Example C.9 The Inversion of Syrinx's Motive from the "Encounter" (a) into "Pan's Reminiscence" (b).

contour inversion or "reflection" of Syrinx's theme into the main motive of the flute solo (example C.9), as well as the return of Chloe, presumably still as Syrinx, at the beginning of that solo. The repetition of Syrinx's musical motive and physical image after she has disappeared for good makes explicit the reproductive activity of memory, while their transformation calls attention to the intertwining of memory and imagination. In particular, the indication in the ballet libretto that Chloe is no longer an autonomous character but "*figure*, par sa danse, les accents de la Flûte" resonates, both in word and concept, with the faun's uncertainty in the poem whether the nymphs "*figurent* un souhait de tes sens fabuleux!" (line 9; italics mine). Bound to Pan's improvisation like a doll to the fingers of a marionettist, the revenant Syrinx is thus best interpreted as the wish fulfillment of Pan's sexual fantasies, made visible.[41] Accordingly, her dance is a dance of seduction, as evident in its slow, mesmerizing accompaniment, which recalls not only the sultry habaneras from the *Rapsodie espagnole* and *L'heure espagnole* (especially Gonsalve's "O impérieuse maîtresse" from scene 14) but also the veil dance of the archdecadent Salome from Strauss's opera, which Ravel admired and knew well.[42]

While Ravel still draws, in the first half of Pan's Reminiscence, from the "supple, undular, gently tinted," and "fluid" sound world of Debussy's *Prélude*, he departs from it in the second half, which explores the violence of sexual desire in a way that the *Prélude* never does; even at the moment of greatest potential violence in the *Prélude*, where it starts to surge with Wagnerian ardor (example C.4), Debussy abruptly truncates it and returns to a sublime version of the faun theme. Although Pan's Reminiscence ultimately represents the faun's desire at its extremes of melancholy and joy, delicate sublimation and indelicate violence, Ravel is still careful to create gradations of mood within the Reminiscence. Chromatic inner voices in the first half gradually compel a modulation from a doleful F♯ minor into its bright parallel major, only to succumb to a second bout of melancholy at the C minor of "Au mouvement" (R178). A brief transition (R179) with trills, arpeggios, and pizzicati ushers in the animated second half, which itself divides into two parts. The flute begins the first part (R180) capriciously—sporting staccati well-suited for a *pas de bourrée*—before swooping up and down in register and finally launching into citations of the bacchanalian War Dance from part two of the ballet (example C.10). Just as the music is about to reach a climax the second part intercedes (R184), apparently seeking to nullify the bacchanal by resetting the music at a slightly more "languorous" pace than the initial tempo

Example C.10 Apparent Citations in "Pan's Reminiscence" (a) from the "War Dance" (b and c).

a)

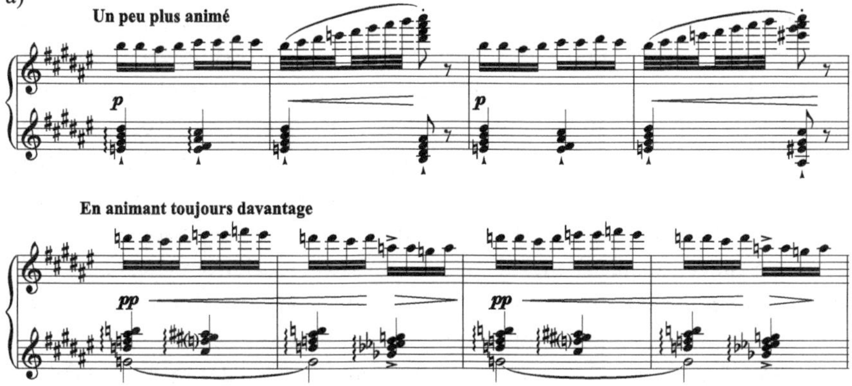

b)

c)

and reprising the dance accompaniment of the first half. However, as presaged by the drunken bitonality of the passage, which resembles the Trio from Waltz VII of the *Valses nobles,* the music soon reverts into a bacchanal. The final acceleration and self-combustion of Pan's Reminiscence not only anticipate the infernal round dance of the numbers in *L'enfant et les sortilèges* but also hark back to the internal climaxes of the two other faun pieces, *Jeux d'eau* and "Ondine," as well as the first movement of the String Quartet. Unlike these pieces, however, Pan's Reminiscence ends before it can regain its initial composure; only in the romance of Daphnis and Chloe—a reincarnation of the myth of Pan and Syrinx that is apparently more naïve than the original—does the violence of lust give way to the tenderness of love. Daphnis's resuscitation of Chloe at the end of the Pantomime thereby atones for Pan's crimes toward Syrinx.

As an interpretation of the myth of Pan and Syrinx, the Pantomime of *Daphnis et Chloé* is generally in accord with Mallarmé's poem but is not perfectly congruent with it. By allotting so much space and importance to memory, both implicitly refute the banal notion that memory is the mere disembodied shadow of experience and suggest instead that it is sensual, vital, and engrossing. However, while the faun in "L'après-midi" ultimately rejects music due to its inadequate expression of and compensation for unrequited desire, the diegetic music of Pan's Reminiscence fails because it keeps stirring up the desire it is supposed to have sublimated. For this reason, Pan's Reminiscence rivals "L'après-midi" in its decadence. For another, its clear demonstration of the faun's split personality reaches back to Baudelaire's decadent subject, which, as we recall from chapter 3, oscillates between the extremes of the "concentration" and "vaporization" of the self. For a third reason, the Pantomime's displacement of Syrinx from reality to fantasy, as well as its capitulation before violent, unmediated desire, bears a debt to Schopenhauer, whose philosophy of solipsism and pessimism was influential for French decadence.[43] Over and above their respective claims on decadence, however, "L'après-midi" remains an invaluable resource for understanding Pan's Reminiscence. As a case in point, the rich ambivalence of the adjective "vaine" (empty, vain, futile) in Mallarmé's "sonore, vaine et monotone ligne" helps us to plot the broad arc of the Reminiscence: from the emptiness of loss and solitude, to the vanity of memory and self-regard, and finally to the futility of sublimation.

The stereotypical, decadent, and typically exotic scenario of heterosexual desire and power, whereby a woman dances before an onlooking male, has already taken place in the ballet. In fact, the Pantomime is its third and final occurrence; since the first instance involved Lyceion dancing for a disinterested Daphnis, and the second involved an unwilling Chloe dancing for Bryaxis, this is actually the first time that the scenario correctly matches Chloe with Daphnis—though in masquerade as Syrinx and Pan. After *Daphnis*, it will recur once more in "Il est doux," the last song in the *Chansons madécasses* (1926). Although the prose poem is a piece of faux exoticism from the eighteenth century, it nevertheless evokes, or even seems to recall, "L'après-midi," a historical paradox that probably made Ravel grin: The first-person protagonist is a despotic male who orders women to entertain him—to sing and then to dance seductively—while he waits out the daytime heat in the shade of a "bushy tree" (*arbre touffu*, bringing to mind the *sommeils touffus* of the faun). Beginning with a languorous solo for the flute and remaining gentle (*doux*) throughout, "Il est doux" is an ode to hedonism closer in spirit to Debussy's *Prélude* than Pan's Reminiscence.

The final example of faun music in Ravel's work is the *Boléro* (1928). At first glance, the notion may seem absurd: How could a piece that Ravel himself described as having "no music in it" be compared to the *Prélude*, which he found "intensely rich in musical matter"?[44] The comparison begins to seem less preposterous, however, once we realize that the *Boléro*, like the *Prélude*, features a sinuous, exotic, improvisatory wind melody—of the "usual Spanish-Arabian kind,"[45] according to Ravel—that he imagined to unfold *en plein air* and whose multiple repetitions provide the basic material for the piece as a whole.[46] Unlike the *Prélude*, the melody of the *Boléro* does not develop freely but rather is restricted to two themes and welded to the two-measure ostinato of the accompaniment. Certain tones in the first theme are prolonged, with the variegate effect of heightening its quality of suspended, *Prélude*-like reverie, lengthening it by two measures, and loosening it from the metrical framework, as shown in example C.11;[47] in fact, its rhythmic abnormality is probably the reason that such a simple melody is notorious for being so hard to accurately reproduce from memory. Further, the melody is as variable in character as the flute in Pan's Reminiscence, evoking, in turn, the panpipes (cf. the flute of R0), the military fife (cf. the "tattoos" of mm. 15–18), and a more strident, exotic instrument, such as the Turkish *zurna* (cf. the high bassoon of R2). Finally, Ravel may not have actually expunged the *Prélude*'s principle of development from the thematic design of *Boléro* but merely sublimated it from pitch into the more refined parameter of timbre by giving each thematic statement a different instrumentation.

In sum, the *Prélude* seems to have provided the *Boléro* with a basic compositional idea that he altered in order to overcome Debussy's "neglect of form."[48] While the unvaried repetition of the melody and its ostinato accompaniment in *Boléro* may make it quite easy for us to say "how it was built up," it also gives the piece the shape and structure that the relatively invertebrate *Prélude* lacked. As a result, Ravel felt comfortable claiming the *Boléro* to be the only piece in which he completely succeeded in realizing his ideas—thereby, we may suppose, creating a work as close to "perfection" as Debussy's *Prélude*, albeit by somewhat different means.[49] Another aspect of the *Boléro* that qualifies it as faun music is its famous appeal to sensuality and sexuality. The appeal is mounted not only by its erotic combination of sinuous melody and rigid accompaniment—simultaneously arousing desire and holding off its satisfaction, as in the beginning of Pan's Reminiscence—but also its large-scale crescendo to the ecstatic E-major climax at its end (R18), recalling the Bacchanales of both *Daphnis* and *La valse*.[50] It comes then as little surprise that Bronislava Nijinska invoked the classic scenario of

Example C.11 The Opening Theme of the *Boléro* (a) and its Putative Normalization (b) through the Abbreviation of Prolonged Tones (*).

heterosexual desire in her choreography for the 1928 premiere of the *Boléro*, which featured Ida Rubinstein dancing alone on a table surrounded by men overcome by their lust for her.[51]

Ravel's putative homages to the fauns of Mallarmé and Debussy are neither idiosyncratic gestures nor isolated events but rather contribute to an unfolding testimonial to French Symbolism and Decadence by the artists and critics who lived during its heady floruit in the 1880s and 1890s. Just as important as the formal studies by literary historians such as André Barre, Henri Moulhiade, Tancrède de Visan, Albert Thibaudet, and Alfred Poizat, which started to appear around 1910,[52] were the more informal memoirs and essays by figures such as Albert Mockel, Henri de Régnier, Adolphe Retté, Gustave Kahn, André Fontainas, Émile Verhaeren, and Édouard Dujardin.[53] In fact, there is a more specific coincidence between Ravel's musical homages and these literary homages. In 1910 Remy de Gourmont—one of the most respected French literary critics of his time, particularly in regard to French Symbolism—published an essay on Mallarmé in *Le temps* that would eventually form part of the "Souvenirs du symbolisme" series in the fourth volume of his *Promenades littéraires* (1912).[54] In this essay he not only described "L'après-midi" as both a "milestone" (*une date*) and a "touchstone" in the history of French poetry but also admonished his readers that "we must not allow this treasure to be lost."[55] Further, the few poems he chose to illustrate Mallarmé's achievement included "Soupir" and "Surgi de la croupe et du bond." Although we will probably never know whether Ravel read this specific essay, it is still curious to note that he was simultaneously devoting himself to preserving the symbolist patrimony, not only composing (between 1909 and 1910) the Pantomime's implicit homage to "L'après-midi" but also setting "Soupir" and "Surgi" to music in 1913. Even if we choose to leave aside the question of the specific impulse behind Ravel's selection of texts for his *Trois poèmes de Stéphane Mallarmé*, we should not fail to recognize the larger testimonial project to which they contributed rather than simply ascribing them to the influence of Stravinsky, his *Three Japanese Lyrics*, and his reportage to Ravel about Schoenberg's *Pierrot lunaire*, as we have grown accustomed to doing.

Couple, adieu; je vais voir l'ombre que tu devins.

With its freestanding final line—"Couple, goodbye; I am going to see the shadow you became"—"L'après-midi" cycles back to the first line, thereby completing a large-scale couplet that frames the entire poem. All that the faun has realized and experienced during his meditation has changed him, however, making a true homecoming impossible. When he awoke, he aspired to "perpetuate" the nymphs and marveled at how clearly he still remembered their rosy flesh; now, as he returns to sleep, the nymphs have become a mere shadow, a twilit memory poised at the brink of oblivion. The coincidence with *Daphnis* is uncanny: not only does the ballet end with a valediction that bids adieu to its beloved couple by reprising the opening music, but the Valediction itself concludes with a twilit memory, the dusky and fragmentary Final Embrace. Though pagan, both the faun and the couple are equally victims of the Fall, implicated in a postlapsarian world of shadowy dialectics. In the hands of their decadent authors they have also become decadent subjects.

NOTES

Introduction

1. Irony and artificiality are identified as essential Decadent principles in Asti Hustvedt, "The Art of Death," 10–29. The most focused recent treatment of irony in Ravel's music is Stephen Zank, *Irony and Sound*, esp. 7–39.
2. A classic analysis of the discourse surrounding cultural degeneration in this period is Robert A. Nye, "Degeneration and the Medical Model of Cultural Crisis," 19–41, elaborated in Robert A. Nye, *Crime, Madness, and Politics*.
3. Nina Gubisch, "Le journal inédit de Ricardo Viñes," 190.
4. Maurice Ravel, "Memories of a Lazy Child," 393–395; here, 395 and 394, resp.
5. Two exceptions are Renato Calza, *Maurice Ravel nella storia della critica*, and Thomas Kabisch, "Ravel." Calza developed his thesis largely from a theory of interart *correspondances* (a "poetics of reflection") advanced by Claudio Casini in radio broadcasts and later consolidated in Claudio Casini, *Maurice Ravel*.
6. For an example of the latter, Gerald Abraham describes Ravel as an anti-Romantic classicist interested in " 'musical structure,' *tout simple*," and, in a volume published a few years later, credits Ravel with introducing "a variety of neo-classicism" that goes back at least to the String Quartet from 1903. Gerald Abraham, "The Reaction against Romanticism," 104, and Gerald Abraham, *The Concise Oxford History of Music*, 804. The description of Ravel as (neo)classicist—with "classicism" helping to sidestep the apparent anachronism of prewar neoclassicism—has become the default interpretation in Anglo-American music historiography, as evident in Robert P. Morgan, *Twentieth-Century Music*, 124–127, Elliott Antokoletz, *Twentieth-Century Music*, 82 and 90–92, and Donald Jay Grout and Claude V. Palisca, *A History of Western Music*, 678 and 685.
7. This critique figures centrally in Richard Gilman, *Decadence*.
8. This psychoanalytical critique is one of the main strands of Donald B. Kuspit, *The Dialectic of Decadence*.
9. Eugen Weber, *France*, 13.
10. Jann Pasler, *Composing the Citizen*, 358–400.
11. Robert A. Nye, "Degeneration," 19–41 passim.
12. This is one of the basic arguments in Debora Silverman, *Art Nouveau in* Fin-de-Siècle *France*.
13. One of the best-known contemporary endorsements of "decadence" is the following testimony from Verlaine: "I love the word Decadence, sparkling with purple and gold. I reject any insulting connotations it might have, and any notion of decline. Of course, on the contrary, this word presupposes highly civilized refined thought, a high degree of literary culture, a soul capable of intense pleasures." Quoted in Ernest Raynaud, *La mêlée*

symboliste: Portraits et souvenirs (Paris: La Renaissance du livre, 1918–1922), 63, which is cited in Robert Vilain, "Temporary Aesthetes," 211.

14. Michèle Hannoosh, *Parody and Decadence*, 36; Pamela A. Genova, *Symbolist Journals*, 84.
15. The specific text under critique by Pierrot is Guy Michaud, *Message poétique du symbolisme* (Paris: Nizet, 1947). In light of the fact that many decadent writers and artists were homosexual, Hanson has identified homophobia as "another reason why the decadents have been dismissed and trivialized by generations of literary critics." Ellis Hanson, *Decadence and Catholicism*, 24.
16. Jean Pierrot, *The Decadent Imagination*, 7; Anatole Baju, *L'école décadente*, 16; Arthur Symons, "The Decadent Movement in Literature," 858–867.
17. This list is culled from important scholarship on the Decadence such as Mario Praz, *The Romantic Agony* (originally published in Italian in 1930), Alfred E. Carter, *The Idea of Decadence in French Literature*; Koenraad W. Swart, *The Sense of Decadence in Nineteenth-Century France*; Pierrot, *The Decadent Imagination*; John R. Reed, *Decadent Style*; Jennifer Birkett, *The Sins of the Fathers*; Louis Marquèze-Pouey, *Le mouvement décadent en France*; Wolfdieterich Rasch, *Die literarische Décadence um 1900*; Matei Calinescu, *Five Faces of Modernity*; Barbara Spackman, *Decadent Genealogies*; David Weir, *Decadence and the Making of Modernism*; Hanson, *Decadence and Catholicism*; and Charles Bernheimer, *Decadent Subjects*. I am grateful to Stephen Arata for sharing with me a bibliography of studies in *fin-de-siècle* Victorian literature that helped to guide my initial research into the Decadence. The notion of the *ange-femme*, whose most famous representative in music is Mélisande, derives from Richard Langham Smith, "Debussy and the Pre-Raphaelites."
18. On this latter point, see Erwin Koppen, *Dekadenter Wagnerismus: Studien zur europaïschen Literatur des Fin de Siècle* (Berlin: de Gruyter, 1974).
19. Friedrich Nietzsche, "The Case of Wagner," 247.
20. The perception of a continuity between the Romantic *mal du siècle* and the Decadence is not specific to Praz alone but is also shared by Croce, Swart, Pierrot, Hanson, and others.
21. Weir, *Decadence*, 15; Nietzsche, "The Case of Wagner," 75. As I gradually transition from Decadence to decadence in this chapter, I begin to move more fluidly between the two terms as necessary, while seeking to remain sensitive to their difference.
22. Bernheimer, *Decadent Subjects*, 55.
23. Liz Constable, Dennis Denisoff, and Matthew Potolsky, "Introduction," 21. Italics in the original.
24. Patrick McGuinness, "Introduction," 7.
25. Thematic cyclicism reaches back at least to Beethoven and was subsequently used by many composers—with Franck and d'Indy as the most prominent among them—whom we would not necessarily designate as "decadent." As we will see in chapter 1, the decadence of Ravel's thematic cyclicism does not lie merely in the fact of its use but rather in the particular ways it is used.
26. One of the few extended discussions of Debussy's decadence is Sharon S. Prado, "The Decadent Aesthetic in France, 1880–1914: Musical Manifestations in the Works of Debussy and His Contemporaries" (PhD diss., University of Cincinnati, 1992).
27. Glenn Watkins is one of the very few textbook authors to have addressed Decadence and related it to modernist music. By linking Decadence to the characters of Salome and Bluebeard, Watkins presents it as an international phenomenon that features the music of Florent Schmitt, Paul Dukas, Béla Bartók, and Richard Strauss. He is nevertheless still unwilling to lend it a fuller independence and chooses instead to describe it as a mere "strain within the Symbolism movement." Watkins, *Soundings*, 130. A related project is Stephen C. Downes, *Music and Decadence in European Modernism: The Case of Central and Eastern Europe* (New York: Cambridge University Press, 2010). Unfortunately, I was unable to review this book before completing my own.

28. Verlaine was not the sole adherent to the *fête galante* in nineteenth-century France, of course; others include Théophile Gautier, Arsène Houssaye, Gérard Nerval, and the *frères* Goncourt.
29. Joris-Karl Huysmans, *Against Nature*, 197.
30. Ibid., 109.
31. Ibid., 84.
32. Ibid., 110.
33. Ibid., 147.
34. Walter Benjamin, "On Some Motifs in Baudelaire," 183. Emphasis on "idéal" in the original translation.
35. Ibid., 182.
36. Ibid. An indispensable source for grasping Benjamin's diagnosis of alienation in Baudelaire is Martin Jay, "Lamenting the Crisis of Experience," 312–360.
37. Ravel, "Memories of a Lazy Child," 394.
38. Lloyd Whitesell has interpreted the move to Montfort-l'Amaury as part of a general strategy of escapism that helped him cope with his putative homosexuality in an inhospitable cultural environment. Lloyd Whitesell, "Ravel's Way," 72.
39. Huysmans, *Against Nature*, 24.
40. Benjamin, "On Some Motifs," 168.
41. Although the two principles of "Oiseaux tristes" achieve a rapprochement in the cadenza on the final page—with the brooder spiraling up imaginatively into the ether on the wings of his *oiseaux*—any hope is snuffed out with the coda ("Encore plus lent"), which replaces the expected plagal cadence in E major with a disorienting fall into E-flat minor, thereby reinstating the initial despair associated with this tonality and its sighing motives.
42. The puzzling melancholy of this opera is raised and addressed—differently than I do here—in Steven Huebner, "Laughter: In Ravel's Time," 225–246. To the list of critics mentioned in Huebner's article I would add Arthur Pougin, whose account brings out the decadence of the work. According to Pougin, *L'heure espagnole* is lugubrious "avec ses mouvements toujours lents, avec son manque d'accent, avec ses complications de rythme, avec son orchestre tarabiscoté [overly ornate], avec ses difficultés d'intonation pour les chanteurs, difficultés provenant d'harmonies étranges et choquantes." Arthur Pougin, *Le Ménestrel* (May 27, 1911), 163, cited in Christian Goubault, *La critique musicale*, 404.
43. Along these lines, compare the following remarks by Donald Kuspit, which apply to both the passage of time and the fluctuation of desire in "Oiseaux tristes" and *L'heure espagnole*: "The sense of time is at the core of the dialectic of decadence—time as a duration which defeats any attempt to gain a perspective. That is, we are decadent and modern because we cannot see *sub specie aeternitatis*, even a semblance of it. . . . The experience of duration—the sense of time as slow or fast—is inseparable from the vicissitudes of desire" (Kuspit, *The Dialectic of Decadence*, 51–52).
44. Bernheimer, *Decadent Subjects*.
45. Swart, *The Sense of Decadence*, 210.
46. Roger Shattuck's assertion that "Proust was more a social critic than a decadent" is valuable for shifting attention to an underexplored aspect of *À la recherche*, but it does little to overturn scholarly consensus about the decadent tendencies of both novel and novelist. Shattuck, *Proust's Way*, xvii. The social object of Proust's scrutiny was, of course, the French aristocracy in a state of decline that reaches its nadir in the "masked ball" at the end of the novel. Marion Schmid has found Proust to obey a more dialectical relation to decadence, assimilating and rejecting it in turn throughout his career, but admits that "de nombreux topoi décadents demeurent dans le grand roman de la vocation: la critique de l'esthétisme et de l'idolatrie, la conception subversive des relations sexuelles et de la sexualité tout court, le portrait des luttes hégémoniques entre une bourgeoisie énergique et une aristocratie déchue sont tous, fût-elle en creux, inspirée de la pensée décadente." Marion Schmid, *Proust dans la décadence*, 240.

47. Michael J. Puri, "Memory, Pastiche, and Aestheticism in Ravel and Proust," in *Ravel Studies*, ed. Deborah Mawer (Cambridge: Cambridge University Press, 2010), 122–152.
48. Frederick Goldbeck, *France, Italy, and Spain*, 24–25; Marcel Marnat, "Vinteuil, peut-être," 20–29; Theodor W. Adorno, "Ravel," in *Musikalische Schriften V*, 273–274.
49. Central texts on memory's intersection with tradition, landscape, and race are, in respective order, Maurice Halbwachs, *The Collective Memory*; Simon Schama, *Landscape and Memory*; and Laura Otis, *Organic Memory*. A seminal critique of tradition, particularly in its contribution to political ideology, is Eric Hobsbawm and Terence Ranger, eds., *The Invention of Tradition*.
50. Standard accounts of the *ars memoriae* in ancient, medieval, and Renaissance contexts include Frances Yates, *The Art of Memory*; Mary Carruthers, *The Book of Memory*; and Anna Maria Busse Berger, *Medieval Music and the Art of Memory*.
51. Pierre Nora, "Between Memory and History: *Les lieux de mémoire*," 12. The original seven volumes of Nora's collaborative project, produced from 1984 to 1992, have been republished as Pierre Nora, ed., *Les lieux de mémoire*, vols. 1–3 (Paris: Gallimard, 1997). One testament to the influence of Nora's project is the subsequent production of its German counterpart, Étienne François and Hagen Schulze, eds., *Deutsche Erinnerungsorte* (Munich: Beck, 2001).
52. Maurice Halbwachs, *Les cadres sociaux de la mémoire* (Paris: Éditions Albin Michel, 1994; orig. Paris: Alcan, 1925). Two main texts by Bergson under critique here are *Matière et mémoire* and *L'énergie spirituelle*.
53. In theorizing the future, Elizabeth Grosz also ascribes transformative potential to the difference between present and past, albeit from a more progressive viewpoint than the *fin-de-siècle* decadent would tend to adopt: "The past is not merely a depleted resource, one robbed of its force or will, but is dynamic insofar as it remains the condition of the present surpassing itself. The past is: The necessary condition for the present; that through which the present has the resources to transform itself; that which must be moved beyond and, if necessary, forgotten." Elizabeth A. Grosz, *The Nick of Time*, 125.
54. "The poetry of memory is not constituted simply by the coincidence of a present moment with a moment in the past but rather by the interposed atmosphere that cannot be measured spatially like other distances since it is the inner distance of a life lived day by day" (Nicht einfach die Koinzidenz eines gegenwärtigen mit einem vergangenen Augenblick im souvenir involontaire macht die Poesie der Erinnerung aus, sondern allererst jene atmosphère interposée, die nicht räumlich gemessen werden kann wie andere Entfernungen, weil sie innere Distanz eines Tag für Tag gelebten Lebens ist.). Hans-Robert Jauss, *Zeit und Erinnerung*, 83. Translation mine.
55. Proust states his dichotomous conception of memory most clearly in an interview with a reporter from *Le temps* in the fall of 1913, which has been translated into English and republished in Roger Shattuck, *Marcel Proust*, 166–172.
56. The seminal discussion of "shock experience" in Baudelaire is Walter Benjamin, "On Some Motifs in Baudelaire," 155–200. Benjamin often compares Proust to Baudelaire in this essay and ultimately finds the notion of memory in the latter to express the alienation of the individual from modern life more radically than that in the former: "The fact that Proust's restorative will remains within the limits of earthly existence, whereas Baudelaire's transcends it, may be regarded as symptomatic of the incomparably more elemental and powerful counterforces that Baudelaire faced" (182).
57. Marcel Proust, *Remembrance of Things Past*, trans. C. K. Scott Moncrieff, Terence Kilmartin, and Andreas Mayor, 3 vols. (New York: Vintage, 1981).
58. Shattuck, *Proust's Way*, 121.
59. In an encyclopedic account of Western cultural-historical memory, David Lowenthal enumerates four aspects of the past that make it attractive to remember: antiquity, continuity, termination, and sequence, all of which can be located somewhere between the poles of pleasurability and factuality, which he calls "instrumental memory." Lowenthal,

The Past Is a Foreign Country, 52–63. For his discussion of instrumental memory Lowenthal relies, in part, on Paul Brockelman, "Of Memory and Things Past," 309–325.

60. This epigraph derives from the final line of the "Avertissement" [Warning] that Régnier incorporates as a preamble into his novel *Les rencontres de M. de Bréot* (Paris: Mercure de France, 1904).
61. Georges Poulet finds the superimposition of temporalities in memory to exemplify a general principle of the "Proustian universe, . . . where everything is juxtaposed," thereby exposing the similarity and difference among things. Poulet, *Proustian Space*, 100.
62. Walter Benjamin, "A Berlin Chronicle," 6. In referring to the text as "Berlin Chronicle" I have chosen to eliminate the indefinite article that appears in Jephcott's translation since it does not appear in the German original ("Berliner Chronik").
63. In a more comic vein, Proust also observes that the rememberer's self-awareness tends to disrupt reminiscence like a "huge shadow . . . obliterat[ing] the figures on the screen of a magic lantern, a shadow which is that of the lantern itself, or that of the operator" (III, 549). These realizations participate in what Shattuck calls "Proust's complaint," which stems from the pathos-inducing knowledge that "our very presence anywhere is a form of intrusion." Shattuck, *Proust's Way*, 88.
64. Ruminating on memory and music from a Proustian perspective, Andreas Dorschel arrived at a similar insight, designating as recollection (*Erinnerung*) only those repetitions that disclose the actual impossibility of reproducing the past in its original form. Dorschel, "Das anwesend Abwesende," 22.
65. Sigmund Freud, "Screen Memories (1899)," *Standard Edition* 3, 301–322, and "From the History of an Infantile Neurosis [The Wolf-Man] (1918 [1914])," *Standard Edition* 17, 3–124.
66. Allusions to the soul, its resurrection, and its immortality are frequent in Proust but do not amount to a doctrine, whether Platonic or otherwise. For slightly amplified discussion, see Puri, "Memory, Pastiche, and Aestheticism," 68–69. For more recent treatment of anamnesis in relation to memory studies, see Jeffrey Andrew Barash, "The Sources of Memory," 707–717, and Richard Terdiman, *Present Past*, 240–288.
67. For example, Terdiman challenges the dichotomy of remembering/forgetting by claiming that the two activities are not "contraries but rather differential modes of existence of the same process in the representation of the past. Forgetting is a form of remembering." Ibid., 250. A recent overview of the truth/fiction dichotomy is Kurt Danziger, *Marking the Mind*, 188–221.
68. Proust's notion of homogeneity has also been proposed as a basis for assessing contemporary French music in Carlo Caballero, *Fauré and French Musical Aesthetics*, 126–169.
69. Théodule-Armand Ribot, *Les maladies de la mémoire* (Paris: Alcan, 1881). The fact that this monograph had undergone eighteen editions by 1906 is a testament to its popularity and importance during the Third Republic.
70. Through Nietzsche, Nordau, and many others, Wagner's music was linked with cultural degeneracy, as discussed in Thomas Grey, "Wagner the Degenerate," 73–92.
71. Nietzsche, "The Case of Wagner," 242.
72. A classic, concise overview of the medical history of nostalgia is Jean Starobinski, "The Idea of Nostalgia," 81–103, which is based on Fritz Ernst, *Vom Heimweh*.
73. Those familiar with Benjamin's writings will note the striking affinity of this passage with the following line from "A Berlin Chronicle": "He who seeks to approach his own buried past must conduct himself like a man digging. This confers the tone and bearing of genuine reminiscences. He must not be afraid to return again and again to the same matter; to scatter it as one scatters earth, to turn it over as one turns over soil." Benjamin, "A Berlin Chronicle," 26. The use of archeological metaphors for the structure and activity of memory is also characteristic of Freud, as discussed in Suzanne Cassirer Bernfeld, "Freud and Archeology," 107–128; Donald Kuspit, "A Mighty Metaphor: The Analogy of Archaeology and Psychoanalysis," 133–151; and, from a much broader theoretical perspective, Ranjana Khanna, *Dark Continents*, 33–65.

74. Gilles Deleuze finds the motion from the material to the ideal to be quintessentially Proustian and claims that "the material meaning is nothing without an ideal essence that it incarnates." Deleuze, *Proust and Signs*, 13.
75. While Proust's remark is closest in time and sentiment to Bergson's critique of the atrophy of *durée* in modern life, it also looks ahead to the present-day "memory boom" in the humanities, which, for Andreas Huyssen, "represents the attempt to slow down information processing, to resist the dissolution of time in the synchronicity of the archive, to recover a mode of contemplation outside the universe of simulation and fast-speed information and cable networks, to claim some anchoring space in a world of puzzling and often threatening homogeneity, non-synchronicity, and information overload." Andreas Huyssen, *Twilight Memories*, 7. For the interrelation between memory and technology in Third Republic France, see Matt K. Matsuda, *The Memory of the Modern*.
76. I have added the first three commas in this quotation to improve its flow.
77. An interpretation of memory in Proust as a solution to the problem of mortal transience and a means to complete happiness appears in Theodor W. Adorno, "On Proust," 312–317.
78. A notable example is Debussy's piano prelude "Des pas sur la neige," in which a direction by the composer to play a certain passage "comme un tendre et triste regret" [like a tender and sad regret, mm. 28–31] motivates us to interpret this passage, as well as the whole piece, from the standpoint of memory. An extended mnemoanalysis of this piece is Steven Rings, "*Mystères limpides*: Time and Transformation in Debussy's *Des pas sur la neige*," 178–208.
79. In a related comment, Jean-Marc Chouvel has defined memory (*la mémoire*) as the mental faculty that gives form to time. Jean-Marc Chouvel, "Avec le temps, il n'y a pas de forme sans mémoire," 47–56.
80. Susan Youens discusses this aspect of memory pieces in an analysis of Luciano Berio's *Recital I (for Cathy)*, arguing that the result of quoting Schubert's "Der Jüngling an der Quelle" in this work is not "to affirm the past as material for use in the present, but to question the effect on performers of prolonged exposure to the past," with the performer potentially endangered by a "preoccupation with fictive inner lives at the expense of her own." Susan Youens, "Memory, Identity, and the Uses of the Past," 242–243.
81. In an editorial Preface for the *Sonatine*, Roger Nichols shares an anecdote personally relayed to him by Manuel Rosenthal, in which Ravel agreed with Carlos Salzedo's judgment of the Massenet-like quality of the opening theme of the first movement when the composer demonstrated it for him. See Nichols, "Preface," 5.
82. Berthold Hoeckner articulates the temporal and formal paradoxes of the "moment" in this formulation: "However short the instant, it may touch eternity; and however minute the detail, it may encompass all." Berthold Hoeckner, *Programming the Absolute*, 4.
83. One of the few texts to suggest a Trio in the midst of this Menuet is Louis Aguettant, *La musique de piano des origines à Ravel*, 435.
84. As evident from plate 27 in Arbie Orenstein, *Ravel: Man and Musician*, which reproduces the first page of sketches for the Sonatine (currently in the private collection of Madame Taverne), this phrase replaced the original transition *en bloc*. Thus, it may seem to redirect musical flow and tonal trajectory because it actually was a compositional intervention. Some scholars interpret example I.8 as the main second theme of the sonata form and view the subsequent theme (mm. 20–23) as a transition to the codetta (mm. 24–28a), but I find this reading insensitive to the interruptive, tonally unstable quality of example I.8 and the relative tonal stability of the theme in measures 20–23. For an example of this alternative interpretation, see Ortrud Kuhn-Schliess, *Klassistische Tendenzen im Klavierwerk von Maurice Ravel*, 122–123.
85. One of the most thorough comparative analyses of the two Forlanes is Martha Hyde, "Neoclassic and Anachronistic Impulses." Among the various possible relations between present and past that Hyde identifies—reverential, eclectic, heuristic, and dialectical—she

finds the "Forlane" to be reverential for following the Couperin with remarkable fidelity. Recently, Andreas Dorschel has presented a more usual interpretation of Ravel's Forlane from the standpoint of memory, finding it to have grotesquely deformed its model upon recalling it and thereby truthfully to have illuminated the unbridgeable gap between past and present (Dorschel, "Das anwesend Abwesende," 22–25). Carolyn Abbate's discussion of the uncannily reanimated quality of Ravel's Forlane—neither living nor dead, just as Nora described the "site of memory"—expands its ambivalent temporality into a spooky ontology. Carolyn Abbate, *In Search of Opera*, 215–222.

86. Although Ravel told Marguerite Long to play the Menuet in the tempo of the "Menuetto" from Beethoven's Piano Sonata, op. 31, no. 3, there does not appear to be any musical basis to consider it to be a significant model for the Menuet. Long, *Au piano avec Maurice Ravel* (Paris: Juilliard, 1971), 126, cited in Nichols, "Preface," 5.
87. Ross Chambers provides a focused account of dilatory, digressive behavior in Decadent literature in his *Loiterature* (Lincoln: University of Nebraska Press, 1999).
88. Walter Benjamin, "The Return of the *flâneur*," 262. In contrast to his discussions of the *flâneur* in "The Paris of the Second Empire in Baudelaire" and "On Some Motifs in Baudelaire," this review is special for emphasizing its relation to memory and fantasy.
89. Svetlana Boym, *The Future of Nostalgia*, 41.
90. Important recent contributions to the study of the interrelation between nineteenth-century nationalism and early French music include Katharine Ellis, *Interpreting the Musical Past*; Anya Suschitzky, "Debussy's Rameau"; and Jane Fulcher, *French Cultural Politics and Music*.
91. "Cloud" is an allusion to the cyclic recurrences of "Nuages" as five-beat measures in the triple-meter passages of the sunny "Fêtes" from Debussy's orchestral suite *Nocturnes* (1901), which Ravel would transcribe for two pianos in 1909. The interrelation of "Nuages" and "Fêtes" is discussed in Sharon Gelleny, "Cyclic Form in Debussy's Nocturnes."
92. This essay was first published as Theodor W. Adorno, "Ravel," *Musikblätter des Anbruch* 12 (April/May 1930): 151–154; the revised version is Adorno, "Ravel," *Gesammelte Schriften*, vol. 17 (Frankfurt: Suhrkamp, 1982), 60–65.
93. Friedrich Nietzsche, "On the Utility and Liability of History for Life," 96. I cite the less literal translation of the German title in the text since it reflects *Nutzen* and *Nachteil* in the similarly paired "Use" and "Abuse."
94. Ibid., 85 and 108–109. At one point Lowenthal implicitly adopts a Nietzschean point of view on modern Western cultural attitudes toward the past and proposes that we preserve it "because we are no longer intimate enough with that legacy to rework it creatively. We admire its relics, but they do not inspire our own acts and works." Lowenthal, *The Past Is a Foreign Country*, xxiv.
95. Nietzsche, "On the Utility," 89.

Chapter 1

1. D'Indy's collaborator for the first two books of the *Cours* was his student Auguste Sérieyx, who helped him compile these two volumes from notes for his classes at the Schola Cantorum between 1897 and 1902.
2. I have defined "cyclic form" in this way to accommodate a variety of understandings. At one end of the spectrum, mere motivic similarity among themes in separate movements is sufficient to qualify as cyclicism, while, at the other the end, cyclicism is only the literal return of a theme from the first movement of a suite in the last. In addition, a specific timbre or instrumentation—separable from a motive or a theme—may recur cyclically in a work, as recently proposed by Marianne Wheeldon in *Debussy's Late Style*, 80–113.
3. Vincent d'Indy, *Cours de composition musicale, deuxième livre—première partie*, 376 and 378, resp. Emphasis in the original.

4. Ibid., 422 and 423, resp. Emphasis in the original.
5. A thorough and insightful analysis of cyclic form in *fin-de-siècle* French symphonism is Andrew Deruchie, "The French Symphony at the *fin de siècle*: Style, Culture, and the Symphonic Tradition," PhD Diss., McGill University, 2008.
6. In two recent articles Benedict Taylor places Mendelssohn at the forefront of experimentation with cyclic form in the first half of the nineteenth century: "Musical History and Self-Consciousness in Mendelssohn's Octet," and "Cyclic Form, Time, and Memory in Mendelssohn's A-Minor Quartet, op. 13." Kip Montgomery discusses cyclic form in its development from Mozart to Brahms, with special emphasis on the latter's Third Symphony and *Ein deutsches Requiem*, in his dissertation, "Cyclic Form in the Music of Brahms." A classic treatment of cyclicism in Schumann, which focuses on works such as the C-major *Fantasie*, *Frauenliebe und -leben*, and the *Davidsbündlertänze*, can be found in Charles Rosen, *The Romantic Generation*.
7. Charles Rosen identifies the same paradox when asserting that "the cyclical return simultaneously attacks and reaffirms the integrity of the individual musical structure." Ibid., 92. Benedict Taylor expands upon this idea to argue that cyclicism allows multiple temporalities to exist simultaneously, but he interprets the coexistence of these temporalities in more harmonious terms than I do—which makes some sense since he and I are analyzing music composed at different historical moments. Taylor, "Cyclic Form," 71. Nonetheless, I do not agree with him when he claims that, "if one really wishes to seek a musical model for Proust, the work that parallels his masterpiece far more closely than any other is the A-Minor Quartet" (79). I disagree not because I think Ravel's music necessarily compares better to Proust than Mendelssohn's but because I do not understand Proust's novel to be as organically unified and closed as he does; my discussion of Proustian "intermittence" later in this chapter encapsulates my alternative viewpoint.
8. My critique of monumental character and invocation of the ruin are indebted to Andreas Huyssen, "Monumental Seduction."
9. Blanche Selva, a student of d'Indy, carves out a middle path between these two possibilities when she asserts that "le thème cyclique . . . n'est pas simplement *rappelé*, mais *transformé*, dans son *expression* même." Blanche Selva, *La sonate*, 186. Emphasis in the original.
10. Roger Shattuck finds intermittence to be so important to an understanding of Proust that he identifies it as the "guiding principle" of the novel. Shattuck, *Proust's Way*, 97.
11. Antoine Compagnon draws a similar distinction between redemptive memory and intermittence (translated from the French here as "intermittency"), suggesting that, "if involuntary memory is the aesthetic foundation of the novel, perhaps intermittency corresponds to its origins in lived experience. Indeed, reminiscence is a kind of transcended or domesticated intermittency, but pure intermittency . . . is too absolute an event to undergo the kind of theoretical taming applied to the madeleine, the paving stones, the spoon or the napkin." Compagnon, *Proust between Two Centuries*, 124.
12. Charles Rosen proposes this criterion in *The Romantic Generation*, 88.
13. Jürgen Braun seems to observe the same tension between past and present in the Duo: "einerseits eine Rückkehr zu deutlicher zyklischer Verknüpfung weniger Themen, andererseits der weitgehende Verzicht auf zyklische Verbindung aller Themen" [on the one hand, a return to marked cyclic linkage of a few themes, on the other hand the broad abstinence from cyclic connection of all themes]. Jürgen Braun, *Die Thematik in den Kammermusikwerken von Maurice Ravel*, 93.
14. Michael Talbot's *Finale in Western Instrumental Music* provides a broad and rich survey of this compositional task but happens not to share our specific concerns (thematic cyclicism, French classical music, Ravel, memory).
15. Edward S. Casey, *Remembering*, 46–47.
16. Susan Stewart, *On Longing*, 140.
17. Walter Frisch, " 'You Must Remember This,' " 584. In the first movement of the Schubert String Quartet, the measures in question are 11–14 (the disintegration) and 15–33 (the recollection).

18. Svetlana Boym, *The Future of Nostalgia*, xiii.
19. Stewart, *On Longing*, 145. The thematic recollection in the Menuet fulfills the same role as a photograph in Stewart's interpretation, which miniatures, idealizes, and distances an event to create "a still and perfect, and thereby interpretable and unapproachable, universe whose signified is not the world but desire" (115).
20. Indeed, the only differences between the Habanera as it appears in the *Sites* and the *Rapsodie* is that the latter is three measures shorter due to the excision of three measures of vamp or simple resonance (mm. 30, 58, and 64 in the *Sites* version) and sports ornamental upward riffs in the second half (harp in mm. 49–50 and clarinets and violins in mm. 53–54). Orenstein's claim that the first version is longer than the second because "several measures were condensed" is inaccurate, mainly because it does not take into account the three measures I have cited, which were simply removed rather than condensed. The measures to which Orenstein is referring are the four (mm. 15, 18, 37, and 40) that Ravel marked with the direction "*bis ad lib.*" Because he interprets this direction—which Ravel did not include in the orchestral version, understandably enough—to add an additional measure, his measure count totals 68 rather than 64. Although it is not entirely clear what this direction asks us to do, nevertheless I am not convinced it is best interpreted as "repeat once." ("Repeat as many times as you like" seems more accurate to me.) Moreover, for the purposes of performance and analysis, I argue that increasing the measure count on its behalf is more confusing than illuminating. Orenstein, *Ravel*, 142n14.
21. Maurice Ravel, *A Ravel Reader*, 30.
22. Ibid., 34–35n13, where Orenstein not only gives his own interpretation but also cites that of Roland-Manuel. Orenstein has drawn this citation from Roland-Manuel's personal notes, which were physically inserted into the December 1938 issue of *La revue musicale* housed in the collection of the Music Division of the Bibliothèque Nationale in Paris. The notes pertain directly to the "Autobiographical Sketch," which was first, and therefore posthumously, published in that issue.
23. For an elaborated discussion of this poem that touches on the racial ambiguity of the Creole woman, see Christopher L. Miller, *Blank Darkness*, 98–107.
24. After having surveyed the Spanish music of both Debussy and Ravel, Parakilas concludes that, before Debussy heard Ravel's Habanera, "he was not evidently drawn to the Spanish exotic. Once he heard it, he reworked the same few ideas from it—and a single extramusical 'image'—in four different 'Habanera' movements, written over the course of a decade and a half. What's more, he began this process, as we shall see, in a work written, like the Ravel, for two pianos [*Lindaraja* (1901)]." James Parakilas, "How Spain Got a Soul," 173. Parakilas subsequently makes claims very similar to mine:

    The third movement of the *Rapsodie* is an orchestration of his earlier two-piano Habanera, a gorgeous piece of orchestration, but retaining the notes of the piano piece exactly, while the date "1895," prominently placed under the title Habanera in the score, stakes his claim to priority over Debussy's "La soirée dans Grenade" in this genre of musical evocation. But then, what is the first movement, the "Prélude à la nuit," but a borrowing in turn of the specific night-in-the-garden scenario of "La soirée dans Grenade"? (185).

25. For Lalo's charges, see his articles in *Le temps* of Jan. 30, 1906, Mar. 19, 1907, and Apr. 9, 1907. Ravel attempted to refute Lalo's claims in two letters, one addressed personally to Lalo on Feb. 5, 1906, and the other addressed to the editor in late March 1907. For the text of both letters, see Ravel, *A Ravel Reader*, 79–80 and 88–89, resp.
26. Another link between "La soirée" and the *Rapsodie* is Ricardo Viñes, who premiered the former and was the dedicatee of the latter. Roy Howat has emphasized that Viñes "maintained the current of musical stimulus between Debussy and Ravel after 1905 when the two composers were no longer in personal contact, playing the latest pieces by each composer to the other." Roy Howat, *The Art of French Piano Music*, 143.

Chapter 2

1. The notion of an introductory formula, especially as it pertains to French musical Symbolism, is indebted to James A. Hepokoski, "Formulaic Openings in Debussy."
2. Jules Combarieu, *Histoire de la musique des origines*, vol. 3, 573–574.
3. As mentioned in the introductory chapter, the major essay on reanimation in Ravel, albeit conceived differently from mine, is Carolyn Abbate, "Outside the Tomb," in *In Search of Opera*, 185–246.
4. With the term *counterchronic* I am paying homage to Gérard Genette's broader category of narrative anachrony. See Gérard Genette, *Narrative Discourse*, 33–85.
5. At a more general level—one removed from the specific assignment of meaning to musical structure—these introductions all share the device of the crescendo, which Stephen Zank has singled out as one of the primary means by which Ravel shapes his compositions. Stephen Zank, *Irony and Sound*, 40–84.
6. Laurence Davies, *The Gallic Muse*, 127.
7. For a more detailed account of the collaboration over *Daphnis*, see Deborah Mawer, *The Ballets of Maurice Ravel*, 81–93.
8. Referring perhaps more to its first half than its second, Marcel Marnat calls the Introduction to *Daphnis* an "introduction quasi abstraite" [quasi-abstract introduction]. Marnat, *Maurice Ravel*, 338.
9. N.a., *Le guide du concert* 25, Apr. 1, 1911, 544. In these program notes, APPEL, NYMPHES, and DC receive the labels "Le thème d'invocation," "le motif des Nymphes," and "Daphnis et Chloé," respectively. Although scholarly discussion of *Daphnis* does not cite this crucial point of reference—which information must come from Ravel since nothing of *Daphnis* had been published by April 1911—they nevertheless generally agree upon the dramatic meaning of these themes. Ravel's tendency to expose his themes so clearly at the beginning of a composition seems to relate to his pedagogical training. For example, in an analysis of Saint-Saëns's *La jeunesse d'Hercule* (Music Division, Bibliothèque Nationale de France, Paris, ms. 17649), dating from his student years, he carefully transcribes and labels the main themes of the symphonic poem, including the "Thème de la vertu," the "Thème des nymphes," and the theme of "Les Bacchantes."
10. Two good discussions of anamnesis are Edward S. Casey, *Remembering*, 1–18, and Jeffrey Andrew Barash, "The Sources of Memory."
11. The *Prélude* is not the sole piece by Debussy evoked by the Introduction to *Daphnis*, of course. The *Chansons de Bilitis* also begin with a flute arabesque that, as Stephen C. Downes has argued, unite past and present under the auspices of eros: "The combination of the piano's imitation of the erotically symbolic sound of the flute with harmonic proximity of 'new' and 'old' material suggests not only the source of musical creation out of desire and recollection but also that Eros might bind the sounds of apparently opposite worlds." Stephen Downes, *The Muse as Eros*, 169. The alternation between two themes prior to an animatory gesture also recalls the slow introduction to the first movement of Debussy's *La mer*, whose main themes Simon Trezise has noted for their "quality of incantation, of ancient voices crying out from the depths of the oceans." Simon Trezise, *Debussy:* La mer, 39.
12. This anonymous reviewer remarked that, at the beginning of the Nocturne (R70), "la flûte solo expose le thème des Nymphes, et tout de suite, invinciblement, on songe à l'Après-midi d'un Faune" [The flute plays the theme of the Nymphs, and, all of a sudden, willy-nilly, we think of *L'après-midi d'un faune*; *L'éclair*, Apr. 3, 1911].
13. The citation appears in Maurice Ravel, *A Ravel Reader*, 346.
14. Representative discussions of rotational form may be found in James A. Hepokoski, *Sibelius: Symphony no. 5*; Warren Darcy, "The Metaphysics of Annihilation"; and James A. Hepokoski and Warren Darcy, *Elements of Sonata Theory*.
15. Marnat, *Maurice Ravel*, 339.

16. Ravel began collaboration with Raoul Bardac to transcribe Debussy's orchestral *Nocturnes* for two pianos, most likely inspired by the premiere of "Nuages" and "Fêtes" on Dec. 9, 1900. In a letter to Florent Schmitt dated Apr. 8, 1901, Ravel mentions that he "was assigned the task of transcribing the third piece, 'Sirènes,' all alone," and continues by declaring it "perhaps the most perfectly beautiful of the *Nocturnes* and certainly the most perilous to transcribe, particularly as it hasn't been heard." See Ravel, *Ravel Reader,* 58–59. From the diary of Ricardo Viñes, we know that Ravel was soon able to remedy this lack by attending the first complete performance of Debussy's *Nocturnes* on Sunday, Oct. 27, 1901, at the Concerts Chevillard; see Nina Gubisch, "Le journal inédit de Ricardo Viñes," 198. Although it may seem strange to suggest that Ravel would have had "Sirènes" on his musical mind eight years after the fact, the transcription was actually first published only in 1909, the year in which he began work on *Daphnis*. Ravel made a further gesture of personal and artistic identification with the *Nocturnes* by giving a premiere performance of his transcription of them at one of the initial concerts of his own Société Musicale Indépendante on Apr. 24, 1911; these biographical details are presented in Orenstein, *Ravel,* 241. Simon Morrison also proposes that the wordless female chorus of "Sirènes" is a strong predecessor for the wordless chorus in *Daphnis;* see Morrison, "The Origins of *Daphnis et Chloé* (1912)," 62–63.
17. Lawrence Kramer, "Consuming the Exotic," 218.
18. A common trope in current critical discourse, the notion of the primal scene is invoked frequently (and casually) across many fields. Some uses in musicology that still demonstrate sensitivity toward its psychoanalytical meaning include Samuel Weber, "Taking Place," and Katherine Kolb Reeve, "Primal Scenes."
19. The classic text for the theory of the primal scene is Sigmund Freud, "From the History of an Infantile Neurosis." Among recent considerations and applications of the concept within the humanities (especially philosophy, literary criticism and theory, film criticism and theory, and gender and sexuality studies), notable examples include Ned Lukacher, *Primal Scenes,* and Kaja Silverman, *Male Subjectivity at the Margins.*
20. On memory and iterability see Richard Terdiman, *Present Past* (Ithaca, N.Y.: Cornell University Press, 1993), 265.
21. Vladimir Jankélévitch, *Ravel,* 47.
22. Nietzsche asserts that the potentially infinite deferral of gratification, "this secret self-ravishment, this artists' cruelty, . . . as the womb of all ideal and imaginative phenomena, also brought to light an abundance of strange new beauty and affirmation, and perhaps beauty itself." Friedrich Nietzsche, *On the Genealogy of Morals,* 87–88. For a discussion of the relation between sensuality and prohibitive law in Nietzsche, see Alenka Zupančič, *The Shortest Shadow,* 46–61.
23. Longus, "Daphnis and Chloe," 288–289. To facilitate comparison between Longus and the ballet scenario, I have chosen Christopher Gill's prose translation of the proem instead of poetic renditions designed to capture the proem's embedded rhymes and parallel phrase structures.
24. Ibid., 296. In the original 1910 piano-vocal score for *Daphnis,* the libretto states at the beginning of the Dance Contest that "Chloe will receive a kiss from the winner" (Chloé recevra au vainqueur un baiser), while the final versions of both piano (1912) and orchestral (1913) scores state that "a kiss from Chloe will be the winner's prize" [un baiser de Chloé sera le prix destiné au vainqueur]. At first glance, the revision might seem counterintuitive and even slightly bold in its ascription of sexual agency to the woman; as Linda Williams has noted in the history of film kisses, it is more usual and conventional (at least in this history) that "the man kisses and the woman receives the kiss, even though she may have orchestrated it all along." Linda Williams, "Of Kisses and Ellipses," 293. However, the revision may also reflect the librettists' desire to be more faithful to the Greek novel, in which it is Chloe that ultimately kisses Daphnis at the end of the contest.

25. Alberto Mantelli, "Maurice Ravel," *Revue musicale* (December 1938), 258.
26. Cited in Morrison, "The Origins of *Daphnis et Chloé*," 55.
27. Riccardo Malipiero, *Maurice Ravel*, 62; Roland-Manuel, *Maurice Ravel et son œuvre dramatique*, 101.
28. The language of "sharply contrasting poses" comes from the following: "Cette dernière figure, où les danseuses ne se montrent que de profil en une série d'attitudes brusquement opposés, devait exercer une influence durable sur les chorégraphes qui succédèrent à Fokine dans la faveur de M. de Diaghilew" (Roland-Manuel, 116–117). The primary choreographer and the choreography to which Roland-Manuel is referring are Nijinsky and his "two-dimensional" choreography for Debussy's *Prélude à "L'après-midi d'un faune,"* which was also premiered during the 1912 season and competed directly with *Daphnis* for rehearsal time and program space.
29. Lynn Garafola, *Rethinking the Sylph*, 6.
30. Ivor F. Guest, *The Romantic Ballet in Paris*, 14 and 112.
31. Richard Langham Smith, "Ravel's Operatic Spectacles," 205.
32. "Mon intention en l'écrivant était de composer une vaste fresque musicale, moins soucieuse d'archaïsme que de fidélité à la Grèce de mes rêves, qui s'apparente assez volontiers à celle qu'ont imaginée et dépeinte les artistes français de la fin du XVIIIe siècle. L'œuvre est construite symphoniquement selon un plan tonal très rigoureux, au moyen d'un petit nombre de motifs dont les développements assurent l'homogénéité symphonique de l'ouvrage." (Ravel, *Maurice Ravel*, 45–46; translation mine.)
33. Roland-Manuel, *Maurice Ravel et son œuvre*, 24.
34. Lynn Garafola, *Diaghilev's Ballets Russes*, 53.
35. Michel Fokine, *Fokine: Memoirs of a Ballet Master*, 196.
36. Ibid., 200.
37. Ibid., 199.
38. According to Charles Mayer, Bakst's trip is supposed to have been "a major stimulus for his change of style. At that time the country was a mixture of Greek, Arab and Turkish cultures, and of antiquity and modernity. It was markedly different from what Bakst had envisioned and after his arrival he confused all that he witnessed with the antiquity he had previously conceived." Charles S. Mayer, *Bakst*, 27.
39. Ibid., 27.
40. Edmond de Goncourt and Jules de Goncourt, *French Eighteenth-Century Painters*, 260–261.
41. Ibid., 6–7.
42. Roland-Manuel, *Maurice Ravel et son œuvre dramatique*, 117. Gerald Larner also makes the same association in *Maurice Ravel*, 117.
43. Longus, "Daphnis and Chloe," 288–289.
44. The cycle of images in the novel's proem is arguably reflected in the history of *Daphnis* as an illustrated book ever since its translation by Jacques Amyot from Ancient Greek into French in 1559. For an account of this history, see Giles Barber, *Daphnis and Chloe: The Markets and Metamorphoses of an Unknown Bestseller*. A "dramatic tableau" is formed when the plot freezes into "an elegant tableau, isolated from the flow of time, or rather concentrating that flow into a charged stasis." Martin Meisel, *Realizations*, 60. Ravel was apparently thinking about his opera *Jeanne d'Arc* in terms of such tableaux. In a 1931 interview he mentioned that "I have been thinking about *Jeanne d'Arc*. The well-known novel by [Joseph] Delteil inspired me, and it is almost mapped out musically. The various episodes in the Saint's life will follow each other 'cinematographically,' or if you wish, as 'images d'Épinal' " (Ravel, *A Ravel Reader*, 474). In a later interview in 1933, he went into further detail:

    I envision the "cuts" adopted by Delteil rather clearly: short scenes in rapid succession, like episodes in a film. First the combat of the children—Delteil calls it the Flower War—which immediately reveals Joan's personality: "of violent temperament, naturally authoritative and brusque gestures, a harsh voice, bold gait, a fiery look, she enjoyed considerable prestige among the boys and girls of her own age! Strong and confident, she did not fail to inculcate her authority with punches." (Ravel, *A Ravel Reader*, 500)

45. This interview from 1913, conducted on the eve of the launch of the first installment of Proust's novel, appears in Roger Shattuck, *Marcel Proust*, 166–172.
46. Proust, *Remembrance of Things Past*, vol. 1, 49.
47. Ibid., 51.
48. Roger Shattuck, *Proust's Way*, 44.
49. Walter Benjamin, "The Image of Proust," 205.

Chapter 3

1. The two definitions are drawn from the fifth entry for "sublimation" in *The Oxford English Dictionary*, 2nd ed.
2. Hans Heinz Stuckenschmidt's *Maurice Ravel: Variations on His Life and Work* likely offers the best promotion of this hypothesis, which culminates in an assessment of *Le tombeau de Couperin* as the site where "Ravel's heart has been transformed into sheer music" (178). More recent examples of biographical claims directly motivated by this hypothesis appear in Michael Stegemann, *Maurice Ravel*, 75, and Christine Souillard, *Ravel*, 78. The phrase "sexual enigma" is drawn from Émile Vuillermoz, "L'œuvre de Maurice Ravel," 65.
3. On sublimation in the "mechanical," see Roland-Manuel, *Maurice Ravel et son œuvre dramatique*, 46; on class membership, see Theodor Wiesengrund Adorno, "Ravel," *Musikblätter des Anbruch*, 153; on orchestration, see Marcel Marnat, *Maurice Ravel*, 328; on choreography, see Simon Morrison, "The Origins of *Daphnis et Chloé*," 74; on Ravel's incipient *dépouillement* [stripping away] of texture, as displayed in the *Trois poèmes de Stéphane Mallarmé* (1913), see Roland-Manuel, *À la gloire de Maurice Ravel*, 121–122, and José Bruyr, *Maurice Ravel*, 144. Sherry D. Lee has recently discussed Adorno's conception of sublimation in relation to his criticism of the music of Franz Schreker; see Lee, "A Minstrel in a World without Minstrels," 648–661.
4. The phrase "Le Dandy doit aspirer à être sublime sans interruption" appears in "Mon cœur mis à nu" [My heart laid bare], 1273. Emphasis mine.
5. Jules Barbey D'Aurevilly, *Du Dandysme*, 65. Comprehensive accounts in English of French literary dandyism include Domna C. Stanton, *The Aristocrat as Art*, and Rhonda K. Garelick, *Rising Star*.
6. Nina Gubisch, ed., "Le journal inédit de Ricardo Viñes," 192.
7. "Der Pfau mit seinem dandyhaften Betragen ist nichts anderes als die Allegorie eines in Wunschträumen befangenen Künstlers des Fin de siècle, wie er damals in Paris häufig anzutreffen war." Hirsbrunner, *Maurice Ravel*, 128.
8. Benjamin Ivry, *Maurice Ravel*, 46.
9. Relevant landmark studies in the history of sexuality include Michel Foucault, *The History of Sexuality*, vol. 1, and David M. Halperin, *One Hundred Years of Homosexuality*. A notable example of musicology to have delved into this history is the work of Jeffrey Kallberg, which includes his *Chopin at the Boundaries* and, among several other essays, his entry "Sex, Sexuality" in *The New Grove Dictionary of Music and Musicians*, 2nd ed., vol. 23, 178–180.
10. Gary C. Thomas, " 'Was George Frideric Handel Gay?' " 163–166. Thomas's 1994 call for scholarly investigation into a "homotextual Handel"—a site of discourse shaped by musical, as well as biographical, consideration—has been impressively realized in Ellen T. Harris, *Handel as Orpheus*.
11. Lloyd Whitesell, "Ravel's Way," 70.
12. Lawrence Kramer, "Consuming the Exotic." Prior to Kramer's essay, Philip Kennicott made some provocative remarks about sublimation, sexuality, and the erasure of the body in Ravel's ballet music—and in *Daphnis*, in particular. See Philip Kennicott, "Ravelation."

13. No pertinent primary source for *Daphnis* provides a title for this dance. The title that I have given it, "The Dance of the Young Girls and Boys," summarizes the general action.
14. See Longus, "Daphnis and Chloe."
15. While the orchestral score, published by Durand in 1913, has "Moins vite" (less fast) here, both the revised piano score and the manuscript of the full score have "Moins vif" (less lively), which is probably correct. Steven Carl Bird recommends the same emendation in Bird, "A Preliminary Comparison."
16. See Roland-Manuel, *Maurice Ravel et son œuvre dramatique*, 105; Jankélévitch, *Ravel*, 46; and Mawer, "Ballet and the Apotheosis of the Dance," 146.
17. For a recent musicological history and analysis of the waltz in the nineteenth and twentieth centuries, see Sevin H. Yaraman, *Revolving Embrace: The Waltz as Sex, Steps, and Sound* (Hillsdale: Pendragon, 2002).
18. See Roland-Manuel, *Maurice Ravel et son œuvre dramatique*, 61.
19. Steven Huebner has associated the sublimation of desire with the music of Massenet, a potentially important precursor to Ravel. Describing Athanaël's dream in *Thaïs*, Huebner suggests that it "elaborates sublimated desire, anticipating the later symphonic interlude where Thaïs mimes the loves of Aphrodite; harp and harmonium scoring lend an especially oneiric aspect to the passage. This is precisely the sort of sexual fantasy that the other monks wish to be spared." Huebner, *French Opera at the Fin de Siècle*, 157–158. Ravel's interest in Massenet's music, at least as an example of compositional craft, is evident in his direction that his student Roland-Manuel analyze the dream of Des Grieux from *Manon*; see Roger Nichols, ed., *Ravel Remembered*, 142.
20. The other three *Triebschicksale* that Freud discusses in "Instincts and Their Vicissitudes (1915)" are "reversal into its opposite," "turning round upon the subject's own self," and "repression." See Freud, "Instincts," 126. Repression and sublimation, the two vicissitudes that receive the clearest treatment in "Instincts" and are referenced most frequently in his work, are also the two that will prove most useful to us in our investigations here.
21. The sexual charge of Ravel's notion of "tendresse" is apparent in a revision he made to *L'heure espagnole*: In a complete copy of the vocal score, signed and dated October 1907, he indicated that Concepcion should sing a passage ("Il vous emporte dans ma chambre!") "très expressif" but exchanged this marking for "très tendre" in the 1911 publication of the full score, arguably to specify Concepcion's emotional relation to the imminent possibility of sex with Gonsalve. The manuscript for the vocal score forms part of the Robert Owen Lehman Collection, which is on deposit at the Pierpont Morgan Library in New York City.
22. Without my indulging in a lengthy analytical digression to undergird this claim, it should suffice here to note that the "Dance of the Young Girls and Boys" falls musically and dramatically into three parts: RR17–20 (girls), 21–25 (boys), and $26\text{–}29^{+3}$ (both), each of which ends with a formulaic series of motives (RR20, 24–25, and 28–29), the last of which is always the jealousy motive. In the final iteration of this series, Ravel postpones the arrival of this motive by interpolating a "false coda"—exactly at the moment that Dorcon, her equally mismatched suitor, goes to kiss her (at "Beaucoup moins vif," $RR28^{+7-9}$)—which then allows Ravel to bring back the jealousy motive under twofold transformation: as Daphnis's "geste brusque" and as the incipient motive for the Dance Contest rather than simply the concluding motive of the "Dance of the Young Girls and Boys."
23. Jean Laplanche and J.-B. Pontalis, *The Language of Psycho-Analysis*, 19.
24. The entity that falls across these bars is the semitonal line that begins with D♭5 in the second flute and ends at the B♭1 of the contrabasses, passing through the D♭4 of the strings and horn in $R29^{+1}$ and the C3 and C♭3 of the "geste brusque" melody in $RR29^{+1-2}$.
25. Mary Ann Doane, "Sublimation and the Psychoanalysis of the Aesthetic," in *Femmes Fatales*, 249–267.
26. See Sigmund Freud, "Deviations in Respect of the Sexual Aim," in *Three Essays*, 22–23.

27. Jacques Lacan, *The Ethics of Psychoanalysis,* 161.
28. In Longus, the Dance Contest is actually a war of words. See Longus, "Daphnis and Chloe," 295–296. As the translator, Christopher Gill, mentions (295n10), verbal contests are tropic to ancient pastoral literature and find their most famous example in the Fifth Idyll of Theocritus.
29. "Le livret de *Daphnis et Chloé* est d'une indigence et d'une banalité surprenantes. On le croirait fait pour l'Opéra, et pour un Prix de Rome. On y voit jusqu'à un concours de danse—ce poncif suprême du genre!—dont le prix est un baiser de Chloé." Gaston Carraud, "Théâtres: Châtelet," *La liberté* (June 11, 1912), n.p.
30. "Bolm triompha dans une danse bouffonne hardiment dessinée où il affirma une précision rythmique réellement héroïque." Vuillermoz, "Les Théâtres: La grande saison de Paris," *Revue musicale de la S.I.M.* (June 15, 1912), 68. A copy of Durand's twelve-page libretto for *Daphnis* is registered in the Bibliothèque de l'Opéra in Paris as Livret 874.
31. Mary Hunter, "The *Alla Turca* Style in the Late Eighteenth Century," 51.
32. While the 1912 (revised) piano score presents the dance as "gracieuse et légère," the 1913 full score describes it as "légère et gracieuse." Although it ultimately does not inflect my argument in any way, I have nevertheless assumed that the later publication incorporates revisions by the composer that the former lacks and have consequently chosen to adopt the 1913 nomenclature throughout.
33. Deborah Mawer describes the transition between the two dances in similar terms, characterizing it as "a progression from the ridiculous to the sublime." Mawer, *The Ballets of Maurice Ravel,* 106.
34. Jankélévitch, *Ravel,* 47. The barcarolle reference at the beginning of Daphnis's dance may betray a debt to Fauré, Ravel's friend and former teacher, who composed his thirteen barcarolles for piano between 1880 and 1915. Features common to Ravel's Dance and Faure's barcarolles include oscillation between compound duple and triple meter; arpeggiated accompaniment that begins low and rises in register; frequent alternation between upper and inner melodies; and scalar coda gestures that cascade down registrally from high to low and back up to high, ending in a trill; Barcarolles 1 (c. 1880), 2 (1885), and 9 (1909) are particularly salient for these comparisons. The author of three books dealing with Fauré—*Gabriel Fauré et ses mélodies* (1938), *Le nocturne* (1957), and *Fauré et l'inexprimable* (a 1974 revised and expanded version of the 1938 volume)—Jankélévitch would surely have been amenable to these comparative efforts on behalf of the barcarolle.
35. "Tes yeux sont doux comme ceux d'une fille, / Jeune étranger, / Et la courbe fine / De ton beau visage de duvet ombragé / Est plus séduisante encor de ligne." The musical stasis in both pieces is arguably also an index of their exoticism--the East as an unchanging realm of infinite pleasure.
36. Debora Silverman, *Art Nouveau in Fin-de-Siècle France,* 28. The notion of rococo ornamentation also links the "Dance of Daphnis" to *Le tombeau de Couperin*: Compare, for example, the recurrent eighth-note figuration of measure 5 (and elsewhere) in the A section of the dance to the recurrent sixteenth-note figuration in measure 7 (and elsewhere) of the "Prélude" to *Le tombeau,* as well as the cadential trill of the former to the cadential trill of the "Menuet" in *Le tombeau.*
37. I am grateful to Bruce Brown for this insight.
38. Jankélévitch's description of the waltz theme as a "valse *gracieuse*" calls attention, whether intentionally or not, to its affinity with the "Danse légère et *gracieuse* de Daphnis," as well as its potential genealogical relation to the dance. See Jankélévitch, *Ravel,* 46. Emphasis mine.
39. Arbie Orenstein suggests that Ravel may have found justification for his refusal to accept the Chevalier's Cross of the Legion of Honor in 1920 in a passage from Baudelaire's *Journaux intimes,* in which the poet argues that official decoration is irrelevant or, worse, opposed to personal merit. It can only strengthen our interrelation of Ravel with the Baudelairean dandy to note that the poet's comment about the dandy's uninterrupted

sublimity, as cited earlier, appears immediately after these comments on decoration in part 3 of "Mon cœur mis à nu." Ravel, *The Ravel Reader*, 199.

40. For a discussion of the dandy's "dichotomous gender," see Jessica R. Feldman, *Gender on the Divide*, 11.
41. Baudelaire, *Œuvres complètes*, vol. 1, 1179. Deborah Mawer translates "léger" in the title of Daphnis's dance as "agile," thereby capturing the practical implications of lightness for choreography. See Mawer, *The Ballets of Maurice Ravel*, 108.
42. It is evident from the reviews of two contemporary critics that Nijinsky incorporated a crook into the choreography of his dance. In a review for *Comœdia illustré*, Henri Gauthier-Villars remarked that "Daphnis's poetic dance, in which the naked arm of Nijinsky, bursting out from [his] immaculate and broadly vented tunic, stretches out elegantly upon the crook that bends the nape of the neck, will count among the most artistic inventions of this stunning creator of visual rhythms." Henri Gauthier-Villars, untitled review of *Daphnis et Chloé*, unpaginated article in *Collection des plus beaux numéros de* Comoedia illustré. Cyril Beaumont also called attention to the "white wand" that Daphnis picks up at the onset of his dance. Beaumont, *Michel Fokine and His Ballets*, 97. Simon Morrison briefly notes Fokin's use of the crook as well in two photographs from the Fokin archive at the State Theatre Library in Saint Petersburg. Morrison, "The Origins of *Daphnis et Chloé*," 72.
43. Cited from Barbey, *Du Dandysme*, 45n2. Irving Wohlfarth finds the same sentiment repeated in Baudelaire's writings on the dandy, in which the poet "rehabilitates leisure" through the figure of the dandy. Wohlfarth, "Aspects of Baudelaire's Literary Dandyism," 170. Walter Benjamin also associates the refrain of Baudelaire's "L'invitation au voyage" with the dandy:

    This famous stanza has a rocking rhythm; its movement seizes the ships which lie moored in the canals. To be rocked between extremes: this is the privilege of ships, and this is what Baudelaire longed for. The ships emerge at the site of the profound, secret, and paradoxical image of his dreams: the vision of being supported and sheltered by greatness. . . . The ships combine airy casualness with readiness for the utmost exertion. This gives them a secret significance. . . . To Baudelaire, the dandy appeared to be a descendant of great ancestors. (Benjamin, "The Paris of the Second Empire in Baudelaire," 59–60)

    To my mind, Benjamin hereby makes explicit an association that Baudelaire seems to offer in a parenthetical pun that is found in the "Fusées" section of the *Journaux intimes*: "These large and beautiful ships, rocking [*dandinés*] imperceptibly upon tranquil waters, these robust ships, with an idle and nostalgic air, don't they say to us in a silent language: 'When are we leaving for happiness?' " Baudelaire, *Œuvres complètes*, vol. 1, 1253.
44. Baudelaire, *Œuvres complètes*, vol. 1, 1184. Tobias Plebuch has compared the difference between the overtone series and its stylization in *Daphnis* to that between real and plastic flowers: "The pose of artificial naturalness is also found in Ravel's early works. The overtone series that he composed out in *Daphnis et Chloé* are, of course, just as 'natural' as well-made plastic flowers" ("Die Pose der künstlichen Natürlichkeit findet sich auch in den frühen Werken Ravels. In *Daphnis et Chloé* hat er Obertonreihen auskomponiert. Doch das ist freilich so natürlich wie gut gemachte Plastikblumen."). Plebuch, "Der stumme Schrecken," 164.
45. Emilien Carassus, *Le mythe du Dandy*, 177.
46. Barbey's description of the dandy as "le Héros de l'élégance oisive" appears in *Du Dandysme*, 32n1.
47. "Die Überbetonung des Körperlichen durch Kleidung und Haltung dient dazu, den Körper als Selbstzweck zu negieren. . . . Der Körper ist also bestenfalls ein gekonnt eingesetztes Instrument, auf dem der Dandy . . . virtuös zu spielen versteht." Klee, *Leibhaftige Dekadenz*, 96.

48. Barbey, *Du Dandysme*, 110. In calling these arpeggios "interjections," Deborah Mawer also presents an understanding of them as elements of verbal discourse. See Mawer, "Ballet," 147.
49. Michel D. Calvocoressi, *Music and Ballet*, 79.
50. Baudelaire, *Œuvres complètes*, vol. 1, 1180. "Idle Hercules" translates Baudelaire's "un Hercule sans emploi."
51. Calvocoressi, *Music and Ballet*, 210–211.
52. Charles R. Batson, *Dance, Desire, and Anxiety*, 186. Compare Batson's description of Nijinsky with Jessica Feldman's quite similar remarks on the dandy-as-androgyne: "To be an androgyne is to sacrifice one's own gender in order to exist outside gender category, neither male nor wholly female, but paradoxically both or neither." Feldman, *Gender*, 118.
53. Mawer, *The Ballets of Maurice Ravel*, 109.
54. The original text reads as follows:

    Fille de la Légèreté et de l'Aplomb . . . [l'Impertinence] est aussi la sœur de la Grâce, avec laquelle elle doît rester unie. Toutes deux s'embellisent de leur mutuel contraste. En effet, sans l'Impertinence, la Grâce ne ressemblerait-elle pas à une blonde trop fade, et sans la Grâce, l'Impertinence ne serait-elle pas une brune trop piquante? Pour qu'elles soient bien ce qu'elles sont chacune, il convient de les entremêler." (Barbey, *Du Dandysme*, 69–70)

    Emilien Carassus also devotes a brief chapter to the dandy's impertinence in Carassus, *Le mythe du dandy*, 119–124.
55. Baudelaire, *Œuvres complètes*, vol. 1, 1273.
56. "Le Ravel qui porte des favoris et sacrifie discrètement, mais assidûment aux exigences de la mode, offre le type achevé du dandy baudelairien: froideur élégante, horreur de la trivialité et de toutes les effusions du sentiment." Roland-Manuel, *À la gloire*, 54.
57. Reprinted in Ravel, *A Ravel Reader*, 448.
58. An English translation of this letter appears in ibid., 53. Arbie Orenstein reproduces the original letter in *Ravel: Man and Musician*, plate 5.
59. Jacques Amyot, the royal preceptor of François I and famous for having first translated Longus's *Daphnis and Chloe* into French in 1559, was also the first French translator of Plutarch's *Lives*, which contains an important biography of Alcibiades. This coincidence should not be too startling, however, since classical civilization was a common and attractive resource for genealogists and mythographers of dandyism—both for its human examples of splendor, deviance, and excess, as well as its (apparently) indifferent relation to the historical present, one that helps to prevent such knowledge from becoming utilitarian.
60. Ravel, *A Ravel Reader*, 82.
61. A basic source for this well-known proclamation is Ravel, "Memories of a Lazy Child" (1931).
62. "Et puis, vous savez, on n'avait jamais fait ça!" Cited in Nichols, ed., *Ravel Remembered*, 181.
63. Baudelaire, *Œuvres complètes*, vol. 1, 1178.
64. Deborah Houk, "Self-Construction and Sexual Identity," 61.
65. Boulenger's *Lettres de Chantilly* (1907) are cited in Carassus, *Le mythe du Dandy*, 274–275.
66. Baudelaire, *Œuvres complètes*, vol. 1, 1179; Wohlfarth, "Aspects," 78; Carassus, *Le mythe du Dandy*, 145.
67. Volney P. Gay, *Freud on Sublimation: Reconsiderations*, 113.
68. On this point, see Franz Kaltenbeck, "Sublimation and Symptom."
69. Freud, "On Narcissism," 94.
70. Feldman, *Gender*, 99.

71. Ravel, *A Ravel Reader*, 38. Upon consulting the original French text, I have slightly modified Orenstein's translation. In the editor's first footnote on the same page, he mentions that "according to Roland-Manuel, this statement concluded the interview which resulted in the Autobiographical Sketch [of 1928]." A recent study of this topic is Steven Huebner, "Ravel's Perfection."
72. Freud, "On Narcissism," 93.
73. Susan McClary, *Feminine Endings*, 80–111.
74. Robert Fink, "Desire, Repression, and Brahms's First Symphony," 284.
75. Harald Krebs, *Fantasy Pieces*, 254.
76. For an overview of displacement dissonance, see ibid., 33–39.
77. Ibid., 253 and 255, respectively.
78. The apparent Wagnerism of the love theme's harmony can be tentatively explained as a way in which Ravel attempted to acknowledge the commission's origin in the Ballets russes, whose collaborative modus operandi derived justification, impetus, and prestige from Wagner's poetic theories (in particular, the notion of the *Gesamtkunstwerk*).
79. Baudelaire, *Œuvres complètes*, vol. 1, 1271.
80. Wohlfarth, "Aspects," 210–211.
81. Bernard Howells, *Baudelaire*, 77.
82. Anne Carson, *Eros the Bittersweet*, 3. Carson's translation of Sapphic Fragment 130 in the 1986 volume differs from the version that she provides in her 2003 volume: "Eros the melter of limbs (now again) stirs me— / sweetbitter unmanageable creature who steals in." Carson, *If Not, Winter*, 265.
83. Christian Thorau has proposed "Leiden im Sehnen," or, alternatively, "Sehnen im Leiden," as synoptic terms that may help to unify the variety of nomenclature that has historically been applied by commentators on *Tristan* to the opening two chromatic motives in the Prelude. Thorau, *Semantisierte Sinnlichkeit*, 190–191.
84. Bruce W. Holsinger discusses the musical symbolism of passion involving both Marsyas and Christ in Holsinger, *Music, Body, and Desire in Medieval Culture*, 54 and 58. Swinburne's poem "Anactoria" is a good example of a literary work that views the subjectivity of the Aeolian harp from a sadomasochistic perspective, as discussed in Lawrence Kramer, *Franz Schubert*, 78–79. Compare Jessica Feldman's description of Baudelaire's "vaporization of the self" as "an extreme of the Romantic image of the self as lyre, played upon by the winds of divine inspiration. Here, the self dies into expression, losing its boundaries." Feldman, *Gender*, 135.
85. "(Sans décomposer)" cancels "(Décomposez)," which appears at the beginning of the "Danse légère" and presumably encourages the musicians to take the necessary time and make the requisite effort to bring out the internal contrasts of the A phrases. We should also note that "décomposer" is aligned with the decadent style through Nisard, Bourget, and Nietzsche (as discussed in the introductory chapter) insofar as the decomposition of the whole shifts attention to its component fragments.
86. Freud, *The Ego and the Id*, 19.
87. In *After the Lovedeath: Sexual Violence and the Making of Culture*, Lawrence Kramer likens the notational convention of the barline to a rod, which is "at once the traditional symbol of authority, discipline, and punishment, and a simple tool for measuring, pointing, upholding, divining, and beating" (61).
88. This nomenclature for octatonicism is taken from Joseph N. Straus, *Introduction to Post-Tonal Theory*, 3rd ed., 144.
89. Richard Langham Smith accounts for the use of this compositional technique in *L'enfant et les sortilèges* (R13) as a representation of the Child's "naughtiness," while Peter Kaminsky interprets the transformation of white-note sonorities into black-note chords in "Nahandove" from the *Chansons madécasses* as a musical-symbolic realization of the transition from "the indefiniteness of imagination" to "the flesh-and-blood act of making love" (Langham Smith, "Ravel's Operatic Spectacles," 207–208; Kaminsky, "Vocal Music and the Lures of Exoticism and Irony," 182).

90. " 'Dire que j'ai gâché des années de ma vie, que j'ai voulu mourir, que j'ai eu mon plus grand amour, pour une femme qui ne me plaisait pas, qui n'était pas mon genre!' " Marcel Proust, *À la recherche du temps perdu*, 305.
91. Ravel heard *L'île joyeuse* before its public premiere in a private performance by Ricardo Viñes at the salon of Madame de Saint-Marceaux on Jan. 13, 1905. He later criticized the piece for resembling a piano reduction of an orchestral score (Ravel, *A Ravel Reader*, 21).
92. Lest one uncritically suppose Nietzsche's conceptualization of the Apollonian/Dionysian dialectic as purely historical in its philology, we should recognize Albert Henrichs's argument that the strong association of Dionysus with suffering, violence, and the loss of self, all of which are involved in the notion of a Dionysian sparagmatics, originated in the nineteenth century and was given new impetus by the classicists Nietzsche and Erwin Rohde toward the end of the century. See Henrichs, "Loss of Self, Suffering, Violence."
93. Gubisch, ed., "Le journal inédit," 190.
94. Ravel, *A Ravel Reader*, 103. The music that so disgusted Ravel on the Mar. 13, 1909, Société Nationale concert included some or all of the following: Marcel Orban's *Symphony in D Minor*, Pierre Bretagne's *Chants d'automne*, Pierre Coindreau's *Le chevalier Moine et les diables dans l'abbaye*, Henri Mulet's *La Toussaint*, Désire-Émile Inghelbrecht's symphonic poem *Pour le jour des premières neiges au vieux Japon*, and the third movement of Paul le Flem's *Symphony in A* (ibid., 104–105).
95. ibid., 345. For further discussion of the SMI and its aesthetic profile, see Jean-Michel Nectoux, "Ravel/Fauré et les débuts de la Société Musicale Indépendante," and Michel Duchesneau, "Maurice Ravel et la Société Musicale Indépendante."
96. Calvocoressi, *Music and Ballet*, 79.
97. Discussions of this opera from the standpoint of musical politics include Martin Cooper, *French Music*, 161, and Jane F. Fulcher, *French Cultural Politics and Music*, 64–75.
98. "Fauteurs d'un art ténu et rare, nous faisons la mode et nous la suivons. Que tout soit abaissé à notre taille. Haine à l'enthousiasme! Haine à l'art idéal! Plus de règles, plus d'études, Faisons petit, faisons original." D'Indy, *La légende de Saint-Christophe*, 99. In his stage directions for *La légende*, d'Indy makes clear that the various guilds are not to be represented by actual performers marching across the stage but rather by the gradual unfolding of a panorama or by "colored projections"; the chorus that sings the various guild songs can be seated onstage but should be hidden from the audience by the placement of the scenery (ibid., 90).
99. Cooper, *French Music*, 161.
100. This list stems, in part, from Pamela A. Genova, "*Le dandysme*: Terrorism with Style," 83.
101. "Verständigungsprobleme zwischen Ravel und nachfolgenden Generationen erwachsen generell daraus, dass Ravel in seinem Leben wie in seiner Musik dem Baudelaireschen Modell des Dandy folgte, dessen Modernität und antibürgerlicher Impuls spätestens seit dem Ersten Weltkrieg nicht mehr unmittelbar nachvollziehbar waren." Kabisch, "Ravel," 1357.
102. Fabio Cleto, "Introduction: Queering the Camp," 2–3. Emphasis in the original.
103. Susan Sontag, "Notes on 'Camp,' " 288. Since its appearance almost fifty years ago, Sontag's essay has been criticized as energetically as it has been celebrated; controversial aspects have included her alleged desexualization and depoliticization of camp, her alignment of camp with bourgeois practices, and her spurious distinction between "naïve" and "deliberate" camp.
104. For a good overview of this group and its artistic principles, see Jann Pasler, "Stravinsky and the Apaches."
105. Baudelaire, *Œuvres complètes*, vol. 1, 1178. This attitude surfaces not only in Ravel's specific choice of epigraph for the *Valses nobles* but also in a letter dated Jan. 10, 1923, in which he recommended that a young Jean Françaix pursue "the 'pleasurable' career" of composition. Ravel, *A Ravel Reader*, 232–233.
106. Gurminder Bhogal has analyzed "Noctuelles" in a similar manner—as an exercise in "trompe l'oreille," whereby sudden shifts in surface texture thwart accruing expectations

of a structural event. See Gurminder Kaur Bhogal, "Arabesque and Metric Dissonance in the Music of Maurice Ravel," vol. 1, 1–33. In addition, Bhogal understands the shifts in texture and meter in the "Danse légère" to portray the uncontrollability of Daphnis's desire, as do I (cf. 208–210). Volker Helbing has also addressed similar musical-structural matters in "*Noctuelles* by Ravel: An Essay on the Morphology of Sound."

107. I find especially attractive the possibility of understanding the inordinately blurry tonal and metrical design in "Noctuelles" as representing the sound of the typically frenetic but titillating conversation among the Apaches, those nocturnally social butterflies.
108. The phrase "gravity in the frivolous" (*gravité dans le frivole*) appears in the chapter on the dandy (9) in Baudelaire's "Le peintre de la vie moderne," in *Œuvres complètes*, vol. 1, 1179.
109. An interesting comparison can be made between "Le paon" (1907) and Debussy's first *Ballade de François Villon*, "Ballade de Villon à s'amye" (1910), a lamentation on love lost, whose climax at bar 20 ("Haro, haro, le grand et le mineur!") bears close affinity to the climax of "The Peacock." Arbie Orenstein presents Debussy's two contrasting comments from 1907 on Ravel's *Histoires naturelles* in *Ravel: Man and Musician*, 53, and reprints the originals in Ravel, *A Ravel Reader*, 86–87.
110. This version of the tale is drawn from the collection *Magasin des enfants* (1756) by Marie Leprince de Beaumont. Ravel's makes explicit the relevant moments of their conversations by including them in the piece as epigraph.
111. This embedded structure is probably what Robert Gronquist was referring to when he described "Futile Petition" as having a "tripartite form." Gronquist, "Ravel's *Trois poèmes de Stéphane Mallarmé*," 517.
112. For a broad treatment of this relation, see Stephen C. Downes, *The Muse as Eros*.
113. For an interpretation of the Pan/Syrinx myth according to the notion of sublimated desire—one that happens to resonate well with Mallarmé's poetics of absence—see Lacan, *The Ethics of Psychoanalysis*, 163.
114. Jennifer E. Goltz, "The Roots of *Pierrot lunaire* in Cabaret," vol. 1, 172–180. Goltz also discusses "Der Mondfleck" (no. 18) in terms of dandyism, whose intricate design ultimately represents for Goltz a parody rather than a celebration of counterpoint.
115. Pierre-Daniel Templier, *Erik Satie*, 84; Steven Moore Whiting, *Satie the Bohemian*, 414. Testimony from two friends of Satie, Charles Levadé and Francis Jourdain, confirms his dandyism; see Robert Orledge, ed., *Satie Remembered*, 15 and 39.
116. It is significant in this context that Theo Hirsbrunner has invoked Pierrot as the figure that best articulates the self-conception of artists in Paris during Debussy's youth. Hirsbrunner, *Debussy und seine Zeit*.
117. Michel Beaujour, *Poetics of the Literary Self-Portrait*, 338.

Chapter 4

1. Scott Messing has accounted for neoclassicism *avant la lettre* in early Debussy and Ravel as a surface allusion to the distant past that proceeds along the lines of their nineteenth-century predecessors (Saint-Saëns, Délibes, Chabrier, et al.) rather than modeling itself directly on Baroque and High Classical repertory. Scott Messing, *Neoclassicism in Music*, 12–59.
2. Deborah Mawer, "Musical Objects and Machines," 55.
3. Carolyn Abbate, *In Search of Opera*, 185–246.
4. Steven Huebner, "Laughter: In Ravel's Time."
5. Mawer, "Musical Objects and Machines," 64 and 66, resp.
6. The idyll and the bacchanal are exotic and fantastical tropes—which, however, only enhances their decadence. Ralph Locke has shed light upon the idyll by observing that, in nineteenth-century exoticism, "any place of purity or refreshing vitality . . . as a 'refuge from [the] overbearing modernity' of real life was understood to be a product of active fantasizing." Ralph Locke, "Cutthroats and Casbah Dancers, Muezzins and Timeless Sands," 49. In another article—one devoted to Saint-Saëns's *Samson et Dalila*, which

features perhaps the most famous bacchanal in Western classical music—Locke cites Edward Saïd on Orientalist art, which is said to include both "idyllic pleasure" and "intense energy" among its characteristic topics. Locke, "Constructing the Oriental 'Other,'" 264.

7. In "Restoring Lost Meanings in Musical Representations of Exotic 'Others,'" a paper delivered at the 2009 National Meeting of the American Musicological Society, Philadelphia, Ralph Locke observed that both the "Danse grotesque" and the "Danse guerrière" share the same source of musical exoticism: the Turkish *usul* rhythm, which I discuss in chapter 3.
8. Recent scholarly testimony to Ravel's intimate knowledge of Russian music is Steven Baur, "Ravel's 'Russian' Period."
9. Despite the fact that Ravel wrote "Ils tombent, ivres" (They fall down, drunk) into the manuscript for the full orchestral score, it was never incorporated into the 1913 Durand publication.
10. In his autobiography, Fokin claims to have asked Ravel, at the outset of their collaboration, to dispense with conventional ballet numbers such as waltzes, polkas, pizzicatos, and galops; see Michel Fokine, *Fokine*, 196. The parodic galop of the War Dance (conjuring up visions of the Cossacks, perhaps) simultaneously satisfies and subverts his request.
11. For a discussion of *Cléopâtre* and the *femme fatale* in Diaghilev's Ballets russes, see Lynn Garafola, *Legacies of Twentieth-Century Dance*, 181–182.
12. For an extensive elaboration of this and related dichotomies in psychoanalysis (the ego and the id, the reality and pleasure principles, etc.) see Herbert Marcuse, *Eros and Civilization*. One of the most powerful and pertinent ideas in this book is his promotion of Orpheus and Narcissus, in contradiction to Prometheus, as archetypes of a utopian and an aesthetic reality:

    If Prometheus is the culture-hero of toil, productivity, and progress through repression, then the symbols of another reality principle must be sought at the opposite pole. Orpheus and Narcissus (akin to Dionysus) . . . have not become the culture-heroes of the Western world: theirs is the image of joy and fulfillment; the voice which does not command but sings; the gesture which offers and receives; the deed which is peace and ends the labor of conquest; the liberation from time which unites man and god, man with nature. (161–162)

13. The relevant sections of the libretto read as follows: After having "fainted at the entrance to the grotto" (R69), Daphnis "is *still* stretched out in front of the grotto of the Nymphs" at the beginning of the Daybreak (R155). Emphasis mine.
14. In Deborah Mawer's typology of dance in *Daphnis*, the War Dance (as well as the dances of Lyceion and Chloe/Syrinx) qualifies as one of the "high-speed" dances. Mawer, "Ballet and the Apotheosis of the Dance," 148.
15. It is difficult to unequivocally determine Daphnis to be a spectator of the nymphs' dance since he is both the agent of his dream and an actor in it—both aware and unaware of the nymphs as they dance. Regardless of Daphnis's superposition of states, the nymphs are certainly viable objects of spectation since they are, like Lyceion, secondary characters that are strongly associated with Chloe and thus share in her desirability.
16. Nigel Simeone tells us that "Durand's records show nothing about this 1910 printing" and concludes that "it is probably fair to assume that neither the composer nor the publisher considered these advance copies to constitute anything more than a provisional publication for copyright purposes (the edition was also deposited for copyright at the Library of Congress)." Nigel Simeone, "Mother Goose and Other Golden Eggs," 65–66.
17. Henri Gauthier-Villars noted that some audience members at the premiere of *Daphnis* in June 1912 "smiled with pleasure upon hearing a citation from *Schéhérazade* pass through the orchestra" ("Faut-il noter que certains auditeurs ont souri de plaisir en entendant

passer dans l'orchestre une citation de Schéhérazade?"). Henri Gauthier-Villars, untitled review of *Daphnis et Chloé*, n.p.

18. According to Henriette Faure, who was one of Ravel's students (as well as the sister of the politician Edgar Faure), the composer wanted the finale of the *Sonatine* played "without prudence or mercy," which feeds directly into what I have been describing as "bacchanalian" music. Cited in Roger Nichols, "Preface," 5.

Chapter 5

1. Although Waltz I may not have greater intrinsic musical value than any other waltz in the set, as the first waltz that the audience hears it has nevertheless acquired special status within the performance history of the *Valses*; Arbie Orenstein briefly discusses this waltz and its attendant controversy in his *Ravel: Man and Musician*, 175–176. In light of a genealogy that Roy Howat has proposed, Ravel may have intended to ruffle feathers with Waltz I by modeling it on the beginning of Debussy's "Ibéria," a piece that Ravel had recently defended in print against hostile critics; see Howat, "Ravel and the Piano," 272–273n26.
2. Michel Fischer reproduces these comments in "Les valses de Maurice Ravel," 118, drawing them from Manuel Rosenthal, *Ravel*, 72–73. Sevin H. Yaraman's suggestion that thematic recollection in the codas of Strauss's orchestral waltzes might have served as a model for the Epilogue is useful but does not address its strangeness and complexity. See Yaraman, *Revolving Embrace*, 94.
3. Deborah Mawer has made the following conjecture about the subtitle and its relation to the scenario: "Although there is no concrete evidence to support the claim, it is hard to imagine that Ravel's scenario is not at some level derived from the highly influential book of the same name, *Le langage des fleurs*, published in 1819 by Charlotte de Latour and itself much indebted to *Emblèmes de flore* by Alexis Lucot, which had appeared earlier in the year." Mawer, *The Ballets of Maurice Ravel*, 129.
4. The full libretto, published as part of his work catalogue, is fully translated into English and reproduced in appendix B of Maurice Ravel, *A Ravel Reader*, 510–511. An earlier draft of the libretto, written in Ravel's hand and housed at the Bibliothèque de l'Opéra in Paris (as item "LAS Ravel 14"), dates the action to "around [*vers*] 1825."
5. The Bibliothèque de l'Opéra possesses a copy of the Durand piano score for the *Valses* (Rés. 2249) with the lines of the ballet libretto (an intermediate draft) written above the staves in Ravel's own hand. Unfortunately, the distribution of lines in the Epilogue is too casual to allow us to make any strong claims about Ravel's intentions concerning the specific coordination of dramatic action to musical structure in this waltz. For one example, he crosses out a long section of the libretto that he has already written in and redistributes it across the third and fourth phrases of the Epilogue (probably to give the dancers more time to perform their pantomime); for another, he bunches up the action toward the end of the fifth phrase, superimposing two libretto lines over a single group of measures, which leaves the dancers with nothing to do during the final phrase. (It is a significant phrase: It is the only literal reprise of the main theme, presents the only citation of Waltz II, and lasts for about a minute in most recordings—a quarter of the length of the entire waltz.) While Ravel generally coordinates the inception of some dramatic action with the beginning of a phrase or subphrase, the musical structure of the Epilogue does not seem to have predetermined its dramatic action, at least not at a detailed level.
6. In other words, the premiere of the ballet on Apr. 22, 1912, was also the premiere of the orchestrated *Valses*, performed by the Orchestre Lamoureux under Ravel's baton at the Théâtre du Châtelet in Paris.
7. Howat, "Ravel and the piano," 88.
8. Jankélévitch, *Ravel*, 152n1.
9. In his "Autobiographical Sketch," Ravel claims that the title alone "indicates my intention of composing a series of waltzes in imitation of Schubert." Ravel, *A Ravel Reader*, 31.

10. Rosen, *The Romantic Generation*, 213 and 235. The special status of the Epilogue within the *Valses*—having its own title but deriving its material largely from previous waltzes—has dissuaded some commentators from describing it as a waltz despite its label of "VIII" within the suite. Rollo H. Myers's description of the *Valses* as "eight waltzes (or rather seven and an epilogue)" expresses this characteristic hesitancy over an appropriate designation for it. Myers, *Ravel*, 168. Deborah Mawer has also singled it out for the larger potential literary and dramatic significance of its title: "An epilogue may denote a speech addressed directly to the audience at the end of a play, or a postscript that provides an update on the fates of the work's characters. On two counts, therefore, the listener may wonder whether Ravel had at least an embryonic sense of programme for this music before its balletic evolution." Mawer, *The Ballets*, 128–129.
11. Ivry, *Maurice Ravel*, 71.
12. Jean-Christophe Branger, "Ravel et la valse," 153.
13. The two themes that overlap and even occasionally interrupt each other in number 12 of *Papillons* previously appeared in numbers 1 and 11, the so-called Grossvater-Tanz.
14. Focused discussions of Schumann reception in France during this period include Elaine Brody, "Schumann's Legacy in France"; Serge Gut, "Schumann und Frankreich"; and Peter Jost, "Schumann in der französischen Musik des 20. Jahrhunderts." Jess Tyre gives an interesting account of Schumann's reception in France as a psychologically troubled Romantic artist in "The Reception of German Instrumental Music in France between 1870 and 1914," 413–428.
15. Eric Frederick Jensen, "Explicating Jean Paul," 127.
16. As I propose in chapter 2, another piece by Ravel that arguably opens on a moonlit, melancholy landscape and explores the power of memory is the *Introduction et allegro* for harp, string quartet, flute, and clarinet (1905).
17. Bergson, *Matter and Memory*, 82–83.
18. "À mesure que la nuit descend sur nous, le souvenir remonte en nous comme une prière." Jankélévitch, *L'irréversible et la nostalgie*, 212. Unless otherwise noted, all translations are mine. While one could translate this sentence without "gradually," I have chosen to include it in order to capture the precise sense of "à mesure que," especially in conjunction with the gradual actions of "ascending" (*monter*) and "descending" (*descendre*), as well as the special reciprocity between memory and nighttime, which seems to me to be at issue in both Jankélévitch's argument and mine.
19. Some readers will recognize this behavior as "rotational" in the sense advanced by James Hepokoski and Warren Darcy insofar as each phrase moves through a prototypical set of ordered elements but is also free to manipulate their order and appearance from one phrase to the next. As mentioned in previous chapters, their most recent exposition of rotational form appears in Hepokoski and Darcy, *Elements of Sonata Theory*.
20. I have chosen to label the thematic material of the Epilogue "~" rather than "VIII" in order to make a clear visual distinction in example 5.1 between it and all extrinsic citations. With "0," on the other hand, I am not implying that these melody-poor measures are worth nothing to the analysis but am rather indicating a specific role that they play in an unfolding musical memory-narrative, as I discuss later.
21. Readers will likely recognize the concept of the musical "sentence" not only from previous chapters—such as chapter 2's discussion of the introductory formula—but also from Arnold Schoenberg, *Fundamentals of Musical Composition*, and the terminology of "presentation" and "continuation" from William E. Caplin, *Classical Form*.
22. As previously mentioned, Proust describes this binarism at greatest length in an interview with a reporter from *Le temps* from fall 1913. An English translation of the entire interview appears in Roger Shattuck, *Marcel Proust*, 166–172.
23. Rosen, *The Romantic Generation*, 112.
24. On this point, compare Abbate: "Nowhere is the machinelike status of human beings more clear than in a musical performance in which someone plays (is played by) someone else's work." Abbate, *In Search of Opera*, 195.

25. Ronald Woodley also notes the "quite radical changes of speed and mood between the fragments." Woodley, "Performing Ravel," 218. This performance has been released on the Pierian label as CD 0013, vol. 4 of the Caswell Collection: "Maurice Ravel: The Composer as Pianist and Conductor."
26. Interpretation of the libretto helps to explain not only the emphasis upon Waltz IV in the Epilogue but also the absence of any reference to Waltz V. During Waltz V in *Adélaïde* the duke declares his interest in the courtesan. She subsequently shows little interest in him until, at the beginning of the Epilogue, she finally dismisses him. Thus, just as the duke has been subtracted from the love triangle during the Epilogue, so, too, does Waltz V fail to appear. On a purely musical level, however, it is not clear to me how one might plausibly account for the conspicuous omission of Waltz V from the Epilogue. Perhaps the idea of an absolutely comprehensive thematic citation was too pedantic for Ravel and compelled him to exclude at least one element.
27. Mawer, *The Ballets*, 133.
28. For example, when the first ghost asks whether the heart of the second "still beats at my name," the latter forecloses further conversation with a simple "no." Then, when the first ghost presses further, recalling "how blue the sky was, and how great our hope!," the second responds that "hope has fled, vanquished, into the black sky." For insightful analyses of Verlaine's poem and Debussy's song, see Susan Youens, "Debussy's Setting of Verlaine's 'Colloque sentimental.' "
29. My association of the quotidian with sentimentality and pleasure is indebted to Linda M. Austin, *Nostalgia in Transition*, in which the author argues for a notion of nostalgia—particularly prevalent in Victorian England but theoretically rooted in Schiller's writings—that is neither psychological nor pathological but rather aesthetic, sentimental, and somatic. It derives its gentle, nonanxious pleasures from the consumption of everyday items of allegedly lesser cultural prestige, some of which we today like to call "kitsch." Although these ideas are certainly pertinent to Ravel's oeuvre as a whole, as well as the first seven waltzes of the *Valses*, I am arguing for a decisive and unmistakable shift into melancholy—a more typical, psychological mode of nostalgia—as we move into the Epilogue.
30. See Brian Hyer, " 'Sighing Branches,' " and Hyer, "Before Rameau and After" (esp. 93–97). Peter Kaminsky offers a similar account of voice leading for the opening of Waltz I in "Composer's Words," 163–164.
31. His library included five piano-vocal scores from the Durand series, edited by Camille Saint-Saëns—*Castor et Pollux, Les fêtes d'Hébé, Hippolyte et Aricie, Platée,* and *Pygmalion*—as well as *Naïs*, which Reynaldo Hahn edited for Durand in 1924. A general discussion of the content of Ravel's personal library, which is on deposit in the Music Division of the Bibliothèque nationale de Paris, is Jean-Michel Nectoux, "Maurice Ravel et sa bibliothèque musicale."
32. My invocation of fire is not casual but precise: It is a site of intersection for the respective metaphor domains of hope and memory. For an account of metaphor in memory discourse and an argument for metaphor as fundamentally constitutive of this discourse, see Aleida Assmann, "Zur Metaphorik der Erinnerung." For a more detailed historical narrative, see Douwe Draaisma, *Metaphors of Memory*.
33. In the copy of the *Valses* (Rés. 2249, Bib. de l'Opéra, Paris) into which Ravel carefully notated a preliminary draft of the *Adélaïde* libretto, at the moment the music suddenly expands to accommodate the second citation of Waltz IV in P4 (m. 41), Adélaïde throws open the windows at the back of her apartment. (In the original libretto, which is also a part of the Opéra's library collection [LAS 14], it is Lorédan who opens the windows from the outside, having scaled the balcony.)
34. The 1911 piano score has "même Mouvement un peu plus las" at this moment (m. 62), while the 1912 orchestral score has "même Mouvement un peu las" (R75). Emphasis on "plus" in the main text is mine.

35. The double circle at twelve o'clock in the lower diagram of example 5.15 represents the overlap between P1 and P6, which is nevertheless not total: In addition to the obvious difference between their continuations, a low, stable tonic pedal in the bass of P6 replaces the higher, less stable supertonic pedal in P1 to signal the end of the tonal process begun in P1.
36. I discovered the heading "Déformation morale" in the manuscript for "Si morne!," whose microfilm copy (Vm. Micr. 860) forms part of the Collection Taverne on deposit in the Music Division of the Bibliothèque nationale de Paris.
37. While Lorédan may indeed be desperate and "sad unto death"—a phrase that, at least for me, brings to mind Kierkegaard's *Sickness unto Death* (1849), a treatise on melancholy and despair—I would nevertheless caution against concluding that the Epilogue is simply a portrait of his mind at work. We must remember, first of all, that Ravel drew up the ballet libretto for *Adélaïde* only well after the *Valses* had been composed, premiered, and published for solo piano. In writing the libretto, Ravel undoubtedly intended Lorédan to personify the melancholic aspects of the *Valses*. Nonetheless, his character seems to me to be irredeemably shallow: As a stock character (the Romantic monomaniac) in a stock situation (a love triangle), he can hardly be matched with the psychological depths and sophistication indicated by the Epilogue. For recent scholarship on the monomaniac in nineteenth-century European music and literature, see Francesca Brittan, "Berlioz and the Pathological Fantastic."
38. In addition to the heaved sigh in the Pantomime, other examples—all of which help to give Ravel's oeuvre a melancholic tint—can be found in the *Menuet antique*, "D'anne jouant de l'espinette," the *Sonatine* (the main cyclical motive), "Oiseaux tristes," "Le gibet," *L'heure espagnole*, and *L'enfant et les sortilèges* (the mother motive). In regard to the two reprises under comparison here, they also differ insofar as the one in the Epilogue is both a reprise of melancholy and a melancholic reprise, whereas the one in the Pantomime is apparently only a melancholic reprise.
39. On this point, compare these comments by Mark S. Muldoon: "Throughout all Bergson's works, duration is consistently described through musical metaphors. The musical metaphor of duration is an apt one since it adequately points to the complete nonspatiality of duration and excludes it from ever being employed for any form of physical measurement." Mark S. Muldoon, *Tricks of Time*, 83.
40. Il y aurait donc enfin deux moi différents, dont l'un serait comme la projection extérieure de l'autre, sa représentation spatiale et pour ainsi dire sociale. Nous atteignons le premier par une réflexion approfondie, qui nous fait saisir nos états internes commes des êtres vivants, sans cesse en voie de formation, comme des états réfractaires à la mesure, qui se pénètrent les uns les autres, et dont la succession dans la durée n'a rien de commun avec une juxtaposition dans l'espace homogène. Mais les moments où nous nous ressaisissons ainsi nous-mêmes sont rares, et c'est pourquoi nous sommes rarement libres. La plupart du temps, nous vivons extérieurement à nous-mêmes, nous n'apercevons de notre moi que son fantôme décoloré, ombre que la pure durée projette dans l'espace homogène. Notre existence se déroule donc dans l'espace plutôt que dans le temps: nous vivons pour le monde extérieur plutôt que pour nous; nous parlons plutôt que nous ne pensons; nous "sommes agis" plutôt que nous n'agissons nous-mêmes. Agir librement, c'est reprendre possession de soi, c'est se replacer dans la pure durée. (Henri Bergson, *Essai sur les données immédiates de la conscience*, 151)

    The *Essai* is often referred to in English as *Time and Free Will*, the title given to it in 1910 by its first English translator, Frank L. Pogson.
41. Suzanne Guerlac, *Thinking in Time*, 91.
42. The critique in Bergson's *Essai* of "spatialized time" for its homogenization, abstraction, and quantification of an essentially heterogeneous, concrete, and qualitative experience could provide a promising point of departure for developing a larger critical perspective on the tools and epistemological tendencies of music analysis.

43. "Le temps de la rêveuse nostalgie et de la flânerie poétique n'est plus cloisonné par les tâches, ni articulé en segments successifs: c'est un temps sans horaire ni calendrier, un temps diffluent et invertébré dont la métronomie entre en fusion et perd tout rigueur." Jankélévitch, *L'irréversible*, 212.
44. "L'expérience du passé, qui est, après tout, une expérience présente, fait partie elle-même de la futurition; notre effort pour susciter 'à nouveau' l'apparition d'une expérience ancienne aboutit en fait à une expérience nouvelle." Ibid., 34.
45. Pierre Nora, "Between Memory and History," 19. Nora's devotion to collective memory and deploration of the historical turn toward what he calls "psychological memory"—memory as a property of the private individual rather than the community or the nation—aligns him strongly with the sociologist Maurice Halbwachs, author of *Les cadres sociaux de la mémoire* (originally published in 1925). Like Halbwachs, he finds the interiorization of memory in Bergson and others to be pernicious; like Bergson, he diagnoses modern society as alienated from itself, to which the melancholic epistemology of the *lieu de mémoire* is testament. Since the felicitous moment of Bergsonian *durée* in P5 is short lived and relatively anomalous within the otherwise melancholic Epilogue, it is not as strange to elucidate it by simultaneous reference to Bergson and Nora as, at first glance, it might seem to a reader well versed in memory studies.
46. Nora, "Between Memory and History," 7. Jankélévitch's notion of musical "charm" might provide an aesthetic supplement to Nora's site of memory: "The charm is labile and fragile, and our presentiments of its obsolescence lend poetic melancholia to the state of grace it has engendered." Jankélévitch, *Music and the Ineffable*, 120.
47. Fischer seems to be thinking along similar lines in describing the clarinet of the Waltz II citation as having a "timbre nostalgique." Fischer, "Les valses de Maurice Ravel," 125.
48. "Ravel dit adieu à la valse comme il a dit adieu à la sérénade, au menuet, à la pavane, à tout l'arsenal des danses classiques devenues symboles sonores de notre civilisation." Marcel Marnat, *Maurice Ravel*, 299.
49. Mawer also associates II with VIII: "Its melodic material resembles strongly that used in waltz II for Lorédan's entrance, and at its more intense presentation (Fig. 67; measures 21ff.)." Mawer, *The Ballets*, 135. If we combine this observation with another—namely, that Waltz VII recalls Waltz I through its cadential rhythms—a double reprise is revealed: The first two waltzes recur in the last two, which is to say that Ravel bookends the *Valses* with two audibly related pairings of "noble" (I and VII) and "sentimental" (II and VIII) waltzes.
50. Ravel's decision to cite the reprise of Waltz II at the end of the Epilogue may have been influenced by the tonic sonority it features. By drawing on and alluding to various conventions of tonal closure (including the tonicization of the subdominant in codas through an applied dominant, as well as the Picardy third), the major ninth chord on G helps to announce in both waltzes that the end of the piece is in sight.
51. The context for this phrase, already cited in a previous chapter, reads as follows: "What an abyss of uncertainty, whenever the mind feels overtaken by itself; when it, the seeker, is at the same time the dark region through which it must go seeking and where all its equipment will avail it nothing. Seek? More than that: create. It is face to face with something which does not yet exist, to which it alone can give reality and substance, which it alone can bring into the light of day." Proust, *Remembrance of Things Past*, 49.
52. Richard Terdiman, *Present Past*, 44. It is also interesting to compare our analysis of memory in the Epilogue with another comment from this volume: "The process of memory carries an uncanny danger, which emerges in the paradigm of dispossession. . . . For the dispossessed, memory stages not recovery but *deficiency*. Its representations make an absence present. Or rather, memory figures the inauthenticity of presentness, the traumatic persistence of an irreversible experience of loss. This is history under the sign of disaster" (108).

Chapter 6 Notes

1. Additional appearances of the waltz in Ravel's oeuvre include Don Inigo's "Mouvement de Valse" in scene 9 of *L'heure espagnole* (1907–1909), the primary theme (m. 32) of "Scarbo" from *Gaspard de la nuit* (1908), "Les entretiens de la Belle et de la Bête" from *Ma mère l'oye* (1908–1910), and arguably a host of numbers from *Daphnis et Chloé* (1909–1912; cf. Lyceion's Dance [R57], the "Danse suppliante de Chloé" [R133], the main theme of the "Lever du jour" [R158], and the Pantomime [R172]), *A la manière de . . . Borodine* (1913), the "Danse des libellules et des sphinx" and the "Danse des rainettes" from *L'enfant et les sortilèges* (1920–1925), and the "Adagio assai" from the G-major *Concerto pour piano et orchestre* (1929–1931).
2. A "sentiment d'adieu." Jean-Christophe Branger, "Ravel et la valse," 151. Michael Stegemann has been more specific on this point by asserting a Schubertian melancholy in both pieces: "As so often in Schubert (and later in Ravel's own *La valse*) one feels [in the *Valses nobles*] the melancholy, if not the morbidity, of an end at hand beneath the 'waltz bliss' of the 3/4 measure." (Wie so oft bei Schubert [und später in Ravels eigener *La Valse*] spürt man unter der 'Walzer-Seligkeit' des Dreivierteltaktes die Melancholie, wenn nicht Morbidität eines nahen Endes.) Stegemann, *Maurice Ravel*, 81.
3. This production was premiered on Feb. 20, 1951, at the New York City Ballet; for an extended discussion, see Mawer, *The Ballets*, 174–181.
4. Cited in Ravel, *A Ravel Reader*, 486.
5. These similarities are also noted in Mawer, *The Ballets*, 175–177.
6. Jankélévitch, *Ravel*, 61–62. Jankélévitch draws the quoted text from the well-known epigraph to the *Valses nobles*. Randolph Eichert locates the historical tragedy underlying *La valse* as memorial in moments further back in history:

   The obliquities of harmony and melody, the disfigured contour of the waltz—as also in the impressive version for piano—speak as well of the victims. No longer does splendor blind the eye, but rather the dead—from the hopes of '48 to the Paris Commune—leave their mark upon the music's image. The World War was able to give the composition only a definitive impetus." (Die Schrägen der Harmonie und Melodie, die entstellte Kontur des Walzers—wie auch in der bedrükkenden Klavierfassung—reden auch von den Opfern. Nicht mehr der Glanz blendet das Auge, sondern die Toten, von den Achtundvierziger Hoffnungen bis zur Pariser Kommune, gehen ein in das Bild der Musik. Der Weltkrieg vermochte nur noch den definitiven Impuls für die Komposition zu geben.) (Randolph Eichert, "Kontrapunkte," 194)
7. Carl E. Schorske, *Fin-de-siècle Vienna*, 3.
8. Ibid., 4.
9. Ibid., 3.
10. Deborah Mawer also describes *La valse* as an ABA' in *The Ballets*, 153–154.
11. The term *wave* is adopted from early twentieth-century theories of musical energetics, which focus on intensifications in instrumental texture, dynamics, and tempo; the *locus classicus* for the concept of the musical wave is the theoretical writing of Ernst Kurth, in particular his massive, two-volume monograph, *Bruckner* (1926). Among analysts of Ravel's music, Wolf-Eberhard von Lewinski makes pointed use of the notion of intensification (*Steigerung*) to discuss musical process in *La valse*. See Lewinski, "Ravels tragischer Abschied," 185–186.
12. "Des nuées tourbillonnantes laissent entrevoir, par éclaircies, des couples de valseurs. Elles se dissipent peu à peu: on distingue (A) une immense salle peuplée d'une foule tournoyante. / La scène s'éclaire progressivement. La lumière des lustres éclate au *ff* (B). / Une Cour impériale, vers 1855." Translation mine. Mawer conjectures the existence of a longer, more elaborate scenario by Ravel, but it has not yet come to light. Mawer, *The Ballets*, 155.

13. The sources of the content of rows 4 and 5 in table 6.1 are Hermann Danuser, *Die Musik des 20. Jahrhunderts*, 74, and George Benjamin, "Last Dance," 433, respectively. If we take the 1921 Durand orchestral score (republished in 1997 by Dover) as our reference, as I have done for table 6.1, George Benjamin has mislabeled the measure number for every rehearsal number that he marks on the figure 1 "time line" in his article. By R9, he has added one measure; by R18, he has added sixty-six measures, a discrepancy he maintains (more or less) until the end of both the piece and his time line, which concludes sixty-eight measures in the black. The 1920 Durand solo piano score for *La valse* is identical in measure length to the orchestral score but differs internally in several respects from the latter: Measure 32 of the orchestral score is interpolated between measures 31 and 32 of the piano score; two measures of the final eight measures of tremolos in the piano score (mm. 746–753) are subtracted upon its transposition into the orchestral score ($R101^{+1-6}$); and the penultimate measure of the piano version (m. 754) is expanded into two measures in the orchestral version ($R101^{+7-8}$).
14. As mentioned in chapter 2, famous settings of this trope include not only the beginnings of Beethoven's *Ninth Symphony*, Wagner's *Das Rheingold*, Strauss's *Also sprach Zarathustra*, and Debussy's *La mer* but also the initial measures of Ravel's own *Daphnis et Chloé*, which, like *La valse*, was intended for Diaghilev's Ballets russes.
15. Tobias Plebuch, "Der stumme Schrecken," 164.
16. "In the search for a particular image, we remount the slope of our past." Bergson, *Matter and Memory*, 81. Elizabeth A. Grosz helps to clarify the arguments of Bergson's book in *The Nick of Time*, 155–184. Rapprochement of past and present through the activity of *remonter* is also characteristic of Proust's metaphorics of memory; for example, see the end of the famous madeleine scene in *Du côté de chez Swann*, as well as the final page of that volume and the beginning of *Albertine disparue*. Proust, *À la recherche*, 46, 342, and 1954, resp.
17. Admittedly writing about Proustian memory in this context, Walter Benjamin adjudges the recovery of a particular memory in Proust to be laborious because of the innumerable associations that beset it:

    > Anyone who wishes to surrender knowingly to the innermost sway of this work must place himself in a special stratum—the bottommost—of this involuntary remembrance, a stratum in which the materials of memory no longer appear singly, as images, but tell us about a whole, amorphously and formlessly, indefinitely and weightily, in the same way the weight of the fishing net tells a fisherman about his catch. . . . His sentences are the entire muscular activity of the intelligible body; they contain the whole enormous effort to raise this catch. (Benjamin, "On the Image of Proust," 247)

18. George Benjamin, "Last Dance," 435. Benjamin also asserts that "the recapitulation . . . can be seen to fall with almost mathematical precision on the golden section of the work" (433).
19. This passage might qualify as an example of a technique in *La valse* that Volker Helbing has described as a "braking" or a "slowing down" of musical momentum and which constitutes at R66 a "final retreat [Ausholen] before the actual climax." Helbing, "*L'impression d'un tournoiement fantastique et fatale*: Aneignung und Verzerrung in Ravels *La Valse*," 193.
20. "Just before section *A'*, the light turns deep green, and Death, clad entirely in black, reappears at the back of the stage with his accomplice. The other dancers are now spellbound in a trance upon the floor, as the white ballerina, vulnerably alone, is seduced by Death." Mawer, *The Ballets*, 178.
21. Mawer, "Balanchine's *La Valse*," 102.
22. Assimilating *La valse* to Strauss's *On the Beautiful Blue Danube* as its putative model, Sevin Yaraman clears out a larger space for the interior waltz suite and divides the thematic succession into five waltzes that begin at RR9, 13, 18, 30, and 41. Yaraman, *Revolving Embrace*,

96–98. While her relation of *La valse* to Straussian norms is valuable, her large-scale groupings underemphasize moments of formal articulation that I find important: R12, R16 (with its Motive 8 as the telos of the opening frame), and the six thematic entrances other than RR30 and 41 that lie between RR18 and 54. Further, her focus on the waltz suite shifts attention away from the two frames, which I find more interesting as compositional experiments and which occupy most of the duration of the piece.

23. Poulenc, *Moi et mes amis*, 179; the relevant passage is translated in Nichols, *Ravel Remembered*, 116–118. We do not currently have further evidence of any formal or informal agreements between Ravel and Diaghilev about a production of *La valse* prior to its preliminary audition; as Mawer notes, it was "intended for the Ballets Russes, . . . though how definite a commitment this was on Diaghilev's part remains open to question." Mawer, *The Ballets*, 151.

24. Garafola, *Diaghilev's Ballets russes*, 22. While many have interpreted the bacchanalian violence of *La valse* against the contemporaneous backdrop of World War I, Garafola interprets Fokin's Bacchanale within the 1905 Russian Revolution, which projects upon the dance a more positive allegorical meaning:

    Fokine's crowds replicated the paroxysm of revolution itself: the fury of masses unchained, the ecstasy of blood, the triumph of instinct over ego, the liberation of the self through collective action. Unlike [ballet historian André] Levinson, who cast a baleful eye on all change, Fokine welcomed the contest of old and new: as much as revolution destroyed, that much it also created. . . . He transformed his living crowd into an image of collective political practice: onstage, the spirit of 1905 continued to live. (23)

25. Marnat, *Maurice Ravel*, 479.
26. Plebuch, "Der stumme Schrecken," 165.
27. Given the usual association of Bacchanales with sexual transgression and abandon, Deborah Mawer's interpretation of the violence done to the waltz in *La valse* as Ravel's attack on heteronormativity potentially adds another dimension to the argument I am building. Mawer, "Balanchine's *La Valse*," 106.
28. Nietzsche, *The Birth of Tragedy*, 104–105.
29. Ibid., 38.
30. These associations are discussed in Pechard, "La Valse," 85–86. They also surface among the reviews amassed by Ravel himself and posthumously collected as the "Fonds Montpensier," on deposit in the Music Division of the Bibliothèque nationale de Paris. Among these reviews appears the following testament in *L'Étoile belge* (no date given) by a certain "G. E." about the (premiere?) performance of *La valse*: "De suggestive, de langoureuse, de gracieuse que cette Valse nous apparaît d'abord, elle tourne peu à peu à une chorégraphie éperdue, à des rafales d'accords et de rythmes, à une délirante apothéose; et ce ne seraient plus d'aimables couples mondains qui se livreraient à pareils ébats, mais bien des satyres et des bacchantes, emportés dans une tourmente dionysiaque."
31. Schorske, *Fin-de-siècle Vienna*, 3–4. Although Schorske does not explicitly associate *La valse* with Nietzsche's notion of the Dionysian, the latter is nonetheless a defining element of the cultural period he is examining. For example, in the same chapter that he begins with the discussion of *La valse*, he describes Arthur Schnitzler's "call to life" (the title of a 1905 Schnitzler play about cultural repression) as "a call to a Dionysian existence, which involves a plunge into the torrent and is thus also a call to death" (11).
32. Ravel, *A Ravel Reader*, 434.
33. Mawer, "Balanchine's *La Valse*," 94.
34. Cited in Baeck and Baeck-Schilders, "La création mondiale du ballet *La Valse*," 369. The recipient of this letter was Sonia Korty.
35. Cited in Ravel, *A Ravel Reader*, 423.
36. Ibid., 80.

37. The volume in question is Nietzsche, *L'origine de la tragédie; ou, Hellénisme et pessimisme*, 2nd ed., trans. Jean Marnold and Jacques Morland (Paris: Société du Mercure de France, 1901). As Christopher Forth and others have shown, Nietzsche's ideas were already broadly disseminated in France by the early 1900s by authors such as Henri Lichtenberger, Ernest Seillière, and Henri Albert, who supervised the *Œuvres complètes* from its inception. For a fuller picture of this reception history, see Christopher E. Forth, *Zarathustra in Paris*; Jacques Le Rider, *Nietzsche en France*; and Douglas Smith, *Transvaluations*. Moreover, even if Ravel had never read a word of Nietzsche and had no inkling of Marnold's translation, his Dionysian descriptions of Greek tragedy in *La valse* are undoubtedly the result of Nietzsche's discursive influence; according to Albert Henrichs, Nietzsche's conception of the Dionysian in *The Birth of Tragedy* was unprecedented and uniquely influential. See Henrichs, "Loss of Self, Suffering, Violence."
38. Historical precedent for this "backward glance" might be found in the short-lived reappearance of the Trio in the final measures of the Scherzo from Beethoven's *Ninth Symphony*. In fact, the similarity between the main motive of the Scherzo and the octave leaps of Motive 14 in *La valse* even suggests the possibility of an intentional allusion—thus, the backward glance as both an inter- and intratextual memory.
39. "Je pense à elle tous les jours, toutes les minutes puis-je dire. Surtout maintenant que j'ai repris le travail et que je me reporte aux moments heureux où je l'ai quittée. . . . Naturellement, je ne me porte pas très bien mais je turbine." Cited in Marnat, *Maurice Ravel*, 473

Conclusion

1. The irony and reflexivity of decadence have received particular emphasis in the work of Charles Bernheimer, who describes Nietzsche, Lombroso, and Freud as "diagnosticians of decadence" in *Decadent Subjects*.
2. Although it might seem strange to separate "je les veux" from "perpétuer" even for the purposes of explication, Mallarmé himself provides a precedent. Toward the beginning of the first version of the poem, the dramatic "Monologue d'un faune," the faun takes big leaps forward while exclaiming about the nymphs, "Je les veux!" Reproduced in Henri Mondor, *Histoire d'un faune*, 107.
3. I propose that we may also approach "perpétuer" through its phonic similarity to "perpétrer" [to perpetrate], which makes us think of the faun's implicit "crime" of rape (line 82), as well as the "certain punishment" (line 104) that he fears it will elicit.
4. Mondor, *Histoire d'un faune*, 107.
5. Ibid., 201.
6. Robert Greer Cohn, *Toward the Poems*, 25. Mary Lewis Shaw bolsters this claim when she observes that Mallarmé's poem differs from many other faun-related scenarios of its time—by Musset, Hugo, Rimbaud, and Banville—in its emphasis on the protagonist's duality, which is so marked that "we might interpret the choice of hero itself as an economical means of expressing the simultaneous unity and discord of the mind and body within the self." Mary Lewis Shaw, *Performance in the Texts of Mallarmé*, 128.
7. As many commentators have noted, the disjointed arrangement of the opening lines also represents the faun's state of mind as he gradually awakens from sleep. Lloyd Austin's use of this point to compare the opening of "L'après-midi" to the beginning of Proust's *Recherche*, as well as Valéry's "La jeune parque," is insightful and effective. Lloyd James Austin, "*L'après-midi d'un faune*," 184.
8. Lloyd Austin explains "fabuleux" by noting that "le Faune, être mythologique, appartient à la 'Fable'; ses sens racontent des choses fausses ou imaginaires; ils sont merveilleux, enfin, splendides, comme dans le monde des fables" [The Faun, a mythological being, belongs to the "Fable"; his senses recount false or imaginary things; they are marvelous,

in fact, splendid, like the world of fables]. Ibid., 185. For our purposes, the most important sense of "fabuleux" is "fictive."

9. The importance of breath in "L'après-midi," which commentators can overlook, stems largely from its ability to interrelate poetry and music. As a case in point, breath occupies a central position in the quatrain of homage that Mallarmé inscribed in the copy of the poem he sent to Debussy in June 1897: "Sylvain d'haleine première / Si ta flûte a réussi / Ouïs toute la lumière / Qu'y soufflera Debussy" [Sylvan of first breath / If your flute has succeeded / Hear all the light / Debussy will blow into it]. Claude Debussy, *Correspondance: 1884–1918,* 266. In "Le tombeau des Naïades," which Debussy set as one of his *Chansons de Bilitis,* Pierre Louÿs has produced a negative counterpart to the image of ruminescence in "L'après-midi d'un faune": Stopping at the tomb, the man in the poem breaks the frozen surface of the nearby spring, holds large pieces of ice to the "pale sky," and peers through them. The act that begins the poem—the attempt to find a faun by following his footsteps in the snow—inspired the title of this chapter.
10. Renato Poggioli denies the famous interpretation in Huysmans's *À rebours* of the "primal fervor" as referring to the faun's erection and declares instead that the lilies of this passage only symbolize "chastity and spiritual purity." Renato Poggioli, *The Oaten Flute,* 302. This allusion to a mystical tradition notwithstanding, I am more sympathetic to Huysmans and ultimately agree with Cohn, who says that the "phallic overtones" of this passage are "clearly a Mallarméan side effect." Cohn, *Toward the Poems,* 20.
11. Since Debussy originally intended to compose a *Prélude, interludes et paraphrase finale pour L'après-midi d'un faune,* scholars have questioned whether it is even appropriate to think of the *Prélude* as setting the poem directly. To my mind, the most convincing response to this issue is by Jean-Michel Nectoux, who finds it "infinitely probable" that the definitive version synthesizes elements from the previous segments since the *Prélude* would have been overlong to merely introduce a recitation that takes about the same amount of time. Nectoux also points to the influence of Franck in the earlier title, a suggestive idea that might help to further account for the strong dependence on thematic cyclicism in the *Prélude.* Jean-Michel Nectoux, "Debussy et Mallarmé," 59.
12. In contrast to the myth of Pan and Syrinx (and in sympathy with Théodore de Banville's *Diane au bois*), the faun's narrative involves two nymphs, and neither is transformed into reeds. Nevertheless, Mallarmé acknowledges the ancient heritage of the scenario in "L'après-midi" by having the faun invoke "maligne Syrinx" (lines 52–53). Various graphic representations of Pan and Syrinx have also been proposed as possible inspirations for Mallarmé's choice of subject matter, in particular the eighteenth-century painting of the same title by François Boucher.
13. William Austin's collation of thematic fragments is probably the clearest illustration of this point. Austin, *Norton Critical Scores,* 76–78.
14. Arthur Wenk interrelates Mallarmé's line and Debussy's theme in a way that accords with our perspective: "Mallarmé's poem may be regarded as a series of digressions upon the opening line, 'Ces nymphes, je les veux perpétuer,' which carry the faun through memory, imagination, supposition, artistic transformation, and finally resignation to dream. Debussy's *Prélude* likewise emanates entirely from the opening flute solo." Arthur B. Wenk, *Claude Debussy and the Poets,* 163.
15. In the most extensive comparison of the *Prélude* and the poem to date, David J. Code has drawn upon a wide range of sources to flesh out their literary and musical contexts. For our purposes, one of his more felicitous discoveries is a passage in a contemporary orchestration treatise by François-Auguste Gevaert that associates the distant quality of the horn with the activities of memory and imagination. David J. Code, "Hearing Debussy Reading Mallarmé," 531.
16. By describing the D♭ major episode as a telos for the *Prélude,* I am slightly resisting Rebecca Leydon's argument that the *Prélude* partakes only of the stasis typical of bucolic narratives rather than the goal-directed dynamism typical of heroic narratives. Rebecca

Leydon, " 'Ces nymphes, je les veux perpétuer.' " The bucolic/heroic dichotomy stems from Thomas G. Rosenmeyer, *The Green Cabinet*.

17. The association between the cantilena of Chopin's nocturne and the interior melody of Debussy's *Prélude* appears in Austin, *Norton Critical Scores*, 73.
18. To associate the repetition and variation of the faun theme with the movement of the remembering mind is different from associating them with the faun's multiple *états d'âme* but does not contradict it. The "soul states" evoked by these thematic variations—which number about fifteen—include languor (mm. 1–4), playfulness (mm. 21–30), passion (mm. 55–73), and plaintiveness (mm. 100–106). In fact, the association of these moments with the activity of memory merely adds a further twist to James Hepokoski's interpretation of the opening sequence of phrases: "In the *Faune* [Debussy] created an eloquent musical analogue to the prevailing Decadent and Symbolist ideal of interior, rather than exterior, growth. . . . The mysterious florification in Debussy's *Faune* is all vertical, inward, involuted, like the closed mind feeding on itself." James A. Hepokoski, "Formulaic Openings in Debussy," 56–57.
19. Ravel, *A Ravel Reader*, 486.
20. Ravel made this comment in private conversation with Manuel Rosenthal, who passed it onto Roger Nichols. Nichols, *Ravel Remembered*, 101.
21. Ravel, *A Ravel Reader*, 486.
22. Ibid., 404.
23. Ibid., 410.
24. Ibid., 421.
25. Recall Ravel's comment, previously cited in chapter 3: "My objective . . . is technical perfection. I can strive unceasingly toward this end since I am certain never to attain it. The important thing is to draw ever closer to it." Ibid., 38.
26. Roland-Manuel accounted for the transcription in this way: "Because it gave him pleasure, and because he wished to pay homage to a man of genius, Ravel transcribed for two pianos [*sic*] the *Prélude à l'après-midi d'un faune*, a work that he himself never tired of calling a masterpiece." Cited in Nichols, *Ravel Remembered*, 101.
27. Ravel, *A Ravel Reader*, 30.
28. Gurminder Bhogal has recently linked the music of Debussy and Ravel through the notion of the arabesque. Her project coincides with mine in some ways—for example, the comparison of Debussy's *Prélude* with various movements from *Daphnis*—but not in others. In particular, she focuses on melodic rhythm and metrical dissonance, while I spend more time on programmatic themes and narrative. See Bhogal, "Debussy's Arabesque and Ravel's *Daphnis et Chloé* (1912)."
29. Although the third water piece, "Une barque sur l'océan" from *Miroirs* (1905), also shares important features with Debussy's *Prélude*—it is marked "d'un rythme souple" and boasts a wealth of themes and textures—it seems to me to be more similar to "Nuages" from *Nocturnes*. Both seem to be organized by thematic rotations whose bounding themes are respectively natural/diffuse and human/melancholic: the "clouds" and the "signal" in "Nuages," and the "ocean" (m. 1) and the "boat" (mm. 46–49) in "Une barque." The labels of "clouds" and "signal" come from James A. Hepokoski, "Clouds and Circles." In addition, my identification of the melody of mm. 46–49 in "La barque" as the "boat" resonates with its description as the piece's "human component" in Siglind Bruhn, *Images and Ideas*, 76.
30. Ravel, *A Ravel Reader*, 30.
31. The presence of "sonata form" as an organizing principle in *Jeux d'eau* is weak and dubious for two additional reasons: A lack of internal tonal and thematic opposition in the first half of the piece makes it impossible to clearly discern anything like the standard two-part exposition; its apparent recapitulation (m. 62) is undermined tonally by the bass G♯, which persists from the previous section, and formally by the subsequent cadenza (m. 72).

32. Wenk, *Claude Debussy and the Poets*, 162–163. After completing this chapter, I was happy to discover that Roy Howat analyzes "Ondine" in a similar fashion: as a combination of gradual thematic metamorphosis and a motivic-thematic palindrome. See table 4.1 in Howat, *The Art of French Piano Music*, 48. My understanding of "Ondine" also interacts in various ways with its analysis in Gurminder Kaur Bhogal, "Arabesque and Metric Dissonance in the Music of Maurice Ravel," vol. 1, 115–187. Bhogal's overall interpretation of it as a musical arabesque that follows "a circular trajectory . . . from the real to the imaginary and back again" (146) matches my sense of it as a *Faune*-like palindrome, as does her reading of it as "the tale of a neurasthenic urban dweller . . . [seeking] refuge for his overstimulated mind and body in an inner world of imaginary freedom" (183)—an epitome of decadent experience, though Bhogal does not actually use this term. However, rather than a tripartite sonata form with a reversed recapitulation, as Bhogal analyzes it, I would suggest that "Ondine" is closer to a binary Type 2 sonata form (as proposed by Hepokoski and Darcy) whose second half begins with a developmental episode, usually based on the primary material, but lacks any recapitulation proper; any literal return to the primary material will usually happen in the coda, which is exactly what occurs in "Ondine." See Hepokoski and Darcy, *Elements of Sonata Theory*, 353–387. Sigrun B. Heinzelmann also analyzes the first movement of Ravel's Piano Trio (1914) as a Type 2 sonata form in her dissertation, "Sonata Form in Ravel's Pre-War Chamber Music," vol. 1, 164–203.
33. Longus, "Daphnis and Chloe," 316.
34. The extent to which the Pantomime is a *pas de deux* is a point of contention that, in the absence of reliable documentation for either Fokin's choreography or Ravel's compositional intentions, cannot be definitively resolved. Roland-Manuel claimed that Ravel had originally composed the scene as if it were to be a classical *pas de deux* but was taken aback when Fokin choreographed it as a pantomime. Roland-Manuel, *Maurice Ravel et son œuvre dramatique*, 116. His claim seems problematic, however, since the libretto, which preceded Ravel's composition, not only lays out the opening pantomime in detail but also omits any direction for Daphnis and Chloe to dance together—a direction that would have been easy to include and obligatory for a *pas de deux*. Based on both the music and the libretto, it makes the most sense to consider "Pan's Reminiscence" as a solo dance for Chloe—on the model of Isadora Duncan, who influenced Fokin—and the framing episodes of the encounter and the resuscitation as opportunities for Daphnis and Chloe to perform some combination of pantomime and dance.
35. Ibid., 112; Jankélévitch, *Ravel*, 93.
36. Paraphrased from Walter Benjamin, "On the Concept of History," 392. I have further altered the passage in English by translating *Barbarei* as "barbarity" instead of "barbarism" since the latter does not adequately convey the subject of the passage—namely, the brutality of the victors toward the conquered.
37. The term *flowing motif* comes from Austin, *Norton Critical Scores*, 75.
38. For an account of Nijinsky's choreography, see Buckle, *Nijinsky*, 237–246. Additional information, documentation, and images can be found in Nectoux, *L'après-midi d'un Faune: Mallarmé, Debussy, Nijinsky.*
39. "Après une brève introduction, la flûte 'en un solo long' nous conte elle-même les merveilles de son origine" [After a brief introduction, the flute itself relates to us the wonders of its origins "in a long solo."]. Roland-Manuel, *Maurice Ravel et son œuvre dramatique*, 112.
40. "Et de faire aussi *haut* que l'amour se module / Évanouir du songe ordinaire de dos / Ou de flanc pur suivis avec mes regards clos, / Une sonore, vaine et monotone ligne." Translation and emphasis mine. In relating the poem to the *Prélude*, David M. Hertz also emphasizes that "high" and "modulate" are to be specifically understood as musical terms. Hertz, *The Tuning of the World*, 83.
41. Poggioli's identification of wish fulfillment in Mallarmé's poem forms an intriguing counterpart to mine: The pastoral faun, even more than the nymph, is but a fantasy, in the

psychological meaning of the term, a wishful projection of the frustrated instinct. . . . The behavior of this figure remains perilously near, even if only in the realm of wish, to that deviation or excess which sexual pathology quite properly designates with the clinical term "satyriasis." (Poggioli, *The Oaten Flute*, 288)

Poggioli is not alone in this interpretation, which coincides with Wallace Fowlie's earlier claim that "satyrs are convenient actors or projections of our more primordial instincts and visions." Fowlie, *Mallarmé*, 151.

42. Chloe's dance is also described as a habanera in Jankélévitch, *Ravel*, 48. There is evidence that Ravel knew Strauss's opera well. In spring 1907 Ravel described *Salome* and *Pelléas* as the most remarkable works of European classical music composed during the last fifteen years. Ravel, *A Ravel Reader*, 232n4. Moreover, in a 1931 interview, Ravel cites a musical theme from *Salome* to demonstrate that "Strauss was the first to superimpose lines which were harmonically incompatible." Ibid., 470. The main touchstones within the decadent imagination for the depiction of Salome include not only Wilde's play and Strauss's opera but also Flaubert's "Hérodias," Mallarmé's "Hériodiade" (which the poet considered as the pendant to "L'après-midi"), Gustave Moreau's series of paintings, and Huysmans's discussion of both Moreau and Mallarmé in *À rebours*.
43. Major French volumes by and about Schopenhauer during this period include Théodule-Armand Ribot, *La philosophie de Schopenhauer* (Paris: Baillière, 1874); Arthur Schopenhauer, *Pensées, maximes, et fragments*, translated, annotated, and preceded by a biography of Schopenhauer by Jean Bourdeau (Paris: Baillière, 1880); and the three-volume translation of *The World as Will and Presentation* by Auguste Burdeau, published between 1888 and 1890. Among decadent writers, Villiers and Huysmans are most closely associated with Schopenhauer's philosophy.
44. The comment about the emptiness of the *Boléro* is reported by Arthur Honegger in his *Incantations aux fossiles* (1948) and cited in Nichols, *Ravel Remembered*, 50.
45. Cited in Arbie Orenstein, *Ravel: Man and Musician*, 201.
46. Reported by René Chalupt in *Ravel au miroir de ses lettres* (1956) and cited in Nichols, *Ravel Remembered*, 49.
47. Example C.11's postulate of lengthened tones in the initial bars of this melody is supported by an initial sketch for the *Boléro*, which is catalogued in the Music Division of the Bibliothèque nationale de Paris as Ms. 21917 (Grande réserve). In this palimpsestic pencil sketch, the held tones, marked by the second and third asterisks in example C.11a, originally seem to have been a shorter by a quarter note, as reflected in example C.11b.
48. Ravel, *A Ravel Reader*, 421.
49. Ibid., 497.
50. At the beginning of this sentence I am invoking the notion of an "aesthetics of eroticism," which Stephen Downes proposes to be "founded on conflicts between fantastic instability and masterful formal manipulation." Downes, *The Muse as Eros*, 13.
51. For an extended discussion of *Boléro* and its choreography, see Mawer, *The Ballets*, 215–248.
52. André Barre, *Le Symbolisme: Essai historique sur le mouvement symboliste en France de 1885 à 1900, suivi d'une bibliographie de la poésie symboliste* (Paris: Jouve, 1911); Henri Moulhiade, *Verlaine et Mallarmé: Le symbolisme et sa floraison poétique de 1860 à 1910* (Le Puy-en-Velay: Peyriller, Rouchon, et Gamon, 1911); Tancrède de Visan, *L'attitude du lyrisme contemporain* (Paris: Mercure de France, 1911); Albert Thibaudet, *La poésie de Stéphane Mallarmé: Étude littéraire* (Paris: Éditions de la Nouvelle revue française, 1912); and Alfred Poizat, *Le symbolisme de Baudelaire à Claudel* (Paris: la Renaissance du livre, 1918).
53. Albert Mockel, *Stéphane Mallarmé, un héros* (Paris: Société du Mercure de France, 1899); Henri de Régnier, *Figures et caractères* (Paris: Société du Mercure de France, 1901); Adolphe Retté, *Le symbolisme: Anecdotes et souvenirs* (Paris: Librairie Léon Vanier, 1903); Gustave

Kahn, *Silhouettes littéraires* (Paris: Editions Montaigne, 1925); André Fontainas, *Mes souvenirs du symbolisme* (Paris: La nouvelle revue critique, 1928); Émile Verhaeren, *Impressions*, 3rd series (Paris: Mercure de France, 1928); and Édouard Dujardin, *Mallarmé, par un des siens* (Paris: Messein, 1936). This is only a select list of such *témoignages*.

54. Remy de Gourmont, "Stéphane Mallarmé," *Le temps* (Oct. 12, 1910), 2–3, repr. in de Gourmont, *Promenades littéraires*, 5–18.
55. De Gourmont, *Promenades littéraires*, 15 and 16, resp.

BIBLIOGRAPHY

Abbate, Carolyn. *In Search of Opera*. Princeton, N.J.: Princeton University Press, 2001.

Abraham, Gerald. *The Concise Oxford History of Music*. London: Oxford University Press, 1979.

———. "The Reaction against Romanticism: 1890–1914." In *The New Oxford History of Music: The Modern Age, 1890–1960*. Ed. Martin Cooper. London: Oxford University Press, 1974. 80–114.

Adorno, Theodor W. "On Proust." In *Notes to Literature*. Vol. 2. Ed. Rolf Tiedemann. Trans. Shierry Weber Nicholsen. New York: Columbia University Press, 1992. 312–317.

———. "Ravel." *Musikalische Schriften V*. Frankfurt: Suhrkamp, 1984. 273–274.

———. "Ravel." *Musikblätter des Anbruch* 12 (1930): 151–154.

Aguettant, Louis. *La musique de piano des origines à Ravel*. Paris: Éditions Albin Michel, 1954.

Antokoletz, Elliott. *Twentieth-Century Music*. Englewood Cliffs, N.J.: Prentice-Hall, 1992.

Assmann, Aleida. "Zur Metaphorik der Erinnerung." In *Mnemosyne: Formen und Funktionen der kulturellen Erinnerung*. Ed. Aleida Assmann and Dietrich Harth. Frankfurt: Fischer, 1991. 13–35.

Austin, Linda M. *Nostalgia in Transition: 1780–1917*. Charlottesville: University of Virginia Press, 2007.

Austin, Lloyd James. "*L'après-midi d'un faune*: Essai d'explication." In *Essais sur Mallarmé*. Ed. Malcolm Bowie. Manchester: Manchester University Press, 1995. 182–200.

Austin, William W. *Norton Critical Scores: Debussy, Prelude to "The Afternoon of a Faun."* New York: Norton, 1970.

Baeck, Erik, and Hedwige Baeck-Schilders. "La création mondiale du ballet *La Valse* de Maurice Ravel à Anvers." *Revue de musicologie* 89.2 (2003): 365–371.

Baju, Anatole. *L'école décadente*. 3rd ed. Paris: Vanier, 1887.

Barash, Jeffrey Andrew. "The Sources of Memory." *Journal of the History of Ideas* 58.4 (1997): 707–717.

Barber, Giles. *Daphnis and Chloe: The Markets and Metamorphoses of an Unknown Bestseller*. London: British Library, 1989.

Barbey d'Aurevilly, Jules. *Du dandysme et de George Brummell (1845)*. Paris: Éditions Balland, 1986.

Batson, Charles R. *Dance, Desire, and Anxiety in Early Twentieth-Century French Theater: Playing Identities*. Aldershot: Ashgate, 2005.

Baudelaire, Charles. "Fusées." In *Journaux intimes. Œuvres complètes*. Vol. 1. Ed. Y.-G. Le Dantec and Claude Pinchois. Paris: Gallimard, 1961. 1247–1270.

———. "Mon cœur mis à nu." In *Journaux intimes. Œuvres complètes*. Vol. 1. Ed. Y.-G. Le Dantec and Claude Pinchois. Gallimard: Paris, 1961. 1271–1301.

———. "Le peintre de la vie moderne." In *Journaux intimes. Œuvres complètes*. Vol. 1. Ed. Y.-G. Le Dantec and Claude Pinchois. Paris: Gallimard, 1961. 1152–1192.

Baur, Steven. "Ravel's 'Russian' Period: Octatonicism in His Early Works, 1893–1908." *Journal of the American Musicological Society* 52.3 (1999): 531–592.

Beaujour, Michel. *Poetics of the Literary Self-Portrait*. Trans. Yara Milos. New York: New York University Press, 1991.

Beaumont, Cyril W. *Michel Fokine and His Ballets*. 2nd ed. London: Beaumont, 1945.

Benjamin, George. "Last Dance." *Musical Times* 135 (1994): 432–435.

Benjamin, Walter. "A Berlin Chronicle." In *Reflections*. Ed. Peter Demetz. Trans. Edmund Jephcott. New York: Schocken, 1978. 3–60.

———. "The Image of Proust." In *Illuminations*. Ed. Hannah Arendt. Trans. Harry Zohn. New York: Schocken, 1968. 201–216.

———. "On Some Motifs in Baudelaire." In *Illuminations*. Ed. Hannah Arendt. Trans. Harry Zohn. New York: Schocken, 1968. 155–200.

———. "On the Concept of History." In *Selected Writings*. Vol. 4, *1938–1940*. Ed. Howard Eiland and Michael W. Jennings. Cambridge, Mass.: Harvard University Press, 2003. 389–400.

———. "The Paris of the Second Empire in Baudelaire." In *Selected Writings*. Vol. 4, *1938–1940*. Ed. Howard Eiland and Michael W. Jennings. Cambridge, Mass.: Harvard University Press, 2003. 3–94.

———. "The Return of the *flâneur*." In *Selected Writings*. Vol. 2, *1927–1934*. Ed. Michael W. Jennings, Howard Eiland, and Gary Smith. Cambridge, Mass.: Harvard University Press, 1999. 262–267.

Berger, Anna Maria Busse. *Medieval Music and the Art of Memory*. Berkeley: University of California Press, 2005.

Bergson, Henri. *L'énergie spirituelle: Essais et conférences*. 5th ed. Paris: Alcan, 1920.

———. *Essai sur les données immédiates de la conscience. Œuvres*. 6th ed. Paris: Presses Universitaires de France, 2001. 1–157.

———. *Matière et mémoire*. 2nd ed. Paris: Alcan, 1900.

———. *Matter and Memory*. Trans. Nancy Margaret Paul and W. Scott Palmer. New York: Zone, 1988.

Bernfeld, Suzanne Cassirer. "Freud and Archeology." *American Imago* 8 (1951): 107–128.

Bernheimer, Charles. *Decadent Subjects: The Idea of Decadence in Art, Literature, Philosophy, and Culture of the* Fin de Siècle *in Europe*. Baltimore: Johns Hopkins University Press, 2002.

Bhogal, Gurminder Kaur. "Arabesque and Metric Dissonance in the Music of Maurice Ravel (1905–1914)." PhD diss., University of Chicago, 2004.

———. "Debussy's Arabesque and Ravel's *Daphnis et Chloé*." *Twentieth-Century Music* 3.2 (2006): 171–199.

Bird, Steven Carl. "A Preliminary Comparison of the Autograph Score of Maurice Ravel's Ballet *Daphnis et Chloé* with the 1913 Edition of the Full Score by Durand et fils." PhD diss., University of Texas, 1989.

Birkett, Jennifer. *The Sins of the Fathers: Decadence in France, 1870–1914*. London: Quartet, 1986.

Bolduc, Benoît. "From Marvel to Camp: Medusa for the Twenty-First Century." *Journal of Seventeenth-Century Music* 10.1 (2006). http://sscm-jscm.press.illinois.edu/v10/no1/bolduc.html.

Boym, Svetlana. *The Future of Nostalgia*. New York: Basic Books, 2001.

Branger, Jean-Christophe. "Ravel et la valse." *Ostinato rigore* 24 (2005): 145–160.

Braun, Jürgen. *Die Thematik in den Kammermusikwerken von Maurice Ravel*. Kölner Beiträge zur Musikforschung 33. Regensburg: Bosse, 1966.

Brittan, Francesca. "Berlioz and the Pathological Fantastic: Melancholy, Monomania, and Romantic Autobiography." *19th-Century Music* 29.3 (2006): 211–239.

Brockelman, Paul. "Of Memory and Things Past." *International Philosophical Quarterly* 15.3 (1975): 309–325.

Brody, Elaine. "Schumann's Legacy in France." *Studies in Romanticism* 13.3 (1974): 189–212.

Bruhn, Siglind. *Images and Ideas in Modern French Piano Music.* Stuyvesant, N.Y.: Pendragon, 1997.

Bruyr, José. *Maurice Ravel.* Paris: Plon, 1950.

Buckle, Richard. *Nijinsky.* London: Weidenfeld and Nicolson, 1971.

Caballero, Carlo. *Fauré and French Musical Aesthetics.* Cambridge: Cambridge University Press, 2001.

Calinescu, Matei. *Five Faces of Modernity: Modernism, Avant-Garde, Decadence, Kitsch, Postmodernism.* Durham, N.C.: Duke University Press, 1987.

Calvocoressi, Michel D. *Music and Ballet.* London: Faber and Faber, 1934.

Calza, Renato. *Maurice Ravel nella storia della critica: Poetiche decadenti raveliane e interpretazioni novecentesche in Francia, Italia, Inghilterra, et Stati Uniti.* Padua: Zanzibon, 1980.

Caplin, William Earl. *Classical Form: A Theory of Formal Functions for the Instrumental Music of Haydn, Mozart, and Beethoven.* New York: Oxford University Press, 1998.

Carassus, Emilien. *Le mythe du Dandy.* Paris: Colin, 1971.

Carraud, Gaston. "Théâtres: Châtelet." *La liberté* (June 11, 1912).

Carruthers, Mary. *The Book of Memory: A Study of Memory in Medieval Culture.* Cambridge: Cambridge University Press, 1990.

Carson, Anne. *Eros the Bittersweet.* Princeton, N.J.: Princeton University Press, 1986.

———. *If Not, Winter: Fragments of Sappho.* New York: Random House, 2003.

Carter, Alfred E. *The Idea of Decadence in French Literature, 1830–1900.* Toronto: University of Toronto Press, 1958.

Casey, Edward S. *Remembering: A Phenomenological Study.* 2nd ed. Bloomington: Indiana University Press, 2000.

Casini, Claudio. *Maurice Ravel.* Pordenone: Studio Tesi, 1989.

Chambers, Ross. *Loiterature.* Lincoln: University of Nebraska Press, 1999.

Chouvel, Jean-Marc. "Avec le temps, il n'y a pas de forme sans mémoire . . ." *Musique et Mémoire.* Paris: L'Harmattan, 2003. 47–56.

Cleto, Fabio. "Introduction: Queering the Camp." In *Camp: Queer Aesthetics and the Performing Subject.* Ed. Fabio Cleto. Ann Arbor: University of Michigan Press, 1999. 1–42.

Code, David J. "Hearing Debussy Reading Mallarmé: Music *après Wagner* in the *Prélude à l'après-midi d'un faune.*" *Journal of the American Musicological Society* 54 (2001): 493–554.

Cohn, Robert Greer. *Toward the Poems of Mallarmé.* Berkeley: University of California Press, 1965.

Combarieu, Jules. *Histoire de la musique des origines au début du XXe siècle.* Vol. 3. Paris: Colin, 1919.

Constable, Liz, Dennis Denisoff, and Matthew Potolsky. "Introduction." *Perennial Decay: On the Aesthetics and Politics of Decadence.* Philadelphia: University of Pennsylvania Press, 1999. 1–34.

Cooper, Martin. *French Music: From the Death of Berlioz to the Death of Fauré.* London: Oxford University Press, 1951.

Danuser, Hermann. *Die Musik des 20. Jahrhunderts. Neues Handbuch der Musikwissenschaft.* Vol. 7. Ed. Carl Dahlhaus. Laaber: Laaber, 1984.

Danziger, Kurt. *Marking the Mind: A History of Memory.* New York: Cambridge University Press, 2008.

Darcy, Warren. "The Metaphysics of Annihilation: Wagner, Schopenhauer, and the Ending of the *Ring.*" *Music Theory Spectrum* 16.1 (1994): 1–40.

Davies, Laurence. *The Gallic Muse.* South Brunswick, N.J.: Barnes, 1969.

Goncourt, Edmond de, and Jules de Goncourt. *French XVIII Century Painters.* New York: Phaidon, 1948.

Debussy, Claude. *Correspondance: 1884–1918.* Ed. François Lesure. Paris: Hermann, 1993.

Deleuze, Gilles. *Proust and Signs: The Complete Text*. Trans. Richard Howard. Minneapolis: University of Minnesota Press, 2004.

Deruchie, Andrew. "The French Symphony at the *fin de siècle*: Style, Culture, and the Symphonic Tradition." PhD diss., McGill University, 2008.

Doane, Mary Ann. *Femmes Fatales: Feminism, Film Theory, Psychoanalysis*. New York: Routledge, 1991.

Dorschel, Andreas. "Das anwesend Abwesende: Musik und Erinnerung." In *Resonanzen: Vom Erinnern in der Musik*. Ed. Andreas Dorschel. Vienna: Universal, 2007. 12–29.

Downes, Stephen C. *The Muse as Eros: Music, Erotic Fantasy, and Male Creativity in the Romantic and Modern Imagination*. Aldershot: Ashgate, 2006.

———. *Music and Decadence in European Modernism: The Case of Central and Eastern Europe*. New York: Cambridge University Press, 2010.

Draaisma, Douwe. *Metaphors of Memory: A History of Ideas about the Mind*. Cambridge: Cambridge University Press, 2000.

Duchesneau, Michel. "Maurice Ravel et la Société Musicale Indépendante: 'Projet mirifique de concerts scandaleux.'" *Revue de musicologie* 80.2 (1994): 251–281.

Eichert, Randolph. "Kontrapunkte: Ravel gegen den Strich gehört." In *Hommage à Ravel 1987*. Ed. Günter Kleinen, Tobias Plebuch, Nicolas Schalz, and Kurt Seibert. Bremen: Hochschule für gestaltende Kunst und Musik Bremen, 1987. 193–195.

Ellis, Katharine. *Interpreting the Musical Past: Early Music in Nineteenth-Century France*. Oxford: Oxford University Press, 2005.

Ernst, Fritz. *Vom Heimweh*. Zurich: Fretz and Wasmuth, 1949.

Feldman, Jessica R. *Gender on the Divide: The Dandy in Modernist Literature*. Ithaca, N.Y.: Cornell University Press, 1993.

Fink, Robert. "Desire, Repression, and Brahms's First Symphony." In *Music/Ideology: Resisting the Aesthetic*. Ed. Adam Krims. Amsterdam: G + B Arts International, 1998. 247–288.

Fischer, Michel. "Les valses de Maurice Ravel: Une étourdissante maîtrise orchestrale du rythme à trois temps." *Ostinato rigore* 24 (2005): 103–143.

Fokine, Michel. *Daphnis et Chloé: Ballet en 3 tableaux*. Libretto. Paris: Durand, 1912.

———. *Fokine: Memoirs of a Ballet Master*. Ed. Anatole Chujoy. Trans. Vitale Fokine. Boston: Little, Brown, 1961.

Forth, Christopher E. *Zarathustra in Paris: The Nietzsche Vogue in France, 1891–1918*. DeKalb: Northern Illinois University Press, 2001.

Foucault, Michel. *The History of Sexuality*. Vol. 1, *An Introduction*. Trans. Robert Hurley. New York: Random House, 1978.

Fowlie, Wallace. *Mallarmé, with Fourteen Line Drawings by Henri Matisse*. Chicago: University of Chicago Press, 1953.

François, Etienne, and Hagen Schulze, eds. *Deutsche Erinnerungsorte*. Munich: Beck, 2001.

Freud, Sigmund. *The Ego and the Id* (1923). Trans. James Strachey. Vol. 19. London: Hogarth Press and the Institute of Psycho-Analysis, 1961.

———. "From the History of an Infantile Neurosis [the Wolf-Man] (1918 [1914])." In *The Standard Edition of the Complete Psychological Works of Sigmund Freud*. Vol. 17. Ed. James Strachey. London: Hogarth Press and the Institute of Psycho-Analysis, 1955. 3–124.

———. "Instincts and Their Vicissitudes (1915)." In *The Standard Edition of the Complete Psychological Works of Sigmund Freud*. Vol. 14. London: Hogarth Press and the Institute of Psycho-Analysis, 1957. 117–140.

———. "On Narcissism: An Introduction (1914)." In *The Standard Edition of the Complete Psychological Works of Sigmund Freud*. Vol. 14. London: Hogarth Press and the Institute of Psycho-Analysis, 1957. 73–102.

———. "Screen Memories (1899)." In *The Standard Edition of the Complete Psychological Works of Sigmund Freud*. Vol. 3. Ed. James Strachey. London: Hogarth Press and the Institute of Psycho-Analysis, 1962. 301–322.

———. *Three Essays on the Theory of Sexuality* (1905). Trans. James Strachey. Vol. 7. London: Hogarth Press and the Institute of Psycho-Analysis, 1953.

Frisch, Walter. "'You Must Remember This': Memory and Structure in Schubert's String Quartet in G Major, D. 887." *Musical Quarterly* 84.4 (2000): 582–603.

Fulcher, Jane F. *French Cultural Politics and Music: From the Dreyfus Affair to the First World War.* New York: Oxford University Press, 1999.

Garafola, Lynn. *Diaghilev's Ballets Russes.* New York: Oxford University Press, 1989.

———. *Legacies of Twentieth-Century Dance.* Middletown, Conn.: Wesleyan University Press, 2005.

———, ed. *Rethinking the Sylph: New Perspectives on the Romantic Ballet.* Hanover, N.H.: University Press of New England, 1997.

Garelick, Rhonda K. *Rising Star: Dandyism, Gender, and Performance in the Fin de Siècle.* Princeton, N.J.: Princeton University Press, 1998.

Gauthier-Villars, Henri. Untitled review of *Daphnis et Chloé. Collection des plus beaux numéros de* Comœdia illustré *et des programmes consacrés aux Ballets et Galas Russes depuis le début à Paris 1909–1921.* Ed. Maurice de Brunoff and Jacques de Brunoff. Paris: Brunoff, n.d. [c. 1922].

Gay, Volney P. *Freud on Sublimation: Reconsiderations.* Albany: State University of New York Press, 1992.

Gelleny, Sharon. "Cyclic Form in Debussy's Nocturnes." *Cahiers Debussy* 20 (1996): 25–40.

Genette, Gérard. *Narrative Discourse: An Essay in Method.* Trans. Jane E. Lewin. Ithaca, N.Y.: Cornell University Press, 1980.

———. *Narrative Discourse Revisited.* Ithaca, N.Y.: Cornell University Press, 1988.

Genova, Pamela A. "*Le dandysme*: Terrorism with Style." In *The Play of Terror in Nineteenth-Century France.* Ed. John T. Booker and Allan H. Pasco. Cranbury, N.J.: Associated University Presses, 1997. 74–92.

———. *Symbolist Journals: A Culture of Correspondence.* Aldershot: Ashgate, 2002.

Gilman, Richard. *Decadence: The Strange Life of an Epithet.* New York: Farrar, Straus, and Giroux, 1979.

Goldbeck, Frederick. *France, Italy, and Spain.* Ed. Nicolas Nabokov and Anna Kallin. London: Weidenfeld and Nicolson, 1974.

Goltz, Jennifer E. "The Roots of *Pierrot lunaire* in Cabaret." PhD diss., University of Michigan, 2005.

Goncourt, Edmond, and Jules de Goncourt. *French Eighteenth-Century Painters.* Trans. Robin Ironside. Ithaca, N.Y.: Cornell University Press, 1981.

Goubault, Christian. *La critique musicale dans la presse française de 1870 à 1914.* Geneva: Slatkine, 1984.

Gourmont, Remy de. *Promenades littéraires, quatrième série.* Paris: Société du Mercure de France, 1912.

Grey, Thomas. "Wagner the Degenerate: *Fin-de-siècle* Cultural 'Pathology' and the Anxiety of Modernism." *Nineteenth-Century Studies* 16 (2002): 73–92.

Gronquist, Robert. "Ravel's *Trois Poèmes de Stéphane Mallarmé.*" *Musical Quarterly* 64.4 (1978): 507–523.

Grosz, Elizabeth A. *The Nick of Time: Politics, Evolution, and the Untimely.* Durham, N.C.: Duke University Press, 2004.

Grout, Donald Jay, and Claude V. Palisca. *A History of Western Music.* 5th ed. New York: Norton, 1996.

Gubisch, Nina, ed. "Le journal inédit de Ricardo Viñes." *Revue internationale de musique française* 1 (1980): 154–248.

Guerlac, Suzanne. *Thinking in Time: An Introduction to Henri Bergson.* Ithaca, N.Y.: Cornell University Press, 2006.

Guest, Ivor F. *The Romantic Ballet in Paris.* Middletown, Conn.: Wesleyan University Press, 1966.

Gut, Serge. "Schumann und Frankreich." In *Robert Schumann und die französische Romantik*. Ed. Ute Bär. London: Schott, 1997. 13–24.

Halbwachs, Maurice. *Les cadres sociaux de la mémoire*. Paris: Éditions Albin Michel, 1994.

———. *The Collective Memory*. Trans. Francis J. Ditter Jr. and Vida Yazdi Ditter. New York: Harper and Row, 1980.

Halperin, David M. *One Hundred Years of Homosexuality and Other Essays on Greek Love*. New York: Routledge, 1990.

Hannoosh, Michèle. *Parody and Decadence: Laforgue's* Moralités légendaires. Columbus: Ohio State University Press, 1989.

Hanson, Ellis. *Decadence and Catholicism*. Ithaca, N.Y.: Cornell University Press, 1997.

Harris, Ellen T. *Handel as Orpheus: Voice and Desire in the Chamber Cantatas*. Cambridge, Mass.: Harvard University Press, 2001.

Heinzelmann, Sigrun. "Sonata Form in Ravel's Pre-War Chamber Music." PhD diss., City University of New York, 2008.

Helbing, Volker. "*L'impression d'un tournoiement fantastique et fatale*: Aneignung und Verzerrung in Ravels *La Valse*." In *Individualität in der Musik*. Ed. Oliver Schwab-Felisch, Christian Thorau, and Michael Polth. Stuttgart: Metzler, 2002. 175–200.

———. "*Noctuelles* by Ravel: An Essay on the Morphology of Sound." *Tijdschrift voor Muziektheorie* 8.2 (2003): 142–151.

Henrichs, Albert. "Loss of Self, Suffering, Violence: The Modern View of Dionysus from Nietzsche to Girard." *Harvard Studies in Classical Philology* 88 (1984): 205–240.

Hepokoski, James A. "Clouds and Circles: Rotational Form in Debussy's 'Nuages.'" *Dutch Journal of Music Theory* 15.1 (2010): 1–17.

———. "Formulaic Openings in Debussy." *19th-Century Music* 8.1 (1984): 44–59.

———. *Sibelius, Symphony no. 5*. Cambridge: Cambridge University Press, 1993.

———, and Warren Darcy. *Elements of Sonata Theory: Norms, Types, and Deformations in the Late Eighteenth-Century Sonata*. Oxford: Oxford University Press, 2006.

Hertz, David Michael. *The Tuning of the World: The Musico-Literary Poetics of the Symbolist Movement*. Carbondale: Southern Illinois University Press, 1987.

Hirsbrunner, Theo. *Debussy und seine Zeit*. Laaber: Laaber, 1981.

———. *Maurice Ravel: Sein Leben, sein Werk*. Laaber: Laaber, 1989.

Hobsbawm, Eric, and Terence Ranger, eds. *The Invention of Tradition*. Cambridge: Cambridge University Press, 1983.

Hoeckner, Berthold. *Programming the Absolute: Nineteenth-Century German Music and the Hermeneutics of the Moment*. Princeton, N.J.: Princeton University Press, 2003.

Holsinger, Bruce W. *Music, Body, and Desire in Medieval Culture: Hildegard of Bingen to Chaucer*. Stanford, Calif.: Stanford University Press, 2001.

Houk, Deborah. "Self-Construction and Sexual Identity in Nineteenth-Century French Dandyism." *French Forum* 22.1 (1997): 59–74.

Howat, Roy. *The Art of French Piano Music: Debussy, Ravel, Fauré, Chabrier*. New Haven, Conn.: Yale University Press, 2009.

———. "Ravel and the Piano." In *The Cambridge Companion to Ravel*. Ed. Deborah Mawer. Cambridge: Cambridge University Press, 2000. 71–96.

Howells, Bernard. *Baudelaire: Individualism, Dandyism, and the Philosophy of History*. Oxford: European Humanities Research Centre, 1996.

Huebner, Steven. *French Opera at the fin de siècle: Wagnerism, Nationalism, and Style*. New York: Oxford University Press, 1999.

———. "Laughter: In Ravel's Time." *Cambridge Opera Journal* 18.3 (2006): 225–246.

———. "Ravel's Perfection." In *Ravel Studies*. Ed. Deborah Mawer. Cambridge: Cambridge University Press, 2010. 9–30.

Hunter, Mary. "The *Alla Turca* Style in the Late Eighteenth Century: Race and Gender in the Symphony and the Seraglio." In *The Exotic in Western Music*. Ed. Jonathan Bellman. Boston: Northeastern University Press, 1998. 43–73.

Hustvedt, Asti. "The Art of Death: French Fiction at the fin-de-siècle." In *The Decadent Reader: Fiction, Fantasy, and Perversion from fin-de-siècle France*. Ed. Asti Hustvedt. New York: Zone, 1998. 10–29.

Huysmans, Joris-Karl. *Against Nature*. Trans. Robert Baldick. London: Penguin, 1959.

Huyssen, Andreas. "Monumental Seduction." In *Acts of Memory: Cultural Recall in the Present*. Ed. Mieke Bal, Jonathan Crewe, and Leo Spitzer. Hanover, N.H.: University Press of New England, 1999. 191–207.

———. *Twilight Memories: Marking Time in a Culture of Amnesia*. New York: Routledge, 1995.

Hyde, Martha. "Neoclassic and Anachronistic Impulses in Twentieth-Century Music." *Music Theory Spectrum* 18.2 (1996): 200–235.

Hyer, Brian. "Before Rameau and After." *Music Analysis* 15.1 (1996): 75–100.

———. "'Sighing Branches': Prosopopeia in Rameau's 'Pygmalion.'" *Music Analysis* 13.1 (1994): 7–50.

Indy, Vincent d'. *Cours de composition musicale, deuxième livre, première partie, rédigé avec la collaboration de Auguste Sérieyx d'après les notes prises aux classes de composition de la Schola cantorum*. Paris: Durand, 1909.

———. *La légende de Saint-Christophe*. Piano-vocal score. Paris: Rouart and Lerolle, 1918.

Irigaray, Luce. *This Sex Which Is Not One*. Ithaca, N.Y.: Cornell University Press, 1985.

Ivry, Benjamin. *Maurice Ravel: A Life*. New York: Welcome Rain, 2000.

Jankélévitch, Vladimir. *L'irréversible et la nostalgie*. Paris: Flammarion, 1974.

———. *Music and the Ineffable*. Trans. Carolyn Abbate. Princeton, N.J.: Princeton University Press, 2003.

———. *Ravel*. Solfèges 3. Paris: Éditions du Seuil, 1956.

Jauss, Hans-Robert. *Zeit und Erinnerung in Marcel Prousts "À la recherche du temps perdu": Ein Beitrag zur Theorie des Romans*. Frankfurt: Suhrkamp, 1986.

Jay, Martin. "Lamenting the Crisis of Experience: Benjamin and Adorno." In *Songs of Experience: Modern American and European Variations on a Universal Theme*. Berkeley: University of California Press, 2005. 312–360.

Jensen, Eric Frederick. "Explicating Jean Paul: Robert Schumann's Program for 'Papillons,' Op. 2." *19th-Century Music* 22.2 (1998): 127–143.

Jost, Peter. "Schumann in der französischen Musik des 20. Jahrhunderts." In *Robert Schumann: Philologische, analytische, sozial- und rezeptionsgeschichtliche Aspekte*. Ed. Wolf Frobenius. Saarbrücken: Saarbrücker Druckerei, 1998. 189–198.

Kabisch, Thomas. "Ravel." In *Die Musik in Geschichte und Gegenwart: Allgemeine Enzyklopädie der Musik*. 2nd ed. Vol. 13. Ed. Ludwig Finscher. Kassel: Bärenreiter, 1994. Cols. 1329–1361.

Kallberg, Jeffrey. *Chopin at the Boundaries: Sex, History, and Musical Genre*. Cambridge, Mass.: Harvard University Press, 1996.

———. "Sex, Sexuality." In *The New Grove Dictionary of Music and Musicians*. 2nd ed. Vol. 23. London: Macmillan, 2001. 178–180.

Kaltenbeck, Franz. "Sublimation and Symptom." In *Art: Sublimation or Symptom*. Ed. Parveen Adams. London: Karnac, 2003. 103–121.

Kaminsky, Peter. "Composer's Words, Theorist's Analyses, Ravel's Music (Sometimes the Twain Shall Meet)." *College Music Symposium* 43 (2003): 161–177.

———. "Vocal Music and the Lures of Exoticism and Irony." In *The Cambridge Companion to Ravel*. Ed. Deborah Mawer. Cambridge: Cambridge University Press, 2000. 162–187.

Kennicott, Philip. "Ravelation." *Dance Magazine* 64 (1990): 68–69.

Khanna, Ranjana. *Dark Continents: Psychoanalysis and Colonialism*. Durham, N.C.: Duke University Press, 2003.

Klee, Wanda. *Leibhaftige Dekadenz: Studien zur Körperlichkeit in ausgewählten Werken von Joris-Karl Huysmans und Oscar Wilde*. Heidelberg: Universitätsverlag Winter, 2001.

Koppen, Erwin. *Dekadenter Wagnerismus: Studien zur europaïschen Literatur des Fin de siècle*. Berlin: de Gruyter, 1974.

Kramer, Lawrence. *After the Lovedeath: Sexual Violence and the Making of Culture*. Berkeley: University of California Press, 1997.

———. "Consuming the Exotic: Ravel's *Daphnis and Chloe*." In *Classical Music and Postmodern Knowledge*. Berkeley: University of California Press, 1995. 201–225.

———. *Franz Schubert: Sexuality, Subjectivity, Song*. Cambridge: Cambridge University Press, 1998.

Krebs, Harald. *Fantasy Pieces: Metrical Dissonance in the Music of Robert Schumann*. New York: Oxford University Press, 1999.

Kuhn-Schliess, Ortrud. *Klassistische Tendenzen im Klavierwerk von Maurice Ravel*. Kölner Beiträge zur Musikforschung 171. Regensburg: Bosse, 1992.

Kurth, Ernst. *Bruckner*. Berlin: Hesse, 1926.

Kuspit, Donald B. *The Dialectic of Decadence: Between Advance and Decline in Art*. New York: Allworth, 2000.

———. "A Mighty Metaphor: The Analogy of Archaeology and Psychoanalysis." In *Sigmund Freud and Art: His Personal Collection of Antiquities*. Ed. Lynn Gamwell and Richard Wells. London: Freud Museum, 1989. 133–151.

Lacan, Jacques. *The Ethics of Psychoanalysis: 1959–1960*. Ed. Jacques-Alain Miller. Trans. Dennis Porter. New York: Norton, 1992.

Laplanche, Jean, and J.-B. Pontalis. *The Language of Psycho-Analysis*. Trans. Donald Nicholson-Smith. New York: Norton, 1973.

Larner, Gerald. *Maurice Ravel*. London: Phaidon, 1996.

Le Rider, Jacques. *Nietzsche en France: De la fin du XIXe siècle au temps présent*. 1st ed. Paris: Presses Universitaires de France, 1999.

Lee, Sherry D. "A Minstrel in a World without Minstrels: Adorno and the Case of Schreker." *Journal of the American Musicological Society* 58.3 (2005): 639–696.

Lewinski, Wolf-Eberhard von. "Ravels tragischer Abschied: *La Valse* als musikalisches Symptom einer Zeit." In *Musik wieder gefragt: Gedanken und Gespräche zum Musikleben von Heute*. Hamburg: Claassen, 1967. 177–186.

Leydon, Rebecca. " 'Ces nymphes, je les veux perpétuer': The Post-War Pastoral in Space-Age Bachelor-Pad Music." *Popular Music* 22.2 (2003): 159–172.

Locke, Ralph P. "Constructing the Oriental 'Other': Saint-Saëns's *Samson et Dalila*." *Cambridge Opera Journal* 3.3 (1991): 261–302.

———. "Cutthroats and Casbah Dancers, Muezzins and Timeless Sands: Musical Images of the Middle East." *19th-Century Music* 22.1 (1998): 20–53.

Longus. "Daphnis and Chloe." In *Collected Greek Novels*. Ed. B. P. Reardon. Trans. Christopher Gill. Berkeley: University of California Press, 1989. 285–348.

Lowenthal, David. *The Past Is a Foreign Country*. Cambridge: Cambridge University Press, 1985.

Lukacher, Ned. *Primal Scenes: Literature, Philosophy, Psychoanalysis*. Ithaca, N.Y.: Cornell University Press, 1986.

Malipiero, Riccardo. *Maurice Ravel: L'enfant et les sortilèges, la valse, Daphnis et Chloé*. Milan: Istituto d'alta cultura, 1948.

Marcuse, Herbert. *Eros and Civilization: A Philosophical Inquiry into Freud*. Boston: Beacon, 1974.

Marnat, Marcel. *Maurice Ravel*. Paris: Fayard, 1986.

———. "Vinteuil, peut-être." *Musical* 4 (1987): 20–29.

Marquèze-Pouey, Louis. *Le mouvement décadent en France*. Paris: Presses Universitaires de France, 1986.

Matsuda, Matt K. *The Memory of the Modern*. New York: Oxford University Press, 1996.

Mawer, Deborah. "Balanchine's *La Valse*: Meanings and Implications for Ravel Studies." *Opera Quarterly* 22.1 (2006): 90–116.

———. "Ballet and the Apotheosis of the Dance." In *The Cambridge Companion to Ravel.* Ed. Deborah Mawer. Cambridge: Cambridge University Press, 2000. 140–161.

———. *The Ballets of Maurice Ravel: Creation and Interpretation.* Aldershot: Ashgate, 2006.

———. "Musical Objects and Machines." In *The Cambridge Companion to Ravel.* Ed. Deborah Mawer. Cambridge: Cambridge University Press, 2000. 47–70.

Mayer, Charles S. *Bakst: Centenary 1876–1976.* London: Fine Arts Society, 1976.

McClary, Susan. *Feminine Endings: Music, Gender, and Sexuality.* Minneapolis: University of Minnesota Press, 1991.

McGuinness, Patrick. "Introduction." In *Symbolism, Decadence, and the Fin de Siècle: French and European Perspectives.* Ed. Patrick McGuinness. Exeter: University of Exeter Press, 2000. 1–15.

Meisel, Martin. *Realizations: Narrative, Pictorial, and Theatrical Arts in Nineteenth-Century England.* Princeton, N.J.: Princeton University Press, 1983.

Messing, Scott. *Neoclassicism in Music from the Genesis of the Concept through the Schoenberg/Stravinsky Polemic.* Rochester, N.Y.: University of Rochester Press, 1996.

Miller, Christopher L. *Blank Darkness: Africanist Discourse in French.* Chicago: University of Chicago Press, 1985.

Mondor, Henri. *Histoire d'un faune, avec un état inédit de L'après-midi d'un faune.* 8th ed. Paris: Gallimard, 1948.

Montgomery, Kip James. "Cyclic Form in the Music of Brahms." PhD diss., SUNY–Stony Brook, 2002.

Morgan, Robert P. *Twentieth-Century Music: A History of Musical Style in Modern Europe and America.* New York: Norton, 1990.

Morrison, Simon. "The Origins of *Daphnis et Chloé* (1912)." *19th-Century Music* 28.1 (2004): 50–76.

Muldoon, Mark S. *Tricks of Time: Bergson, Merleau-Ponty, and Ricoeur in Search of Time, Self, and Meaning.* Pittsburgh: Duquesne University Press, 2006.

Myers, Rollo H. *Ravel: Life & Works.* Westport: Greenwood, 1973.

Nectoux, Jean-Michel, ed. *L'après-midi d'un faune: Mallarmé, Debussy, Nijinsky.* Paris: Éditions de la Réunion des musées nationaux, 1989.

———. "Debussy et Mallarmé." *Cahiers Debussy* 12–13 (1988–1989): 54–66.

———. "Maurice Ravel et sa bibliothèque musicale." *Cahiers Maurice Ravel* 3 (1987): 53–64.

———."Ravel/Fauré et les débuts de la Société Musicale Indépendante." *Revue de musicologie* 61.2 (1975): 295–318.

Nichols, Roger. "Preface." In *Sonatine* by Maurice Ravel. London: Hinrichsen Edition, Peters Edition, 1995. 4–5.

———, ed. *Ravel Remembered.* London: Faber and Faber, 1987.

Nietzsche, Friedrich W. *The Birth of Tragedy, and the Case of Wagner.* Trans. Walter A. Kaufmann. New York: Vintage, 1967.

———. "The Case of Wagner: A Musician's Problem." In *The Anti-Christ, Ecce Homo, Twilight of the Idols, and Other Writings.* Ed. Aaron Ridley. Cambridge: Cambridge University Press, 2005. 231–262.

———. *On the Genealogy of Morals.* Trans. Walter A. Kaufmann and R. J. Hollingdale. New York: Vintage, 1967.

———. "On the Utility and Liability of History for Life." *Unfashionable Observations.* Trans. Richard T. Gray. Stanford, Calif.: Stanford University Press, 1995. 83–167.

———. *L'origine de la tragédie.* 2nd ed. Trans. Jean Marnold and Jacques Morland. Paris: Société du Mercure de France, 1901.

Nora, Pierre. "Between Memory and History: *Les lieux de mémoire.*" *Representations* 0.26 (1989): 7–25.

———. *Les lieux de mémoire*. Vols. 1–3. Paris: Gallimard, 1997.

Nye, Robert A. *Crime, Madness, and Politics in Modern France: The Medical Concept of National Decline*. Princeton, N.J.: Princeton University Press, 1984.

———. "Degeneration and the Medical Model of Cultural Crisis in the French Belle Époque." In *Political Symbolism in Modern Europe: Essays in Honor of George L. Mosse*. Ed. Seymour Drescher, David Sabean, and Allan Sharlin. New Brunswick, N.J.: Transaction, 1982. 19–41.

Orenstein, Arbie. *Ravel: Man and Musician*. New York: Dover, 1991.

Orledge, Robert, ed. *Satie Remembered*. Portland, Ore.: Amadeus, 1995.

Otis, Laura. *Organic Memory: History and the Body in the Late Nineteenth and Early Twentieth Centuries*. Lincoln: University of Nebraska Press, 1994.

Parakilas, James. "How Spain Got a Soul." In *The Exotic in Western Music*. Ed. Jonathan Bellman. Boston: Northeastern University Press, 1998. 137–193.

Pasler, Jann. *Composing the Citizen: Music as Public Utility in Third Republic France*. Berkeley: University of California Press, 2009.

———. "Stravinsky and the Apaches." *Musical Times* 123.1672 (1982): 403–407.

Pechard, Laurence. "La Valse." *Revue international de musique française* 24 (1987): 83–86.

Pierrot, Jean. *The Decadent Imagination, 1880–1900*. Trans. Derek Coltman. Chicago: University of Chicago Press, 1981.

Plebuch, Tobias. "'Miroirs,' Ansichten zum Werk Ravels." In *Hommage à Ravel 1987*. Ed. Günter Kleinen, Tobias Plebuch, Nicolas Schalz, and Kurt Seibert. Bremen: Hochschule für gestaltende Kunst und Musik Bremen, 1987. 91–104.

———. "Der stumme Schrecken, Ravels *Frontispice*." In *Hommage à Ravel 1987*. Ed. Günter Kleinen, Tobias Plebuch, Nicolas Schalz, and Kurt Seibert. Bremen: Hochschule für gestaltende Kunst und Musik Bremen, 1987. 155–165.

Poggioli, Renato. *The Oaten Flute: Essays on Pastoral Poetry and the Pastoral Ideal*. Cambridge: Harvard University Press, 1975.

Poulenc, Francis. *Moi et mes amis: Confidences recueillies par Stéphane Audel*. Paris: La Palatine Ligugé, 1963.

Poulet, Georges. *Proustian Space*. Trans. Elliott Coleman. Baltimore: Johns Hopkins University Press, 1977.

Prado, Sharon S. "The Decadent Aesthetic in France, 1880–1914: Musical Manifestations in the Works of Debussy and His Contemporaries." PhD diss., the University of Cincinnati, 1992.

Praz, Mario. *The Romantic Agony*. Trans. Angus Davidson. 2nd ed. Cleveland: Meridian, 1956.

Proust, Marcel. *À la recherche du temps perdu*. Ed. Jean-Yves Tadié. Paris: Gallimard, 1999.

———. *Remembrance of Things Past*. Trans. C. K. Scott Moncrieff, Terence Kilmartin, and Andreas Mayor. New York: Vintage, 1981.

Puri, Michael J. "Memory, Pastiche, and Aestheticism in Ravel and Proust." In *Ravel Studies*. Ed. Deborah Mawer. Cambridge: Cambridge University Press, 2010. 122–152.

Rasch, Wolfdieterich. *Die literarische Décadence um 1900*. Munich: Beck, 1986.

Ravel, Maurice. *Maurice Ravel: Lettres, écrits, entretiens*. Ed. Arbie Orenstein. Paris: Flammarion, 1989.

———. "Memories of a Lazy Child (1931)." In *A Ravel Reader: Correspondence, Articles, Interviews*. Ed. and trans. Arbie Orenstein. New York: Columbia University Press, 1990. 393–395.

———. *A Ravel Reader: Correspondence, Articles, Interviews*. Ed. and trans. Arbie Orenstein. Mineola, N.Y.: Dover, 2003.

———. *Songs 1896–1914*. Ed. Arbie Orenstein. New York: Dover, 1990.

Reed, John R. *Decadent Style*. Athens: Ohio University Press, 1985.

Reeve, Katherine Kolb. "Primal Scenes: Smithson, Pleyel, and Liszt in the Eyes of Berlioz." *19th-Century Music* 18.3 (1995): 211–235.

Régnier, Henri de. *Les rencontres de M. de Bréot*. Paris: Mercure de France, 1904.

Ribot, Théodule-Armand. *Les maladies de la mémoire*. Paris: Alcan, 1881.

Rings, Steven. "*Mystères limpides*: Time and Transformation in Debussy's *Des pas sur la neige*." *19th-Century Music* 32.2 (2008): 178–208.

Rodger, Gillian. "Drag, Camp, and Gender Subversion in the Music and Videos of Annie Lennox." *Popular Music* 23.1 (2004): 17–29.

Roland-Manuel. *À la gloire de... Maurice Ravel*. Paris: Éditions de la Nouvelle Revue Critique, 1938.

———. *Maurice Ravel et son œuvre*. Paris: Durand et fils, 1914.

———. *Maurice Ravel et son œuvre dramatique*. Paris: Éditions musicales de la Librairie de France, 1928.

Rosen, Charles. *The Romantic Generation*. Cambridge, Mass.: Harvard University Press, 1995.

Rosenmeyer, Thomas G. *The Green Cabinet: Theocritus and the European Pastoral Lyric*. Berkeley: University of California Press, 1969.

Rosenthal, Manuel. *Ravel: Souvenirs de Manuel Rosenthal*. Ed. Marcel Marnat. Paris: Hazan, 1995.

Sannemüller, Gerd. *Maurice Ravel, Daphnis und Chloé, 1. und 2. Suite*. Munich: Fink, 1983.

Sappho. *If Not, Winter: Fragments of Sappho*. Trans. Anne Carson. New York: Random House, 2003.

Schama, Simon. *Landscape and Memory*. New York: Knopf, 1995.

Schmid, Marion. *Proust dans la décadence*. Paris: Champion, 2008.

Schoenberg, Arnold. *Fundamentals of Musical Composition*. Ed. Gerald Strang and Leonard Stein. New York: St. Martin's, 1967.

Schorske, Carl E. *Fin-de-siècle Vienna: Politics and Culture*. New York: Knopf, 1979.

Selva, Blanche. *La sonate: Étude de son évolution technique historique et expressive en vue de l'interprétation et de l'audition*. Paris: Rouart and Lerolle, 1913.

Shattuck, Roger. *Marcel Proust*. Princeton, N.J.: Princeton University Press, 1974.

———. *Proust's Way: A Field Guide to* In Search of Lost Time. New York: Norton, 2000.

Shaw, Mary Lewis. *Performance in the Texts of Mallarmé: The Passage from Art to Ritual*. University Park: Pennsylvania State University Press, 1993.

Shreffler, Anne. "Phantoms at the Opera: The Ghosts of Versailles by John Corigliano and William Hoffman." *Contemporary Music Review* 20.4 (2004): 117–135.

Silverman, Debora. *Art Nouveau in Fin-de-Siècle France: Politics, Psychology, and Style*. Berkeley: University of California Press, 1989.

Silverman, Kaja. *Male Subjectivity at the Margins*. New York: Routledge, 1992.

Simeone, Nigel. "Mother Goose and Other Golden Eggs: Ravel and Durand." *Brio* 35.2 (1998): 58–79.

Sisman, Elaine. "Memory and Invention at the Threshold of Beethoven's Late Style." In *Beethoven and His World*. Ed. Scott Burnham and Michael P. Steinberg. Princeton, N.J.: Princeton University Press, 2000. 51–87.

Smith, Douglas. *Transvaluations: Nietzsche in France, 1872–1972*. New York: Oxford University Press, 1996.

Smith, Richard Langham. "Debussy and the Pre-Raphaelites." *19th-Century Music* 5.2 (1981): 95–109.

———. "Ravel's Operatic Spectacles: *L'heure* and *L'enfant*." In *The Cambridge Companion to Ravel*. Ed. Deborah Mawer. Cambridge: Cambridge University Press, 2000. 188–210.

Sontag, Susan. "Notes on 'Camp.'" In *Against Interpretation and Other Essays*. New York: Dell, 1961. 275–292.

Souillard, Christine. *Ravel, 1875–1937*. [Paris]: Éditions Gisserot, 1998.

Spackman, Barbara. *Decadent Genealogies: The Rhetoric of Sickness from Baudelaire to D'Annunzio*. Ithaca, N.Y.: Cornell University Press, 1989.

Stanton, Domna C. *The Aristocrat as Art: A Study of the* honnête homme *and the Dandy in Seventeenth- and Nineteenth-Century French Literature*. New York: Columbia University Press, 1980.

Starobinski, Jean. "The Idea of Nostalgia." Trans. William S. Kemp. *Diogenes* 14.54 (1966): 81–103.

Stegemann, Michael. *Maurice Ravel*. Reinbek bei Hamburg: Rowohlt Taschenbuch, 1996.

Stewart, Susan. *On Longing: Narratives of the Miniature, the Gigantic, the Souvenir, the Collection*. Durham, N.C.: Duke University Press, 1993.

Straus, Joseph N. *Introduction to Post-Tonal Theory*. 3rd ed. Upper Saddle River, N.J.: Pearson Prentice Hall, 2005.

Stuckenschmidt, Hans Heinz. *Maurice Ravel: Variations on His Life and Work*. Trans. S. R. Rosenbaum. Philadelphia: Chilton, 1968.

Suschitzky, Anya. "Debussy's Rameau: French Music and Its Others." *Musical Quarterly* 86.3 (2002): 398–448.

Swart, Koenraad W. *The Sense of Decadence in Nineteenth-Century France*. The Hague: Nijhoff, 1964.

Symons, Arthur. "The Decadent Movement in Literature." *Harper's New Monthly Magazine* (November 1893): 858–867.

Talbot, Michael. *The Finale in Western Instrumental Music*. Oxford: Oxford University Press, 2001.

Taylor, Benedict. "Cyclic Form, Time, and Memory in Mendelssohn's A-Minor Quartet, Op. 13." *Musical Quarterly* 93.1 (Spring 2010): 45–89.

———. "Musical History and Self-Consciousness in Mendelssohn's Octet, Op. 20." *19th-Century Music* 32.2 (2008): 131–159.

Templier, Pierre-Daniel. *Erik Satie*. Trans. Elena L. French and David S. French. Cambridge, Mass.: MIT Press, 1969.

Terdiman, Richard. *Present Past: Modernity and the Memory Crisis*. Ithaca, N.Y.: Cornell University Press, 1993.

Thomas, Gary C. " 'Was George Frideric Handel Gay?': On Closet Questions and Cultural Politics." In *Queering the Pitch: The New Gay and Lesbian Musicology*. Ed. Philip Brett, Elizabeth Wood, and Gary C. Thomas. 2nd ed. New York: Routledge, 2006. 155–203.

Thorau, Christian. *Semantisierte Sinnlichkeit: Studien zu Rezeption und Zeichenstruktur der Leitmotivtechnik Richard Wagners*. Stuttgart: Steiner, 2003.

Trezise, Simon. *Debussy:* La mer. Cambridge: Cambridge University Press, 1994.

Tyre, Jess. "The Reception of German Instrumental Music in France between 1870 and 1914." PhD diss., Yale University, 2000.

Vilain, Robert. "Temporary Aesthetes: Decadence and Symbolism in Germany and Austria." In *Symbolism, Decadence, and the Fin de Siècle: French and European Perspectives*. Ed. Patrick McGuinness. Exeter: University of Exeter Press, 2000. 209–224.

Vuillermoz, Émile. "L'œuvre de Maurice Ravel." In *Maurice Ravel par quelques-uns de ses familiers*. Ed. Roger Wild. Paris: Éditions du Tambourinaire, 1939. 1–95.

———. "Les Théâtres: La grande saison de Paris." *Revue musicale de la S.I.M.* (June 15, 1912): 62–68.

Watkins, Glenn. *Soundings: Music in the Twentieth Century*. New York: Schirmer, 1988.

Weber, Eugen. *France, Fin de Siècle*. Cambridge, Mass.: Belknap Press of Harvard University Press, 1986.

Weber, Samuel, "Taking Place: Toward a Theater of Dislocation." In *Opera through Other Eyes*. Ed. David J. Levin. Stanford, Calif.: Stanford University Press, 1994. 107–146.

Weir, David. *Decadence and the Making of Modernism*. Amherst: University of Massachusetts Press, 1995.

Wenk, Arthur B. *Claude Debussy and the Poets*. Berkeley: University of California Press, 1976.

Wheeldon, Marianne. *Debussy's Late Style*. Bloomington: Indiana University Press, 2009.

Whitesell, Lloyd. "Ravel's Way." In *Queer Episodes in Music and Modern Identity*. Ed. Sophie Fuller and Lloyd Whitesell. Urbana: University of Illinois Press, 2002. 49–78.

Whiting, Steven Moore. *Satie the Bohemian: From Cabaret to Concert Hall*. Oxford: Oxford University Press, 1999.

Williams, Linda. "Of Kisses and Ellipses: The Long Adolescence of American Movies." *Critical Inquiry* 32.2 (2006): 288–340.

Wohlfarth, Irving Norman. "Aspects of Baudelaire's Literary Dandyism." PhD diss., Yale University, 1970.

Woodley, Ronald. "Performing Ravel: Style and Practice in the Early Recordings." In *The Cambridge Companion to Ravel*. Ed. Deborah Mawer. Cambridge: Cambridge University Press, 2000. 213–239.

Yaraman, Sevin H. *Revolving Embrace: The Waltz as Sex, Steps, and Sound*. Hillsdale, N.Y.: Pendragon, 2002.

Yates, Frances. *The Art of Memory*. London: Routledge and Kegan Paul, 1966.

Youens, Susan. "Debussy's Setting of Verlaine's 'Colloque sentimental': From the Past to the Present." *Studies in Music* 15 (1981): 93–105.

———. "Memory, Identity, and the Uses of the Past: Schubert and Luciano Berio's *Recital I (for Cathy)*." In *Franz Schubert—Der Fortschrittliche? Analysen-Perspektiven-Fakten*. Ed. Erich Wolfgang Partsch. Tutzing: Schneider, 1989. 231–248.

Zank, Stephen. *Irony and Sound: The Music of Maurice Ravel*. Rochester, N.Y.: University of Rochester Press, 2009.

Zupančič, Alenka. *The Shortest Shadow: Nietzsche's Philosophy of the Two*. Cambridge, Mass.: MIT Press, 2003.

INDEX